Windows Programmer's Guide to

DLLs and Memory Management

Windows Programmer's Guide to

DLLs and Memory Management

Mike Klein

SAMS

A Division of Prentice Hall Computer Publishing
11711 North College, Carmel, Indiana 46032 USA

To my fiance, Hanna Fleck.

International Standard Book Number: 0-672-30236-5

Library of Congress Catalog Card Number: 92-64087

Composed in New Baskerville and MCPdigital by
Prentice Hall Computer Publishing

Printed in the United States of America

Publisher
Richard K. Swadley

Managing Editor
Neweleen A. Trebnik

Acquisitions Editor
Joseph Wikert

Development Editors
Ella Davis
Jennifer Flynn

Production Editor
Cheri Clark

Copy Editor
Gayle Johnson

Editorial Coordinator
Becky Freeman

Editorial Assistants
Rosemarie Graham
Lori Kelley

Project Coordinator
San Dee Phillips

Technical Editor
Timothy S. Monk

Cover Designer
Jean Bisesi

Production Director
Jeff Valler

Production Manager
Corinne Walls

Book Designer
Michele Laseau

Production Analyst
Mary Beth Wakefield

Imprint Manager
Matthew Morrill

Proofreading/Indexing Coordinator
Joelynn Gifford

Graphics Image Specialist
Jerry Ellis, Dennis Sheehan,
Sue VandeWalle

Production
Keith Davenport, Christine Cook,
Mark Enochs, Kate Godfrey,
Tim Groeling, Dennis Clay Hager,
John Kane, Carrie Keesling,
Linda Quigley, Angie Trzepacz,
Julie Walker, Kelli Widdifield,
Allan Wimmer

Indexer
Jeanne Clark

About the Author

In addition to numerous magazine articles and the book you're currently holding, Mike Klein has written three other books, all about languages (generic BASIC/assembly) and operating systems long past: *The Commodore-64 Experience, The VIC-20 Experience,* and *The IBM PC Experience.* Current projects include an extensive control class library, and a powerful memory manager for Windows. When not vehemently cursing at Windows or his computer, the author enjoys several forms of skating, target shooting, and exploring San Francisco.

Overview

Contents

Acknowledgments

First and foremost, this book is dedicated to my fiance, Hanna Fleck. Through rain, sleet, and snow, she put up with all of my quirks, rantings, and late-night/early-morning cappuccino-driven hours while I compiled the information for and wrote this book. She helped console me through periods of utter chaos, and in short, made the book possible. Thanks, sweetheart!

I'd also like to get a special computer-related "shot" out to several other friends who in one way or another helped me research and compile information for the book: John Patterson, truly a BIOS/DOS/assembly hacker extraordinaire; Paul Headley, for the Windows' internals, OOP-stuff, and for getting me started with the NRA and target shooting (what an excellent release after staring at a monitor all day!); Scott Esters, for the OS/2 tidbits and various other stuff, as well as for several late-night ice-skating sessions to release book-induced mind-stress; and Joel Johnstone, for the "hairy" type-casting problems and other K&R C stuff that nobody else seems to have down straight.

Additionally, I'd like to thank authors/developers Michael Geary, Paul Yao, Richard Hale Shaw, Ray Duncan, Gordon Letwin, and Charles Petzold, for writing key magazine articles and books over the years. In Gordon's case, it's for writing a whole operating system—thanks, G!

A thanks goes out to my online CompuServe "buddies": Kyle Sparks, Alistair Bankes, Tammy Steele, Matt Leber, and Brian Lieuallen, for answering my many questions and for their continued support of developers. A definite thanks also goes to Arthur Knowles for editing early drafts of the book and providing valuable feedback.

Thanks goes to Nu-Mega Technologies for allowing me to use their series of DOS and Windows development tools, including Soft-ICE/W and Bounds Checker. It really is great having the right tool for the job! Probably one of the only companies whose future products I could recommend buying without even knowing what they do first!

Last, I'd like to thank my previous employers (and still friends!): Jim Day, Paul Atkinson, and Courtney Krehbiel of Chaparral Computers/Networks; Chris Beck of Forte; and the staff at *Dr. Dobb's Journal*. These guys took chances with me, and in general helped me get a start in the early days. Without good friends, life isn't worth a whole heck of a lot, no? I value friendships totally, and truly appreciate theirs.

Trademarks

Introduction

Is the third time the charm? Or is it three strikes and you're out? In either case, with Windows 3.1, Microsoft has finally managed to deliver what it had been promising since the first release of Windows: a usable and productive graphical user interface. PC users had long been clamoring for an interface similar to the Macintosh, and at last that dream was realized.

Windows has finally become more than just a "mega" application. Indeed, instead of running Windows for the sole purpose of executing a single application, users run Windows purely for the benefits that Windows itself provides. Applications are slowly becoming icing on the cake. Although Windows is still built on top of a crippled (but improving) platform—DOS— it is rapidly improving with each release. Indeed, the future of Windows, Windows NT, won't even require DOS.

Several features have contributed to Windows' success, including virtual memory, protected mode, multitasking, DDE, the clipboard, fonts, an all-around modular design, and an attractive visual interface. Part of Windows' success must be attributed to the support that enhanced versions of DOS have provided. Under DOS 5.x it is possible to get an unheard-of amount of free memory available, with most 80x86 systems reporting more than 620K free. With Microsoft using a protected-mode CPU as a base for extending future versions of DOS, its robustness and potential for success can be guaranteed. Backward compatibility (real-mode, DOS) with software and hardware must be sacrificed at some point for speed and power, and now's the time!

Windows 3.1 has extended the offerings found in Windows 3.0 significantly. New features and upgrades with the 3.1 release include

- TrueType scalable fonts. Now what you see on-screen is really what you get on the printer.

- Improved windowing speed and paint message handling. Most noticeable is how Program Manager can "snap" its windows on the screen much faster than the 3.0 version.

- The FastDisk driver for speeding up disk I/O, allowing it to be performed almost entirely in protected mode.

- An enhanced, sound API and a few sound utilities. Best yet, they function almost flawlessly with everything except DOS boxes.

☐ A series of additional developer utilities, libraries, and templates. Perhaps the most important is ToolHelp.DLL, which offers a peek at the lists of data normally reserved for internal use by Windows.

☐ An improved API that fills in the gaps with the 3.0 SDK, improving type-checking and adding (and finally documenting) much-needed messages for dialogs and controls.

☐ An improved, speedier File Manager.

☐ The Object Linking and Embedding (OLE) library, as well as DDEML.DLL, a Dynamic Data Exchange library that vastly improves the DDE interface for developers.

☐ Robust error-checking. When a program crashes, Windows finally handles it gracefully, allowing a program to be edited, recompiled, and debugged—all without the user having to reboot the machine.

As a long-time character-mode DOS user, I was very interested in the new GUI that Microsoft was offering. The more I worked with Windows, the more I wanted to learn, and the more I could see its potential. Windows' building-block design and almost-object-oriented architecture give it an incredibly open-ended feel.

My problems with this new environment didn't include mastering more than 800 API calls, and they didn't include this supposedly new concept of an event-driven architecture. My problems were with a lack of good documentation. At first glance, the Microsoft-supplied manuals seemed like a good teaching aid; however, the more I dug into Windows, the more I wanted to climb out of the hole I found myself in. The manuals "spread" and cover the topics well enough, but not nearly enough attention is devoted to each topic, especially the crucial ones such as DLL design, memory management, custom controls, and messaging. This is not to say that there aren't problems with working in such a different environment, because there are. However, I think you'll find that working with events and messages is infinitely easier than trying to generate an equivalent application in DOS' procedure-driven environment.

After hacking through the Windows jungle (with a very large, sharp machete) for a few years now, I finally feel comfortable enough and have developed enough subject matter to write a book on some of the more important Windows topics, which not coincidentally are DLL design, memory management, custom controls, and messaging. I guarantee that each of these topics is equally crucial in laying the foundation for any future applications development.

What's in This Book/Disk

The book/disk package includes the source for a number of custom control libraries, with several being built from the ground up and not using superclassing. These controls include

- BITMAP.DLL, providing panning and pixel editing of any device-dependent bitmap

- BUTTON.DLL, providing regular and graphical styles of push buttons, checkboxes, and radio buttons.

- SPLIT.DLL, providing a vertical or a horizontal "grab" bar that can be used to resize any number of attached client windows

- STDWIN.DLL, providing a flexible parent window class

Modified Windows control classes include COMBOBOX.DLL, EDIT.DLL, and LISTBOX.DLL, which are much more efficient than their SDK equivalents. The STDWIN DLL also contains APIs for bitmaps, printing (includes a somewhat-WYSIWYG print dialog), and the clipboard. Source is also included for a "hotkey" library/hook application as well as other related utilities that help examine principles discussed in this book. All the source code is provided on the disk included with this book.

Who This Book Is For

This book is not in the slightest way a replacement for the SDK, nor is it for someone wanting a beginning tutorial on the SDK. This book is targeted at the intermediate-to-advanced Windows programmer. At times, certain concepts in this book might seem to be at too low a level for someone concerned with Windows and the C language, but this really is not the case. You'll find that having a knowledge of such low-level system-related details will greatly improve your debugging skills. Sometimes it's better to have the background knowledge required to solve problems than to be given simple flat answers to specific questions. You'll find that with an in-depth knowledge of such low-level internals, you, not someone else, will be the one answering the majority of your questions. Think of it this way: If you understand how Windows' memory management and messaging systems work, reading about and understanding DDE becomes a piece of cake, because you already understand its

supporting foundation of code. You must understand the basic concepts behind module design, messaging, and memory management well to acquire new Windows skills rapidly and proficiently.

System Configuration

My programming (and writing) environment for this book consisted of the following software and hardware: Microsoft Windows 3.1 and 3.0 (under protected mode), Microsoft C 6.0 and the SDK; Nu-Mega Technologies' Soft-ICE/W debugger; Solution Systems' Brief programming editor; Gimpel Software's PC-lint; an 80386/33 processor with 64K cache; 180M IDE hard disk; Headland Technology's Video 7 VRAM video adapter (running at 640x480x256); and a Zenith flat-screen VGA color monitor. All the examples in this book are compiled for Windows 3.1. For obvious reasons, this book caters to Windows running under protected mode. I based this decision on the fact that support for real mode was discontinued with Windows 3.1, and the fact that it does not represent the kind of processor environment necessary for large-scale applications development. You will find numerous descriptions and references to real mode throughout this book, however.

How This Book Is Organized

Chapter 1, "Windows Fundamentals," discusses in-depth the foundation that Windows is built on, including module layout and messaging. Chapter 2, "Processor and Memory Fundamentals," discusses processor internals, covering important CPU-related topics such as address spaces, segmentation, paging, and virtual memory. Chapter 3, "Program and Module Fundamentals," discusses program/module architecture. Chapter 4, "Memory Management," covers memory and resource management; Chapter 5, "Library Design Ideas," discusses various aspects involved in library design; and Chapter 6, "Dialog and Custom Control Design," covers a multitude of topics surrounding dialog and window design. The appendixes contain source code for the several custom controls discussed in this book. The appendixes also discuss improvements that can be made to the design of each control and library. All the controls and functions given in the source are ready for instant implementation. To prove it, I've included a sample application that uses the controls listed in this book. Taking full use of DLLs is akin to the ultimate form of recycling. Make a resolution to file all your `SpecialLittleSomething()` functions in a single, reusable (and always-being-tested) DLL. It's amazing what you can do with the time you save because you've quit repeating mistakes.

Conventions Used in This Book

Throughout this book, certain conventions are followed:

- *Italics* are used to introduce a new term.
- A special `monospace` font is used to highlight code examples and code in the text.
- Windows API functions are shown in a **`monospace bold`** font.
- A special icon, shown to the right, is used to identify discussion of features new to Windows 3.1.

I'm extremely conscious about the quality of my source code and comments, so rest assured that I've given everything a thorough testing. The entire book and its examples have been technically edited as well. I sincerely hope that this book's information, correctness, and subject matter meet with your approval.

PART

I

Core Windows
Development
Concepts

Windows
Fundamentals

It has been said that writing good Windows applications requires a different way of thinking—at least for the tried-and-true DOS programmer. This is entirely untrue. A good DOS developer, with the same amount of effort, can become a good Windows programmer. It takes exactly the same set of skills, just a reapplication of them. Not that there aren't differences, though. Not only is your environment totally different, but there are not nearly as many tools to help you when you're stuck somewhere in the middle of the development process.

This chapter discusses

- Application and library modules

- The library-based architecture of Windows

- Messages

- Object-oriented concepts

The Windows environment provides a number of services for applications, and each has an impact (good and bad) on the programming cycle. The biggest *initial* differences and hurdles to developing under Windows are

- Event-driven architecture/messaging

- Poor documentation

- Windows itself

Under DOS, programmers have virtually complete control over their program's execution. Under Windows it's somewhat different, because an event-driven model is used for program flow, not a syntax- or procedure-driven model. Not everything about your environment can be assumed as it is in DOS. If you try taking anything for granted, your application is likely to be terminated or close shop for the night! The event-driven architecture can be the biggest hurdle. A developer can no longer single-step and trace through CodeView and be assured that he or she is watching the current thread of execution. Calling a Windows function from Module A can (possibly unbeknownst to you) cause code in a different module to start executing. A certain level of "peripheral vision" must be acquired to effectively debug under Windows.

Windows' messaging system, such as how and when certain messages get sent, is another source of confusion for the developer. When it comes down to it, Windows itself is the biggest culprit. Just as in DOS, Windows uses several undocumented functions and messages that are restricted from use by the developer. Windows also routinely violates many of its own messaging rules, especially in the areas of the Multiple Document Interface (MDI) specification and custom controls.

Developing successfully under Windows requires that a programmer understand the operating system completely, because application idiosyncrasies are no longer tolerated as they were under DOS. Source code must be written cleanly from the ground up. Such a request requires a complete understanding of Windows. This chapter is devoted to gaining a better grasp of some of the more basic concepts regarding the design of Windows, and messaging. The "Object-Oriented Concepts Under Windows" section at end of this chapter briefly discusses several object-oriented principles and how they relate to the Windows operating system.

Modules: Applications and Libraries

The Windows environment works with two fundamental program units: applications (.exe executable files) and dynamic link libraries (.dll, .drv, .exe, and .fon). Both are sometimes referred to as loadable or executable modules (see Figure 1.1). From here on, the term *program* is used to refer to either an application or a library, and the terms *library* and *DLL* are used interchangeably.

Applications differ from DLLs in that multiple copies or *instances* of an application can be run. Each copy of the application is referenced by a single instance handle. DLLs, which are loaded into memory once, have only a single instance handle. The instance handle is actually used by Windows as a handle to the program's default data segment. The reason is simple. Because Windows shares code and resource segments, the data segment is really the only segment left that can be used to differentiate between instances of a module.

Under Windows 3.1, all applications and libraries run at ring level 3, which is the norm for nonsystem code (see Figure 1.2). This contrasts with Windows

3.0, which runs all user programs at ring level 1. In either version, ring 0 is reserved exclusively for Windows' virtual memory manager and virtual device drivers. Programs running at ring 0 can see all of linear memory and have unhindered access to all system resources.

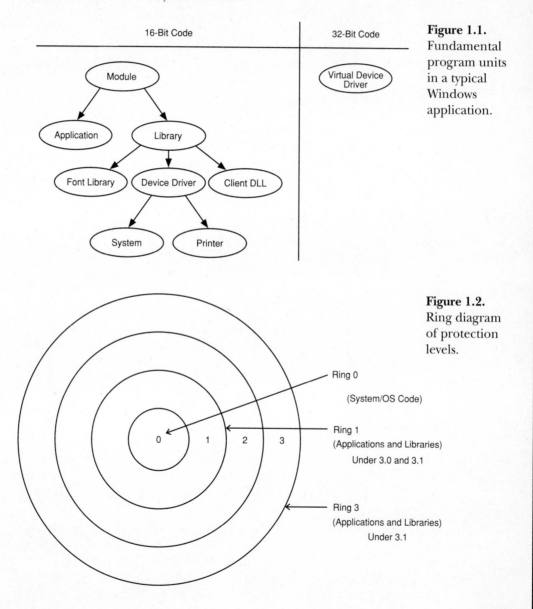

Figure 1.1. Fundamental program units in a typical Windows application.

Figure 1.2. Ring diagram of protection levels.

The module/instance and class/window pairings are very similar, because there can be multiple instances of a module (applications only) or multiple windows of a certain class. The terms *class* and *module* in this case both refer to a collection of information (database) needed to make a live object of that particular type.

Instance/Module == Window/Class

When an application or a library is first loaded into memory, Windows creates a data structure known as *module database*. The module database, like all other program segments (code, data, and resources), is stored in the global heap. The module database contains information found in the new-style .exe header of applications and DLLs. This well-documented header contains a wealth of information regarding all the program's exported functions, resources, and other unique, unchangeable information. Under Windows, a module database is kept track of with a *module handle*. Along with every instance of a specified application, Windows also associates a single task, which is referenced by a task handle. This task handle points to the application's *task database* (TDB). The TDB contains instance-unique information such as a DOS file handle table, the current DOS path, and a pointer to an application message queue. Its function is similar to DOS's program segment prefix (PSP). In fact, the TDB actually contains a PSP.

DLLs have no TDB, which is part of the reason for associating all windows created by a library with the currently active task (which must always be an application). This is also why so many API calls are application-centered. This single task is a kind of thread that runs through the application, as well as through any libraries attached to the application. Although future versions of Windows, specifically NT, will allow multithreaded applications, libraries still will be driven by a calling process (application) and won't have a "life" of their own. However, libraries will be able to spawn individual tasks on behalf of an application. The words *process* and *task* are interchangeable under Windows 3.x.

Task, instance, module, and window handles can be thrown together to form a simple tree. The fanned-out lower levels of the tree are traversed upward to determine ownership and other responsibilities (see Figure 1.3). There's only so much you can do programming-wise with a handle of any type, so by association the developer can get another handle in the tree that provides access to the needed information. For example, if an application is scanning desktop windows and wants to know the applications that created them, it couldn't find out with just a window handle. The window handle must be associated with an instance handle, and then the instance handle can be used to determine the upper step in the rung—the module's full pathname.

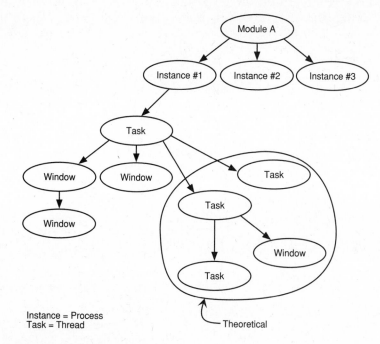

Figure 1.3.
The relationship among task, instance, module, and window handles.

Applications

Applications are referred to as *tasked executables*. This is because every application under Windows is driven by a single task and responds to a series of external events (messages). Currently only one task exists per instance of an application, but eventually Windows will become multithreaded, allowing the initial (and possibly only) task or process in an application to spawn multiple threads.

In a sense, a Windows application can be thought of as kickstarted by code and then driven by messages. All applications initially gain control by way of their WinMain() function, which has several responsibilities. Because multiple instances of your application can be run, the first thing to do inside WinMain() is to call any module initialization code. This is strictly *one-time* use code that applies to all instances of your application. Basically, it's used for registering application-bound window classes and initializing global data. WinMain()'s

second job is to call instance-specific creation code, which usually means creating windows. `WinMain()` is called by Windows with just four parameters: the instance handle of the application, the instance handle of another currently running copy of the application (if one exists), a long pointer to the command line the application was invoked with, and an integer value indicating how the application should be shown (that is, minimized, normal, or maximized) when it first executes.

As soon as your program has created at least one window, control is usually passed to `WinMain()` so that the application can enter its central message processing and dispatching loop. If, for some reason, no windows end up getting created (through error or for another reason) and the `WinMain()` loop is still entered, the application might never relinquish control. The message loop will never be broken or return control to the application because no application-created windows exist on the desktop to feed messages to the loop. Most critically, the loop will never process a `WM_QUIT`, the message that is used to terminate the message loop and thus the application. The only exception to this rule is when `PostAppMessage` is used to send a message to an application, as a task handle and not a window handle is specified as the receiver of the message. This technique is discussed later in this chapter.

The `WinMain()` message loop is the heart of every application, because its job is to pump messages out to all the windows created just a few lines of code earlier. Applications are free to create, maintain, and destroy as many windows as they want. There does, however, appear to be a system-wide limitation of about 500–700 windows (your mileage may vary). As soon as a window makes a call to **`PostQuitMessage()`**, Windows posts a `WM_QUIT` to the application, and control then breaks out of the message loop. At this point, cleanup code might be called, and the application terminates. Figure 1.4 illustrates this message flow and shows a (figuratively) segmented view of a basic Windows application.

Figure 1.4.
Message flow
in a Windows
application.

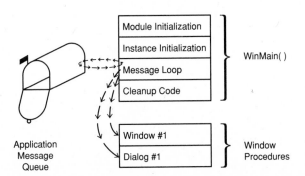

Dynamic Link Libraries

DLLs sometimes are referred to as *nontasked executables* because they are driven by the task (synonymous with application) of the caller. Libraries also don't have their own stack, nor do they have a message processing loop or a message queue, because they borrow everything from the calling application. This is because DLLs really aren't meant to stand on their own. They rotate around the lives of their client applications and libraries. A DLL's main purpose is to provide a guaranteed always-callable library of functions or resources. Barring no programming mishaps, a DLL isn't freed until the last module referencing the DLL has itself been unloaded from memory. DLLs are used for the following purposes:

- Registering and storing global window classes
- Creating device drivers and interrupt-driven code
- Housing large quantities of resources (bitmaps, icons, dialogs)
- Creating hook/filter code for system-wide mouse, keyboard, and message filtering
- Providing a library of instantly usable, debugged code

DLLs are a great place to put code for supporting system-wide window classes. As a matter of fact, they're the only place. This makes sense, because Windows gives DLLs preferential treatment over applications, with the operating system virtually guaranteeing their availability at all times.

The best things about DLLs are their plug-and-play nature and the high level of abstraction they can provide from an application's source code. After all, the ideal Windows application is not one big mass of all-encompassing code; rather, it's just the right amount of glue and support code needed to bind together a series of top-level windows and controls. Ideally, the only code that should be written is a simple switch statement for each window procedure, with a case statement for every message that needs to be acted on. DLLs should be (intelligently) used by the developer to store all of his or her common code. This reuse factor is one of the major benefits of applying object-oriented analysis and design principles in this somewhat limited object-oriented environment. It's been said by numerous O-O proponents that reuse can approach an unbelievable 80 percent in certain circumstances. Therefore, 80 percent of all your future code could already be written! This model, of course, assumes that the developer is making extensive use of libraries and is using

applications to hold only "uncommon" code, or roughly 20–30 percent of the actual application. This is why this book focuses on libraries and not on applications.

Device drivers always must be implemented as DLLs because of a certain property they have: They're always loaded and callable for any module acting as a client. In Windows 3.0's real-mode EMS 4.0 memory configuration, certain portions of a DLL were guaranteed not to get swapped into banks of expanded memory. This is good news if you're trying to service interrupt code. Windows also gives DLLs preferential treatment when it comes to low-memory situations because they're considered more crucial to the system as a whole than are individual applications. For holding a large number of resources such as icons, dialogs, and bitmaps, DLLs can't be matched.

Windows provides several message hooks that can be used inside DLLs and applications. Windows 3.0 restricted most hooks to libraries. However, Windows 3.1 allows most hooks to be task-specific (application-specific) or system-wide (library-based). The hooks control everything from function to message filtering, allowing a DLL to intercept messages before they're even delivered to an application's message queue. All the hooks affect system performance and as such should be used with some caution. Basically, setting up a hook involves sticking a function into an existing chain of filter functions. Hook code then optionally processes or passes messages down the chain, similar to the way a window passes messages to another window to inherit certain behaviors. Two of the hooks Windows provides are for journaling, a function demonstrated by Windows' Recorder utility. This utility allows messages to be looked at as they're being generated, enabling the developer to record them and then play them back later.

DLLs have different file extensions, depending on whether they're font resources (.fon), device drivers (.drv), or operating system files (.exe). All operate on the same basic principles. After all, they're still DLLs. Some unique differences are with device drivers and fonts. Device drivers are always loaded into the lower bowels of DOS conventional memory, and their segments are marked as fixed and page-locked so that memory can't move or be paged to disk. This is because device driver code services interrupts and must always be in memory at exactly the same place every time it is called. Font libraries are unique because they contain no code or data segments, only resource segments that contain fonts. Only font libraries can be resource-only. All other resource libraries (containing icons, bitmaps, and so on) created by a developer must contain at least one code segment holding the library's entry point (LibEntry) and exit point (WEP).

When a DLL is first loaded into memory, its assembly-language-defined entry point, LibEntry(), is called. LibEntry()'s job is to (possibly) initialize the DLL's local heap, link in C startup code (again, this is optional), and then make a call to LibMain(), the DLL's C-based initialization function. LibMain() is where the majority of the initialization for the DLL usually is done. When LibMain() finishes its job and returns to LibEntry(), control is returned to Windows and the library can be accessed. A DLL does not regain control again until a module calls into it or until it is unloaded from memory, which is when the library's WEP() exit procedure is called for any final needed cleanup. Figure 1.5 breaks down a simple DLL.

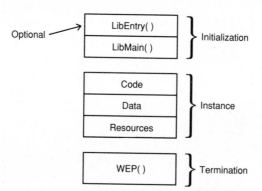

Figure 1.5. Initialization, sustanance, and termination of a simple DLL.

Windows' Library-Based Architecture

After Windows starts and protected mode is entered, several device drivers, font files, and OS libraries, shown in Table 1.1, are loaded into memory.

Table 1.1. Various DLLs and their purposes.

DLL	Purpose
comm.drv	Serial communications
display.drv	Video display
keyboard.drv	Keyboard input

continues

Table 1.1. continued

DLL	Purpose
mouse.drv	Mouse input
sound.drv	Sound output
system.drv	Timer
gdi.exe	Graphics Device Interface (referred to as GDI)
krnl386.exe	Multitasking, memory, and resource management (referred to as Kernel)
user.exe	Window management (referred to as User)
typeface.fon	Various font resources

Note: This list also includes any modules specified in WIN.INI's `load=` or `run=` lines or in the Windows 3.1 Program Manger's AutoStart folder.

These libraries form the hub around which Windows operates, providing services to each other and to any other loaded modules. Newer services, such as the MultiMedia Extensions to Windows, DIB driver, and OLE and DDE extensions, always consist of .drv and .dll replacements and additions to the previously mentioned drivers. With a slight modification of the SYSTEM.INI system configuration file, a completely different environment is possible. To most applications and libraries, Windows' Kernel, GDI, and User libraries represent the front end to the operating system, because these three files contain most of the functions called by application or library code. See Figure 1.6 for an illustration of this concept.

Note: Future references to the terms *DLL* and *library* refer to libraries created with the .DLL extension.

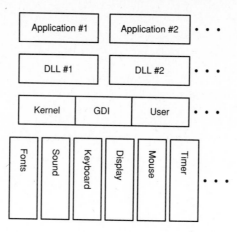

Figure 1.6.
Windows'
building block
architecture.

GDI

The GDI (Graphics Device Interface) module is responsible for exporting the painting, drawing, plotting, printing, and color functions of Windows. GDI stores the overhead for all its graphics objects, such as brushes, pens, and regions, in its own local heap, which has a theoretical maximum of just less than 64K. The raw data for larger GDI objects, such as bitmaps, icons, and cursors, usually is stored in the global heap, which has no similiar size limitation. Available local heap space is always less than the maximum when the heap is contained in the module's primary or automatic data segment, which is the case with GDI. This generally isn't much of a problem with this particular module, because the life of most graphics objects, such as pens and brushes, tends to be fairly short. An object that is created and destroyed in four lines of code isn't much of a threat.

User

The User module controls everything in Windows involving window creation, communications, hardware, and messaging. User, like GDI, uses its local heap to store all class and window data, with menus stored in a separate heap segment. The memory limit is felt more in User than in GDI, because the life of a window tends to be quite long. One nightmare scenario is a desktop consisting of three highly graphical and window-oriented multiple-document interface (MDI) applications (for example, network management, factory control, and accounting). If each application creates an easy minimum of

300 windows, you'll quickly have a locked-up desktop. The solution is easy. Don't create so many windows. Sadly enough, this is your only recourse. Don't expect the problem to be fixed until a 32-bit version of Windows is released.

Actually, there is a way that you can circumvent the per-session window limit; however, it isn't the easiest fix in the world. The solution involves creating just one window per class and dynamically moving and updating the window as the user tabs and clicks through the different windows and dialogs in the application. Using this method requires that the developer maintain a list in memory of the size, position, parent window, and data for every window in the class to be represented by this "floating" window. For example, when the user clicks a mouse somewhere within the window, the developer must scan the rectangular regions represented by each control, checking for a hit. When a hit is found, the edit control is moved and repainted to indicate that a new control has received the focus. Likewise, the old control is painted as having lost the focus. This technique is most practical for industrial-strength data entry forms, which can potentially require hundreds of single-line and multiline edit controls. This method also has the benefit of removing the 255-control-per-dialog limit enforced by Windows. This technique also works well for MDI child windows, although the implementation is a little different. When you use this method, the same kind of list is kept; however, this time it must contain only a handle to an icon and an MDI client-relative screen position. This requires that the developer handle all dragging, dropping, painting, and opening of the minimized window. Naturally, using any window-on-the-fly method like this prevents a function from calling `GetWindow()` or any of the `EnumWindow*()` series of functions. This isn't really a problem, however, just an observation.

Kernel

Windows functions involving memory management, multitasking, and re-sources belong to the Kernel module. Kernel exports functions for string management, resource management, local and global heap management, module management, task management, and even a series of selector values (0h, 40h, a000h, b800h, and so on), which can be used to directly access physical locations in the lower 1M of memory. Memory management under Windows basically consists of Kernel's heap manager on the front end and Windows' virtual memory manager, using the DOS Protected Mode Interface (DPMI) version .9, holding up the rear.

Device drivers export various functions indicative of their level of support for Windows' functionality. Kernel, GDI, and User pick up the slack for whatever functions the drivers don't export themselves. If a printer, such as the HP LaserJet III, supports enhanced functionality (bit blitting and pixel plotting) above and beyond what the GDI module can "generically" provide, then it will export functions to provide those features.

Device Drivers

Windows device drivers fall into three basic categories: system drivers, printer drivers, and virtual device drivers (VxDs). Virtual device drivers are (primarily) 32-bit flat model programs. The only exception is some 16-bit real mode and 16-bit protected mode Windows startup code. The other device drivers are 16-bit segmented model programs. System device drivers support things such as the mouse, parallel ports, and serial ports. Printer drivers depend solely on the services of one of the system drivers, which control parallel and serial port access.

Virtual device drivers (.386) are loaded along with Windows while it's still in real mode and in the process of switching to protected mode. The job of a VxD is to serialize access to hardware, providing a buffer between the system drivers and hardware devices. Most device drivers are characterized as either *block-* or *character-mode device drivers.* This term is an indication of how they handle associated data. Parallel and serial ports are examples of character-mode device drivers, whereas floppy and hard disk drivers and video display drivers are examples of block-mode device drivers.

Believe it or not, custom VxDs are used quite a bit in end-user applications, such as screen savers and in the Norton Desktop for Windows. VxDs are so common because they can talk to and see everything in memory at all times. Sometimes this kind of functionality is required especially when the DOS-to-Windows boundary must be bridged. An example of such an instance is when a Windows-based screen saver kicks in while the user is in an active DOS window. Several base VxDs are bundled with Windows' 32-bit virtual machine manager to form the file WIN386.EXE. If a single file were to be held responsible for Windows' being what it is, this would be it. Windows' virtual machine manager is composed of several units, including a scheduler (primary and time-slicer), I/O emulation, virtual memory manager, general interrupt handler, and an event servicer. The virtual memory manager acts as a DPMI front end (or host) to various virtual device drivers and to Kernel, a DPMI client. Kernel then uses these DPMI services and some extra code to

create a heap manager front end to modules running in the system. Having Windows' virtual memory manager acting as a DPMI host does not prevent either a VxD or a DLL from accessing DPMI services directly. A VxD can, because it runs at ring level 0 and has access to the entire 4G address space as well as all VMs at all times. DLLs can access DPMI functions too, but they should limit themselves to functions that Windows does not provide itself.

Of Messaging and Messages

Messages are at the heart of any object-oriented system, coursing through all the objects on the system like blood through the human body. Without a constant stream of messages, an object can be thought of as "dead." Although it still might function on its own, it will never seem "alive," responding to external events. Under Windows' nonpreemptive multitasking model, when a single application stops the flow of messages, all windows on the desktop come to a screeching halt, effectively lying dead. Fortunately, Windows 3.1 provides the ability to detect when an application has gone belly up and stopped the flow of messages, allowing a local reboot of the application. Under Windows 3.0, this same situation required a reboot of the entire computer instead.

As Figure 1.7 illustrates, Windows generates and acquires messages from several sources. At the lowest level are the messages generated by the keyboard, mouse, and timer, which are all placed into the system-wide hardware message queue. From there, these messages are posted to the individual message queues of each instance of an application. The reason these messages are posted is that device drivers cannot call `SendMessage()`, which could cause other messages to be invoked, thus inadvertently calling the device driver again. `PostMessage()` is safe to call for virtually any type of program, because it merely places a message into a queue and immediately returns. The only requirement for `PostMessage()` is that the application's queue has been created.

Messages are also generated by the different functions in the Windows API, with most of these messages being sent and not posted. Almost every function can be thought of as a "messaging macro," meaning that a single function call wraps up at least one and possibly several messages. Messages are also (obviously) generated by running applications. An application or a library can post messages to its own queue (of the application) or to the queue of another application, and it can send messages directly to its own windows or to the windows of another application. However, an application is also required to process messages intended for the desktop window. Because no individual task exists for this processing, it must be handled by the currently active application.

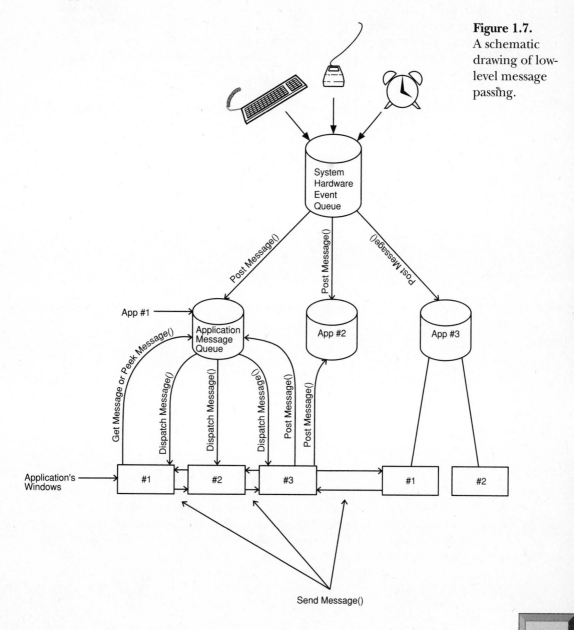

Figure 1.7.
A schematic drawing of low-level message passing.

Additionally, an application or a library can read and optionally remove and process messages from its own queue. To do this same thing with a foreign application requires that a messaging hook be established, which is discussed in depth in Chapter 5. Generally, messages must be read and processed on a first-in, first-out basis. Windows provides no simple mechanism of treating the messaging queue like an array, with access to individual elements. Doing such a thing would more than likely severely undermine the stablity of an application and would represent one of the worst possible hacks that could be done under Windows.

Messages provide an indirect method of sending commands to a window and represent a key object-oriented construct. Figure 1.8 illustrates the several methods that modules can use to communicate with each other. Windows supports the sending of messages to window objects only, unlike other object-oriented environments that support messaging with objects that don't necessarily have an associated visual component. Brushes, bitmaps, pens, and window classes all could benefit from a message-based interface.

Figure 1.8.
Methods of communication among application and DLL modules.

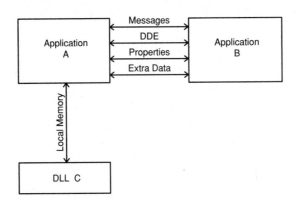

Due to Windows' nonpreemptive nature, a single application can easily spin its gears in a section of code and never return control to Windows. If a WM_ACTIVATE message (deactivating the current application) is in the queue but never processed, the other application will never receive control, nor will Windows (unless Yield() or some other Windows messaging function is called). Because mouse and keyboard input are serialized in the system queue, other applications cannot receive control because the messages are targeted only to the queue of the currently running task. A 32-bit multithreaded version of Windows solves this problem by dedicating a thread to handling mouse and keyboard input, thus freeing applications from the responsibility.

The Window Function

Every window on the desktop has at least two functions that process its messages: a private method handler, which is the function passed to **RegisterClass()**, and a common method handler (**DefWindowProc()** or **DefDlgProc()**). Regardless, all window functions must follow a particular format. All window functions must be declared FAR, because Windows will need to change code segments when it actually invokes the window procedure. Window functions also are declared PASCAL simply because the PASCAL convention is already used by Windows, and it was chosen because it reduces code size considerably. (See Chapter 3, "Program and Module Fundamentals," for more on calling and naming conventions.) The following line lists the format of a window function:

```
ReturnValue WINAPI WndProcName(HWND hWnd, UINT Msg, WPARAM wParam, LPARAM lParam);
```

So what happened to the FAR PASCAL keywords? The 3.1 SDK offers several new typedefs and macros that alleviate some of the cryptic syntax required with the 3.0 SDK. They include:

Typedef	Use
WINAPI	Defined as _FAR _PASCAL. Used to declare a window procedure.
CALLBACK	Defined as _FAR _PASCAL. Used to declare a callback function.
WPARAM	Defined as an unsigned integer. Used for first message parameter.
LPARAM	Defined as a long. Used for second message parameter.
LRESULT	Defined as a long. Used for a window procedure return value.
WNDPROC	A pointer to a window function.

Macro	Use
MAKELPARAM(low, high)	Constructs a window procedure lparam parameter value.
MAKELRESULT(low, high)	Constructs a window procedure return value.

Part of the reason these new typedefs and macros are included with the SDK concerns portability to Windows NT. The Windows 3.0 windows.h include file was extremely sloppy when it came to type checking. As a result, the newer include file with 3.1 more strongly types all definitions. Because many common values have been widened to 32 bits under NT, the new typedefs can help mask the width of the value, providing a level of indirection that can be taken advantage of when the program is recompiled for Windows NT.

The astute observer will notice that under Windows 3.1 many of the parameter types have been changed from words to integers. This was done because a compiler treats an integer as the most fundamental unit that the computer can handle. In the case of a 16-bit operating system (Windows 3.x), this value is 16 bits wide, which also happens to be the size of a word. However, under a 32-bit operating system like Windows NT, this value is now 32 bits wide. To have parameters "float" to this new size, they were changed from words to integers. True, this could have been done with earlier versions of Windows, but it wasn't. Windows 3.1 has also included a new strict definition for prototyping, which involves a separate winstric.h include file, as well as a header file containing portability macros and message encapsulator crackers, which is contained in windowsx.h.

Additionally, different window function return types are needed, depending on how the window was created:

Return Value	Use
LRESULT	For windows and modeless dialogs created with a developer-supplied window class.
BOOL	For modeless dialogs created with Windows' internal dialog class.
int	For modal dialogs using Windows' internal dialog class.

The Message

A message, as it is received by a window procedure, is broken down into four distinct portions: a window handle (hWnd) specifying the destination of the message, an unsigned integer value representing the message (wMsg), and an extra word (wParam) and long (lParam) representing additional information to be associated with the message. The wParam value often is used either as an index, as a true/false flag, or as the control ID of a window, whereas lParam often is used as a long pointer to a string or a function, as a start/stop value, or as a combination notification code and window handle. Generally, the message is processed in a switch and case statement in the window procedure, with each case statement in the switch acting on a different message.

The following code snippet illustrates the format of a simple window procedure:

```
LRESULT WINAPI MainWndProc
(
    HWND hWnd, UINT Msg, WPARAM wParam, LPARAM lParam
)
{
    switch(Msg)
    {
        case WM_CREATE :

            CreateMethod();         // Call create/init stuff for window
            break;
        case WM_CLOSE :

            DestroyWindow(hWnd);
            return(0L);

        case WM_DESTROY :

            PostQuitMessage(0);     // Post WM_QUIT to terminate app
            break;

        case WM_COMMAND :

            switch(wParam)          // wParam contains child ctrl ID
            {
                case IDC_SOMECTRL :

                    ProcessSomeCtrlMsg();
                    return(0L);

                default :

                    break;
            }
            break;

        default :
```

```
        break;
    }

    // Process any default messages for window

    return(DefWindowProc(hWnd, Msg, wParam, lParam));
}
```

A message is stored in the following structure:

```
struct MSG
{
    HWND    hWnd;      // Window receiving the message
    UINT    message;   // Integer value representing message code
    WPARAM  wParam;    // Parameter associated with message
    LPARAM  lParam;    // Parameter associated with message
    DWORD   time;      // System elapsed-time when message was posted
    POINT   pt;        // Cursor position when message was posted
}
```

Note that window functions are declared as passing only four members of the message structure (`hWnd`, `wMsg`, `wParam`, and `lParam`), yet there are six members in all (including the missing entries `pt` and `time`). This just reflects on the overhead involved with function calls and a little on the importance of those two items relevant to the message as a whole. If the time and position of the message actually is important, the message should be intercepted just after the `GetMessage()` call in the application's `WinMain()` loop, before it is dispatched to a window procedure. Intercepting the message before it is dispatched allows access to the two "hidden" message parameters. The last two elements in the structure can also be obtained by calling the functions `GetMessageTime()` and `GetMessagePos()`.

A common problem for developers involves the fact that messages are passed only in response to events that have already occurred. Many times a more direct (synchronous) route is required, especially when keyboard input is involved, because keystrokes (such as mouse and timer events) normally are given to the application in the form of a series of posted messages. Windows, however, provides the `GetAsyncKeyState()` function, which gets the current state of the keyboard, not its state at the time of the receipt of the message. Functions such as `GetInputState()` return keyboard status only at the time of the event. They aren't much use when you want to check whether the user currently is pressing a key.

Processing Events in the Queue

Generally, you either process a message or you don't. There usually are no gray areas. Messages can be processed internally, passed to a default handling procedure for external processing, logged, not acted on, halted, or any combination thereof. Intercepting a message is not the same as processing the message. If you aren't doing specifically what the message requires (which isn't always clear in the documentation), you should pass control to a default window function.

After WM_COMMAND messages are processed, control can immediately be returned to Windows without further processing control being passed to a default message handler. This is because WM_COMMAND messages are completely private to the application, and Windows would have absolutely no idea of what to do with the message. With other types of messages, however, a little trickery can be performed. When multiple methods must be handled for a message, usually the default method is called first, and then the additional method is performed, providing extra behaviors. This is commonly done when certain painting effects need to be achieved, and in general whenever a control is superclassed or subclassed. For example, when processing the message WM_GETDLGCODE for a superclassed or subclassed stock Windows control (edit, listbox, and so on), your code would perform something similar to this:

```
case WM_GETDLGCODE :

    // call original method handler for message

    OldVal = CallWindowProc(lpfnCtrlProc, hWnd, Msg, wParam, lParam);

    ...perform additional processing here...

    return(OldVal | SomeNewValue);
```

This is needed because stock controls respond differently to WM_GETDLGCODE. To add an additional layer of processing for this message, the developer must first determine and accommodate the original response to the message. A similar technique is used for the nonclient painting performed by the custom dialog class code presented in the appendixes. In this case, the WM_NCPAINT message is first sent to Windows (with certain nonclient style bits removed from the window temporarily). Then new painting methods are invoked after the default painting has been performed and the style bits re-added to the

window. Superclassing a stock button control and at the same time providing a new visual look for the control (without using owner-draw) requires a block of code similar to the following block:

```
case WM_KEYDOWN     :

    // If a spacebar was pressed, enable Windows to check or push the button,
    // yet prohibit it from painting the control. You want to do that part.

    if(wParam != VK_SPACE)
    {
        break;
    }

case WM_LBUTTONDOWN :
case WM_LBUTTONUP   :

    RedrawOff(hWnd);

    // call original message handler, enabling it to set extra data correctly

    CallWindowProc(lpfnCtrlProc, hWnd, Msg, wParam, lParam);

    RedrawOn(hWnd);

    InvalidateRect(hWnd, NULL, TRUE);   // Cause a paint to occur, giving the
    UpdateWindow(hWnd);                 // button your own look and style

    return(0L);

case WM_PAINT :

    ...perform painting of control...

    return(0L);
```

This code effectively prohibits the original button code from repainting the control, yet it allows the original code to handle all mode and state settings for the button. The reason owner-draw isn't a viable option with buttons is because after owner-draw is implemented, Windows automatically assumes that the control is a push button, allowing no checkbox or radio button functionality. By imaginatively using messaging and default processing, you can perform neat time-saving tricks and effects—and all are perfectly legal.

Default Message Processing

Whether a message is processed or not, the Windows "buck" must end somewhere. How and when you return control to Windows or to a window class procedure is very important. The answer is fairly complex, because it all depends on the type of message being processed and whether your window function is for a modal dialog, dialog, or window. Several layers of code can be involved in the process, as illustrated by Figure 1.9. The process of messages being passed down through layers is known as *inheritance*. By not processing a message, other processes "inherit" the capability to process and act on the message, possibly providing different results.

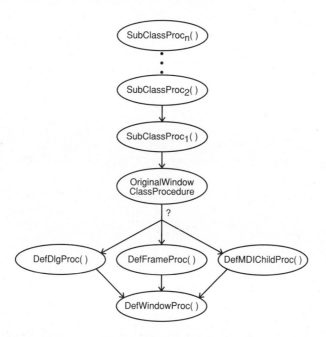

Figure 1.9. Message-handling layers.

Depending on the window type (control, dialog, MDI frame, or MDI client) and, more important, whether the message needs further processing, the Windows API provides the following functions for the handling of default window behaviors:

Default Window Function	Use
CallWindowProc()	Called by a window procedure to pass processing of a message to a lower layer in the chain. The lower layer might then call DefWindowProc() or DefDlgProc(). Used when subclassing and superclassing a window.
DefDlgProc()	For dialogs created with an application-registered class.
DefFrameProc()	For processing MDI frame window messages.
DefMDIChildProc()	Default processing for MDI client windows.
DefWindowProc()	Provides default processing for windows with an application-registered class.

The developer should pass message handling control only to window procedures of the same class. Although it would be nice to tell another control class to paint itself on top of your control, that's not possible. This is because virtually every stock control uses the class and window extra data to hold state information for the control. When this data isn't there, or is in the wrong format, a crash or other weird result occurs. A button control uses its extra data to indicate whether it is in a pushed state, whereas the dialog class uses its extra data to locate the default button in the dialog, and the control with focus. When superclassing existing stock Windows control types, you must preserve any existing class or window extra data. The function GetClassInfo() can be used to get this information before the new class is registered. In fact, you should call this function and use the resulting WNDCLASS structure as a template for your new control, merely filling in changed fields. Note that when you use this method, it's entirely legal to increase the amounts of per-class and per-window extra data—however, you can't decrease them.

Posting Versus Sending Messages

Messages are sent to a window in one of two ways: by *posting* or by *sending*. An application receives posted messages indirectly via its application message queue. When a message is posted, it is placed in this queue and a TRUE or a

FALSE is immediately returned to the caller, indicating the success or failure of this function. Completion status depends on whether the application message queue was full at the time of the posting. Under Windows 3, applications come with a default, fixed queue size of eight messages. Windows 3.0 had a bug that prevented the queue size from growing any larger, but normally, an application should have no need to adjust the size of its queue. A future version of Windows will dynamically adjust the message queue as needed.

All the initial "early" messages going to a window, such as WM_CREATE and WM_GETMINMAXINFO, must be sent to the window (rather than posted) for reasons other than requiring a return value. This is primarily because the message dispatching loop in WinMain(), which is key to distributing posted messages, might not have been entered yet. When per-instance initialization code (which usually means window-creation code) is being executed, enough messages are sent to the window to allow the window to come online. After this is done, calls to **ShowWindow()** and **UpdateWindow()** are usually made, and the application enters its message processing and dispatching loop, where created windows are now ready to receive posted messages.

Posting a message into a queue guarantees that the active task will be uninterrupted, because control is always returned immediately after placing the message in the target application's queue. Sending a message, on the other hand, bypasses an application's message queue and instead goes straight for the jugular, giving the message directly to the destination window's window function. The window function then usually returns a value immediately, relinquishing control at the same time. If the called window function doesn't want to relinquish control, it can always respond to the **SendMessage()** call with a call to **ReplyMessage()**, instead of just using the return() function to return a static value. **PostMessage()** is fully reentrant, and it is actually the only messaging-related API call that can be used by an interrupt service routine (ISR) to notify a DLL that processing needs to occur. **PostMessage()** usually is a safe function to call, even inside of what are normally restrictive sections of code, such as a DLL's LibMain() or WEP() routines.

Not all the messages that Windows generates for an application are posted. In general, input messages such as keyboard, mouse, and timer messages are posted, whereas window management messages such as WM_PAINT and WM_ERASEBKGND are always sent. This makes sense, because in every WinMain() procedure, windows are created before the message processing loop is even entered. If the messages were posted (some of which can't be posted because they require a return value), there would be no way for the application to process them. Additionally, Windows 3.1 posts WM_COMMAND messages, instead of sending them as under Windows 3.0.

Any messages such as WM_ERASEBKGND that require a return value are always sent to the task. Sending messages is by far more common for a developer than posting. This is because of the nature of a message itself. Usually you expect some sort of answer from the window procedure, and **SendMessage()** is the only way to get it. Messages posted by a task generally are processed by Windows shortly after the task that posted the messages relinquishes control. However, this can't be counted on. One message that is always posted and never sent is WM_QUIT. That's because WM_QUIT is acted on only in the task's message processing loop and never in a window procedure. If you sent WM_QUIT, the message loop would never see it. Posted messages commonly are messages whose return value is of no concern, such as WM_QUIT and WM_CLOSE.

Posting a message puts the message into the target application's message queue, where several things can happen. Ultimately, the message is dispatched to one of the windows on the desktop, but until that point, several layers of translation can occur. For starters, the message might be translated and stolen by the function **IsDialogMessage()**, which handles many of the keystroke messages and common behaviors for dialogs, such as tabbing, the default button, and arrow keys. **IsDialogMessage** also calls **TranslateMessage** and **DispatchMessage** if required, which is the reason they are effectively skipped inside this application's messaging loop. The application also can call **TranslateMessage()** to map virtual key codes into actual character codes, leaving the messages in the queue to be processed. Accelerators can be processed at this stage in the game, as can certain forms of background processing.

Ultimately, the message is dispatched to the appropriate window procedure, where it is finally acted on. If the message doesn't end up getting processed by the window that the message was sent to, it usually is passed (via a function, not another message) to the next procedure associated with the window. The following code snippet illustrates a basic message dispatching loop for an application:

```
while(GetMessage( &msg, NULL, NULL, NULL) != WM_QUIT)
{
    if(hDlgActive)
    {
        if(IsDialogMessage(hDlgActive, &msg))
        {
            continue;              // Msg was handled by dialog
        }
    }

    TranslateMessage( &msg);      // Translate virtual key codes
    DispatchMessage( &msg);       // Send to window procedure
}
```

In the preceding example, a static window handle is used to keep track of the currently active dialog window. Every dialog function in your application should trap the message WM_ACTIVATE and set the value of hDlgActive according to the wParam value. If it's not zero, the dialog is being activated and hDlgActive should be set to the dialog's window handle. If wParam is zero, then hDlgActive is set to NULL.

Setting the variable hDlgActive from within a library is done a bit differently. Because only functions, and not variables, can be exported by an application, another means must be developed to let the application know that a library-created and library-housed dialog is coming online. A simple method that can accomplish this feat involves a custom message, but not one created with **RegisterWindowMessage()**. This message is task-based, which means you can pick any value for the message. All that must be done is for the library to call **PostAppMessage()**, passing the task handle of the application owning the library. A task message is required because this message isn't bound to a particular window created by the application; rather, it applies to a window created by the library. Although the application is servicing and dispatching messages for this window, it knew nothing about its creation. Therefore, the application must be notified that it needs dialog-style support. The application identifies the message as task-based, because the message structure returned by **GetMessage()** or **PeekMessage()** in its message dispatching loop will contain a NULL HWND value. When the message is received, the application can use the wParam value passed by the library (containing the new value for hDlgActive) and set its global variable accordingly.

Multitasking via Messaging

A task yields control to Windows, allowing it to process messages placed in other applications' queues, via one of four messaging functions: **GetMessage()**, **PeekMessage()**, **WaitMessage()**, or **Yield()**. When any of these four functions is called, control is returned to Windows, where the messages in other queues can finally be serviced. If none of these functions is called for a long period, performance of the system as a whole suffers, because of the nonpreemptive multitasking model, which relies on tasks voluntarily relinquishing control frequently. The functions **DialogBox()**, **DialogBoxIndirect()**, **DialogBoxParam()**, **DialogBoxIndirectParam()**, and **MessageBox()** also yield control to Windows.

A call to **GetMessage()** relinquishes control to Windows and returns to the calling task only when a message has been placed in the queue. **GetMessage()** is commonly used inside the WinMain() message dispatching loop, and it shouldn't be used when some form of background processing is desired. For this, the developer should use `PeekMessage()`. `PeekMessage()` polls the application's message queue for messages (if any are present) and fills a passed message structure with the results, optionally removing the message from the queue if desired. From this point, the message can be either translated and dispatched or merely discarded. By using another flag, `PeekMessage()` can optionally *not* relinquish control to Windows when it is called. Unlike `GetMessage()`, `PeekMessage()` doesn't have to wait for a message to be placed into the queue in order to return.

An application should not use `PeekMessage()` unless processing needs to be done in the background. If the application is just waiting for an event to occur, it should call either `GetMessage()` or `WaitMessage()`. `WaitMessage()` is like `GetMessage()` in that it waits for an event to enter the message queue before control is returned. Unlike `GetMessage()`, however, `WaitMessage()` does not remove the message from the queue. Microsoft warns against using `PeekMessage()` in messaging loops because the task will constantly be rescheduled by the Windows scheduler. This practice could wreak havoc with laptop-based power management software that depends on the system's going idle. `Yield()` is unique compared to the other messaging functions in that control is relinquished to Windows only when no messages exist in the task's queue.

The following code snippet illustrates a more advanced message dispatching loop that provides a form of background processing. A loop similar to this would be used for an application that required constant polling of the serial port. If notification needs to occur the other way around, and the device needs to signal an application that an event has occurred, it can call `PostMessage()` to put the event in the application's queue.

The following message loop shows one method of background processing:

```
while(TRUE)
{
    while(PeekMessage( &msg, NULL, NULL, NULL, PM_REMOVE))
    {
        if(msg.message == WM_QUIT)
        {
            break;
        }

        if(hDlgActive)
        {
            if(IsDialogMessage(hDlgActive, &msg))
            {
```

```
                    continue;                   // Msg was handled by dialog
            }
        }

        TranslateMessage( &msg); // Translate virtual key codes
        DispatchMessage( &msg);  // Send to window procedure
    }

    if(msg.message == WM_QUIT)
    {
        break;
    }
    if(BackgroundProcessingRequired)
    {
        ProcessingFunc();                 // Handle bkgrd processing
    }
    else
    {
        WaitMessage();                    // Return when msg is in queue
    }
}
```

The `PeekMessage()` function accepts one of possibly several flags that affect how the message is intercepted in the queue and how control is relinquished after the call. They include the following flags:

PeekMessage Flag	Description
PM_NOREMOVE	Puts the pending message into the MSG structure but does not remove the message from the queue.
PM_REMOVE	Puts the pending message into the MSG structure and removes the message from the queue.
PM_NOYIELD	Does not relinquish control (as is normally done) after the call.

New with Windows 3.1 is the messaging function `GetQueueStatus()`, which, like `PeekMessage()`, is used to check for pending events in the message queue. Unlike `PeekMessage()`, `GetQueueStatus()` is quite fast, and often it is used to determine whether `GetMessage()` or `PeekMessage()` should be called at all. `GetQueueStatus()`, when passed a message type, returns a dword value indicating two things: whether any new messages exist in the queue since the last call to

`GetQueueStatus()` (or `GetMessage()`/`PeekMessage()`) and what type of events currently are in the queue. `GetQueueMessage()` can trap for the following events:

Flag	Description
QS_KEY	Checks for keystroke messages (for example, WM_CHAR).
QS_MOUSEMOVE	Checks for mouse movement messages (for example, WM_MOUSEMOVE).
QS_MOUSEBUTTON	Checks for mouse button messages (for example, WM_?BUTTONDOWN*).
QS_MOUSE	Checks for all mouse messages.
QS_POSTMESSAGE	Checks for posted messages other than those listed.
QS_TIMER	Checks for WM_TIMER messages.
QS_PAINT	Checks for WM_PAINT messages.
QS_SENDMESSAGE	Checks to see whether a message sent by another application is in the queue.
QS_ALLINPUT	Checks for any type of message in the queue.

Due to the way that Windows handles message processing, a call to `GetQueueStatus()` is not guaranteed to indicate that messages will be "pullable" from the queue, because Windows internally handled or reorganized some messages. For this reason, `GetQueueStatus()` should be used only as an indicator that events might be waiting to be processed.

User-Defined Messages

Although messages normally are sent to a single window at a time, Windows does provide the capability of broadcasting a single message to all top-level windows and dialogs on the desktop. Any call to `PostMessage()` or `SendMessage()` with an `hWnd` value of 0xffff (or in Windows 3.1, the `#define HWND_BROADCAST`) will accomplish this very feat. For a developer, this functionality often is useful only for developer-defined messages. Private messages can be defined and sent in one of two ways. The most common is to send "submessages" via the `WM_COMMAND` message, which already is registered by Windows and completely private to the application. The only restriction is that private messages sent via `WM_COMMAND` don't interfere with messages intended for window controls, which also use WM_COMMAND. Another method for creating "same application" private messages is to use message values from WM_USER (0x0400) to 0xBFFF. These are guaranteed to be private and available to any application. However, WM_USER can only be used with custom window classes, not dialogs or superclassed "stock" controls provided by Windows. this is because messages like LB_GETTEXT and BM_SETCHECK use WM_USER to define their own messages. For messages that need to be sent to different applications or to any type of window, there's the function **RegisterWindowMessage()**, which registers a system-wide message guaranteed to be unique while Windows is running. Any message registered in this manner will remain registered until Windows terminates. Messages registered in this manner return values from 0xC000 to 0xFFFE.

All the custom controls (as well as the custom dialog class) presented in the book use the function **RegisterWindowMessage()** to create custom messages for handling the drawing of control labels and working with the virtual client areas of the dialog class and bitmap class control types, among other things. Because these messages are dynamically created and have varying values, they cannot be processed inside the normal switch()/case block; rather, they must be trapped for and processed inside a series of if() statement blocks located either before or after the switch statement.

Message Priority and Queue Optimization

Actually, the description given **GetMessage()** a few paragraphs ago is somewhat incorrect. **GetMessage()** does not necessarily return control to an application as soon as a message has been placed in its queue. If other applications have messages waiting to be processed that are of a higher priority, **GetMessage()** yields control again. Low-priority messages include WM_PAINT and WM_TIMER. This is part of the reason that when an application is closing down, the screen painting can get rather garbled for a second. In this flurry of activity before shutdown, paint messages are hardly getting processed, if at all. Until a window is actually painted, WM_PAINT messages are accumulated, merged together, and forced to the bottom of the message queue.

Why is WM_TIMER a low-priority message, you ask? After all, shouldn't it be one of the highest priority messages? Actually, because Windows is nonpreemptive, it has no control over task switches and the amount of time spent processing each task. Because of this, timer messages should be used strictly for noncritical needs, such as simple animation, or noncritical polling of a device.

Other than low-priority messages, Windows 3.0 had fairly little in the way of message queue optimization. For Windows 3.1, the reverse holds true. The real reason behind the instant "snap" of a window up on the desktop (especially evident in Program Manager) is because of the elimination of superfluous window messages. Windows 3.0 sometimes sent WM_PAINT and WM_ERASEBKGND messages under inappropriate circumstances, often to hidden, disabled, or soon-to-be-destroyed windows. And because an unnecessary number of calls to `UpdateWindow()` were being made, they too have been removed, resulting in an additional level of performance. It's because of these optimizations that developers must test all paint- and scroll-related aspects of their applications. Windows 3.1 has changed several rules regarding the validating/invalidating and painting of display contexts and the ordering and presence of messages that end up getting sent in the process.

Message Ordering

The Windows SDK manual states quite clearly in several places that no assumptions are to be made about the order of messages in the queue during a specified event. Try studying the start-to-finish message flow going to a specified window, using Spy or CodeView. For an experiment, try this on a variety of modal and modeless dialogs—ones created with a private class and with Windows' internal dialog class. Don't limit the experiment to top-level windows; try it on child controls as well. Message flow can be quite unpredictable at times, although admittedly Windows 3.1 has fixed many of the problems.

Window Messages and Notification Messages

Messages are grouped into two basic categories: window messages and control notification messages. Window messages are sent to the window in which the event occurred, whereas control notification messages are sent to the parent of the child control where the event occurred.

Window messages fall into one of two varieties: *generic* and *dependent*. Generic window messages (prefixed with WM_) describe every possible event that can happen to almost every kind of window. This includes messages for painting, erasing, and mouse and keyboard activity. Dependent messages are sent to child controls and are prefixed in a manner to indicate the control type (LB_, CB_, EM_, and so on). These messages aren't generic to all windows, existing only to provide functionality for the controls for which they were created. Generally, messages deal with events involving the window's client and nonclient areas. Several other categories of messages exist, however, including system notification messages for when the WIN.INI file or other system resources are changed.

Notification messages are provided merely as a convenience to the parent window. Without notification messages, the developer might have to manually subclass each child control. A much easier method is to have the child control selectively pass certain messages to its parent—all without having to do any subclassing. Window messages are prefixed with a WM_, and control notification messages are prefixed with an abbreviation of the control class name (for example, BN_ for buttons and CB_ for comboboxes). Control notification messages are passed to the parent window via a WM_PARENTNOTIFY or a WM_COMMAND message.

Only one button notification message is sent to the parent through WM_COMMAND: BN_CLICKED. Generally, however, any message sent to the parent window of a button control is usually assumed to be a click message, because most source code doesn't explicitly check for BN_CLICKED. Notification messages for other controls, such as comboboxes and listboxes, are more numerous.

The message WM_PARENTNOTIFY is used for notification messages common to all child window types. This message is sent whenever a child window is created, destroyed, or clicked with the left, middle, or right mouse button. In this case, the wParam value of the WM_PARENTNOTIFY message contains the actual window message applicable to the current state of the control (that is, WM_CREATE, WM_DESTROY, WM_?BUTTONDOWN). When the create message is sent through this method, it is done just before the return of the **CreateWindow()** call that created the window. When the destroy notification message is sent, it's done just before the child window is about to be destroyed, allowing the parent window a chance to perform any additional cleanup. The only time WM_PARENTNOTIFY isn't sent to a window is when the child window in question is created with the extended window style WS_EX_NOPARENTNOTIFY.

An important and common window message is WM_COMMAND. Whenever any menu, accelerator, or child control is selected or in some way acted on, a WM_COMMAND message is fired off to the parent window, instructing it of the event that just occurred. With WM_COMMAND messages, wParam represents the ID of the menu, child control, or accelerator, and lParam is used for miscellaneous data. When a child control sends a WM_COMMAND-style notification message to its parent, it uses the HIWORD of the lParam value to store the notification message

and the LOWORD to store the control's window handle. Menus store a zero in the low-order word of lParam, whereas accelerators store a one in the high-order word. Windows 3.0 used to send WM_COMMAND messages to an application, whereas Windows 3.1 now posts WM_COMMAND messages. This was done to help the developer prevent certain reentrance problems that might have occurred otherwise.

Emulating Functions via Messages

A module should never try to duplicate the sequence of messages required to emulate many of the functions in the Windows API, which generally encapsulates several messages into a single call and should always be used when provided. Not only do the functions provide a much-needed level of indirection, but they're also guaranteed to work. Microsoft commonly issues warnings to developers about assuming anything about messaging. This includes not only message ordering and priorities, but also implies the number and type of messages required to emulate an API function.

For example, to set the focus to a particular control in your window, you shouldn't send a WM_KILLFOCUS and a WM_SETFOCUS. Use Windows' **SetFocus()** function instead. This ensures that the appropriate paint messages and caret maintenance is taken care of. You'd be surprised at the number of messages that a single Windows API function might invoke. Unless it is specifically mentioned in the SDK documentation that the message can be sent "as is" to a window, don't try it. Or at least don't get too upset when it doesn't work.

Trying to manually control a foreign application via messages is extremely difficult. Windows' macro recorder utility is successful only because it uses journaling, which means that you've already captured a stream of successfully sent keystrokes. Controlling an application dynamically is much more difficult.

To help ease the pain, however, Windows has provided new computer-based training (CBT) and shell messaging hooks (in addition to the already-present keyboard journaling hooks) that make it easier to control "foreign" applications. These new hooks send notification messages whenever a top-level window is created, destroyed, moved, or otherwise manipulated, making it easier to determine in developer-based code when to perform certain actions. Incidentally, Microsoft has also released a new product, Microsoft Test, which is used to provide automated testing and control over a foreign application. This product makes it infinitely easier to construct a series of test suites and then hammer the application repeatedly until it drops or survives the tests.

A Windowless Application

Although the text you've read so far has implied for the most part that an application must create at least one window to "live and breathe" under Windows, this isn't entirely true. The windowless application situation is desirable when an application's sole purpose is to load a library. Most developers, to get around this kind of situation, create at least one desktop window, either minimizing it at the bottom of the desktop or hiding it from view altogether.

There is one other option, at least for applications that have an accompanying library. In fact, this method is used by the HotApp/HotKey hook example given in Chapter 5, "Library Design Ideas," which uses a small stub-application to load a library containing a keyboard hook. The keyboard hook is used to test for various key combinations, through which full-screen and windowed-DOS windows can be launched. Another key combination unloads the application. This is why this kind of code is needed. Obviously, if the application never needed to be unloaded, you could just wait until Windows exited. Consider the following example:

```
int PASCAL WinMain
(
    HINSTANCE hInstance, HINSTANCE hPrevInstance, LPSTR lpCmdLine,
    int nCmdShow
)
{
    MSG msg;

    InstallHook();

    //
    // Spin gears waiting for a WM_QUIT from library, done via
    // call to PostAppMessage
    //

    while(GetMessage(&msg, NULL, NULL, NULL))
        {
            TranslateMessage(&msg);
            DispatchMessage(&msg);
        }

    //
    // Remove the hook. This could have been in the library,
    // but for symmetry reasons, it's in the application.
```

```
//

RemoveHook();

//
// Hasty banana!
//

return(FALSE);
}
```

In the HotKey library is the following portion of code that terminates HotApp:

```
PostAppMessage(hTaskClient, WM_QUIT, 0, 0L);
```

The `hTaskClient` variable is a global that was initialized when the hook was first installed. When this message is posted, the `GetMessage()` loop in `WinMain()` aborts, and the hook is removed and the application is terminated. When a message is sent via `PostAppMessage()`, the receiver's MSG structure is given an HWND of null, indicating the receipt of a task message as opposed to a window message.

The Windows API contains a number of messaging-related functions, including the following functions:

Function	Purpose
`DispatchMessage()`	Dispatches a message to the window created by the current task.
`GetInputState()`	Retrieves the input state of the entire keyboard at the time the keyboard event was placed in the queue.
`GetMessage()`	Waits for and retrieves a message from the application message queue.
`*GetMessageExtraInfo()`	Returns extra information associated with a message.
`GetMessagePos()`	Returns the cursor position at the last message gotten by `GetMessage()`.
`GetMessageTime()`	Returns the elapsed time since the last message gotten by `GetMessage()`.
`*GetQueueStatus()`	Indicates types of messages (if any) that are sitting in the queue.

Function	Purpose
`InSendMessage()`	Used in a window function to determine whether it is processing a message sent to it via `SendMessage()`, as opposed to `PostMessage()`.
`PeekMessage()`	Used by a task to check for and optionally read messages in its queue. Control is not necessarily relinquished, nor is the message automatically removed from the queue.
`PostAppMessage()`	Posts a message to a task, not a window. When the message is received, the HWND value is NULL.
`PostMessage()`	Posts a message to a target window's application message queue.
`PostQuitMessage()`	Called by the window during WM_DESTROY to shut down the application. Posts a WM_QUIT message in the application's queue.
`*QuerySendMessage()`	Determines whether the `SendMessage()` call originated from within the current task.
`RegisterWindowMessage()`	Registers a guaranteed unique message to be used by cooperating Windows applications. The message can be sent using `SendMessage()` or `PostMessage()`.
`ReplyMessage()`	Used by the recipient of a `SendMessage()` to respond to the message without yielding control to the calling task.
`SendDlgItemMessage()`	Same as `SendMessage()`, except oriented for child dialog controls.
`SendMessage()`	Sends a message directly to a target.
`SetMessageQUEUE()`	Creates a new, possibly larger message queue for a task. By default, queues are made large enough to hold eight messages.

continues

Function	Purpose
`TranslateAccelerator()`	Translates keyboard accelerator messages into `WM_COMMAND` and `WM_SYSCOMMAND` messages.
`TranslateMDISysAccel()`	Same as the preceding, but for MDI window keyboard accelerators.
`TranslateMessage()`	Translates virtual key message into character messages. Translates `WM_*KEYDOWN`/`UP` pairs into a single `WM_*CHAR` message.
`WaitMessage()`	Yields control until a message is deposited in the application's queue.
`Yield()`	Yields control only when no messages are waiting in the queue.

*Specific to Windows 3.1

Object-Oriented Concepts Under Windows

Over the past several years, much ado has been made about the benefits of object-oriented programming and design techniques. The excitement over object-oriented programming is evident on computer store shelves, because just about every conceivable product these days advertises some level of "OOPness" in its design or user interface. In many cases, the product is simply an everyday Windows application. Just because Windows offers a few object-oriented extensions doesn't mean that any application running under it is "object-oriented." One of the things causing this confusion is that there really is no concrete specification detailing what is needed to label a piece of software as object-oriented. In fact, use of the term could backlash, much like the overused terms *artificial intelligence* and *multimedia* did.

Whether the software in question is a programming language, database, or desktop environment, any of several basic object-oriented principles can be implemented, including

☐ Classes, objects, and messages

☐ Inheritance

☐ Data encapsulation/abstraction

☐ Dynamic binding

Classes and Objects

The use of classes and objects is one of the fundamental tenets of object-oriented programming. The benefit of classes and objects is that they enable the developer to take any real-world problem and easily categorize and define the software components needed to solve the task. An object such as a building might be broken down into several subcomponents, such as a floor, roof, foundation, walls, and so on. Working with classes and objects is very similar to how problems (usually) are solved in the real world. A topic is never tackled in its entirety; it is always broken down into manageable portions. Each of these resulting objects is then fine-tuned and possibly broken down into more objects. At some point, the classification procedure stops, and each object is assigned its behaviors.

Whereas most object-oriented languages support objects based on any type, Windows supports only window objects—that is, only objects that have a visual front end. Sometimes this isn't always desirable, because a developer might want to create a "supervisor" object that has no window component. Using Windows and the C programming language, this just isn't possible. A window front end must be created, even if it's made invisible upon creation. If strict O-O principles are that critical to the design of your application, you should consider another language such as C++.

An object really is nothing more than raw bytes that describe some kind of unique entity. At the lowest level, an object such as a GDI brush or a Kernel memory object is nothing more than a collection of data. At a higher level, an object can be composed of data and code, like a window object from the User module is. Obviously, because window objects are the only objects with code dedicated to supporting them, these are the only objects that can be sent messages.

Even though Windows provides support for "visual" objects and classes to create those objects, support is not as complete as it should be. In some cases, it is quite primitive. Under Windows, a window class doesn't exist as a separate entity until at least one window of the class has been created. However, the

ToolHelp DLL included with Windows 3.1 does let the developer find out about registered classes before an instance of the class is created. Classes also can't get sent messages or be manipulated in the same way that a window can. When the attributes of a window on the desktop need to be modified, a message is sent directly to the window. When the attributes of a window class need to be read or modified, however, a window handle still is passed to the function. This is because Windows associates a handle with an ASCII name only, and not with registered window class. Windows does provide API functions, such as `GetClassInfo`, that do not require a window handle. However, to modify class information, a window is always required. What's really needed in the API is a function called `SetClassInfo`.

Inheritance

Inheritance is an object's capability to leverage off of the services and attributes of lower-level "subobjects," and it involves the terms *subclassing* and *superclassing*.

Subclassing is when the flow of messages being sent to a window is intercepted and rerouted. There are two types of subclassing available to the developer: global subclassing and instance subclassing. Both are quite similar; they differ only in scope and how the window procedure is hooked. Instance subclassing involves the function `SetWindowLong()`, which is used to establish a new window procedure for the window, and in return, identify the old procedure associated with the window. All messages normally directed to this procedure now go to the new window function, which can optionally decide to process the message or return default control to the original window function, whose address is normally kept inside a global variable. Global subclassing involves the function `SetClassLong()` and affects an entire class of windows—not just one. Although a single window handle is passed to `SetClassLong()`, the changes are perpetuated throughout all current and future members of the window class.

Subclassing does have its problems. The main problem with instance subclassing is that a window can be subclassed only after it has been created, which means that certain key messages for the window may be missed. True, the parent window can intercept WM_PARENTNOTIFY to know when the child window is being created, and subclass it at this point. Even here, however, there are certain messages that have already been sent and are unavailable to the subclassing procedure, such as WM_NCCREATE, WM_GETMINMAXINFO, and a few others. One of the main problems with global subclassing is when more than one application attempts to globally subclass a stock windows control. In this situation, TaskA installs its class procedure, and then TaskB rewrites this with its own class procedure, remembering the class procedure installed by TaskA. The problem occurs when TaskA unhooks itself, substituting the original class procedure for the window class, rather than the newer class procedure installed by TaskB. This unhooks TaskB from the class message filtering chain of procedures. This is why Microsoft recommends against global subclassing for stock controls, instead recommending it only for subclassing application-local window classes. If global subclassing is still required for a stock control, superclassing is a better alternative.

Superclassing is when an entirely new class of window is created. However it's a class that leverages off of the methods of an existing class, such as a listbox or edit control. This technique involves the functions `GetClassInfo()` and `RegisterClass()`. The first function is used to get the default elements of the window class structure, which are then modified appropriately with new values, and the resulting structure is then passed to `RegisterClass()`. Superclassing an existing "stock" Windows control requires that any class or window extra data be preserved, because your new class is to emulate the existing one. Not preserving these values results in a crash or other undefined weirdness. Except for having a new class name and being first in line for all messages (from start to finish), a superclassed window is just like a subclassed one, in that when a method isn't processed, control must be passed to the original class procedure associated with the window, which then handles the method. Superclassing cannot be used on scroll bars, because Windows uses the class name to produce certain behaviors. Using superclassed edit controls inside a dialog resource poses a similar problem. Windows will force the edit control data into the local heap, regardless of the presence or absence of the `DS_LOCALEDIT` style bit for the dialog. In this case too, Windows depends on the "edit" class name when determining where to store the data.

Subclassing or superclassing a stock Windows control can range from simple to difficult, to near impossible, depending on the type of new behaviors the developer is trying to provide. If it's simply catching keystrokes or some other benign activity, there's generally not a problem. However, if the intent is to provide entire new major methods for a control, such as changing the way a button control or nonclient window area paints itself, difficulties can arise. This is due to the way the window changes its states. Not all painting for a control is done from a `WM_PAINT` message. Quite commonly, at least in the case of a button control, `WM_LBUTTONDOWN`, `WM_MOUSEMOVE`, and a host of other messages are all used to perform painting. This requires that the developer trap and emulate these messages as well, which very quickly leads to a hairier situation because no source code exists showing how the control expects its window and

class extra data to be modified during these messages. When radical changes need to be made to a control, often the developer is best put to write a completely new window class.

When an object (or window) of any specified class is first created, it is assigned a handle to uniquely distinguish it from other objects. The object also has a single procedure (or messaging loop) that intercepts and processes all commands destined to go to the object. If a developer doesn't like the behaviors of a particular object, one can simply add another "message processing" layer to the object. This is known as creating a subclass. Any messages that your routine decides not to process for the object are then passed down to another layer. This is known as inheritance, because the object is inheriting from the capabilities provided by others. Multiple-inheritance is when the object might have several different code paths to traverse down to fulfill and process the message.

Windows' support for inheritance is provided via the several message handling functions mentioned earlier (`DefWindowProc()`, `DefDlgProc()`, and `CallWindowProc()`). When a message cannot be processed by the current window, it is passed to a lower-level window procedure associated with the object. Many Windows programs limit inheritance to two levels. There is the initial code for the object, which usually is completely encapsulated and out of reach by the programmer, and there is the code that comes down the pike later to modify any errant behaviors with the original object.

Inheritance is not a feature that can be used with abandon. Just because you don't want to handle paint messages for your object doesn't mean you can blindly pass control to the paint method of another class. Along with any specified message, the task processing the message usually expects window or class extra data and maybe a property or two in order to process the message correctly. If the window was subclassed, inheritance of behaviors usually isn't a problem, because the window is presumed to have been created and initialized before the developer even gets to work with it. When superclassing, the developer is assumed to have established the class parameters for the window, including class and window extra data. This invariably means that the window's data and configuration will not be in the format expected by the original method for the window. Whenever superclassing is used to create a new window class based on an existing stock control class, it is important to preserve any expected class and window extra data. The function `GetClassInfo()` can be used to determine default minimum values for these numbers.

Data Encapsulation/Abstraction

Data encapsulation and abstraction can be thought of as the level of "tidiness" for a specified object. (I'm sure true O-O types are cringing at this description.) Both are key to effective object design. Are all the variables and data used by the object contained completely inside the object's address space and unavailable to other procedures? Does the object have a simple interface? When both of these prinicples are followed, the answer is a definite yes. Data encapsulation and abstraction are key to large-scale projects and automatically help the developer in writing reentrant code. Windows provides several simple methods for incorporating encapsulation and abstraction techniques, including the use of dynamic-link libraries, local allocations, local variables, class and window data, and window properties.

Dynamic Binding

Dynamic binding is the process of resolving function names with addresses at runtime rather than at compile or link time. This is also referred to as *late binding* or *dynamic linking*. This feature allows applications to dynamically alter their behavior and services at runtime. With static linking, the library's code is linked with program code, effectively binding the application to a certain version and revision of the library. When a newer library then becomes available, the original source code must be manually recompiled by the developer and redistributed. Dynamic binding is much more efficient, allowing the new library to be seamlessly incorporated at runtime, freeing the developer from worrying about such details. Windows' method of implementing dynamic binding is discussed in more detail in Chapter 3, "Program and Module Fundamentals."

Summary

This chapter covered some of the most fundamental aspects of Windows: its basic architecture and modular design, its messaging system, and several key object-oriented concepts and how they apply to the Windows operating system. Each of the sections in this chapter, especially the one on messaging, are key to being productive under Windows and understanding the following chapters and source code included with the book. The messaging system should be completely understood, because it represents one of the basic units under which Windows operates. Without a full comprehension of its intricacies, including the differences between sending and posting messages, the developer is doomed to create the same mistakes over and over again.

Processor and Memory Fundamentals

One of the first things I did when I wanted to start exploring more of the technical side of Windows was to purchase a book—Intel's *Programmer's Reference Guide* for the 80386 processor. Reading the manual put me in shock. Comparing the raw potential of the 80386 to the present capabilities in Windows just isn't possible, because Windows doesn't even come close to fully implementing the 32-bit functionality of the 80386 or 80486 processors.

This chapter discusses

Several of the hardware and other structure-based issues involving Windows, including its use of different processors (808x, 80286, 80386/80486) and processor operating modes (real and protected)

Different types of memory (conventional, expanded, extended)

Memory managers (DOS, XMS, EMS, VCPI, and DPMI)

Software operating modes (real, EMS, standard, and enhanced)

Throughout the chapter, several references are made to real mode (both the processor's real mode and Windows' use of real mode) and expanded (EMS) memory. Although Windows 3.1 has officially dropped support for both of these 808x relics, they are still discussed in depth. Likewise, whenever the 80386 is mentioned, assume that the same features apply to the 80486. To be concise, references usually refer to just the 80386, although in every case the 80486 processor could just as easily be substituted. Additionally, the chapter covers in depth the differences between the processor's use of real and protected mode, and Windows' different operating modes: real (3.0 only), EMS (3.0 only), standard, and enhanced. The two groupings of terms are not to be confused and intermingled. The first are modes the processor provides, and the second are modes (based on the type of processor) that Windows provides.

One major difference in the way Windows operates versus the capabilities of the processor is with multitasking. Under Windows, multitasking is nonpreemptive. Simply put, the operating system doesn't have the total control over processes the way it should. Under Windows, control must be voluntarily relinquished by an application, or all other running applications come to a screeching halt. Windows does not force task switches to different

applications. This differs from an operating system such as OS/2, which supports multitasking and other processor-specific and protected-mode features.

Windows also doesn't isolate applications from each other in the manner a protected OS normally does. Windows generates protection faults only under the following circumstances: writing to a read-only segment, reading or writing past the end of a segment, or using an invalid selector to a segment. Note that this list doesn't include "writing into another application's address space." This is because Windows uses a single local descriptor table for all applications running under Windows and provides no task-to-task protection. This makes life difficult for the programmer because bugs might pop up that are totally unrelated to the problem currently being worked on. Under DOS, a programmer doesn't need to worry about other applications unless a TSR is loaded in memory.

About the only high-end features that Windows incorporates from the 80386 and 80486 processors are a larger linear address space, paging/virtual memory, and virtual 808x mode. Windows does not use the larger segment sizes associated with these processors, or the flat memory model, because all of Windows' code and data segments are flagged as USE16, which specifies that all segments are based on the 64K segment limit of the 80286. Windows retains compatibility with 80286 code because of this and the fact that 80286 segment descriptors are a "subset" of 80386 segment descriptors.

Naturally, Windows' functionality varies, depending on the type of CPU used. Table 2.1 illustrates some of those differences across three of Windows 3.x's basic operating modes.

Table 2.1. Differences between memory management performed by processor and Windows.

Feature	808x***	80286	80386
Virtual memory	1M	16M	64T
Linear memory	1M	16M	4G
Segment size	64K	64K	4G
Protection	No	Yes	Yes
Virtual machines	No	No	Yes

Feature	Real***	EMS 4.0***	Standard**	Enhanced
Virtual memory	1M	33M	16M	512M
Linear memory	1M	1M	16M	512M
Segment size	64K	64K	64K	64K
Largest alloc	64K	64K	1M*	16M*

Due to internal overhead, the amount is 64K lower than shown. Allocation is the result of selector tiling.

**Using the 80386 in standard mode, the amounts in this column are equal to their enhanced mode counterparts.*

***Windows 3.0 only.*

Windows can be forced into a particular mode by specifying the following parameters at runtime:

Mode	Command Line
Real (808x)	win /r
Standard (80286)	win /2
Enhanced (80386)	win /3

The Windows function `GetWinFlags()` can be used to determine both the computer's processor type and the current operating mode of Windows. This is kind of the read-only "hardware" equivalent of the Windows 3.1 function `SystemParametersInfo()`, which reads and writes several system-wide parameter settings. `GetWinFlags()` returns one or more of the following 32-bit values:

Value	Meaning
WF_80x87	Math coprocessor found
WF_CPU086	8086 processor found*
WF_CPU186	80186 processor found*
WF_CPU286	80286 processor found
WF_CPU386	80386 processor found
WF_CPU486	80486 processor found

continues

Value	Meaning
WF_ENHANCED	Windows is running under the enhanced-mode configuration
WF_LARGEFRAME	Windows is running under the large frame EMS configuration*
WF_PAGING	Windows is implementing virtual memory (paging); always set**
WF_PMODE	Windows is running in protected mode
WF_SMALLFRAME	Windows is running under the small frame EMS configuration*
WF_STANDARD	Windows is running in standard mode
WF_WIN286	Same as WF_STANDARD
WF_WIN386	Same as WF_ENHANCED
WF_WLO	Identifies a Windows Libraries for an OS/2 (WLO) application running under OS/2**

*Windows 3.0 only

**Windows 3.1 only

The Segmented Memory Model

The segment is a fundamental unit in Intel's 808x and 80x86 series of processors; everything revolves around segments. A segment merely defines a logical mapping over a range of memory, with possibly multiple segments overlapping and mapping the same section of memory. The overlap can be due to aliasing or, in the case of real mode, due to the way addresses are generated by the processor. Segments are defined by a starting address, a length, and a number of properties, such as read-only, read-write, execute-only, execute-read, and other combinations. Segments can also represent code, data, and resources (for Windows only), with these terms indirectly specifying the attributes associated with the segment (that is, code segments are execute-only or execute-read).

Under the segmented memory model, segments are mapped into a linear address space. In the case of protected mode, if a segment has not been mapped (represented by a descriptor in a descriptor table), or if the offset portion of an address extends past the length of the segment, the address is considered invalid. Because real mode lacks the memory access and protection services provided by protected mode's segment descriptor tables, all memory under 1M is available to any running application, with no explicit allocation or mapping of segments required—it's just not possible. Under real mode, addresses are generated with a 16-bit segment value and a 16-bit offset. The segment value is shifted left by four bits (a paragraph) and added to the offset value, resulting in a 20-bit address capable of reaching anywhere in the first megabyte of physical memory. Because of this method of generating addresses, 64K segments (overlapping every paragraph) are accessible in the first megabyte of physical RAM. This also means that the highest address that can be generated by a processor when in real mode accesses a segment starting just a paragraph before the 1M boundary, extending past the 1M boundary by 64K (minus one paragraph). This extra chunk of memory is what's used by 80x86 processors (when running in real mode) to generate the area of memory called the HMA (high memory area). When 808x processors run in real mode, the address merely wraps around to the start of memory, thus not yielding the "extra" RAM.

The amount of addressable physical memory (RAM) available to a processor is determined by the number of address lines going to the processor. The 808x CPU has 20 address lines, yielding 1M (2^{20}) of directly addressable memory. The 80286 has 24 address lines, yielding 16M of memory, and the 80386 CPU has 32 address lines, providing 4G of addressable physical memory. The physical address space of a processor (its RAM) represents the maximum amount of memory that can be accessed without having the processor perform any virtual-memory trickery. As mentioned in the preceding paragraph, in real mode, logical addresses (addresses generated by software) are statically mapped into linear addresses, whereas in protected mode the address is first routed through a descriptor table before a linear address is returned. In real mode, linear addresses equal physical addresses. However, in the protected mode of the 80386, when paging is enabled, another layer of translation takes place, whereby some linear addresses are mapped (through the processor's paging unit) into physical addresses. Unmapped linear addresses generate a page fault when accessed, causing the the processor to halt the application, swap the 4K page into physical RAM, and restart the application where the page fault was first generated.

As mentioned, in protected mode access to linear memory is done differently because the 80x86 processors use descriptor tables to govern access to available, mapped segments. Each descriptor in the table is an 8-byte value describing a mapped segment. Segment descriptors for the 80286 have a 24-bit base address (pointing anywhere within 2^{24} or 16M of memory) and a 16-bit limit (restricting the segment to 64K), whereas segment descriptors for the 80386 have a 32-bit base address (pointing anywhere within 4G of memory) and a 20-bit segment limit. At first, the 20-bit length would seem to restrict 80386 segment sizes to 1M. However, this is not the case, as through a special bit (defining byte or 4K page granularity for the segment), a 1M or 4G length can be assumed. Regardless, with the 80386 running in 32-bit protected mode, multiple segments can be mapped to this large 4G linear address space, or the processor can effectively be switched to a flat addressing model in which all the system registers (CS, DS, SS, ES) are mapped to the same range of linear address space. This effectively removes all segmentation issues. The flat model is actually quite similar to the tiny memory model, which maps all the program registers to the same 64K segment. With the absence of virtual memory features provided by the 80386, the segmented memory model provides important features, including task isolation and simple code relocation. By default, segments provide a unique address space, and as such are protected from manipulation by prying tasks. Leaving the segmented model behind, however, provides more potential for code portability, because most processors on the market use a flat model architecture.

PC Memory Types

Windows can enter several modes (real, standard, and enhanced) and can use several types of memory (conventional, extended, and expanded). See Figure 2.1. Each type of memory is accessed differently, and each has its advantages and disadvantages.

Conventional Memory

Conventional "real-mode" memory ranges from address 0–1M and represents the only form of memory that can be accessed by all makes and models of a PC. Available memory is somewhat limited because of this. The first 10 to 20K of lower RAM is used to hold the interrupt vector table, TSRs and device drivers, and MS-DOS, and the upper 384K is used for video RAM/ROM and the system ROM BIOS. Conventional memory is critical because so many things absolutely depend on it, such as device drivers, portions of DLLs, and any other applications wanting fixed segments, DOS-accessible memory, or interrupt-driven code. Windows 3.0 running in real mode had a tough time trying to fit so much into so little. After all, the whole global heap consisted of a space far less than 640K minus the memory used in lower RAM. This space, referred to as the *Transient Program Area,* had to include not only any possible network driver software and a small portion of Windows, but every DLL and application on the desktop as well.

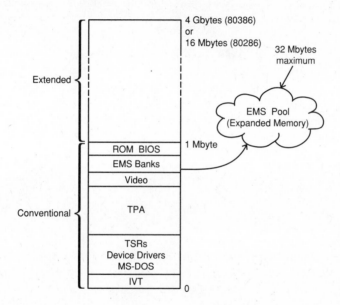

Figure 2.1. Representation of conventional, expanded, and extended memory in a PC.

Memory that needs to be allocated out of conventional memory can be done with a Windows call to `GlobalDOSAlloc()`; otherwise, you can never be sure where your memory is coming from. (Normally, you shouldn't care.) Conventional memory should not be used for anything unless absolutely necessary. Often conventional memory is so precious that the only way a real-mode memory buffer can be created is when it's done first by a TSR that's loaded before Windows.

Sandwiched between the video memory tidbits and the ROM BIOS is a prime piece of real estate referred to as the *upper memory blocks* (UMBs). This section of memory normally is reserved by "loadhi" utilities, such as those found in MS-DOS 5 and QuarterDeck's QEMM. Many network drivers load their code and data into swappable banks of expanded memory. Upper memory blocks usually are not allocated directly by the developer.

Also worth mentioning when discussing conventional memory, even if it's actually extended memory, is the high-memory area. The HMA is real-mode accessible by any 80286 and above processor. This is made possible via an addressing/wrap-around trick involving address line 20 on the processor. The trick has the processor addressing almost 64K of RAM past the end of memory instead of wrapping around to 0:0, as on an 808x machine. Like the UMBs, the developer does not allocate memory from the HMA directly. Like the UMBs, it is a space usually stolen by programs that can load themselves high.

Expanded Memory

Expanded memory, specifically under the EMS 4.0 configuration, can give a starving application as much as 32M of extra memory. Windows uses expanded memory for its own internal use too. Unfortunately, it can be accessed only in small 16K chunks, and it is efficient only for certain types of programs. Also unfortunate is that expanded memory is accessed through a window frame located in conventional memory, making conventional memory even more precious than it already is.

Another limitation is that expanded memory is really useful for storing only data and not code. The use of expanded memory is slowly being phased out for two reasons: extended memory is much more powerful, and there is a lack of real-mode computers on the corporate desktop. As mentioned earlier, the different EMS specifications originally were designed with 808x computers in mind. Because Windows 3.1 has "officially" dropped support for real mode, application support for expanded memory will slowly wither away as well.

Extended Memory

Extended memory consists of all memory located above conventional memory's 1M line. This includes the HMA space, as well as the rest of physical memory. This means a maximum of 15M of extended memory on an 80286 processor, and as much as 4G (minus 1M) of extended memory on the 80386 and above processors. Windows and its client applications use extended memory almost exclusively.

Although accessing extended memory requires the use of protected mode, it has numerous benefits that other forms of memory can't provide. First, as shown earlier, extended memory can be quite plentiful. Even if there isn't much around, 80386 systems can page out extended memory to give a larger-than-actual address space. Extended memory also can be used to emulate expanded memory (if so desired). More important, extended memory also can easily hold, run, and access both code and data. Both conventional and extended memory represent forms of physical memory. When added together, they represent the total amount of memory available to the processor.

Memory Management Drivers

Normally, memory is not accessed or allocated from a particular block or section directly—at least it isn't when your application is running under Windows. Windows must be in control of and know of just about everything. Except in the case of device drivers or other programs that require conventional memory, a program shouldn't care where or how it gets its memory. Several drivers are used by Windows to control the flow of memory.

DOS

Conventional memory, specifically the memory in the TPA, is managed by DOS and a series of memory control blocks (MCBs), also referred to as *arena structures,* which form a link throughout the TPA. The MCBs are constantly updated as memory is allocated and freed. Public-domain utilities that map system memory are merely walking the MCB chain, determining ownership (using the Program Segment Prefix) and listing program entries from first to last, as it finds the MCBs in memory. The Windows utility Heap Walker walks a similar list of structures when perusing the global heap. Normally, when an application is run under DOS, it is given all available memory, as DOS is, and thinks of itself as a single-tasking system. Likewise, when Windows is loaded it is given the remaining memory available in the TPA, and then more than likely does away with MCBs and DOS for managing this area of memory, using its own allocation method and structures instead.

EMS

Expanded memory, as mentioned earlier, is managed by an EMS driver, which maps memory above 640K into a series of pages, swapping them in and out of memory as needed. Windows 3.0 provides two EMS operating modes—small frame and large frame. Both are discussed more in depth later in the "Small- and Large-Frame EMS Mode and Banking" section.

XMS

The XMS, or *extended memory specification,* was designed to allow 80286, 80386, and 80486 processors to manage conventional memory's upper-memory blocks, the 64K HMA, and the extended memory blocks located just past the HMA. XMS memory is similar to EMS memory in that allocated blocks of memory must first be copied to conventional memory before they can be accessed. XMS support is provided by the HIMEM.SYS driver included with both DOS and Windows. It is also provided by QuarterDeck's QEMM386.SYS driver. Although the UMBs are controlled by the XMS specification, it is rare to find them available on DOS 5 systems. This is because DOS 5 usually grabs this section of memory at boot time and loads DOS into it. Both Windows 3.1 and 3.0 use XMS version 2.

VCPI

The VCPI, or *Virtual Control Program Interface,* was the first extended-memory API introduced solely for the 80386 and higher processors. Developed by Pharlap Software and QuarterDeck Systems, VCPI united several DOS extender technologies and expanded memory managers, later adding support for XMS memory as well. VCPI routines deal with 4K pages of memory rather than the 16K memory pages used by EMS. This works out well, because it coincides with the page size used by the 80386 and 80486 processors to implement virtual memory. Virtual DMA services are even part of the VCPI specification. The VCPI was lacking only in that it couldn't multitask DOS extender technologies, had no support for the 80286 processor, and saw no implementation by Windows.

DPMI

The DPMI, or *DOS Protected-Mode Interface,* was developed by Microsoft specifically for DOS multitasking, memory management, and the virtualization of PC hardware. Windows' virtual memory manager, WIN386.EXE, is a ring 0 DPMI host that provides low-level memory allocation and management services for DPMI clients, which include virtual device drivers and DLLs. Windows' Kernel module and all DOS boxes are DPMI clients. DOS boxes fall into this category due to the ring 0 monitor code required to initialize the virtual machine and handle interrupts. Windows 3.1 and 3.0 both use DPMI version .9. For more information on the DPMI specification, contact Intel Corp. at (800) 548-4725 and ask for part number JP-26.

Direct support of DOS and ROM BIOS interrupts was removed from the original DPMI specification to enable its portability across different non-DOS platforms. DPMI is different from VCPI because it includes support for the 80286 and can be run at a higher privilege level than its clients, as opposed to a VCPI server, which runs at the same privilege level as its clients. This lets a DPMI host support virtual memory and provide a higher level of enforcement over the actions of its clients. Fortunately, the DPMI specification was generalized enough that DOS extenders were quick to jump on the bandwagon. The result is that any DOS-extended programs running in Windows' DOS box can have access to DPMI-provided memory. For memory management, Windows uses its own services, those provided by the DPMI host and XMS, and the memory management provided by the 80386 processor—specifically, paging and virtual memory management.

All these memory managers are manipulated directly by Windows, and never directly by an application. (DLLs and device drivers are exempt from this rule if the DPMI service they request is not already provided by Windows.) Windows' stock memory management API is the most likely interface for a task requiring memory.

Windows implements the DPMI specification using the file DOSX.EXE in standard mode and the file WIN386.EXE in enhanced mode. Note that in standard mode DPMI functionality is only emulated.

61

CHAPTER

2

Real Versus Protected Mode

Before we launch into a discussion of Windows' real, standard, and enhanced modes of operation, we first need to look at the different modes or states that the processor is capable of entering—mainly, real mode and protected mode. The word *real* in real mode refers to the fact that all program-supplied addresses reference physical, "real" memory. A system running under real mode is limited to conventional memory and possibly the HMA. Under protected mode, access to memory is governed by a set of processor-protected descriptor (segment) tables. Protected mode allows access to the processor's entire linear address space. In real mode, a table called the *Burgermaster* is used to function as a protected mode descriptor table equivalent. Whereas real mode provided only memory management, protected mode provides both memory management and memory protection.

In every version of Windows, real mode is used as a kickstarter to get into protected mode, which can be entered only when a global descriptor table has been created and initialized with the appropriate structures (Interrupt Descriptor Table, OS code/data segment, Local Descriptor Table, and Task State Segment). Protected mode can be run in two ways—16-bit and 32-bit. This refers to the type of selectors used for code and data segments. If 16-bit protected mode code is running, 64K code and data segments are used (USE16). If 32-bit protected mode code is being executed, all segments are assumed to be 32 bits wide (4G).

Protected mode is what Windows uses to break the 1M barrier and perform simple memory protection. Addressing memory under protected mode involves the use of several segment lookup tables, known as *descriptor tables*. Under protected mode, all access to segments and linear memory is governed by these tables. If you try to access a segment not in one of your tables, your application is terminated.

Protected mode comes in two flavors, 16-bit and 32-bit. Naturally, 16-bit protected mode is what the 80286 processor runs under, and 32-bit protected mode is the domain of 80386 and 80486 processors. The differences mainly involve the size of segments that can be allocated. In 16-bit protected mode, 64K segments are the norm, and in 32-bit protected mode, 4G segment sizes and a flat model can be incorporated. Most of Windows itself and all applications and libraries run in 16-bit protected mode as a means of achieving compatibility with the large installed base of 80286 processors. The two modes can easily coexist, because the descriptors for 16-bit protected mode are merely a subset of the descriptors for 32-bit protected mode. Windows' virtual memory manager and all virtual device-drivers, however, run under 32-bit protected mode.

Virtual Machines

A form of protected mode called a *virtual machine* (VM) also exists. A virtual machine consists of both real- and protected-mode code. The real-mode portion of the VM totally emulates an 808x system, right down to the shifted-segment addressing, interrupts, and video memory. The main difference between real and virtual 808x mode is that access to all interrupts and hardware is virtualized. This includes serial ports, parallel ports, and video memory. Hardware is not accessed directly by the application as it is in real mode. In a virtual machine, the processor restricts access to I/O ports through the use of an I/O permission bitmap located in the task state segment. This mask determines which ports and devices the virtual machine has access to.

The 80386 implements hardware-enforced multitasking through the round-robining of virtual machines. Windows also adds a Virtual Machine Manager whose job it is to manage and coordinate access between VMs and the rest of the system. Under Windows 3, all applications and DLLs are run in the protected-mode portion of a single "system" virtual machine, and each DOS application is run in its own virtual machine. This is the reason that DOS applications perform "true" multitasking and that Windows applications don't. The real-mode portion of the system virtual machine is copied whenever a new virtual machine is being created. This ensures that fresh copies of DOS, vectors, and so on are present for every DOS VM. All virtual machines can be broken into several distinct portions, including a ring 3 real-mode virtual 808x portion, a ring 0 V86 control program, and a protected-mode section that runs at ring level 3 under Windows 3.1 (protected-mode Windows programs ran at ring level 1 under Windows 3.0). See Figure 2.2 for an illustration.

All V86 ring 3 portions of a virtual machine start out with a copy of an IVT, DOS, device-drivers, and so on, just like the first megabyte of real mode. In the case of a DOS VM, this also includes the now-loaded DOS program's code and data. The ring 0 section is the V86 control monitor, whose job is to handle any exception or interrupt processing for the VM. When the control monitor gets an interrupt, it first checks the IDT to see whether the vector has been hooked.

If it hasn't, control is instead passed to the IVT vector in the VM that generated the offending instruction. The control monitor also contains some initialization code for the VM.

Figure 2.2.
Windows'
enhanced-mode
virtual machine
layout.

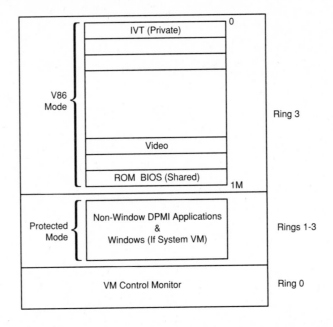

Windows 3.1 includes support for a special batch file named WINSTART. This file is used to preload the system virtual machine, not DOS virtual machines, alleviating some of the RAM cram found "inside" a DOS box. Normally, when a TSR or other memory-resident software, like a network driver, is loaded before Windows, it affects all running applications—Windows or non-Windows. This is because a snapshot of real mode is taken before Windows goes into protected mode, and this snapshot is used to preload any new DOS virtual machines and is copied into the system virtual machine. Using WINSTART.BAT enables the user to specify applications that should only be loaded into the system virtual machine. This means that DOS boxes will be preloaded only with what was in the lower 640K when Windows was first brought online. Preloading an individual DOS virtual machine is simple, requiring that a batch file or .pif file be established that preloads the VM before entering DOS. The file WINSTART.BAT should be located in the Windows system directory, but all memory-resident software might not work with this method.

Real Mode

Real mode is synonymous with Intel's 808x processor, although you don't necessarily need one to run in real mode. Real mode is what the first version of Windows ran under, offering 1M of addressable linear memory and a 64K segment size. In real mode, the CPU treats linear addresses as physical addresses and does not virtualize the interrupt table. In real mode, access to everything is direct, and nothing is masked. Segment addressing is unique under real mode as well, because segment addresses are referenced directly by a static value and not looked up in a descriptor table as in protected mode. Figure 2.3 shows the memory configuration used by Windows in real mode.

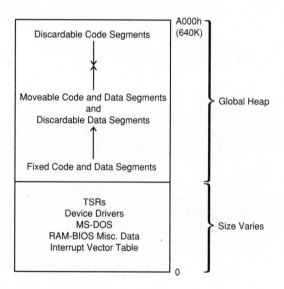

Figure 2.3.
Memory
configuration
of Windows in
real mode.

Standard Mode

Like real mode, standard mode is synonymous with another Intel processor, the 80286. Standard mode (16-bit protected mode) adds several features, including protection, a 16M linear address space, and 1M allocable blocks from the global heap. Protected mode means that linear addresses are generated indirectly by a selector pointing to an entry in a descriptor table and are not addressed directly by a segment/offset pair as in real mode. In standard mode, global heap handles are limited to 4096. This is half the amount in enhanced mode, because standard mode allocations require a

selector for the arena entry and a selector for the allocation itself. Because standard mode (the 80286) doesn't support the virtualization of I/O, all DOS boxes are run in full-screen real mode. The full-screen mode is required because screen addresses cannot be virtualized and trapped, which is required when screen writes must be intercepted. All is not lost with standard mode, however, because this lack of capabilities makes standard mode a bit faster than enhanced mode. For an end-user this is an option, but for a developer it's not, because any debugger worth its salt requires enhanced mode for operation. Figure 2.4 shows the memory configuration used by Windows in standard mode.

Figure 2.4.
Memory configuration of Windows in standard mode.

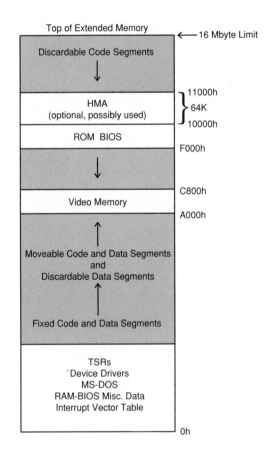

Enhanced Mode

Protected-mode capabilities provided by the 80386 include a 64T virtual address space and 4G segments. Windows' enhanced mode does things a little differently, however. Because the 80286 and the standard PC-AT bus are limited to 16M, Windows Kernel was coded around this fact, resulting in a system capable of 16M global heap allocations and addressing a total of 64M of memory. The 16M allocation limit is because of the way global heap allocations and selector tiling are implemented. Kernel uses a single byte to hold the number of possible 64K selectors making up an allocation, with this yielding approximately 16.3M of memory at a single time. Windows 3.1 is supposed to have broken the 64M "total" allocation limit. However, I haven't verified this. Because Windows 3.1 still runs enhanced mode in the processor's 16-bit protected state, programs still are dealing only with 64K segments—code, data, task, or otherwise. In enhanced mode, global heap handles are limited to 8192, because only a single descriptor is used for each mapped segment. The separate arena structures segments are no longer required because virtual memory and page table structures essentially remove the need. Figure 2.5 shows the memory configuration used by Windows in enhanced mode.

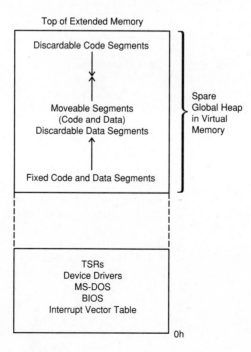

Figure 2.5.
Memory configuration of Windows in enhanced mode.

Small- and Large-Frame EMS Mode and Banking

The EMS specification originally was designed to enable Intel 808x computers to access more than 1M of memory. Expanded memory is accessed through a chunk of memory referred to as a *page frame*. A page frame consists of several (possibly noncontiguous) 16K pages of memory, and it usually is located above 640K. The total pool of EMS memory (up to 32M) is divided into several 16K pages. When EMS memory is needed, a request is made to allocate a certain number of pages. These pages are then swapped into the different sections of the page frame as needed.

When Windows is running on a system using a single page frame, it's referred to as *small-frame EMS mode*. With small frame EMS, the page frame is located above the 640K line, and everything between the bottom of lower memory and 640K is used as the global heap. *Large-frame EMS mode* involves multiple page frames locatable virtually anywhere in the first megabyte of memory. Figure 2.6 shows the EMS 4.0 memory configuration used by Windows in real mode.

Figure 2.6.
EMS 4.0 memory configuration of Windows in real mode.

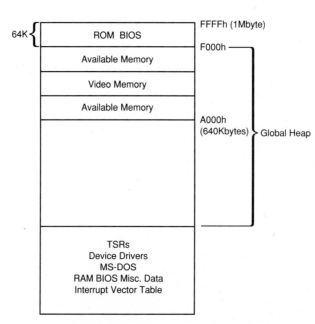

EMS is used by Windows applications and even by Windows itself. When Windows is run in real mode and it detects expanded memory, banked EMS memory is used to hold objects residing above a certain portion of the global heap, referred to as the *EMS bank line*. The location of the bank line, and the amount of memory to be banked, is determined by the size of the global heap. If the global heap is too small, Windows uses the small-frame EMS mode, moving the bank line high in memory to A000h. This means a relatively small amount of bankable memory, as soon as you subtract everything that has already been used in the UMBs.

Most of the segments in an application, and certain segments in a DLL, are all bankable into expanded memory. Banking is performed whenever Windows performs a task switch between applications, swapping out the prior task's pages and swapping in the new task's pages. Banking is performed only on a per-application basis and is not used to swap in individual pages for an application. Thus, adding expanded memory does not increase the overall space available to an application. It does, however, increase the number of applications that can be banked in and out and handled at one time by Windows. See Figure 2.7 for an example of EMS banking and the bank line.

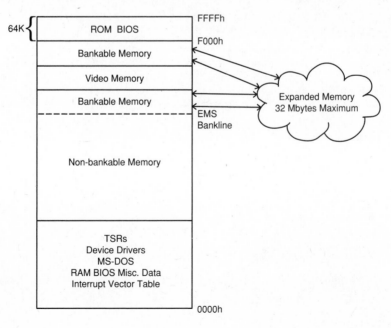

Figure 2.7. Mapping to expanded memory.

Discardable objects are always located below the bank line because it's considered more efficient to discard an object rather than bank it into expanded memory. The only exceptions to this rule are a library's discardable segments, because these are banked by Windows. This is because a DLL segment, whatever its type, probably will see much action, and swapping banks of EMS memory is much quicker than reloading discardable segments from disk. This also frees up more space in lower memory. Of course, if the library compiles its resources with the private option (using `rc -p`), the library is assumed to be used by only one application. As a result, segments are automatically located above the bank line. The reasoning is that if no other tasks need the library's segments, they'll get banked.

The way a library is loaded by another module also affects the placement (relative to the EMS bank line) of any global memory segments that are dynamically allocated on behalf of the library. Libraries that are dynamically loaded via `LoadLibrary()` automatically place global memory segments below the bank line. For implicitly (the make file) or explicitly (`IMPORTS`) loaded libraries, the segments are placed above the bank line in large-frame EMS mode, or below the bank line in small-frame EMS mode. To control the placement of global heap objects for libraries, the resource compiler has an `-e` option that automatically forces all global segments above the bank line. Of course, this global setting can always be overridden with a `GMEM_NOT_BANKED` or `GMEM_LOWER` flag during the call to `GlobalAlloc()`.

As if all of this weren't enough, an additional override to all the rules just mentioned is that any objects that cannot be banked above the EMS line will be loaded below it. Table 2.2 summarizes the different global heap objects and how they fit into Windows' EMS-based banking method of memory management.

Table 2.2. Position of global heap objects in relation to bank line.

Object	Small-Frame	Large-Frame
Task Database	Below	Below
DLL Module Database	Below	Below
DLL Data Segment	Below	Below*
DLL Code Segment (FIXED)	Below	Below*
DLL Code Segment	Below	Above
DLL Resource	Below	Above

Object	Small-Frame	Large-Frame
`GlobalAlloc()` Memory	Below	Above
Task Module Database	Below	Above
Task Data Segment	Below	Above
Task Code Segment	Above	Above
Task Resource	Above	Above

*Located above if private library (rc -p)

The Windows API also provides the `LimitEMSPages()` function, which is used to limit the number of expanded memory pages available to an application. This function has no effect when expanded memory isn't installed or being used by Windows, and it can't be used to limit the amount of memory available by calling INT 67H.

Virtual, Logical, Linear, and Physical: Of Addresses and Address Spaces

Several terms are bantered about when discussing the implementation of various types of memory, when referring to the addressable portions of these memory ranges, and when actually generating addresses to access memory. Starting from the top, I'll cover each term and how it applies to both Intel's processors and the Windows operating system.

When a program generates an address to access some portion of memory, this is always referred to as a *logical address*. Sometimes the term *virtual address* is used instead. Regardless, a logical address can actually be a linear address, a physical address, or neither, which is the basic premise here—the program shouldn't know the difference. In real mode, a logical address consists of a 16-bit segment and 16-bit offset value. Both of these values are statically mapped (no translation) into a linear address, which under real mode also happens to equal the physical RAM address of the memory to be accessed.

Under protected mode, a logical address is dynamically mapped (with translation performed through a descriptor table) into a linear address, which can then be used to access any desired section of memory. In both cases, a linear address points to directly addressable RAM on the computer. Of course, if the 80386 is used and paging is enabled, then linear addresses (through a series of page tables) can contain another layer of translation, being mapped to different locations in RAM or unmapped, thus indirectly referencing locations on disk.

Address spaces (and memory) can be referred to as *virtual, linear,* and *physical.* An address space refers to a not-necessarily-contiguous range of memory. The physical address space of a computer refers to all directly addressable RAM, period. Conventional, expanded, and extended memory are all forms of physical memory. The linear address space usually is the same as the physical address space, except (as mentioned earlier) when paging is enabled. In this case, a linear address space can be uncontiguous and fragmented, as it is broken up into a series of mapped and unmapped 4K pages. In protected mode, potentially, multiple descriptors can be mapped to the same section of linear memory, or individual descriptors can be mapped to their own 4G linear address space. A virtual address space represents the theoretical maximum amount of memory a single task can address (physical RAM plus possible disk space). In this case, the processor could possibly be juggling multiple and separate linear address spaces (4G per descriptor). On the 80386 this means 16K of descriptors (the 8K in the GDT plus another 8K in an LDT) multiplied by a 4G segment size per descriptor. This yields 64T, an imposing amount. Of course, right now this number is an absolute dream, partly due to the sheer cost of the RAM and disk hardware involved, partly due to Windows' design, and most important, partly due to the imposing design issues faced by chip manufacturers. Figure 2.8 shows how different processors manipulate and interpret the different address spaces.

Figure 2.8.
How different processors interpret virtual, linear, and physical address spaces.

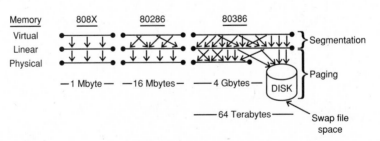

Virtual memory can be a good thing and it can be a bad thing. It's a good thing because it's like insurance; it's a bad thing because, just like insurance, when you need it you end up really feeling the effects.

Virtual memory is made possible by the 80386's memory paging mechanism, which maps the entire linear address space into a series of 4K pages that get swapped between physical RAM and the hard disk, effectively giving tasks more memory than is really available. Even though a task has more memory available to it, all is not cherries and cream. Accessing the extra memory can be extremely slow when the pages are stored on disk and not in RAM. Try performing a multimegabyte global allocation with the GMEM_DISCARDABLE and GMEM_ZEROINIT flags set, and watch how the hard drive goes off into never-never land, while it is zeroing out three or so megabytes of memory on the hard disk. This is not very fast, to say the least.

The 80386 implements paging in hardware and does its virtual memory magic pretty much unbeknownst to any running applications. When a task requests access to a section of memory that happens to reside on disk, a page fault occurs and the memory is demand-loaded invisibly and put into RAM. Windows even restarts the task at the offending instruction, so an application never even becomes aware that the rug has been pulled out from under it and replaced with a different one.

Memory is swapped to and from the disk in 4K pages. This number is no coincidence; it is one of the basic units of granularity used by the 80386 and also the cluster size found on most hard disks. When running under the segmented memory model, a page can contain multiple segments, and a single segment can span multiple swapped and unswapped pages.

The CPU maintains all virtual paging information in a single page directory and several subtables kept on disk. With paging enabled, a linear address must be translated into a physical address. On the 808x and 80286 processors, which have no memory paging, linear addresses equal physical addresses. See Figure 2.9 for an example of a 32-bit linear address. Before a linear address is parsed, the control register CR3 is used to specify the base of the page directory. Next, a portion of the linear address is used to specify an entry within the page directory, which points to a page table. Another portion of the linear address is used to specify an entry within the page table (see Figure 2.10), which points to a page frame. The last portion of the linear address then is used as an offset into the page frame pointed to by the page table entry. See Figure 2.11 for an overall illustration of the 80386's paging mechanism.

Figure 2.9.
80386 linear
address format.

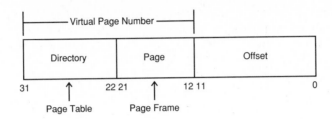

Figure 2.10.
80386 page
table entry.

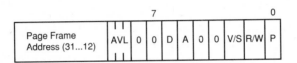

Figure 2.11.
80386 paging
mechanism.

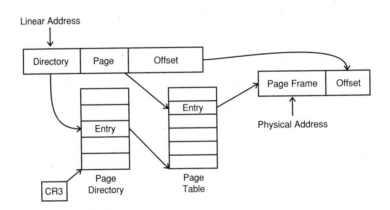

The different paging structures associated with virtual memory are manipulated on the fly continually by Windows. Many neat tricks can be done in this fashion. For instance, with DOS boxes, the pages mapped to video memory are flagged as write-protected, meaning that they are not present in memory. This lets the processor trap any writes to video memory and ultimately have them rerouted to a nice graphics-mode DOS box instead. Windows' current implementation of paging allows four times the amount of physical memory to be reserved in a swap file. However, with Windows 3.1 this limit has been removed.

Fixed memory on an 80386 is an interesting subject, because it really is not as "fixed" as you might think. With paging enabled on an 80386, even fixed memory can end up getting swapped to disk. After all, when the memory is needed, it's simply paged back in, right? Normally this would be just fine, except in the case of device drivers and other interrupt-driven code. When an interrupt occurs, the processor expects to be able to jump directly to a specified address, without doing any memory management magic first. This means that memory cannot have moved or been paged to disk—it must be in the same place every time it is accessed. To prevent the paging of fixed or any other kind of memory blocks in enhanced mode, memory can be designated as page-locked.

> **Tip:** Page locking is recommended only for use with device drivers, which usually are loaded quite low in memory anyway. This helps minimize the "sandbar" effect that page-locked segments have on Windows' virtual memory manager.

Segments and Registers

Intel's protected-mode processors divide segments into two basic categories—system segments and application segments. System segments include local descriptor tables, task state segments, call gates, task gates, interrupt gates, and trap gates. Application segments include code segments, read-write data segments, and read-only resource data segments. All these segments are tracked by a series of different descriptor tables, descriptors, and registers.

The user and system registers keep track of the many different segments possibly in use at one time. These registers include developer-accessible registers such as CS, DS, ES, and SS and the "hidden" registers such as GDTR, LDTR, IDTR, and TR, which are used to locate the global descriptor table, the current local descriptor table, the interrupt descriptor table, and the current task's TSS. Some registers are set directly by program instructions, and some are set automatically by the processor. The DS register is an example of an always-modifiable register. The CS register can be set only indirectly by transferring execution to a different code segment. The 80386 allows as many as six different segments to be accessible at one time, via the data registers CS, DS, ES, FS, GS, and SS. If access to another segment is required, the selector for the segment must be hand-loaded into the appropriate register by the developer. In a flat model, all the segment registers (at least CS and DS) are mapped to the same section of address space, effectively eliminating the segmentation issue.

The 80386 also includes four control registers, CR0–CR3. These low-level registers contain and control some important system functions, such as the disabling of paging, caching, and protection, and the control of task switches, the math coprocessor, and default alignment. The values of the hidden or system registers cannot be changed by programs and are handled instead by the operating system.

Alignment

Alignment is the process by which segments and other data structures are placed in memory at specific boundaries. The data usually is word-, dword-, paragraph-, or page- (or otherwise) aligned. Objects usually are aligned at object boundaries, meaning that pages get aligned at page boundaries, and paragraphs are aligned at paragraph boundaries. Instead of letting the data structures "fall where they may," the linker often is passed on its command line a specific alignment value, making it easier for the processor to fetch data in a single operation. Alignment is more of an issue with 808x processors, and you shouldn't worry about it when developing with C and writing end-user Windows applications. For device-driver programs written in assembly language, however, alignment is crucial, because timing and performance can be everything.

Alignment also affects data structures and the way they're accessed. Without specifying a packing level for data structures, the compiler will automatically try to align items in the structure to certain boundaries. For example, word values are aligned on word boundaries, and dword values are aligned on dword boundaries. This doesn't really present a problem when referencing structure elements by name. When simple arithmetic is being performed on the structure elements, however, alignment can wreak havoc with your calculations.

To control program segment alignment, the Microsoft linker provides the /Alignment command-line switch, which can be used to set alignment values to any power of 2. The default alignment is 512 bytes, but a value of 16 for paragraph alignment is commonly used instead. Under most circumstances, alignment doesn't need to be changed. To control the default packing method of data structures in memory, the compiler comes with a /Zp switch and a #pragma pack() statement. Specifying /Zp, /Zp1, /Zp2, or /Zp4 on the compiler's command line alters the default packing of structures for the entire module, assuming either byte, byte, word, or dword alignment. The pack pragma, which, like all #pragmas, is placed in program source code, allows the module-wide default to be changed structure by structure. The value between the pragma's parentheses determines how tightly structures are packed in memory. With no value given between the parentheses in the pragma, the default structure packing method initially passed to the compiler is used.

Selectors, Descriptors, and Descriptor Tables

In protected mode, items called *selectors, descriptors,* and *descriptor tables* govern access to a specified memory location and segment. Each of these protected-mode mechanisms is virtually the same on either the 80286 or 80386 and above processors. The only difference is with the 80286, which uses a subset of the data structures used by 80386 and above processors. This is one of the reasons 80286 protected-mode code is compatible with the 80386 processor.

Selectors

A *selector* is a 16-bit handle that selects a segment descriptor in a table. Which descriptor is determined by taking 13 bits of the selector and multiplying the value by eight (the size of a descriptor). This offset value is added to the base address of the descriptor table and is used to select a descriptor for an already allocated segment. Which table is determined by bit 3 of the selector. If it's 0, the system-wide global descriptor table is used, and if it's 1, the current local descriptor table is used instead. The first two bits of every selector represent its *requested privilege level* (RPL), the privilege level of the program that created the selector. Figure 2.12 shows the format of a protected-mode selector.

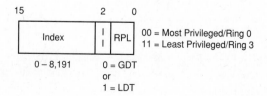

Figure 2.12.
Format of a protected-mode selector.

Windows' Kernel module exports predefined selectors that can be used to access locations in the first megabyte of linear memory. They include the following selectors:

Selector	Description
0000h	Points to the start of linear memory, which includes (among other things) DOS' interrupt vector table (IVT).
0040h	Points to BIOS/DOS areas.
A000h	Points to the start of video graphics memory.
B000h	Points to the start of video text memory.
B800h	Points to the start of video text memory.
C000h	Points to the start of video BIOS.
D000h	Points to the location commonly used by EMS and other drivers.
E000h	Points to the location commonly used by EMS and other drivers.
F000h	Points to the area normally reserved for the ROM BIOS.

These selectors can be verified by using either WDEB386 or Soft-ICE/W to dump the contents of the LDT. In it (as well as in the GDT) you will find "precreated" selectors pointing to common blocks of memory. Here's an example using a sample dump of the LDT:

```
100D  Data16  Base=00000000  Lim=0000FFFF  DPL=1  P  RW
1015  Data16  Base=000F0000  Lim=0000FFFF  DPL=1  P  RW
101D  Data16  Base=000A0000  Lim=0000FFFF  DPL=1  P  RW
1025  Data16  Base=000B0000  Lim=0000FFFF  DPL=1  P  RW
102D  Data16  Base=000B8000  Lim=0000FFFF  DPL=1  P  RW
1035  Data16  Base=000C0000  Lim=0000FFFF  DPL=1  P  RW
103D  Data16  Base=000D0000  Lim=0000FFFF  DPL=1  P  RW
1045  Data16  Base=000E0000  Lim=0000FFFF  DPL=1  P  RW
```

Notice that every handle value is separated by 8 bytes. This reflects the fact that a single 8-byte descriptor is required for every enhanced-mode global heap allocation. In standard mode, the handle symmetry is similar, although the difference between them is 16 bytes apiece, because one descriptor is for an arena entry and the other is for the actual application segment being allocated. The GDT also contains at least two precreated selectors, one for

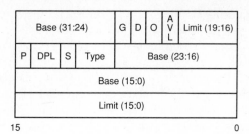

Figure 2.13.
General format
of a segment
descriptor.

The base bits of the descriptor are added together to form the segment's starting address in linear memory. A 32-bit base allows the segment to be mapped anywhere in the 4G linear address space, whereas the 24-bit base specified by an 80286 descriptor allows the segment to be mapped anywhere inside a 16M linear address space. Because the 80286 uses only 16 bits for a segment limit, 64K segments are used. The 80386, however, uses an extended 20-bit segment width, which would seem at first to limit all segment sizes to 1M, but this isn't true. The 80386 uses a special **G**(ranularity) bit in the high word of the descriptor that specifies byte or 4K (page) granularity for the segment. If the G bit is clear (as is always the case with an 80286), a 1M segment size is assumed for the 80386. If the G bit is set, however, a segment size of 1M x 4K, or 4G, is used.

The **D**(efault) bit in the descriptor is used by the processor to indicate whether the segment is a 32-bit segment (D = 1) or a 16-bit segment (D = 0). The **P**(resent) bit is used to indicate whether the segment is currently in memory. It is used by Windows' virtual memory manager to demand-load discarded code and resource segments. Even if the segment is flagged as being in memory, portions of it might still be paged to disk. The **S**(egment) bit is used to differentiate between application and system segment descriptors. The final and last interesting bit is the **A**(ccess) bit, which is set and cleared to determine the access frequency of segments. The access bit is used in lieu of the code segment "trip" bytes found in the module databases under real-mode Windows. Other miscellaneous bits in the descriptor describe the segment in even further detail.

Descriptor Tables

A *descriptor table* is a protected-mode 64K (maximum) segment containing a variable number of eight-byte entries called *descriptors*. Each descriptor in the table references an application code segment, application data segment, or

system segment allocated by the processor. Intel's protected-mode processors support three types of descriptor tables—global, local, and interrupt. In protected mode, access to segments is controlled exclusively through these tables. In real mode, Windows keeps track of allocated segments differently. In this case, a table called the Burgermaster is used to track all moveable and discardable memory segments. The Burgermaster did a fair job of emulating in software what protected-mode processors provide in hardware, but with one serious limitation: Only Windows and Windows-aware programs benefited from its implementation. A DOS-level TSR or network software did not know of the existence of the Burgermaster for translating addresses. As a result, fixed, unmoveable memory is required for any kind of communications buffer between a Windows and a DOS application. In protected mode, the opposite is true, because merely running in protected mode the program is assumed to be using a local or a global descriptor table to translate segment addresses.

Global Descriptor Table

The single system-wide global descriptor table is supposed to be used to keep track of system segments and any "shared" memory segments. System segments include things such as local descriptor tables, task state segments, and the like. However, Windows uses the global descriptor table in a manner inconsistent with the processor's guidelines. Instead of being used to track shared memory between modules, the GDT is used by Windows and the DPMI driver for internal purposes only. A single LDT is used to track all allocated system memory (including GMEM_SHARE/GMEM_DDESHARE memory) for all Windows programs. The 80386 processor has a special register known as the *global descriptor table register* (GDTR), which contains the starting address and limit of the global descriptor table in memory. The first entry in the GDT is always set to NULL and is never used.

To first enter protected mode, a program residing in real mode must create and set up a global descriptor table and interrupt descriptor table. The GDT must include a task state segment, operating system code and data segments, and either an LDT or application code and data segments.

Following is a sample partial dump of the GDT used by Windows:

```
GDTbase = 8010011C          Limit = 010F
```

Selector Value	Selector Type	Base	Limit	DPL	Present	Attributes
0008	Code16	00007360	0000FFFF	0	P	RE
0010	Data16	00007360	0000FFFF	0	P	RW
0018	TSS32	80010390	00002069	0	P	B
0020	Data16	8010011C	0000FFFF	0	P	RW
0028	Code32	00000000	FFFFFFFF	0	P	RE
0030	Data32	00000000	FFFFFFFF	0	P	RW
0039	Code16	80018240	000002FF	1	P	RE
0041	Data16	00000400	000002FF	1	P	RW
0048	Code16	00004DE0	0000FFFF	0	P	RE
0051	Data16	00000000	FFFFFFFF	1	P	RO
0059	Data32	80482000	00000FFF	1	P	RW
0061	Data16	00000522	00000100	1	P	RW
0068	LDT	80530000	00001FFF	0	P	
0070	Reserved	00000000	00000000	0	NP	
0078	Reserved	00000000	00000000	0	NP	
⋮	⋮	⋮		⋮		
00F8	Reserved	00000000	00000000	0	NP	
0100	Reserved	00000000	00000000	0	NP	
0108	Reserved	00000000	00000000	0	NP	

Notice how the first entry in the GDT isn't at an offset of 0, but rather is at an offset of 8, implying (as is the case) that the first descriptor in the GDT isn't used. Also notice that, similar to the LDT example given earlier, two precreated "guaranteed" selectors (numbers 28 and 30) map to the entire 4G range of flat linear memory. One selector is used for code and the other is used for data. These two selectors are used by 32-bit flat-model programs such as Windows' Virtual Machine Manager and various VxDs.

Local Descriptor Tables

Local descriptor tables normally are provided on a per-task basis, and they are used to store descriptors for an application's code, data, resource, and dynamically allocated private memory segments. Windows, however, uses a single LDT for all applications, so no task isolation of segments is really provided. Whenever a program requests from Kernel a global heap allocation greater than 64K, a series of tiled selectors in the LDT is used to satisfy the request. A future 32-bit version of Windows will probably provide an LDT per-task, giving each task its own 4G linear address space. The 80386 processor has a special register known as the *local descriptor table register* (LDTR), which contains the starting address and limit of the current local descriptor table, plus an additional 16-bit selector value representing the LDT's GDT selector.

Systems that use an LDT for each task break the LDT into a series of interleaved private and shareable selectors. The interleaving (2:1 or 3:1) was done to provide some kind of easy, uniform method for determining private versus shared selectors. With the implementation of paging and virtual memory, however, this strategy can be changed to mirror how memory is allocated in a flat address space, with private memory at the beginning of the address space and shared memory at the end. Using the "indirect" mapping features provided by page tables, a system can allocate private selectors from the beginning of the LDT and shared selectors from the end of the LDT. In a flat-model 4G address space, usually a smaller section at the bottom (for example, 512M) is used for memory private to the process, and the rest of the address space is mapped for shareable memory, libraries, and kernel routines. At first, this would seem like a waste of space (what's a 64K LDT among friends?). When you use the indirect mapping method of pages, however, only necessary pages at the bottom and top of the LDT actually need to be committed.

Of IVTs and IDTs

Real mode's interrupt vector table and protected mode's interrupt descriptor table play crucial roles under Windows. Both are used to hold addresses of routines designed to service a particular interrupt. The IVT is located in the first 400h bytes of real mode and in every virtual machine. The IDT is located via the IDTR register. Its location in memory is determined by its descriptor and is not fixed in memory as is the IVT.

When an interrupt or exception occurs, the current contents of CS:IP and the flags are saved. Then control is turned over to an interrupt handler, in either the IVT or the IDT. Which one depends on the currently executing mode of Windows—real, protected, or virtual machine. When an interrupt occurs in real mode, control immediately is transferred to an IVT entry. When an interrupt occurs in protected mode, control is transferred to an entry in the IDT. When an interrupt occurs in a VM, however, it can be serviced in one of possibly two ways. First, the interrupt is passed to the VM's ring 0 control program, which decides what to do with the interrupt. If it's a DOS, BIOS, or user-defined interrupt, it gets passed through to the virtual machine's IVT. If the interrupt or exception was generated in response to a page fault or some other non-DOS fault, a vector in the IDT is used. To locate the IDT table in memory, protected mode uses the IDTR system register.

Interrupts and Exceptions

All members of the Intel processor family are capable of generating processor, software, and hardware exceptions. An *exception* is a forced switch to a procedure or a task invoked when the processor cannot interpret an instruction. Exceptions include faults, traps, and aborts. Interrupts tend to be user-initiated and can involve hardware and software. Software interrupts can be further broken down into two categories—predefined (like INT 21) and user-defined. Exceptions return control to the offending instruction that caused the exception in the first place, whereas interrupts return control to the point just after the offending instruction. Several types of exceptions and interrupts are shown here:

Processor	Hardware	Software
Divide by zero	Floppy/hard drive	INT 21
Page fault	Mouse	INT 9
Segment not present	Parallel/serial port (Any IRQ device)	(Any other INT)

One of the nice features of the 80386 and above processors is the restartability of opcodes when an exception is generated. This effectively lets Windows fix

the situation that generated the exception and return control to the task to let it try the whole thing all over again. This restartability is required for implementing virtual memory effectively. There are a couple of means of generating interrupts under Windows. Following is a list of several interrupt-related functions and the way they are to be used:

Function	Description	Usage
DebugBreak()	Issues an INT 3h to switch to the debugger	C
DOS3Call()	Issues a DOS INT 21h interrupt	Assembly
INT ##	Issues regular interrupt	Assembly
NetBIOSCall()	Issues a NetBIOS INT 5Ch interrupt	Assembly
SetErrorMode()	Controls whether Windows should handle DOS INT 24h errors or whether the application should handle them	C

The DOS3Call() and NetBIOSCall() instructions execute somewhat faster than their INT ## counterparts, because control is automatically switched to an interrupt gate instead of having Windows try to "reflect" the interrupt through various mechanisms.

Gates enable the transfer between different, privileged sections of code. The different types of gates all have in common the fact that they are contained in a GDT, LDT, or IDT, and that each references a segment selector in the GDT, LDT, or IDT. A *call gate,* for example, defines two items—the entry point of a procedure and the privilege level required to access the procedure. Call gates contain a selector pointing to a "destination" executable code segment where control is (possibly) to be transferred.

A *task gate* contains information on the task it represents, including a selector to a task state segment in the global descriptor table. *Interrupt* and *trap gates* contain a selector to the executable code segment of the routine that is to service the interrupt. When a gate descriptor of any type is jumped to, transfer to the gate is controlled and permission is either granted or denied. All gates use their own stack for protection purposes. Figure 2.14 illustrates the gate principle.

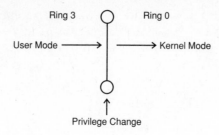

Figure 2.14.
The gate
principle.

Protection

Intel's PC processors implement protection through segmentation (all processors) and paging (80386/80486 only). Protection levels are represented by the four-ring diagram in Figure 2.15. The lower the number, the higher the privilege rating. Ring 0 commonly is used for Kernel and other core components of an operating system, rings 1 and 2 are used for any device driver code, and ring 3 is used for applications. Windows 3.1 runs all applications, DLLs, and DOS boxes at level 3, with system-level code running at level 0.

Figure 2.15.
Windows'
implementation
of Intel's ringed
protection level
scheme.

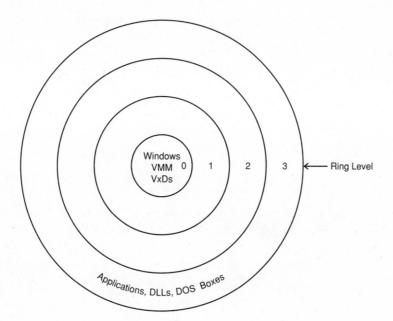

Protection is enforced through several mechanisms, all of which are performed in parallel with the processor's address translation, so a performance hit is never taken by the task. Five basic protection checks are performed, including the following checks:

- ☐ *Type* controls the access method of the segment (execute-only is x-o, read-only is r-o, and read-write is r-w).

- ☐ *Limit* establishes segment boundaries in linear memory.

- ☐ *Restriction of addressable domain* is protection levels provided by CPL, RPL, and DPL.

- ☐ *Restriction of procedure entry points* is provided by gate descriptors.

- ☐ *Restriction of instruction set* means that privileged opcodes are monitored by the processor.

Segments support protection in several ways. First, providing task protection is the concept of a segment as a private address space. By default, no task can access the segments of another task without express permission. If the desired segment isn't in the program's local *or* global descriptor table, access to the memory is denied. Second, the execute-only, read-only, and read-write properties are associated with code, resource, and data segments, respectively. These attributes define the basic access method of the segment. Third, the processor traps any read and write operations outside the segment's boundaries, generating an exception. This includes exceptions such as specifying an "out of range" address, as well as trying to read a word value at the byte before the end of a segment, or a dword value one, two, or three bytes before the end of the segment.

Several processor structures have a privilege level associated with them, including:

- ☐ Tasks, which have a *current privilege level* (CPL) associated with them, an attribute located in the currently executing code segment

- ☐ Segments, which have a *descriptor privilege level* (DPL) associated with them, which represents the privilege level needed to access the segment

- ☐ Segment selectors, which have a *requested privilege level* (RPL) associated with them, which represents the privilege level of the task that generated the selector

Yet another acronym is the EPL, or *effective privilege level*. This level is the result of mating a selector and a descriptor and determining the higher of the two values. This possibly less-privileged level is where access to the segment occurs.

Privilege levels are always represented by a two-bit (0-3) value, which generates a corresponding protection ring level.

The processor also implements protection in the form of restricted opcodes. All the registers and opcodes dealing with global, local, and interrupt descriptor tables are restricted and as such are exempt from manipulation. Protection also is provided via call, trap, interrupt, and task gate descriptors, which check protection levels before transferring execution to a different segment.

The 80386's memory paging mechanism implements protection as well, because every page table contains a two-bit value indicating its security level and read-write status. The security level indicates whether the page is owned by a "supervisor"-level task or a "user"-level task. Application tasks cannot access pages flagged as supervisor-owned. This supervisor bit is equal to a CPL of 0-2. A level of 3 specifies user status for the page. In the future 32-bit flat-model version of Windows, ring level protection schemes will be done away with because segmentation will no longer exist. Instead, page-level security and protection will be all that is needed. In fact, this is the reason for Windows' implementing only two ring protection levels (0 and 3), as it mirrors the security levels used when paging is enabled.

Multitasking

Multitasking is an interesting issue when comparing the capabilities of protected-mode processors such as the 80386 and the 80486 with the current capabilities of Windows. Intel's 80386 and 80486 protected-mode processors provide the capability for preemptive hardware-based multitasking between virtual machines. At any time, the processor can force a switch between tasks. Windows 3 implements only nonpreemptive multitasking, in which the active task must voluntarily relinquish control to the CPU. When this doesn't happen, the system quickly comes to a screeching halt. Windows actually runs the entire system as a number of virtual machines. All Windows applications, DLLs, and device drivers are run in a single system VM, and each DOS box is given its own VM. This is why DOS boxes are preemptively multitasked and applications aren't. As soon as each application is given its own VM and separate address space, you have full preemptive multitasking. Sandwiched between the virtual machines is Windows' Virtual Memory Manager, which also interfaces with any loaded virtual device drivers. See Figure 2.16 for an illustration of this concept.

Figure 2.16.
A layout of
Windows'
"virtual" envi-
ronment in
enhanced
mode.

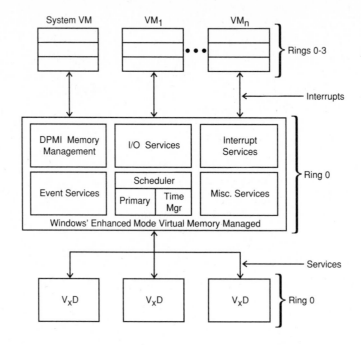

A task switch is much different from a function call, because of the amount of processor-state information saved. A normal procedure call uses the stack in a manner that allows the procedure to call itself again, but tasks don't push any data on the stack and are not reentrant. A task switch saves and loads entirely new register values, LDTs, and different paging structures used to map the task's linear memory. Note, though, that not all of this is necessarily done by Windows 3.

The 80386 and 80486 processors provide several structures and registers to fully support multitasking environments, including

- A local descriptor table (located in the GDT) for each task, providing task address space protection

- Task state segments (a system segment in the GDT) containing task-related information

- A task register, which contains a GDT selector pointing to the task state segment of the current task

- Task gate descriptors, providing an indirect method of switching tasks

- A special descriptor for task state segments that includes a bit setting to indicate whether the task is busy, available, or idle

The designers of Windows have not incorporated several of the 80386 processor's built-in mechanisms for implementing multitasking. The OS/2 kernel design team (is there a big difference here?) has followed suit by not incorporating Intel's full suite of multitasking offerings. Apparently some features, such as multiple task state segments, will never be used because of overhead and performance issues. Could this possibly be a flaw in the processor's design? I can't imagine a chip feature that wouldn't be used (except for segmentation), although I guess it's entirely possible and human to err in chip design, just as in software design. Actually, the TSS is of little use in high-performance multitasking situations, partly because it has its roots in the segmented world. An examination of the global descriptor table shows that only a single TSS and task gate descriptor are present and accounted for. A future version of Windows more than likely will take better advantage of the 80386's multitasking features. The Intel 80386 manual, however, states that "full" task switches using processor-provided mechanisms can be quite slow, relative to the whole scheme of things, and recommends that in certain cases, certain sections of multitasking code should be emulated in software with a few private data structures.

Summary

This chapter covered what many would consider the "unportable" aspects of Windows. True, many of the details have been at a fairly low level, and they aren't issues when you use a newer version of Windows on a different environment. For the immediate future, however, they're very important to understand, because they help you better understand the internal organs making up Windows' soft (extremely soft, some would say) underbelly.

Program and Module Fundamentals

You can look at a completed program in several ways. You can discuss its interaction with the operating system or with other programs, or discuss its internal interaction. It's easy to look at a section of source code—a function, for example—and think of everything as one big object or block of memory. However, a high degree of manipulation, organization, and structure go into a program when it is compiled and linked and has resources, libraries, and a header bound to it. Figure 3.1 illustrates the program-making process.

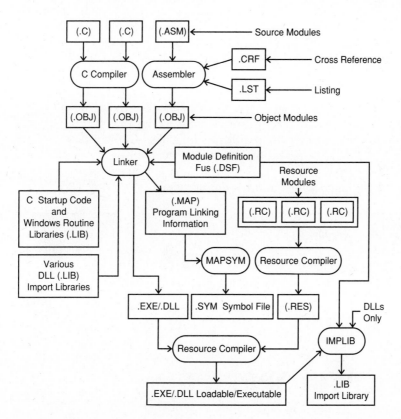

Figure 3.1.
Module creation process.

This chapter discusses in-depth

The architecture and issues surrounding the loadable module, whether application or library

■ All three development stages of the module's life: source, object, and loadable/executable

■ The different types of segments making up an application—code, data, and resource—with information and ideas on how they can best be "tweaked" to create more efficient programs

■ Several more language-oriented issues, including topics on naming and calling conventions, and typecasting and promotion

It's important to fully understand every aspect of program design, because each smaller portion of the module has a major impact on the module as a whole. Not understanding portions of the make file, .DEF file, and linker can cause much grief. For example, a developer's lack of understanding of segmentation issues could lead to a program's having too many fixed or page-locked program segments, which could wreak untold havoc with Windows' memory manager. The attributes assignable to a segment are numerous—pick the wrong ones and a module could end up exhibiting either poor performance or, quite possibly, no performance. Naturally, default values always work in a pinch, but default values aren't always desirable values. A lack of knowledge concerning the make file process makes it difficult to track down the numerous build-related problems that can occur during the development cycle, including linkage errors to external functions, improperly (or redundantly) rebuilding modules, and version problems.

> **Note:** Although Chapter 1, "Windows Fundamentals," refers to applications and libraries as modules, the term *module* actually applies to all three stages of the development process. The developer starts with source file modules, compiles them into object file modules, and finally links them into executable (or loadable) file modules.

Program Segments

Under the segmented memory model, when a program is linked, code and data are separated and organized into one or more named segments. The number of allowable code and data segments depends on the memory model used to compile and link the program. Then, the resource compiler adds resources to the end of your program, effectively adding additional segments. The beginning of the program also contains what is known as an .EXE header, which, despite its name, is applicable to both applications and libraries. This header contains information tying together all the program's code, data, and resource segments. As described later, the data in this header block is key to Windows' implementation of dynamic linking and code and resource sharing. Figure 3.2 illustrates the relationship among the module segments of applications and those of libraries. By the end of this chapter, not only should you be familiar with each of these segments and with other program structures, but you also should have a better understanding of the module-loading and linking process in general.

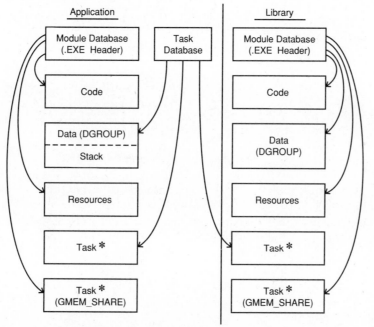

Figure 3.2. Ownership among module segments.

* Task segments created by way of GlobalAlloc( )

The total number of segments in any Windows program can never exceed 254 (excluding an internally used segment). At first this might seem like a limitation, but it can be overcome easily by storing additional functions and resources in DLLs. Except for developer-created segments, no program code, data, or resource segments can grow in size or increase in number. Each segment also contains a certain level of protection, because code segments are flagged as execute-only or execute-read, data segments as read-write, and

resource segments as read-only. Microsoft provides a utility, EXEHDR.EXE, that can be used to dump the structure of applications and libraries. The output from EXEHDR is useful to the developer for several reasons. First and foremost, it represents the easiest way to get an "architectural" view of a program. When you are fine-tuning a module's segments, the output from EXEHDR (as well as a map file) is invaluable. Figure 3.3 is a Heap Walker display that illustrates the program segments required to support the Heap Walker application itself.

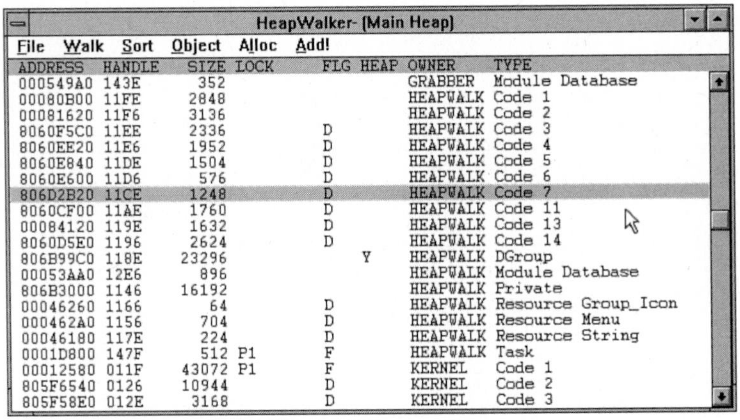

Figure 3.3.
The Heap
Walker's
program
segments.

```
─                       HeapWalker- [Main Heap]              ▼ ▲
 File   Walk   Sort   Object   Alloc   Add!
 ADDRESS   HANDLE   SIZE LOCK      FLG HEAP OWNER      TYPE
 000549A0  143E      352                    GRABBER   Module Database   ▲
 00080B00  11FE     2848                    HEAPWALK  Code 1
 00081620  11F6     3136                    HEAPWALK  Code 2
 8060F5C0  11EE     2336         D          HEAPWALK  Code 3
 8060EE20  11E6     1952         D          HEAPWALK  Code 4
 8060E840  11DE     1504         D          HEAPWALK  Code 5
 8060E600  11D6      576         D          HEAPWALK  Code 6
 806D2B20  11CE     1248         D          HEAPWALK  Code 7
 8060CF00  11AE     1760         D          HEAPWALK  Code 11
 00084120  119E     1632         D          HEAPWALK  Code 13         �N
 8060D5E0  1196     2624         D          HEAPWALK  Code 14
 806B99C0  118E    23296            Y       HEAPWALK  DGroup
 00053AA0  12E6      896                    HEAPWALK  Module Database
 806B3000  1146    16192                    HEAPWALK  Private
 00046260  1166       64         D          HEAPWALK  Resource Group_Icon
 000462A0  1156      704         D          HEAPWALK  Resource Menu
 00046180  117E      224         D          HEAPWALK  Resource String
 0001D800  147F      512 P1      F          HEAPWALK  Task
 00012580  011F    43072 P1      F          KERNEL    Code 1
 805F6540  0126    10944         D          KERNEL    Code 2
 805F58E0  012E     3168         D          KERNEL    Code 3          ▼
```

Although fine-tuning a program's segments was an issue only under real mode, in protected mode a couple of basic steps still have to be taken. The main thing is to ensure that the parameters in the module-definition file are near normal for your module's intended purpose. This includes ensuring that as much code as possible (maybe all) is flagged moveable and discardable (except for WEP()), and that enough stack (at least 8K) and heap size (at least 1024 bytes) have been declared. Keeping code segments under 4K is also advisable, because this size represents the block size used by the enhanced mode paging mechanism of Windows.

Every code and data segment in a compiled program is assigned a name— usually the defaults of _TEXT and _DATA. Additionally, the different possible source modules (.C, .ASM) making up a single executable image or library are assigned names as well, although in this case the names are used only during error processing at the program compilation stage. Following are the default segment names assigned by the compiler:

Model	Code	Data	Module
Small	_TEXT	_DATA	n/a
Medium	module_TEXT	_DATA	*filename*
Compact	_TEXT	_DATA	*filename*
Large	module_TEXT	_DATA	*filename*

See the C compiler switches at the end of this chapter for information on the /ND, /NM, and /NT parameters for overriding the naming of data segments, modules, and text (code) segments.

Code Segments

Code segments represent sections of address space that contain all or a portion of a program's instructions. Code segments, like any other segments, are mapped into sections of linear address space, and it is there, and only there, that instructions are actually executed. A code segment must contain whole functions; a function cannot span several code segments. As a program is linked, its compiled source modules are put into a certain number of segments, determined solely by the chosen memory model and the amount of code in your program.

The order and placement of functions within different code segments can be handled in a default way by the linker, or it can be handled more directly by the developer, who has complete control over the naming and attributes of segments and the grouping of functions within those segments. (See make and .DEF file descriptions later in this chapter.) With the abolishment of real mode and its many associated problems, the fine-tuning of code segments is not as much of an issue as it used to be. Windows' least recently used (LRU) memory management and the 80386's paging mechanism for virtual memory really should be the ones in control of such an issue, not the developer. Why should a developer have to worry about such a low-level detail?

Functions are placed alphabetically into code segments in all but two cases: when the function is too large to fit into the current code segment, or when the function's segment placement has been overridden with #pragma alloc_text or the .DEF file's SEGMENTS statement. All the DLLs mentioned in this book use the alloc_text pragma to place LibMain() into the segment associated with startup code. LibMain() is forced into INIT_TEXT because it's called only once, just like the startup routines. Windows actually does an additional trick: It promotes the INIT_TEXT segment to the beginning of the discard list with a call

to `GlobalLRUOldest()`. The only restriction on the pragma is that it be used before the definition of the function it is referencing. See the following example.

```
#pragma alloc_text(INIT_TEXT, LibMain) // INIT_TEXT is for startup code

int FAR PASCAL LibMain
(
    HINSTANCE hInst, WORD DataSeg, WORD HeapSize, LPSTR CmdLine
)
{
    ...one-time startup code...
}
```

Code segments usually are flagged as moveable and discardable. This helps Windows' memory manager maintain a fluid and dynamic heap. The only exceptions are the code segments of device drivers, which are usually page-locked to prevent the segment from being swapped to disk. As mentioned earlier, ideally a code segment should be under 4K.

Due to Windows' use of 16-bit protected mode, code segments are limited to 64K in size, and after they are allocated, a code segment's size can never increase. If a single source file generates more than 64K of code, it must be broken into separate modules and compiled separately. This really isn't much of a limitation, because not many functions approach the 64K or 4G segment limit. A single function this large would be unreasonably difficult to maintain, requiring at least two days just to page through the source listing. Not being able to reallocate and resize a code segment isn't really a problem either, because code, for the most part, tends to remain static.

Data Segments

Data segments are read-write sections of address space that contain all or a portion of a program's data. Unlike code and resource segments, data segments can grow in size. Being writable and exempt from all but a few memory protection techniques, data segments are quite easy to corrupt with a stray pointer. Memory protection is provided only on a segment level by Windows and the processor, and it doesn't guard against the overwriting of individual objects inside the segment. The Windows operating system doesn't bother enforcing memory protection inside segments, only across segments. Such a great amount of overhead would unnecessarily burden an application.

Data segments usually are flagged as just moveable, because discardable data (except for resources) would be more of a hassle than a benefit. For DOS applications, data segments always are in fixed memory, because "dumb" DOS applications have no mechanism for using descriptor tables or the Burgermaster. With the exception of certain DLLs, all modules contain at least one data segment (usually just one). This is referred to as the *automatic data segment*, or *DGROUP*. Here you can find a program's static variables, stack, dynamic variables (because they're stack-based), local heap space, and local atom table. The automatic (also known as default) data segment is treated as special by Windows, because the operating system never allows the segment to be flagged as discardable. The automatic data segment also is special because it is used to uniquely identify a particular instance of a module. See Figures 3.4 and 3.5 for diagrams of the automatic data segment for applications and libraries.

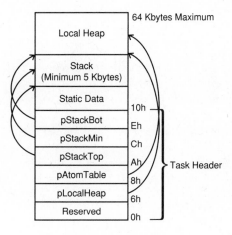

Figure 3.4.
The layout of an automatic data segment for an application.

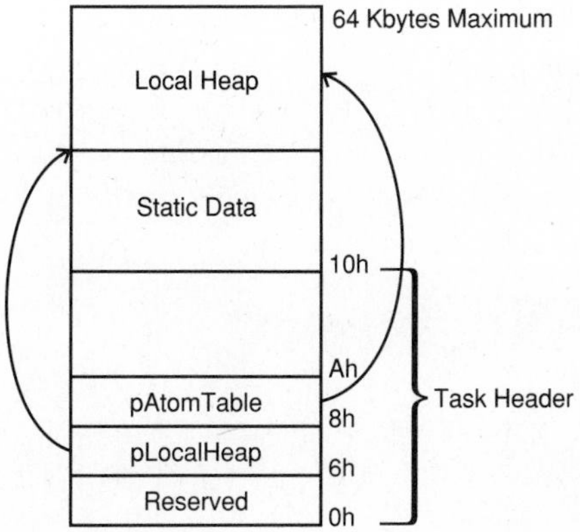

Figure 3.5.
The layout of an automatic data segment for a library.

The first 16 bytes of every data segment (*task header*) are reserved much in the same manner as a relocation table at the end of every program code and data segment. Both serve basically the same service—to locate objects inside the segment. Windows fills in the task header automatically for default data segments. Startup code takes care of stack and heap creation, and the atom table will be set up in the data segment on demand by Windows. For libraries, the startup code stops short of filling in the stack pointers in the task header and reserving stack space, because libraries always use the stack of a calling application.

An application that dynamically allocates segments (r-w global heap objects) to use for local heap space or atom storage must manually call `LocalInit()` and `InitAtomTable()` to create a local heap and atom table, because Windows won't do it automatically in this case. All data segments, whether the automatic data segment or dynamically created ones, can possibly move and grow in memory to satisfy additional local heap allocations. If Windows doesn't have enough additional space in linear memory at the end of the data segment, Windows moves it to an area in memory that does have enough space.

For dynamically allocated data segments, a size of at least 4K to 8K should be used, and the segment should be declared as moveable, because the local heaps in fixed data segments can never grow or move in memory. Almost any Windows call can cause a module's data segment to move in memory, thus invalidating far pointers. In real mode, the movement of a data segment wreaked havoc on far pointers to data items within the segment. In protected mode, however, no such problems exist because descriptor tables are used to govern access to segments.

Due to Windows' use of 16-bit protected mode, program data segments are limited to 64K in size. In this case the segment size does present a problem, because most automatic data segments very quickly get pinched for space. With certain fixed areas of the data segment reserved for static variables and the stack, the local heap often has far less than 64K to work with. It is for this reason that most local heap calls tend to be for small, dynamic character array allocations. A technique for allocating multiple local heaps is discussed in more detail in Chapter 4, "Memory Management."

Resource Segments

Like data segments, resource segments are sections of address space that contain portions of a program's data. Unlike data segments, resource segments are read-only, cannot grow in size, and can be larger than 64K (using tiled selectors). Every object listed in a program's .RC file is loaded as a global heap object, including icons, cursors, bitmaps, menus, dialogs, string tables, text files, and custom data structures. Resource segments almost always are flagged as moveable and discardable, whereas most data segments are merely moveable. This just reflects that resources can be demand-loaded at any time, whereas with privately generated data, the Windows loader has no idea of what to re-create. Like the name *demand-loaded* implies, extensive use of resources can be extremely efficient. Figure 3.6 is a Heap Walker dump showing the various resource segments for Windows' File Manager utility.

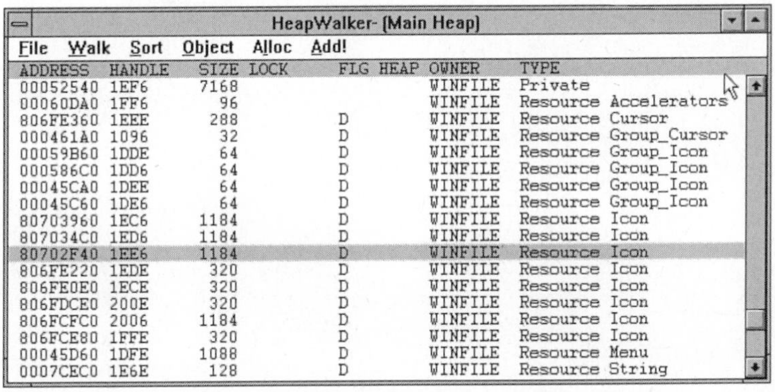

```
                    HeapWalker- [Main Heap]
 File   Walk   Sort   Object   Alloc   Add!
 ADDRESS   HANDLE   SIZE LOCK      FLG HEAP OWNER      TYPE
 00052540  1EF6      7168                   WINFILE    Private
 00060DA0  1FF6        96                   WINFILE    Resource Accelerators
 806FE360  1EEE       288          D        WINFILE    Resource Cursor
 000461A0  1096        32          D        WINFILE    Resource Group_Cursor
 00059B60  1DDE        64          D        WINFILE    Resource Group_Icon
 005B86C0  1DD6        64          D        WINFILE    Resource Group_Icon
 00045CA0  1DEE        64          D        WINFILE    Resource Group_Icon
 00045C60  1DE6        64          D        WINFILE    Resource Group_Icon
 80703960  1EC6      1184          D        WINFILE    Resource Icon
 807034C0  1ED6      1184          D        WINFILE    Resource Icon
 80702F40  1EE6      1184          D        WINFILE    Resource Icon
 806FE220  1EDE       320          D        WINFILE    Resource Icon
 806FE0E0  1ECE       320          D        WINFILE    Resource Icon
 806FDCE0  200E       320          D        WINFILE    Resource Icon
 806FCFC0  2006      1184          D        WINFILE    Resource Icon
 806FCE80  1FFE       320          D        WINFILE    Resource Icon
 00045D60  1DFE      1088          D        WINFILE    Resource Menu
 0007CEC0  1E6E       128          D        WINFILE    Resource String
```

Figure 3.6.
A screen from Heap Walker showing resource segments for File Manager.

Task Segments (Dynamically Allocated Data Segments)

Task segments represent read-write sections of address space that contain globally allocated (not necessarily shared) program data. This is not the same as the "Task" segment reported by Windows 3.1 Heap Walker, which actually is the task database for an application. Task segments are virtually indistinguishable from program data segments. The main difference is in their potential size and how they are allocated and freed. Whereas static program data segments are created during the program compilation stage and destroyed along with the application, task segments are created dynamically during the execution of a program with calls to functions such as `GlobalAlloc()`. Task segments are created to hold dynamically created bitmaps, arrays, or any other kind of data.

Unlike code and data segments, which for compatibility reasons (USE16) are limited to 64K, task segments can grow to just less than 16M in size. Technically, task segments are limited to 64K, but Windows does a fair job of masking the fact that large dynamic allocations really consist of a series of smaller 64K segments. When Kernel starts doling out selectors, it creates a linked list of *tiled* selectors to point to the 64K allocated segments. Tiled just means that the selectors are guaranteed to follow each other in memory. Part of the reason for a 16M allocation limit under enhanced-mode Windows is the fact that Kernel uses as many as 255 of these selectors for any specified global heap object. Given a 64K limit for segments, this yields an allocation size of just less than 16M–64K. For large allocations, selectors are tiled according to some preset value (__ahincr). This value must be added to the selector value whenever a 64K boundary in the object is crossed. This technique is discussed in more depth in the section entitled "Near, Far, and Huge Pointers."

Task segments allocated by an application are automatically freed when the application terminates. As implied by the name, when allocated, task segments belong to the currently active task, which is always an application. There is one exception to this rule. When a library making a global heap allocation wants the memory for itself and not the currently active task, the GMEM_SHARE and GMEM_DDESHARE attributes can be used to override ownership, allowing the library to retain the memory until explicitly freed or until the library terminates. When an application allocates memory using this GMEM_SHARE attribute, the memory is owned by the application's module database rather than by its task database. This allows the memory to be retained until the last instance of the application terminates.

Program Registers

Program registers include any of the common processor registers used by a task during its execution (AX, DX, DS, CS, and so on). So why aren't program registers mentioned in Chapter 2, "Processor and Memory Fundamentals," where processor and memory internals are discussed? The answer is that this chapter puts them in a better context.

When a program is running, different processor registers are used for different things, with some registers being paired for a specific need. Effective debugging requires at least a basic knowledge of registers, register pairings, and how they're used. When a program crashes or, better yet, symbols haven't been loaded and, heaven forbid, no C source code is present, you must be able to fall back (ever so slightly) on your assembly language knowledge. Being able to trace down into the bowels of a Windows API function is another thing entirely. Most of the time, however, all that's really required is a little knowledge of assembly language—just enough that you have a basic idea of what's going on when the source code has been yanked out from beneath your debugger.

Registers fall into two categories: user modifiable and system-reserved. The reserved system registers (mentioned in Chapter 2, "Processor and Memory Fundamentals") point to things such as the current LDT, TSS, and other system data structures. However, the modifiable registers are, in a manner of speaking, free for the taking, including the data registers, index/base registers, and segment registers. The 80386 registers are merely a superset of their 80286 sibling. Just prepend an E to the register name and you've got the whole 32-bit value (that is, EAX, EBX).

Data registers are used to hold a variety of static values, or near pointers to data. All data registers have a high and a low byte portion, each referenced by a separate register name (that is, AH/AL, BH/BL, CH/CL, DH/DL). Other registers are not split in this way. Table 3.1 shows data registers.

Table 3.1. Various registers, their uses, and pairings.

Register	Type	Description
AX (accumulator)	Data	One of the most common temporary registers. Used for arithmetic operations and port I/O and used by procedures to hold word or byte return values.
BX (base)	Data	Used as a starting address for data structures.
CX (count)	Data	Used frequently as a counter for looping and bit-shift operations.
DX (data)	Data	Used for arithmetic operations.
SI (source index)	Index	Used with string instructions.
DI (destination index)	Index	Used with string instructions.
BP (base pointer)	Base	Used to mark stack frames. If BP pushed as even, stack frame is for a near function. If incremented first and then pushed as odd, the stack frame marks a far function.
SP (stack pointer)	Base	Used as an offset to the top of the stack, which is where the next pop/push instruction will affect.

continues

Table 3.1. continued

Register	Type	Description
CS	Segment	Used to hold the currently executing code segment.
DS	Segment	Used to hold the current data segment.
SS	Segment	Used to hold the current stack segment. For applications, DS == SS. For DLLs, SS != DS.
ES	Segment	Used as a backup data register.

Pairing	Description
CS:IP	Segment and offset of the next instruction to be processed by the current task.
SS:SP	Segment and offset of the top of the stack, where all push and pop opcodes will occur.
DS:SI	Used with ES:DI as pointers to string values during execution of string processing opcodes.
ES:DI	See preceding line.
DX:AX	Used to hold dword and larger procedure return values. AX is used for word and byte return values.

A couple of last notes about the loadability and different addressing modes of certain registers are in order. Loadability isn't an issue when you're debugging, only when you're programming, as Intel enforces a set of rules on how registers are to be loaded. Some registers, such as the code segment register (CS), cannot be loaded directly. The code segment register is always loaded as the result of a task transfer or a jmp or call instruction. Other rules include a restriction on memory-to-memory operations. This explains the somewhat jumbled procedure by which registers are loaded.

A line of assembly language code is broken into two portions—an *opcode* and an *operand*. The opcode generally contains the "command," and the operand generally contains the "target" of the command, which can be a register, static data immediately following the opcode, or an indirectly specified location in memory. The following assembly language instructions are an example of the different addressing modes:

```
MOV  AX,BX     ; Register to register
MOV  AX,1      ; Immediate to register
MOV  AX,[BX]   ; Memory location in BX to register (indirect)
```

Indirect addresses can be specified in one of several ways:

```
MOV  AX,[BX + 2]   ; (Value pointed to by ES:BX) + 2
MOV  AX,[BX] + 2   ; Same as the preceding


MOV  AX,[BX].Name  ; Memory to register (for structures)
```

A mode known as *indexed addressing* provides easy access to array structures. The format of an indexed address, similar to the C statement for accessing an array, is as follows:

```
MOV  SI,2
MOV  AL,String[SI]  ; Get byte 3 from character array
```

Whenever registers such as BX or BP are used to specify an indirect address, the compiler assumes a certain default segment value to go along with it. In the case of BX it's DS, and with BP it's SS. In certain cases, an override is required to generate the correct address. Following is an example:

```
MOV  AX,[BP]       ; Assumes SS--is this what's wanted?
MOV  AX,DS:[BP]    ; Overrides and uses DS rather than SS
```

Indirect addresses also can specify another register to help generate an end address, generating what is known as *based indexed mode addressing*. Following are equivalent examples of the same instruction:

```
MOV  AX,[BX + DI + 2]   ; (Value pointed to by DS:BX) + DI + 2
MOV  AX,[BX + 2][DI]    ; Same as the preceding
MOV  AX,2[BX + DI]      ; Same as the preceding
MOV  AX,[BX][DI][2]     ; Same as the preceding
```

An interesting thing to do when tracing through compiled code is to notice the number of special shortcut instructions that might not be totally intuitive at first. These can be either the result of optimizations or merely regular compiler-created code. With optimizations turned off, not many shortcuts will get implemented. There are still some instructions that might seem somewhat puzzling at first glance, however:

```
XOR  AX,AX     ; Quicker in clock cycles than MOV AX,0


PUSH DS        ; Sometimes this is used rather than MOV AX,DS
POP  AX        ; or vice-versa
```

Just as it sometimes can be difficult for a developer to step through fully optimized code, the same applies to CodeView, Soft-ICE/W, and any other source-level debugger. Optimizations must be forced off with the /0d compiler switch, or the debugger has a difficult time matching compiled program instructions with lines of source code.

The Stack

A stack is a temporary data storage area associated with tasked modules (applications). The stack is used for storage during function calls (holding parameters and a return address) and any other time that storage for temporary values (such as local variables) needs to be created. All Intel processors contain built-in instructions that push and pop word-length values on and off this first-in, last-out queue. The processor also contains instructions that can be used to access the stack similar to an array.

A stack is an expand-down data array usually contained in a program's automatic data segment (DGROUP), which yields the term SS == DS, implying that the stack segment is equal to the data segment. At all times, the processor maintains a stack segment register, which always can be used to find the segment address of the current stack, and a stack pointer, used to index into the current stack segment.

The stack is most commonly used during function calls, where it's used as storage for the calling procedure's parameters and return address. The called procedure then uses the stack to establish a frame pointer, possibly save a few registers, and finally, reserve space on the stack for local variables. Although all global variables are automatically initialized to zero (or null), local stack-based variables follow no such rule. This is in part due to the way they are created. When local variables need to be created, instead of pushing "zero" values onto the stack, the stack pointer is merely decremented by a certain amount. Because local variables reference locations within this "uninitialized" section of the stack, there is no telling what values will be there.

Although the stack is potentially a 64K segment, it is often limited to approximately 5K or 10K. Anything less and Windows automatically switches to a 5K stack. Higher values for a stack size are needed for programs making many nested or recursive function calls. Also, applications using the common dialogs provided by Windows 3.1 should use an 8K stack. Many developers will find that an 8K stack size is more appropriate than the default of 5K. Stacks have the distinction of being the most used and abused aspect of programming.

When an application calls into a DLL (which has no stack), only code and data segment registers are reloaded by Windows, which yields the term SS != DS, because the data segment of the library was loaded but the stack segment of the application was retained. This presents a problem for the DLL when it tries to pass by reference any local variables pushed onto the stack. Even if another DLL was making the call, an application was at some point initially responsible for providing a stack. The problem results because the compiler has no way to differentiate between stack-based and data segment-based near pointers. When the call is made and the near pointer is pushed, the function tries to use the near stack pointer as a near pointer into the module's data segment—but it's not. It's a pointer within the current stack segment. This call will fail because virtually all functions assume that SS == DS. The usual solution is to make the variable global by prepending a `static` where the data is first declared. This forces the data to be stored in the module's data segment, and not on the stack.

Sometimes the current stack isn't used during a function call. This usually happens when a less-privileged piece of code calls into a higher-privileged section. In this case, parameters are copied off the stack and onto the stack of the more-privileged task. The number of words to be copied is specified by the `p-words` option for the `EXPORTS` statement in the module-definition file. This option is rarely used in Windows applications. The ToolHelp DLL included with Windows 3.1 includes several functions for tracing through the stack of a task. See the section entitled "Prologue and Epilogue Code" for a related discussion on stack frames. Most stack-related functions don't see much use in end-user applications, but rather in debuggers and other developer-oriented tools.

Program Initialization and Cleanup

Initialization and cleanup code can be performed in any of multiple areas in an application or a DLL. For applications, initialization code (registering classes, creating windows, loading DLLs, and so on) usually exists in an early section of `WinMain()` just before the message dispatching loop, whereas per-window initialization code (extra data, properties, GDI or Kernel objects, and so on) usually is done inside the methods of several key window messages. These messages are so important because they're guaranteed to be received before the window is shown. Messages that can be trapped on and used for

housing per-window initialization code include WM_INITDIALOG, WM_CREATE, WM_NCCREATE, and the first WM_PAINT message. The fact that these messages are guaranteed to be received before the window is shown is the only thing you should assume about the ordering or use of messages and the messaging system. For DLLs, initialization code (registering classes, loading other DLLs, and so on) usually exists in either LibEntry() or LibMain().

Cleanup code also can be located in multiple areas in a module. For applications, cleanup code is done just after the **GetMessage()** loop in WinMain(). This usually consists of unloading any DLLs loaded via **LoadLibrary()** at the beginning of WinMain(), and possibly freeing up any global memory or procedure instances. Per-window cleanup, however, usually is done in either the WM_CLOSE or (more commonly) WM_DESTROY method of the window. The kind of code you find here usually is concerned with removing window properties and freeing the global or local objects referenced by handles stored in window extra data or property handles. For libraries, cleanup code "officially" is done inside WEP(). Quite often, however, a separate routine is used because WEP() is incapable of calling very many functions. In fact, at termination time, Windows itself often is incapable of calling WEP(). This problem has supposedly been fixed with Windows 3.1.

The C and Windows Runtime Libraries

The C and Windows runtime libraries represent a different kind of initialization and cleanup routines for a module. These routines deal with more low-level, internal kinds of initialization and cleanup than do WinMain() or LibMain()— and they're executed first. Just because they're internal, however, doesn't mean you can't benefit by understanding their use.

The C startup libraries are used to link in runtime variables such as environ, psp, osmajor, arg, and argc, and the entire C library of functions. Applications and libraries dynamically link to these libraries in their make file, using either ?libcew.lib for applications or ?dllcew.lib for libraries. The question mark is replaced with the alphabetic character representing the intended memory model (s, c, m, l). The different sets of libraries (application versus DLL) are a direct result of the fact that DLLs aren't tasked, and therefore shouldn't have access to certain runtime variables such as environ and psp. They're also different because for applications, the runtime libraries define _astart as the module's entry point. For DLLs no entry point is automatically specified, which is why the DLL's LibEntry routine declares itself as the entry point. If a module doesn't require the overhead of the environment variables or the C runtime functions, the C runtime library can easily be dropped by specifying a different form of the library in the make file, using either ?nocrt.lib for applications or ?nocrtd.lib for libraries. This is commonly done with font- and other resource-only libraries.

The C runtime libraries for applications define _astart as the entry point for the module. The job of _astart is to initialize certain C features, make calls to the Windows runtime functions InitTask(), WaitEvent(), and InitApp(), and finally make a call to the application's WinMain starting point. When WinMain finally returns and the application has "officially" terminated, certain termination routines in the Windows startup library are called to do things such as destroy message queues and, finally, kill the task.

DLLs are laid out quite differently, because no starting point is automatically defined for the DLL. Whereas the C and Windows runtime application libraries contain external links to the functions _astart and WinMain(), the runtime libraries for DLLs know nothing at all about _astart, LibEntry(), or even LibMain(). This is the reason for the inclusion of the assembly language routine LibEntry(), which not only defines itself as the starting point for the module, but, like the runtime functions, also performs a number of initialization features, such as creating a local heap and calling LibMain().

In addition to the C runtime code normally required for applications, Windows also requires the use of certain startup and termination routines. These routines are used to create message queues, initialize tasks and applications, and basically let Windows know about the new module that's loaded and about to come online. Unlike the C runtime libraries, Windows' startup code is for applications only. This code should never be discarded because it has made a call to WinMain() and is still waiting for control to return. A DLL's startup code is different, because control is returned immediately after the call to LibMain(). At this point the initialization code can be jettisoned (and is) with a call to **GlobalLRUOldest()**. After all, when it comes time for a DLL to terminate, Windows automatically calls the library's WEP() termination routine. Unlike applications, DLLs can keep startup and termination code in different segments.

The Module-Loading Process

Before a program is loaded into memory by Windows, its module header is checked for certain key bits of information. This "new-style .EXE" header contains everything you need to know about the layout of a module—specifically, the number, size, attributes, and location of any code, data, and resource segments. If the module has not been loaded into memory yet, Windows uses this information to allocate and read in (at a minimum) the program's default code and data segments, plus any segments marked as PRELOAD in the resource file (.RC) or module-definition file (.DEF). Just as the linker can override certain segment attributes specified at compile time, while Windows is in the process of loading segments it too can override certain segment attributes. If a prior instance of the module were already loaded in memory, only a new copy of the module's data segment is created. Additionally, if the module contains any implicit or explicit links to other modules, they too are loaded in the same manner and gain control before the original module. At some point during the loading of the module, Windows automatically creates two additional global heap objects to provide support to the module—a *module database* and a *task database*.

The Module Database

Windows creates a module database entry in the global heap on loading the first instance of any application or library. The module database contains information from the .EXE header and any other pieces of information applicable to every running instance of the program. Obviously, the majority of this information is related to code and resource segments, which represent the shared units in Windows. For real mode, when the module database is loaded into memory, each item in the entry table of the .EXE header is expanded into a full-fledged call thunk, with all of them residing in the module database. In real mode, the module database also contained an array of bytes (one for every discardable segment) to use as "access trips." Additionally, when memory moved or was discarded, Windows would patch up the values in all the call thunks to keep them current. Protected mode Windows needs no such mechanism in the module database because protected mode of the processor contains a "segment not present" fault, which is used to generate a software interrupt to the Windows loader, where the loading of the segment is handled automatically.

Deep inside Windows, lists are kept for just about everything imaginable: program segments, tasks, modules, windows, global heap segments. You name it and there's probably a list. Prior versions of Windows allowed very little manipulation or access to these lists. Windows 3.1 and ToolHelp, however, radically change all of this. The following functions are provided by Windows for module management:

Function	Purpose
`FindExecutable()`	Returns the executable file and path associated when given a file.
`FreeLibrary()`	Decreases the reference count of a library, unloading if the count is zero.
`FreeModule()`	Frees instance-related data of a module. Not a commonly used function.
`GetModuleFileName()`	Returns the module name when given a module handle.
`GetModuleHandle()`	Returns the module handle when given a module name.
`GetModuleUsage()`	Returns the reference count of a loaded module.
`GetProcAddress()`	Returns the address of a function in the specified library.
`LoadLibrary()`	Loads a library (if it is not already in memory) and increases the reference count.
`LoadModule()`	Loads a Windows application and increases the reference count.
`WinExec()`	Loads a Windows or a DOS application and increases the reference count.

New with Windows 3.1 and ToolHelp are the following module-related functions and structure:

Function	Purpose
`ModuleFirst()`	Fills struct with info on first module in system.
`ModuleNext()`	Fills struct with info on next module in system.
`ModuleFindHandle()`	Fills struct with info on module specified by handle.
`ModuleFindName()`	Fills struct with info on module specified by name.

```
typedef struct tagMODULEENTRY
{
    DWORD  dwSize;                          // Size of ME struct (reqd.)
    char   szModule[MAX_MODULE_NAME + 1];   // Module name
    HANDLE hModule;                         // Module handle
    WORD   wcUsage;                         // Usage (reference) count
    char   szExePath[MAX_PATH + 1];         // Fully qualified module
path
    WORD   wNext;                           // Internal use
}
```

The Task Database

Windows creates a *task database* (TDB) entry in the global heap for each instance of an application. The TDB is used by Windows to keep track of task-specific information such as the current DOS path, message queue, file handle table, dynamically allocated segments, an array of instance thunks (`MakeProcInstance()`), a private interrupt vector table, and handles to the TDB's associated module database, data segment, and DOS program database (also known as the program segment prefix). Many of these items are represented by separate selectors, whose values are stored inside the TDB.

Task handles are commonly used by applications and libraries to keep track of individual programs, to determine whether a client module has terminated or crashed without calling a "goodbye" function. True, in this case the instance handle could always be used for the same purpose, because Windows associates only one task and one instance handle with every running application. However, the Windows API provides far more task-related functions than instance-related functions. Simply by running through an array of task handles and calling the function `IsTask()`, a module can quickly determine whether an application is up and running. Additionally, Windows 3.1 provides notification functions (and shell messaging hooks) that can be used to determine when an application is coming on- or off-line.

The following task-related functions are provided by Windows related to task management:

Function	Purpose
EnumTaskWindows()	Returns via a callback function all windows created by a specified task.
GetCurrentPDB()	Returns the handle (selector) of the current program database.
GetCurrentTask()	Returns the handle of the currently running task.
GetInstanceData()	Allows access to another module's data segment (not recommended).
GetNumTasks()	Returns the number of currently executing tasks.
GetClassWord()	Can be used to return the handle of the module that registered a window class.
GetWindowWord()	Can be used to return the instance of the module that owns a specified window.
IsTask()	Determines the validity of a task handle.

New with Windows 3.1 and ToolHelp are the following module-related functions and structure:

Function	Purpose
TaskFirst()	Fills struct with information on the first task in the list.
TaskNext()	Fills struct with information on the next task in the list.
TaskFindHandle()	Fills struct with information on the specified task.
TaskGetCSIP()	Gets the current execution address of the sleeping task.
TaskSetCSIP()	Sets the current execution address of the sleeping task.
TaskSwitch()	Switches to a specific address in the current task.

```
typedef struct tagTASKENTRY
{
    DWORD       dwSize;             // Size of TE struct (reqd.)

    HTASK       hTask;              // Handle to task
    HTASK       hTaskParent;        // Handle to task's parent
    HINSTANCE   hInst;              // Instance assoc. with task
    HANDLE      hModule;            // ModuleDB assoc. with task

    WORD        wSS;                // Task's Stack segment. A stack is
                                    // the only thing unique to a task.
    WORD        wSP;                // Task's SP
    WORD        wStackTop;          // Stack checking pointers
    WORD        wStackMinimum;
    WORD        wStackBottom;

    WORD        wcEvents;
    HANDLE      hQueue;             // Handle to message queue of task
    char        szModule[...];      // Module that created task
    WORD        wPSPOffset;         // Offset to program segment prefix

    HANDLE      hNext;              // Handle to next task
}
TASKENTRY
```

Like most ToolHelp functions and structures, these are listed merely for informational purposes and aren't used by the code in this book or by most end-user applications, only by development tools such as debuggers.

Dynamic Linking and the .EXE Header

The dynamic linking and relocation of code is made possible through a variety of implemented mechanisms. Much behind-the-scenes work needs to occur when functions are called and memory is accessed. The majority of this work occurs during function calls and task switches. Under Windows 3, however, only function calls are really involved in this process, because there are no forced task switches.

References to near code and data need no special hand-holding or fix-up, because all references are relative to the beginning of the segment, regardless of where it is mapped in memory. For far references to code and data, some kind of fix-up mechanism and common storage area for shared segments must be implemented. The storage area is the .EXE header present in every Windows module. The .EXE header contains almost all the information needed to share code and resources. Not only the linker generates code and data segment information from the module-definition file (.DEF), placing it in the .EXE header. The resource compiler does the same thing, generating information on resource segments and placing it in the header as well. This database is the focus point for all kinds of segment fix-up and sharing information. Among other things, the .EXE header contains the following data structures:

Structure	*Description*
Header information block	The header information block contains several pieces of static information, most regarding the executable file in general. The header block also contains information on the various tables listed as follows, indicating their size, and an offset value to locate the table.
Segment table	The segment table contains information on every segment in the module, indicating whether the segment is code or data and describing its attributes (fixed, discardable, and so on). The table also specifies whether the segment contains relocation data.
Resource table	The resource table contains information that describes each resource in the module.
Resident-name table	The resident-name table holds two items for every exported far function in a module—an ASCII string name and an ordinal, which is used as an index into the entry table.
Module-reference table	The module-reference table contains a series of word offsets into the imported names table. Each offset references a different library name.

continues

Structure	Description
Imported-name table	The imported-name table contains the ASCII names of any modules imported by the application or library.
Entry table	The entry table contains groups of entry points into the module. Each entry point is represented by a six-byte data structure describing the moveable entry point (far function reference) in the module.
Non-resident-name table	Like the resident-name table, the non-resident-name table holds an ASCII string name and an ordinal into the entry table for every exported far function. In this case, however, the segment containing the names is not guaranteed to stay in memory.

Before you continue, a little more light needs to be shed on the entry table used to track a program's moveable entry points. As mentioned, the entry table contains a series of groups, each describing one or more entry points in the module. Generally, a group is created for every segment in the module. Associated with each group is a two-byte value indicating whether the segment the group describes is fixed or moveable, and the total number of entries in the group. Moveable entry points are described by the following six-byte structure:

Offset		Description
0h	Bit 0 set	The entry is exported.
	Bit 1 set	The entry uses a shared global data segment.
	Bits 3–7	Indicates whether ring transitions occur. If they do, these bits count the number of words making the stack. This information is used because the normal stack segment is not privileged enough to enter most areas of the "kernel." In this case, the appropriate number of words on the stack is copied to a higher-privileged procedure, the work is performed, and then at some point the original stack is restored and the return value is copied to the original stack.

Offset	Description
1h	Two bytes representing the instruction INT 3Fh.
3h	The segment number.
4h	The segment offset.

The structure describing fixed entry points is similar, although somewhat smaller. A fixed entry point is represented by the following three-byte structure:

Offset	Description	
0h	Bit 0 set	The entry is exported.
	Bit 1 set	The entry uses a shared global data segment.
	Bits 3–7	Indicates whether ring transitions occur.
1h	Specifies an offset.	

Also present in the module, after every code and data segment, is a relocation table. The purpose of the relocation table is to resolve all references to far functions, both internal and external. The exehdr utility, when used with the /Verbose option, displays the relocation table for each segment. The module's map file also can be used to view public, external symbols. Relocation information is really useful only in an "FYI" kind of context, and it isn't used during normal debugging or program development.

The first two bytes of each relocation table contain a count of the number of entries in the table, with each entry taking up eight bytes of storage. The first byte in the structure describes the relocation address type. Possible values are shown here:

Value	Description
0	Relocation item is the low byte at the specified address.
2	Relocation item is a 16-bit selector.
3	Relocation item is a 32-bit pointer.
5	Relocation item is a 16-bit offset.
11	Relocation item is a 48-bit pointer.
13	Relocation item is a 32-bit offset.

The second byte describes the relocation type itself, with the following possible values:

Value	Description
0	Internal reference
1	Imported ordinal
2	Imported name
3	Operating system fix-up

Bytes three and four in the structure pinpoint the offset of the relocation within the segment. If the relocation type is an internal reference for a fixed memory segment, the fifth byte is the segment number, the sixth byte is zero, and the last two bytes specify an offset into the segment. If the relocation is an internal reference for a moveable memory segment, the fifth byte is 0xFFh, the sixth byte is zero, and the last two bytes are used to hold an ordinal number found in the entry table. If the relocation type is for an imported ordinal, the fifth and sixth bytes are used as an index into the module-reference table, with the last two bytes specifying a function ordinal. Finally, if the relocation is for an imported name, the fifth and sixth bytes specify an index into the module-reference table, and the last two bytes are used as an offset into the imported-names table.

As far as the different segment types are concerned, only data and code segments are routinely fixed up, because the stack segment remains constant throughout an application and is changed by Windows only during task switches. In real mode, Windows requires a series of thunks (instance, call, and return) to fix up code and data segments. See Figure 3.7 for a simple illustration. Thunks are sections of code used to load or set up a segment register, and then jump to some target location. The relocation tables found at the end of every code and data segment actually contain addresses to fixed-memory call thunks (also known as "load thunks") found in the module database. The call thunks are responsible for loading segments from disk, using interrupt 3Fh. If the segment is already loaded in memory, the INT instruction is replaced with a simple JMP.

Call thunks increase the size of the moveable entry-point structure (mentioned earlier) by two bytes, placing them just before the INT 3Fh or JMP instruction. The two bytes are used to hold the instruction SAR CS:[xxxx],1. In real mode, the module database contains an "access" byte for every discardable code segment. The SAR instruction is used to trip this access byte. Because the call thunks exist in a fixed memory segment, whenever a code segment is loaded into memory, only the call thunks need to be patched, not addresses in the actual application. Instance thunks fix up the appropriate value for DS, then call either a call thunk or, in the case of a fixed code segment or protected mode, the address of the actual routine in memory.

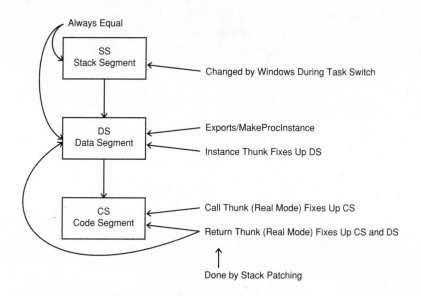

Figure 3.7.
Segment register fix-up mechanisms.

Real mode also requires another operation known as *stack patching*. During the execution of a function, segments can be moved and discarded from memory. There's really no guarantee that the return address specified on the stack will be valid at the end of the function. Stack patching involves tracing through the stack (see the "Prologue and Epilogue Code" and "Stack Frames" sections), changing the values of any references to segments that have been moved or discarded. References to segments that have been moved merely need to be altered, whereas references to discardable segments must be patched to point to a section of code known as a return thunk. A return thunk is just like a call thunk, except instead of jumping to an address, a return (RET) is done. Return thunks also use an invalid segment of zero, to let Windows know that a RET and not a JMP is required. Segment zero in an application is reserved exclusively for return thunks. A return thunk also contains a data segment handle, because it too might have been moved around in memory.

Call and return thunks aren't needed in protected mode for several reasons. When a program is loaded in protected mode, all references to internal and external far functions are immediately fixed up to point to "valid" locations. If a JMP or some other instruction is done on a segment that doesn't happen to be loaded in memory, the processor issues a "segment not present" fault. This issues a software interrupt to Windows' memory manager, notifying it of the segment that needs to be loaded. When the segment is reloaded into memory, the CS:IP where the instruction failed is restarted. A similar mechanism is used for virtual memory pages not present in physical RAM.

Whereas code segments must be fixed up whenever segment boundaries are crossed, data segments must be fixed up whenever module boundaries are crossed. Naturally, for near functions the data segment is assumed to be unchanged. For exported or other far functions, however, the current data segment probably belongs to somebody else. A C compiler automatically generates the correct prologue and epilogue for far functions when the /Gw compiler switch is used. This switch alters the prologue to fix up the data segment on entering the function. The following section discusses instance thunks and the purpose of the prologue and epilogue code.

Prologue and Epilogue Code

Prologue and *epilogue code* are sections of code added to the beginning and end of the functions in most high-level languages, such as C, Pascal, and FORTRAN. Prologue code is used to construct a procedure call, which can include setting up a stack frame, whereas epilogue code is used to destruct a procedure call, possibly cleaning up the stack. Normally, the C programmer is insulated from this layer of code, because the compiler generates it automatically. When interfacing to assembly language, however, or when Windows is added to the picture, the developer is made acutely aware of its existence. Figure 3.8 shows how the prologue and epilogue code serve a function.

Figure 3.8.
Prologue and epilogue code serving a far function.

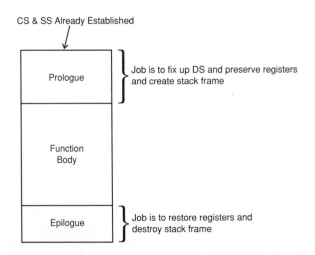

Whether it's a small in-line assembly routine that needs to be written or a debugging session with no source code, the prologue and epilogue code must be fully understood if the developer is writing or debugging code that needs to access any of the function's parameters or local variables. For all functions declared as far in Windows applications, the standard prologue and epilogue code preserve and restore the value of DS at the beginning and end of the function. The compiler automatically generates this code with the -Gw switch. With the -GW switch, the prologue and epilogue are the same as indicated in Figure 3.8, except that DS isn't fixed up at entry and exit—only BP. This is useful when DS is not expected to change, which is the case when you're dealing with single-instance, protected-mode applications. Trimming code like this actually saves more time than you might think. This is because any code that reloads a segment register always incurs a substantial time hit. When the discussion is centered around functions for window procedures, you can be assured that Windows will be calling the function enough that streamlined prologue and epilogue code will definitely make a difference.

Following is the Windows prologue and epilogue for a simple near function, where DS does not get preserved:

```
PUSH BP                 ; Preserve BP upon entry
MOV  BP,SP              ; Establish new BP frame pointer
SUB  SP,localvarsize    ; Adjust the stack for newly created local vars

...function body...

MOV  SP,BP              ; Restore old SP, destroying local variables
POP  BP                 ; Restore old BP value
RET  #                  ; If Pascal, then # is size of parms on stack
```

A near function is always located in the current code segment. For that reason, a reload of the current data segment is not required, because it is assumed that the value is already valid. For a far function in an application, the prologue and epilogue are somewhat different, because the data segment is assumed to have changed somewhere along the line, and thus must be reloaded. The compiler generates code to ensure this. See the following code:

```
PUSH DS                 ; Do-nothing code that doesn't hurt. Ensures
POP  AX                 ; that ax == ds. Ignore for now...
NOP

INC  BP                 ; Increment before pushing to indicate far call
PUSH BP
MOV  BP,SP
```

```
PUSH DS                ; Preserve original DS
MOV  DS,AX             ; Put AX (which should have a valid DS) into DS

SUB  SP,localvarsize
PUSH DI                ; Save whatever registers get messed with
PUSH SI                ; Ditto

...function body...

POP  SI                ; Restore old values
POP  DI

SUB  BP,+02            ; Push BP back two to pick up DS on a POP
                       ; and effectively wipe out local vars
MOV  SP,BP
POP  DS                ; Restore original DS value
POP  BP                ; Restore pushed BP
DEC  BP                ; Make BP even again

RETF #                 ; Far return
```

The do-nothing code at the top of the prologue is there because the prologue code can take on any of several formats. For exported far functions, the format of the prologue and epilogue changes. This time the first three instructions are replaced with NOPs. This lets the incoming value of AX determine the default data segment to be used with the function. That incoming value is established with the **MakeProcInstance()** function, which generates a code snippet somewhere in fixed memory similar to this:

```
MOV AX,datasegaddr ; Windows fills in this value
JMP segment:offset ; Dest. addr is call thunk or actual routine
```

Windows maintains separate instance thunks for each function in every instance of your application that you ask for. They need to be separate because in each case the data segment getting reloaded is different. An interesting alternative to **MakeProcInstance()** and the use of the EXPORTS command is FIXDS, a utility by Windows developer Michael Geary. A veteran of the early versions of Windows, Michael noticed that because SS == DS for applications, and because SS will always be constant throughout the life of the application and any loaded libraries (which have no SS), the code for procedure instances could be thrown away entirely. FIXDS changed code to this:

```
MOV AX,SS          ; Stack segment value is always set
NOP

INC BP             ; Stack frame stuff
```

```
PUSH BP
MOV  BP,SP

PUSH DS               ; Save old DS
MOV  DS,AX            ; Set current DS (which == SS)

SUB  SP,localvarsize
PUSH DI               ; Save whatever registers get messed with
PUSH SI               ; Ditto

...function body...

POP  SI               ; Restore old values
POP  DI

SUB  BP,+02
MOV  SP,BP
POP  DS
POP  BP

RETF #
```

Depending on the linker, the following code might also be generated:

```
INC  BP               ; Stack frame stuff
PUSH BP
MOV  BP,SP

PUSH DS               ; Save old DS
PUSH SS               ; Push current app's Stack segment
POP  DS               ; Set DS according to the current SS (app)

SUB  SP,localvarsize
PUSH DI               ; Save whatever registers get messed with
PUSH SI               ; Ditto

...function body...

POP  SI               ; Restore old values
POP  DI

SUB  BP,+02
MOV  SP,BP
POP  DS
POP  BP

RETF #
```

Various instructions can be used to achieve the same effect. It all depends on the brand of linker used on the module. Because these FIXDS statements overwrite the first couple bytes of prologue code, it isn't necessary to EXPORT the function. Nor is it required to call **MakeProcInstance()**, because the thunk code is no longer required—it has been made a part of the prologue. For libraries, the prologue code is quite similar to the FIXDS example shown earlier. Because DS will be constant throughout the life of the DLL, the following introduction part of the prologue code can be used:

```
MOV  AX,datasegaddr ; Move constant DS value of library into AX
NOP
...
```

MakeProcInstance() isn't required for libraries because DS never changes for the life of the library. **MakeProcInstance()** isn't required for exported window procedures because Windows automatically loads DS into AX when a message is sent to a window. This is also why exported functions can't be called directly. Calling an exported function from within an application doesn't correctly set up AX.

With the release of Windows 3.1, the prologue and epilogue for applications can be changed yet again because the INC and DEC BP instructions can be dropped. Any program (such as a debugger) taking advantage of the ToolHelp DLL included with Windows 3.1 does not require these instructions. A newer, smaller form of the prologue and epilogue is shown next:

```
PUSH BP
MOV  BP,SP

PUSH DS
MOV  AX,SS
MOV  DS,AX
SUB  SP,localvarsize

PUSH DI            ; Save whatever registers get messed with
PUSH SI            ; Ditto

...

MOV  DS,[BP-2]

LEAVE              ; A processor instruction that does a MOV SP,BP
                   ; and POP BP
RETF #
```

To get an idea of how important the stack is, you should know that Intel's protected mode processors provide special instructions specifically for the stack, including ENTER and LEAVE. LEAVE, as shown in the preceding code, is used to destroy a stack frame, whereas ENTER is used to establish a stack frame. Stack frames are discussed in depth in the following section. Here is the code simulating ENTER:

```
PUSH BP          ; ENTER 5,0
MOV  BP,SP
SUB  SP,5
```

Unfortunately, the ENTER instruction cannot be used in Windows programs because it sets up local variables before the value of DS has had a chance to get saved on the stack.

Another trick for prologue and epilogue functions involves the keyword _loadds, which generates prologue and epilogue similar to this:

```
PUSH BP
MOV  BP,SP

PUSH DS                  ; Save current DS
MOV  AX,DS_CONST         ; Load single-instance DS into AX
MOV  DS,AX               ; Set up new DS
```

As shown, a constant value for DS is inserted into the epilogue code. This is why _loadds is valid only with single-instance protected mode applications. The /GW compiler switch must also be used so that the compiler knows to generate a prologue that doesn't interfere with DS.

Stack Frame

Knowledge of exactly how the stack works during function calls is crucial during debugging, because the stack is used to hold the parameters passed to the function, the return address, local variables, and possibly a few other registers, such as DS, SI, and DI. All these items are essentially wrapped up into what is known as a stack frame, shown in Figure 3.9.

Whenever a function is called, a certain number of significant events occurs. Excluding any code or data segment fix-ups, three distinct steps emerge. First, the caller's parameters are pushed onto the stack, with the ordering dependent on the calling convention used by the language. If it is Pascal, parameters are pushed onto the stack from left to right, whereas with C, parameters are pushed onto the stack from right to left. Next, after a jump to the destination address, a near (16-bit word) or far (32-bit dword) return address gets pushed onto the stack. At this point, control has shifted from the caller to the callee. The first thing the callee does is to preserve the value of BP, the base pointer. BP is used by CodeView as a reference point for tracing through the stack. Depending on whether BP is incremented before it is pushed (producing an odd value), CodeView will know whether to pop a dword or word return address off the stack. The INC and DEC of BP is not required for Windows 3.1 applications because they are assumed to be using the ToolHelp DLL to find out such information.

Figure 3.9.
Pascal stack frame.

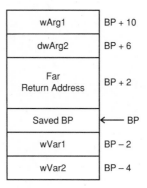

Depending on the type of function (near or far) after the original base pointer has been preserved, the value of DS might be preserved and then changed. Regardless of whether this is done, BP can now be used as a placemarker for the beginning of local variables. Local variables are easily referenced through a negative offset to BP, and caller-supplied parameters are referenced through a positive offset to BP. Knowing how to dump stack parameters and local data in this manner can be extremely helpful while debugging, making it easier to catch typecasting and promotion errors.

Additionally, the amount of reserved local data space must be subtracted from SP so that no other routine walks over it. When the body of the function has finished executing, the local data storage is "erased" and all the registers are restored. At this point, the only thing left to do is clean up the stack (if it is Pascal) and return control to the caller.

The redistributable ToolHelp DLL included with Windows 3.1 offers the following functions: `StackTraceCSIPFirst()`, `StackTraceFirst()`, `StackTraceNext()`, and the following structure for walking the stack:

```
typedef struct tagSTACKTRACEENTRY
{
    DWORD  dwSize;    // Size of STACKTRACEENTRY struct
```

```
    HTASK  hTask;       // Task associated with stack

    WORD   wSS;         // Value of stack segment register
    WORD   wBP;         // Value of base pointer register. Used with SS
                        // to determine next stack trace table.

    WORD   wCS;         // Value of code segment register
    WORD   wIP;         // Value of instruction pointer. Used with CS to
                        // determine return address

    HANDLE hModule;     // Module associated with function
    WORD   wSegment;    // Segment number of current selector
    WORD   wFlags;      // Type of stack frame--FRAME_FAR or FRAME_NEAR
                        // If FRAME_NEAR, then CS is NULL.
}
STACKTRACEENTRY;
```

These functions are used only for debuggers and other development-related tools. They don't see much use in end-user applications. They are listed here only for reference purposes.

Inter- and Intra-Process Communications

Communication and data transfer between programs can be a great source of frustration for the Windows developer. Compounding the problem are the many possible methods of inter- and intra-process communications. Some work now but will change with a future versions of Windows, and some methods are guaranteed to work with any future implementation.

When an application is communicating with portions of itself, any communication method can be used: function calls, local heap memory, private and shared global heap memory, DDE, the Clipboard, messaging, class and window extra data, and window properties. This is just a given. Complications arise, however, when the communications involve another instance of the same application or a foreign application. Assuming that the application in question is named "App A, instance #1," review the most common methods it has for sharing data and communicating with the following programs:

AppA/Inst#1	AppA/Inst#2	AppB/Inst#1	DLL C
1. DDE	1. DDE	1. DDE	1. Function calls
2. Clipboard	2. Clipboard	2. Clipboard	2. Global, shared memory
3. Function calls	3. Messaging	3. Messaging	3. DLL's data segment
4. Messaging	4. Extra data	4. Extra data	
5. Local heap		5. Properties	5. Properties
6. Global heap	6. Global variables*		
7. Global variables			
8. Extra data			
9. Properties			

This method involves the call `GetInstanceData()`, which is used to access another instance's data segment. This call is not recommended, because it violates the concept of a private address space.

Microsoft strongly recommends that only the Clipboard and the DDE be used as a means of communication between applications for both Windows 3.1 and 3.0. Windows NT, however, will offer several IPC mechanisms, including named pipes and mail slots, both of which provide an extremely simple method for sharing global memory. In addition, Windows 3.1 now offers the new DDEML library for making DDE much simpler and quicker to implement.

Tip: In Windows NT, all methods of communication between differing applications will and can be restricted for security reasons. The target application must give consent even for simple message passing.

Many of the problems surrounding process communications involve ownership. Owner A will never be able to understand anything belonging to Owner B, period. Each application has a module database it uses to determine access to memory, open files, and program segments (code and resources). If a program just flat-out tries to access data in another program's segment, it might fail. It is true that all programs share the same LDT, yet if Windows has nothing to link you to another program's segments, there's no guarantee they'll be loaded for your program on demand. The resources quite possibly could be discarded and won't be automatically loaded for you. These kinds of links are established by loading a library "into" your program's address space. For example, when `LoadLibrary()` (or an IMPORT statement) is used by ModuleA to load ModuleB, Windows automatically adds the segments of ModuleB to the list of segments "known" by ModuleA. Implicitly loading a library works similarly. Whenever a task switch occurs, Windows switches to the appropriate module segment list. In fact, the resource loader used by Windows examines this list whenever a module calls LockResource to access a resource segment. This is why you can't always just grab an application on the desktop and start accessing its segments willy-nilly.

Another problem of data transfer involved real mode, which really isn't a problem anymore because support for real mode was dropped with Windows 3.1. In real mode, when a message was sent to a window (within the same application) and a long pointer to memory was passed via the lParam parameter, there was a chance that memory might move, thus invalidating the pointer. Unfortunately, Windows can't "walk the parameter list" as it can walk the stack. Windows has no way of telling whether a parameter points to a segment or contains some arbitrary value. This required that memory pointed to by far pointers be locked before it was passed to another function.

Except for DDE and `GetInstanceData()`, the custom controls included with the book illustrate just about every other form or process communications.

Choosing a Memory Model

You'll find as much debate and confusion over which memory model to choose as you will over source code formatting styles. It's not a matter of which memory model you want; it's a matter of choosing a memory model that best reflects the needs of your program. Table 3.2 illustrates the segment restrictions imposed by the different memory models and the compiler switches required to generate code for the model.

Under DOS it was pretty much a free-for-all. You chose tiny model for relocatable single-segment .COM programs, and small, medium, compact, large, or huge model for executables. With Windows, choosing the correct memory model is all the more critical, because certain models pose a definite problem–specifically, ones that allow multiple data segments. This includes both the compact and the large models. In both of these cases Windows allows only one instance of the application to run, because the Windows loader cannot resolve instance fix-ups for memory models allowing multiple data segments. This is part of the reason that extra data segments are loaded by Windows as fixed, overriding the (possibly) moveable attribute specified by the developer.

Table 3.2. Compiler memory models.

Model	Code	Data	Arrays	Switch
Small	Single	Single	< 64K	/AS or /Asnd
Medium	Multiple*	Single	64K	/AM or /Alnd
Compact	Single	Multiple*	64K	/AC or /Asfd
Large	Multiple*	Multiple*	64K	/AL or /Alfd

No more than 254 code and data "program" segments can exist in a single module.

An additional problem was that under Windows 3.0 all fixed segments are additionally page-locked. This was probably done under the assumption that any library using fixed memory required it because it was servicing interrupts, and it would automatically require that the memory be page-locked. The locking of memory presented a problem only to real mode; however, the virtual memory manager used in enhanced mode is definitely hindered in its manipulation of the heap when it has to handle page-locked segments. Fortunately, Windows 3.1 fixes the page-locking bug, and it has removed real mode, eliminating the first problem as well. Ultimately, one memory model— the medium model—prevails over all others. In fact, the majority of large applications on the market today were all built with the medium model.

Any memory model specifying a single code segment (small and compact) ensures that all functions in the source module are assumed to be near. Of course, window procedures and other callbacks still need to be declared as far and exported. However, by default all other functions are assumed near unless explicitly cast otherwise. Use of a memory model that specifies multiple code segments (medium and large) means that all functions will be automatically made far, unless otherwise specified. Far calls incur a fair amount of overhead (see the "Prologue and Epilogue Code" section) because reloads of segment registers are quite expensive relative to the clock cycle times of other instructions.

The memory model specified on the compiler command line specifies only a default for code and data access. Like most compiler and linker switches, these "global" rules can easily be changed through use of a simple #pragma, or by specifically declaring certain variables and functions as near, far, or even huge (for data only). Programs break memory model restrictions all the time, accessing both code and data using a combination of near, far, and huge references. When a program uses the small or medium memory models and dynamically declares functions and data as near or far, this is referred to as a *mixed memory model*. Different calling conventions such as C or Pascal are used and mixed together quite frequently as well. The second compiler switch in Table 3.2 illustrates a second method of specifying a compiler memory model. This method provides a little more flexibility when assigning the default rules by which code and data are referenced.

The concept of a memory model is based on Intel's use of the segmented memory model for its processors. In a flat memory model, all the issues surrounding the use of different memory models could easily vanish, depending on how the linker and Windows' loader adapt for the new flat environment.

Near, Far, and Huge Pointers

Any pointer to memory, whether it's a function or data, can be referenced by any of several kinds of pointers: near, far, and huge (data only). Near pointers, which are merely 16-bit segment offsets, are used to point to a location within a 64K segment. Near data is data assumed to be located in the current data segment, whereas a near function is assumed to be in the current code segment. Near references have the benefit of not requiring a reload of any of the segment registers, which substantially increases the time to perform a specified function—at least when it's done often enough. By default, all functions in single-code segment memory models are declared near, and as such have an extremely simple function prologue and epilogue.

By default, all functions in multiple-code segment memory models are declared far. A far function is called under the presumption that the code segment register will have to be reloaded before the call can be initiated. Although this might not necessarily be the case (because a medium memory model program can still have just one code segment), it will happen by default. All window procedure functions and other Windows callback functions are automatically declared as far, because it is assumed that a Windows-owned code segment will be calling the function and that a new program code segment will need to be reloaded. Windows does include special mechanisms for treating "auto-designated" far functions as near (see the discussion of the /Farcalltranslation linker option in the the "Compiler and Linker Options" section). Far pointers to data are required for any data not residing in the current data segment. Far data pointers are most commonly used to pass data between functions declared as far. Far data pointers are also obviously required whenever a far or a huge data object is accessed. Prefixing a data declaration with _far or _huge forces the data into a different data segment than the automatic data segment, causing the ES register be loaded with the new data segment value.

In protected mode, passing far pointers is no longer the problem it was in real mode. This is because in protected mode, all segments are indirectly referenced with one of the descriptor tables, and as such can be moved without invalidating the address used to specify the segment. For discardable segments, however, the segment must be locked when a far pointer is to be passed. Obviously, discardable segments need this so that they aren't discarded as a result of having to load in a code segment.

Like a far pointer, a huge pointer is composed of both a segment and an offset. Two important differences still remain, however. First, huge pointers are used only with data. Second, the destination of a far pointer is assumed to be a single 64K segment. A huge pointer makes no such assumption. It is used quite frequently to point to data objects larger than 64K. All global heap objects larger than 64K are in reality composed of multiple, tiled 64K segments in the LDT. In C, using huge pointers ensures that a fix-up will occur when the pointer is incremented past a segment boundary and that the next selector in the series of tiled selectors will be chosen. For assembly language, Kernel exports the value __ahincr, which can be added to a pointer between segment boundaries. When the memory is first allocated, the memory manager assigns tiled selector values according to the value of __ahincr. Standard mode allows up to 1M of tiled selectors, whereas enhanced mode allows 16M (less 64K) worth of tiled selectors.

The following example in C illustrates the correct usage of huge pointers:

```
HGLOBAL  hObject;
BYTE HUGE        *hpObject;

...

if(hObject = GlobalAlloc(GMEM_MOVEABLE, 0x40000L))  // Alloc 4M
{
    if(hpObject = (BYTE HUGE *) GlobalLock(hObject))
    {
        // Now you can peek and poke data pointed to by hpObject
```

```
    ...

    GlobalUnlock(hObject);
  }

  GlobalFree(hObject);
}
```

In assembly language the following code can be used:

```
EXTRN __ahincr:abs  ; Make sure exported ahincr is available

MOV  AX,ES          ; ES contains data segment being addressed
ADD  AX,__ahincr    ; Add "increment" value to segment in AX
MOV  ES,AX          ; ES correctly fixed up across segment boundary
```

Static data can also be given a _huge or _far designation, as shown by the following:

```
static int _huge Array1[10000];
static int _far Array2[10500];
```

Source code like this, however, has the unfortunate distinction of forcing the program into large model, meaning that the application is limited to a single instance. Whenever data like this is accessed in program code, the ES register is used to temporarily hold the new data segment value that needs to be loaded. When the _huge or _far keywords aren't used on a huge object, the compiler might respond with an error, indicating that the item exceeds the automatic data segment's 64K limit. Two other limitations on huge data arrays are that no element in the array can cross a segment boundary, and that in arrays larger than 128K, all elements must have a size that is a power of 2 (that is, 2, 4, 8, 16). Obviously, huge arrays must be created from static, not automatic (stack-based), data.

Program Data Storage

Every Windows application and DLL has one of eight choices when it comes to program storage of data items: static data, automatic data, the local heap, the global heap, resources, atoms, window properties, and window and class extra data. Each location is used under different circumstances, with each having its advantages and disadvantages.

Data Type	Overhead
Static data	Automatic data segment
Automatic data	Stack space in automatic data segment
Local heap	Data segment
Global heap	Kernel
Resources	Kernel
Atoms	Kernel
Properties	User
Extra Data	User

Most of the storage areas overlap either in where their overhead is stored or in how they're accessed. Each area is different enough, however, that it warrants a small discussion. Full descriptions of the local heap, global heap, resources, and atoms appear in Chapter 4, "Memory Management." Likewise, class and window extra data and window properties are both discussed in more detail in Chapter 6, "Custom Controls," thus limiting this chapter's discussion to program-internal data, including static and automatic data.

Static Data (Global Variables)

The term static data describes any variables created out of permanent program storage space in the static data area of the default data segment. Static variables are most frequently used when a value needs to be shared frequently by functions—so frequently that passing as a parameter isn't a viable option. Usually, at least three static variables are kept by every Windows application: one for the current program instance, one for the main application window, and one for the currently active window or dialog.

Declaring variables as static is as simple as declaring them outside of a function, or by actually declaring them with the keyword static. However, when the keyword static is added, it implies that the variable is private to the source module and cannot be referenced by another source module through an extern statement. It also includes variables declared as extern. Variables declared inside program functions often use the static designation to avoid the overhead and limitations of being created out of space on the stack. This usually is done for long byte arrays (possibly a file path) and any local variables in a DLL passed to functions by reference. Static variables, as their name implies, are created out of the default data segment's static data area, which is limited to 64K. Any reference in source code to a static variable, pointer or otherwise, points to a location in the static data area. Because of the 64K data segment limitation, large arrays should be created dynamically out of the global heap, which has no similar size limitations.

Automatic Data (Local Variables)

Automatic data includes any variable declared inside a function without the static keyword. Local variables, as their name implies, are created local to the function that requires them. Because functions don't have a reserved section of the data segment available to them, the stack is used during function calls as storage space. This is how the name *automatic data* is derived, because storage space for the variable is created automatically at each function call. A large number of local variables, especially long byte arrays, can easily overflow the stack, crashing your program. The solution is to use either static data or dynamically allocated local or global heap space. A better description of how local variables are stored on the stack is given in this chapter's "Stack Frame" section.

Not as well known about local variables is the fact that they can be created inside any group of program statements enclosed in curly braces. An example of this, as well as other types of variable creations, is given in the following example:

```
extern DWORD MyCode;      // Static data defined by another module

static BYTE TestByte;     // Static data. Also prevents other modules
                          // from "extern"ing and accessing value

DWORD TestNum;            // Static data--permanent allocation

int PASCAL TestFunc(HWND hWnd, BOOL x) // hWnd and x are stack-based
{
    int y;                // Automatic data on the stack--temporary

    static int s;         // Static data (but unique to function)

    if(TRUE)
    {
        int r = 10;       // Automatic data created on the stack--temp
    }
}
```

The Module-Definition File

The module-definition file (.DEF) is used to establish certain unchangeable program-wide characteristics, including giving the module a name, declaring heap and stack sizes, exporting functions, and establishing attributes for code and data segments. The module-definition file (along with the program make file) has a profound affect on the organization and structure of a completed module.

The module-definition file, module database, and .EXE header have much in common. Each of these structures contains program-wide information. For example, when a program is compiled and linked, information from the module-definition file (and other sources, such as the non-instance-specific resource file) is culled and placed near the beginning of the module's binary image. This block of memory, which is present for every application or library, is referred to as the "new-style" .EXE header. It contains, like the .DEF file, module-wide information that can be shared between program instances—except that in this case, it includes information about resource segments as well as code and data segments. When a program is finally loaded into memory by Windows, it creates a global heap entry called the module database, which contains much of the information found in the .EXE header. Module databases and the .EXE header format are discussed in more detail earlier in this chapter.

The following is the format of a module-definition file. Curly braces ({}) indicate mandatory elements, and square brackets ([]) indicate optional elements. Any item within braces or brackets separated by a comma is one of several possible choices.

```
; The module name should always be uppercase! Otherwise, the library
; might not be freed when its time has come...

{NAME,LIBRARY} MODULENAME     ; Use NAME for apps, LIBRARY for DLLs.
EXETYPE        WINDOWS        ; Always WINDOWS
DESCRIPTION    'Module Title'
STUB           'WINSTUB.EXE'  ; Not needed for libraries

; CODE attribute sets defaults for ALL code segments, likewise
; for DATA.

CODE  [PRELOAD,LOADONCALL] [FIXED,MOVEABLE] [DISCARDABLE,NONDISCARDABLE]

DATA  [PRELOAD,LOADONCALL] [FIXED,MOVEABLE] [DISCARDABLE,NONDISCARDABLE]
      [SINGLE,MULTIPLE,NONE]
```

```
; Local heap optional for DLLs. Minimum of 1024 bytes should be used

HEAPSIZE  xxxx

; For applications only. Minimum of 5K enforced

STACKSIZE xxxx

; The segment names used by SEGMENTS must have been created
; either via the #pragma alloc_text option or by naming
; individual modules with the /NT parameter. A class name of CODE
; is assumed, so otherwise specify DATA

SEGMENTS
    [']SegName['] [CLASS 'classname'] (continue line...)
    {PRELOAD,LOADONCALL} {FIXED,MOVEABLE} {DISCARDABLE,NONDISCARDABLE}
    ...


; For EXPORTS, InternalName is the name as it's referenced inside the
; module, and FunctionName is the name as it's exported to others.
; If no ordinal number is specified, they are assigned automatically.
; RESIDENTNAME specifies that the name cannot be discarded or paged
; to disk and must remain resident in memory at all times. The NODATA
; option is for DLLs that want to assume the calling module's DS as
; well as SS.

EXPORTS
    FunctionName [=InternalName] [@ordinal# [RESIDENTNAME]] [NODATA]
    ...


; For IMPORTS, InternalName is the name used by the module when
; referring to the function. By default, InternalName equals
; FunctionName. ModuleName is the name of the module where the
; function is stored. If an ordinal# rather than name is given,
; InternalName is required.

IMPORTS
    [InternalName=]ModuleName.{FunctionName,ordinal#}
```

The STUB statement is used to identify an application that is run when an attempt is made to run a Windows application under DOS. The default file normally used is WINSTUB.EXE, which prints a simple error and returns to the DOS prompt. In fact, the entry point of this application is responsible for the ___EXPORTEDSTUB statement that's visible when exehdr is run on a module or when you view a module's map file. The statement isn't required for libraries, and it saves a few bytes when removed. More advanced stubs are available from various sources that handle the error differently. One possibility is to run the application under Windows, even while the user is still at the DOS prompt.

The CODE statement provides a means of specifying the default attributes for every code segment in the module. Depending on the module type (application or library), certain code segment attributes are not permissible. Obviously, the fixed and moveable attributes cannot be combined. A number of more subtle restrictions exist, however—all for good reason. In libraries, for example, code cannot be flagged as moveable without being discardable. In this case, the resource compiler automatically flags the code as discardable.

Similar to the CODE statement, the DATA statement specifies the default data segment attributes for a program. Unlike the CODE statement, the DATA statement attributes usually apply only to a single segment, because the majority of Windows applications do not use memory models that allow multiple data segments.

In fact, the SINGLE, MULTIPLE, and NONE options don't apply to the number of allowable data segments for a program, as you might think. Instead, they determine whether multiple, single, or no "instances" of data segments are allowed. Remember that the number of allowable program data segments per program is specified by the memory model, not by the DATA statement. This is why MULTIPLE is always specified by applications and SINGLE (or NONE) is specified by DLLs. Actually, except in the case of wanting to use the keyword NONE, these attributes don't need to be specified at all, because the default and only allowable values will automatically be assumed by Windows. Note that the SINGLE attribute for data segments doesn't actually prevent multiple copies of the application from being run. To do that, the developer must place code inside WinMain() to check the previous instance passed at runtime. Then, a decision can be made whether to activate the primary instance or to respond with an appropriate message.

The segment directives CODE, DATA, and SEGMENTS have one additional option (SHARED, NOSHARED) that was defined for OS/2 and that could apply to future versions of Windows. For now, the default is SHARED. After all, everything is sharing the same LDT. Libraries also have an interesting option that's not defined for Windows—yet. It's INITGLOBAL or INITINSTANCE, an optional parameter following the uppercase LIBRARY name. This interesting option could (in the future) possibly control how the library is initialized, whether singly or every time it is loaded by another module. This would allow the library to establish a different default data segment for each client module or any of a number of other options. Many DLLs require that client modules call an initialization function before using functions in the library. This library option would effectively eliminate that problem. In fact, libraries in Windows

NT have just such an option, making it quite easy to establish per-instance heaps for each application loading the library.

The EXPORTS and IMPORTS statements define how the module interfaces with other applications and libraries, controlling which functions are published for the use of others and which functions need to be imported from other modules. From within a library, a developer actually can use both the EXPORTS and IMPORTS statements to transparently intercept Windows system calls from within a module. This technique involves importing the target function, realiasing the name, exporting the new function with the same name as the function being intercepted, and then at some point in the new function, calling the original function to do the processing. This technique is discussed in depth in Chapter 5, "Library Design Ideas."

For applications, the EXPORTS statement is used for functions called by Windows, such as a window procedure or some other callback function. For libraries, functions listed in EXPORTS are primarily functions called by other libraries and applications. For any exported function, the linker automatically nulls the first few bytes of the prologue, allowing the incoming value of AX to establish the data segment register. When Windows calls an exported window function, AX is guaranteed to contain the application's correct data segment. With other kinds of callback functions, this is not the case, which is the reason for the separate call to MakeProcInstance(). It creates an instance thunk that establishes DS. Of course, any calls by an application into a library require no MakeProcInstance() call because libraries are restricted to a single instance. Therefore, no fix-up of the data segment register is required. The only reason the EXPORTS statement is used by libraries is that, just like an application, their name needs to be flagged as "public" and available to other functions. All this does is set some bits in one of several entry table groups that are created for any far functions in a module.

Although the C compiler provides the _export keyword for functions, using the module-definition file to control the exporting of functions is preferred for several reasons. When _export is used, the developer has no control over the function's ordinal value, the aliasing of the name, specifying NODATA, or declaring the name as resident. Although this might seem like a problem, it really isn't. Most of the time, a function needs only to be exported, and the developer doesn't need to modify any of the other options. The only regular exception to this rule is a DLL's WEP function, which must be exported and declared RESIDENTNAME.

A function can be exported by name or by ordinal. Whether it actually gets imported in this manner (by name or ordinal) is determined by how the library itself is loaded (either dynamically, implicitly, or explicitly). Functions that are assigned an explicit ordinal are always imported by ordinal, and functions that are implicitly assigned an ordinal might or might not be imported by ordinal, depending on how the library is loaded. When the linker is processing a module, any functions not assigned an explicit ordinal are implicitly given an ordinal value using the gaps between or after any already-assigned ordinals. If a library is dynamically loaded (using `LoadLibrary()`), the developer has the option of using `GetProcAddress()` with either an ordinal or a name. If a library is explicitly loaded (using an IMPORTS statement), the function is imported in the manner that the IMPORTS statement specifies, which can be by ordinal or by name. When a function is imported by ordinal, it must be explicitly assigned a new name. Finally, if a library is implicitly loaded (using the program's make file), functions are always imported by ordinal, whether originally exported by ordinal or not. Functions assigned an explicit ordinal always execute faster than functions exported and imported by name. This is due to the lookup difference, because obviously, indexing an integer value into a table is much simpler than doing an alphanumeric lookup.

All functions are exported both by ordinal and by name. Explicitly specifying an ordinal value for an exported function allows Windows to find the function faster, but it is far less intuitive than an alphanumeric. The use of ordinals can be a benefit when function names are apt to change. If an exported function is always imported via its ordinal value and not its name, then there will never be any name-resolution problems. If not explicitly specified, all exported functions are assigned consecutive ordinal values. When the function exported by ordinal is required by another module, the module merely imports the function by ordinal and aliases the name to something more readable.

Following are valid examples of the EXPORTS command:

```
EXPORTS
    WEP @1 RESIDENTNAME       ; Normal WEP export; name is resident
    TestFunc                  ; 'Normal' export
    GlobalAlloc=MyGlobalAlloc ; Export using alias
```

The IMPORTS statement represents one of three ways a function can be "imported" from another module. Resolving references to functions in this manner causes an explicit load of the module that contains the function. That is, any module listed by the IMPORTS statement is automatically loaded into memory (if it is not already loaded) *before* the application. The libraries then get unloaded after the application has terminated. The other methods involve dynamically loading the DLL and implicitly linking the library in with the linker. These two methods are preferred, although sometimes no choice exists but to use the IMPORTS statement. The primary time that a function would need to be resolved explicitly is when an import library doesn't exist for a DLL.

This prevents the module from linking the library in at compile time. In this case, however, the dynamic loading method could be used, although it is a bit more tedious than using a simple IMPORTS statement.

Imported functions represent "external" names that cannot be resolved by the linker at compile time. They must be resolved by Windows dynamic linking mechanism at runtime. In protected mode, when a module is loaded in memory, all references to IMPORTed functions are immediately patched, setting up the link for the rest of the program's life. There is no limit to the number of functions that can be imported in this manner. The only restriction is that the space reserved for their names not exceed 64K. The different methods of loading libraries (explicit, implicit, and dynamic) are discussed in more detail in Chapter 5, "Library Design Ideas."

Following are valid examples of the IMPORTS command:

```
IMPORTS
    TestDLL.TestFunc                  ; 'Normal' import
    MyGlobalAlloc=Kernel.GlobalAlloc  ; Import using alias
    TestFunc2=MyDLL.2                 ; Aliased import by ordinal
```

The Make File

A make file is associated with almost every module. It can be thought of as an intelligent macro used for compiling and linking code. A make file scours through all its listed source files, determining via a series of relationships which files need to be recompiled and relinked. The make file does all of this automatically by spawning calls to the compiler and linker. By following a particular format, quite elaborate and time-saving make files can be produced. With a little use of #defines and macro variables, a program can be rebuilt in an entirely different way almost instantly. Using a make utility is far better than any project management system that can be created with batch files. A make file can get quite complex, so it is best not to try to create one from scratch. Instead, use a make file from one of the SDK's source file examples.

The make files used for the common DLL (stdwin.dll) and custom controls described in this book need only a single variable to be established, containing the name of the module. Because the make files of all the libraries don't use the generic name "makefile," the variable is passed not only as a make file name to the make program, but also as a setting for the variable lib, which is used by almost every command in the make file. Here is an example:

```
compile=-c -W3 -Od -AMw -Gsw2 -Zipe // Set compiler macro flags
link   =/align:16 /CO /NOD           // Set linker macro flags

all: $(lib).dll                      // Needed for NMAKE

$(lib).res: $(lib).rc $(lib).h       // If .rc file changes, recompile
  rc -r $(lib).rc                    // a new .res file

libentry.obj: libentry.asm           // If libentry.asm changes,
  masm -Mx libentry,libentry;        // make a new libentry.obj

$(lib).obj: $(lib).c $(lib).h $(lib)     // Ditto for .c to .obj
  cl $(compile) $(lib).c

// Do you need to rebuild/relink the .dll file?

$(lib).dll: libentry.obj $(lib).obj $(lib).def
  link $(link) /M $(lib) libentry, $(lib).dll,, libw mdllcew, $(lib).def
  rc -t $(lib).res $(lib).dll        // Add compiled resources to .dll
  implib $(lib).lib $(lib).def       // Create import library

  copy $(lib).dll w:                 // Copy .dll to Windows directory
  copy $(lib).h i:                   // Copy header file to include dir
  copy $(lib).lib l:                 // Copy import lib to lib directory

  // Copy various items to RAM disk 'E:' for speed-up and inputting
  // executables/source filenames in CodeView

  copy $(lib).h e:
  copy $(lib).lib e:
  copy $(lib).dll e:
  copy $(lib).c e:

$(lib).dll: $(lib).res               // Did just the .RES file change?
  rc -t $(lib).res $(lib).dll // Recompile the resrcs into the DLL
  copy $(lib).dll w:                 // Copy .dll to Windows directory
  copy $(lib).dll e:                 // Copy to ram disk for debugger
```

The DOS copy commands at the end of the make file should be included only if the computer has had the appropriate substituted drives created. Developing DLLs requires that you distribute components of the DLL throughout the computer. Unless your program is meant to be totally self-contained in a single directory, it's a good idea to copy the DLL to the Windows system directory. Likewise, you should put your include files and import library files in a place where other applications can locate them during their "build" cycle.

Because a parameter is now required for the make program, you might use a make batch file to initiate the whole make process, helping to establish the `lib` variable referenced throughout the make file. An example is as follows:

```
m.bat:

@echo off                  // Turn off command printing
CALL ram                   // Set up ram disk if not already set up
nmake @library > c.err     // Make using the text file 'library'
if exist c.err type c.err  // Redirect errs to file and type it
```

The make file and the preceding m.bat batch file are used by all the custom controls mentioned in this book (stdwin, bitmap, button, combobox, and listbox). Supporting a large number of custom controls with many common make file attributes can get somewhat tedious as the number of supported custom controls increases. The advantage to the setup just shown is that the only dependent file that must be created is one called "library," which is located in the directory along with the source files composing the module. This simple ASCII file has the following format:

```
library:

"lib = stdwin" stdwin
```

Its purpose is to set the macro variable `lib` and to specify a make file target for the batch file m.bat. Of course, there probably are an infinite number of methods for creating stream-lined make files, including the use of a nice version control package and some other program make facility besides the NMAKE program included with Microsoft C. There's absolutely no telling how much pain and grief will be saved over the long haul by spending a few days implementing relatively airtight make and version control procedures. For many single-developer and simpler cases, however, the "homegrown" method just mentioned works quite well.

Compiler and Linker Options

It's fortunate for most beginning Windows developers that Microsoft includes sample source along with the SDK. The sample source is valuable in two ways. The sample sources not only provide numerous examples of Windows programming techniques, but, more important, they also provide fairly complete examples of how to set up the compiler, linker, and make files for writing Windows programs. For many, this is a more daunting issue. It's probably much easier to originate from scratch a simple Windows application than it would be to scan through the several sources of compiler, linker, and .DEF and make file reference sources. Debugging is also simplified when you're assured that compiler and linker settings are at default values and aren't the cause of your problems.

Compiler

Format: `cl [options] sourcefile`

Example: `cl -c -W3 -AM test.c`

Switch *Description*

/A{S,M,C,L,H} Selects small, medium, compact, large, or huge memory model for module compilation (see the section entitled "Choosing a Memory Model").

/Af Assumes 32-bit far data pointers. Used to customize a memory model.

/Ah Assumes 32-bit huge data pointers. Used to customize a memory model.

/Al Assumes 32-bit far code pointers. Used to customize a memory model.

/An Assumes 16-bit near data pointers. Used to customize a memory model.

/As Assumes 16-bit near code pointers. Used to customize a memory model.

/Ad Assumes SS == DS. The default for standard memory models.

/Au Assumes SS != DS for module. DS is reloaded on entry. It is the DS of the *first* instance of the module, however.

/Aw Assumes SS != DS for module. DS isn't reloaded on entry. Used with DLLs.

/c Compile only. Used when compiling multiple source modules in a make file.

Switch	Description
/Fa	Creates .ASM assembly listing of source module. Useful for checking function prologues and epilogues, and the casting of variables in equations and function calls.
/Fc	Creates mixed source/assembly listing (.COD) of source module.
/Fl	Creates object-file listing (.COD), mixing assembly and raw object-code.
/Fm	Creates map file listing (.MAP) showing program segments, imported and exported functions, and program entry point.
/Fs	Creates source-file listing (.LST) containing line-numbered program source and detailed information on both public and local symbols.
/G{0,1,2}	Target processor for code generation (0 = 808x, 1 = 8018x, 2 = 80286).
/Gc	Specifies the Pascal/FORTRAN calling convention for the source file.
/Gd	Specifies the C (_cdecl) calling convention for the source file.
/Gs	Removes stack probes, making programs run slightly faster.
/Gw	Adds required Windows prologue/epilogue code to all functions in module. Code fixes up DS and increments BP on entry. Required for all functions called by Windows.
/GW	Adds required Windows prologue/epilogue code to all functions in module. Code doesn't fix up DS, but only increments BP on entry. Can be used with modules containing far functions not called by Windows, or in combination with the keyword _loadds for single-instance protected-mode only applications. Code is faster than using /Gw because a segment register reload isn't required.
/NDname	Used to name a module's data segment.
/NMname	Used to override the default name of the module, which normally is the filename.

continues

Switch	Description
/NTname	Used to name a module's code segment.
/Od	Disables all optimizations. Mandatory during the debugging process, because optimizations wreak havoc with CodeView source code line information.
/P	Writes preprocessed output to a file (.I). Useful for debugging problems related to macro expansion.
/W3	Moderate error-checking. All errors and warnings are reported. Truly superfluous error messages are suppressed, however. Recommended warning level.
/W4	Strictest level of error-checking. Not quite like lint, but a step in the right direction.
/Zd	Used to embed line information in object modules. Used by SYMDEB, WDEB386, and other debugging utilities.
/Zi	Puts symbolic debugging information into object file. Used by CodeView.
/Zp[1,2,4]	Controls structure-packing. Using /Zp and /Zp1, structures are packed on byte boundaries. Using /Zp2 and /Zp4, structures are packed on word and dword boundaries. This switch is required for any source code performing "structure arithmetic."

Linker

Format: `link [options]objfiles, [exefile], [mapfile], [libfiles], deffile`

Example: `link /CO /NOD /MAP test,,,libw mlibcew,test.def`

options   A series of space-delimited parameters, with each parameter prefixed with a forward slash (/) or a dash (–). See the following switches table.

objfiles   A series of space-delimited object (.obj) files to be linked. This list usually includes the names of every source module in a make file. For large numbers of object files, the linker supports command line redirection from a text file.

exefile Optionally specifies a different name for the resulting executable or loadable module.

mapfile If a map file has been created (with the /M compiler option), optionally specifies a different name for the map file from the default of MODULE.MAP.

libfiles A series of space-delimited object or import library (.lib) files to be linked in with the resulting executable module. Object libraries include the C runtime and start-up libraries (mlibcew.lib), whereas import libraries include the library used to resolve functions to all Windows API functions (libw.lib).

deffile Specifies the module-definition file (.DEF) to be used during linking.

Whether it is used on the command line or from a make file, the linker can redirect its input from a text file in addition to using the DOS command line. The advantage is that a text file is capable of handling parameter lengths not allowed by DOS. This is done by using link in the following manner, and creating the shown linker file:

```
c:\> link @module.lnk
```

module.lnk:

```
object-file1+
object-file2+
object-file3+
...
object-filen+
/NOD /CO

libw+
mlibcew
module.def
```

Switch	Description
/AL[ignment]:#	Controls alignment of segments. The default value of 512 really should be changed to 16, resulting in a slightly smaller code size. Number must be a power of 2.

continues

Switch	Description
/CO[deview]	Tells linker to embed symbol and line-number information in executable. Required for debugging with CodeView. Also requires that /Zi be used on the compiler. Use of this option increases code size and should be removed when the development process is finished.
/F[arcalltranslation]	Optimizes far calls to locations within the same segment by pushing the current code segment (CS) instead of reloading a "new" one.
/INF[ormation]	Used to show progress of linker. Includes information detailing the processing, ordering, and location of program segments.
/LI[nenumbers]	Includes line numbers and addresses in map file listing. Object files must have been compiled with /Zd. Required by SYMDEB and other real-mode debugging utilities.
/M[ap]	Generates an ASCII .MAP file of all public symbols. Report is sorted by name and by address. Useful for debugging, and required by SYMDEB and other real-mode debugging utilities. The utility MAPSYM uses this file to create a .SYM symbol file.
/NOD[efaultlibrarysearch]	Ignore default libraries when resolving references. Used because of the differences in the C and Windows libraries.
/NOE[xtdictionary]	Ignore extended dictionary. Used when the linker issues warnings indicating that a symbol is defined across multiple libraries.
/?	Generates help listing.

Keywords

Keywords are reserved terms that prefix the declarations of both functions and data. Keywords either declare or modify the meaning of the object being referenced. Keywords include those defined by the ANSI C committee and those defined by Microsoft. Per ANSI C guidelines, all Microsoft and other

OS-specific extensions must be prefixed with an underscore. A summary of the most common keywords and their meanings is given in Table 3.3.

Table 3.3. Keywords.

Keyword	Description
_asm	Tells the C compiler that what follows is an assembly-language instruction to be processed by MASM. If followed by a set of curly braces {}, all instructions inside the braces are processed by MASM. Each assembly language instruction must not end with a semicolon.
auto	Declares a stack-based local variable. Because this is the default for variables located at the beginning of function blocks, it is rarely used.
_cdecl	Declares a function as using the C calling convention. The windows.h typedef for the function is CDECL.
const	Declares unmodifiable data or pointers to unmodifiable data.
_export	Used as an alternative to EXPORTing functions in the module definition (.DEF) file. This alternative doesn't provide as much control over the exported function.
extern	Declares an object (function or variable) as static. This means that storage space for the object has already been allocated and that the name can be resolved by the linker.
_far	Declares functions or data as requiring a code or data segment fix-up to be accessed. The compiler automatically adds special prologue and epilogue code to all functions declared as far. When applied to data, it places the object in its own data segment. The typedef defined by windows.h is FAR.
_huge	Used to declare data (and pointers to data) that requires huge arithmetic. Huge arithmetic is different from far arithmetic because pointers are incremented correctly when crossing segment boundaries. Like _far, when applied to data, _huge places the object in its own data segment.
_loadds	Used to fix up DS on entry to function. The data segment used for the fix-up, however, is always that of the first program instance. This keyword can be used in conjunction with /GW for single-instance protected-mode programs.
_near	Declares functions or data as being in the same segment. Eliminates the overhead associated with far arithmetic, including the prologue and epilogue added to all far functions. The windows.h typedef is NEAR.

continues

Table 3.3. continued

Keyword	Description
_pascal	Declares a function as using the Pascal calling convention. Overrides any module default set by a compiler switch. The windows.h typedef is PASCAL.
static	For data, specifies that variables are to be created out of permanent storage space in the default data segment. When the static prefix is used on data declared outside of a function or on function declarations themselves, it specifies that the name is not to be known to the linker, and thus is unavailable for use by other source modules.

Reserved Data Types/ Common Definitions

The SDK provides special types, macros, and typedefs to simplify access to data. Predefined data types are valuable because they mask (in a static way) access to data. It's a very simple type of indirection available only at compile time. The common data types shown in Table 3.4 are provided by the SDK.

Table 3.4. Data types.

Type	Description
BOOL	Defined as an integer.
FALSE	Defined as 0.
TRUE	Defined as 1.
char	An 8-bit signed value.
BYTE	An 8-bit unsigned value.
PBYTE	A near pointer to a byte value.
LPBYTE	A far pointer to a byte.
int	A 16-bit signed value.

Type	Description
UINT	An unsigned integer.
PINT	A near pointer to an integer.
LPINT	A far pointer to an integer.
WORD	A 16-bit unsigned short.
PWORD	A pointer to a word.
LPWORD	A far pointer to a word.
LONG	A 32-bit signed value.
PLONG	A near pointer to a long.
LPLONG	A far pointer to a long.
DWORD	An unsigned long value.
PDWORD	A near pointer to a dword (unsigned 32-bit value).
LPDWORD	A far pointer to a dword.
PSTR	A near pointer to an array of characters.
NPSTR	A near pointer to an array of characters.
LPSTR	A far pointer to an array of characters.
LPCSTR	A far pointer to a const(ant) array of characters.
CALLBACK	Specifies a FAR PASCAL value. Used for all Windows callback functions, including window, enumeration, timer, and hook procedures.
WINAPI	Specifies a FAR PASCAL value to be used with any function called by Windows.
WPARAM	Represents first block of additional per-message data. Second is LPARAM. WPARAM under Windows 3 is a word. Under NT, however, it is 32 bits wide.
LPARAM	Represents second block of additional per-message data. First is WPARAM.
LRESULT	A 32-bit window procedure return value.
FARPROC	A 32-bit pointer to a function.

continues

Table 3.4. continued

Type	Description
NEAR	See the description for the keyword _near.
FAR	See the description for the keyword _far.
HANDLE	An identifier used to reference an object, whether a file or a GDI object. Items referenced by handles usually need some sort of cleanup. Currently a 16-bit value. Under Windows NT, however, handles will be 32 bits wide.
PHANDLE	A pointer to a handle (type set according to memory model).
SPHANDLE	A near pointer to a handle.
LPHANDLE	A far pointer to a handle.
NULL	Indicates an uninitialized pointer or handle. Windows defines NULL to be 0.
LPVOID	A long pointer to a void. Requires an explicit cast on every reference. Used by functions that accept multiple parameter types (memcpy).
VOID	A return type for functions that don't return a value and a parameter type for functions accepting no parameters.
CDECL	See the description for the keyword _cdecl.
PASCAL	See the description for the keyword _pascal.

The macros for data conversion, shown in Table 3.5, also are provided by the SDK.

Table 3.5. Macros.

Macro	Return Value
LOBYTE(word)	The low byte of the word
HIBYTE(word)	The high byte of the word
LOWORD(dword)	The low word in a double word
HIWORD(dword)	The high word in a double word
MAKELONG(low, high)	Constructs a long (double word) value

Language Implementation Issues

Any language, such as C or Pascal, imposes a collection of rules other than the obvious command and syntactical differences. These rules include things such as naming conventions, calling conventions, and parameter-passing requirements. Most compilers and Windows itself fully support the use of mixed-language calls, although it's usually limited to the languages C and Pascal. Pure assembly programming imposes no particular language restrictions, because higher-level languages are compiled into assembly code. Whenever you want to bridge C, Pascal, assembler, or some other high-level language, however, you must fully understand all language implementation issues.

Naming Convention

The term *naming convention* refers to the way the compiler treats names when a module is being compiled. For the linker to perform any kind of name resolution, compatible naming conventions must be used. Without the appropriate fix-up, mixed language calls cannot be performed. With the Pascal naming convention, every character in the name is translated to uppercase. The C naming convention is quite different. With C, no name translation is done; however, a leading underscore is placed in front of the name. Whenever a C function is imported through a module's .DEF file, the name should be aliased to remove the underscore.

Recognizable name lengths also vary from language to language, as illustrated here:

Language	Code	Parameters	Conversion	Name Length
C	_cdecl	right to left	FuncA to _FuncA	31 characters
Pascal	_pascal	left to right	FuncA to FUNCA	8 characters

A name can be used in three different contexts: when it is defined, when it is exported, and when it is imported. The name can change at each of these stages, although it references the same location.

Calling Convention

The term *calling convention* is used to describe the manner in which a particular language, such as C or Pascal, implements the mechanisms for calling functions. Basically, a calling convention affects the way the compiler generates code for passing parameters and cleaning up the stack during function calls. Windows programs routinely use both the Pascal and C calling conventions.

With the Pascal calling convention, parameters are pushed onto the stack in the order in which they appear (from left to right). The Pascal convention also specifies that stack cleanup is the responsibility of the called procedure. The C calling convention works in the opposite manner, pushing parameters from right to left, and putting the burden of stack cleanup on the caller. One advantage of the C calling convention is that function calls can be made with a variable number of arguments. This is possible because the first parameter is always referenced at the top of the stack (after all, it was the last one pushed), no matter how many parameters were actually pushed. Conversely, although the Pascal convention can't be used to pass a variable number of arguments, it does result in slightly smaller and faster code because cleanup responsibilities are localized within the actual procedure and are not duplicated among every call into the procedure.

Parameter Passing

In addition to understanding how parameters are organized on the stack during a procedure call, you should also understand exactly how those parameters are passed to another procedure. Microsoft languages support two basic methods of parameter passing—by value and by reference.

Passing parameters by value effectively creates a new copy of the data, pushing it onto the stack. With this method, the called procedure knows the value of the original variable but cannot modify it because no pointer back to the original data exists, only the copy. Passing by reference, however, does offer a link back to the caller's data, because the called procedure is passed an actual pointer to the data and not just a copied value that exists on the stack. The type of pointer required to pass data by reference depends on the memory model and any explicitly cast types in the function's definition.

Microsoft languages support two methods of passing by reference—near and far. Both terms refer to the location, or perceived location, of the code. When both the caller and the callee are in the same module, only a near pointer reference is required to pass modifiable parameters to a procedure. If the callee isn't in the same module, a far reference is always required. Sometimes the function might be in the same module and still be declared far, because functions in different modules might need to call the function. In this case, you too must adhere to the same rules and pass by far reference.

Typecasting and Promotion

Typecasting and promotion rules are important topics to the Windows developer. *Typecasting* refers to the process of modifying a value's meaning on the fly. You (usually) don't actually change the value; rather, you change how the value is interpreted. The only exception is when you typecast a word to a dword or a near pointer into a far pointer. In this case, the size of the value is changed. Typecasts in code done for "interpretation," such as casting a WORD value to a HANDLE, are done primarily to satisfy the compiler.

The C compiler automatically promotes near pointers to far pointers if the called function's definition expects a far pointer, freeing the developer from having to typecast manually most of the parameters being passed to Windows API functions. There are only two exceptions to this rule: C-based variable-argument functions such as wsprintf, which require the full typecast (LPSTR for strings); and functions such as **SendMessage()**, which expect a long or dword value as a parameter. In this case, the compiler expects that the value will be cast to a DWORD or LONG and will specify a far typecast of the pointer (such as LPRECT or LPSTR).

Promotion refers to how the compiler automatically casts values in expressions. Whenever uncast variables are used together in a common expression, the compiler automatically promotes the uncast elements according to a pre-defined set of rules. If the value in question is an uncast pointer, it is promoted according to the rules of the current memory model. If the value is some kind of "static" number of variable, it is promoted according to neighboring elements in the expression. For a complete rundown of promotion and other "C" rules, consult one of the C "blue books." When in doubt, cast. It's always best to cast every value in an expression. If words and integers are added together, the integer values (which can be negative) could adversely affect the intended total. That's why it's best to convert them to word values first or to cast the word values in the expression to INTS, depending whether the intended total can be a signed value or not. Typecasting and clean compiled output still dog the Windows developer.

The biggest problem is encountered when float or double values are used alongside integer and word values in an equation. Elements of any subexpression (values grouped together in parentheses) are always promoted according to the largest element in the expression, unless explicitly cast otherwise. In the WYSIWIG print dialog included with STDWIN, an Aspect button allows the printed image to retain its proportions after being stretched by the mouse. To correct for a lopsided aspect ratio, a new height was created for the stretched image based on the proportions of the original width and height and "stretched width," all of which are integers. The stretched width remains the same; only the stretched height is changed.

Check the following example:

```
int Height, Width;
int OrigHeight, OrigWidth;

...

Height = (int)
(
     (float) Width * (float) OrigHeight / (float) OrigWidth
);
```

Casting all values to floats ensures that the division operation yields a float and not an integer value. Of course, this expression could be cast in a number of different ways, but this is one of the clearest.

Summary

This chapter covered just about every aspect of constructing a module, whether loadable or executable—from how segments are laid out and constructed, to how they're put together, compiled and linked, and, to an extent, how modules interact with each other and the operating system. This kind of information is especially important when you need to answer questions like "Is it my problem or a Windows problem?" Knowing from the beginning that a module is designed somewhat correctly helps eliminate many obvious bugs and questions later. The Windows operating system can be difficult enough without including module design, build, compile, and link issues.

Memory
Management

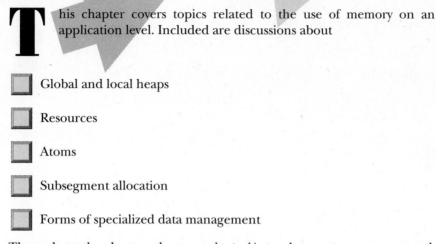

This chapter covers topics related to the use of memory on an application level. Included are discussions about

- Global and local heaps

- Resources

- Atoms

- Subsegment allocation

- Forms of specialized data management

Throughout the chapter, the terms *heap object* and *segment* are encountered frequently. It is important to remember the differences between the two. When the word *segment* is encountered, it always refers to objects allocated out of the global heap and the local descriptor table, whereas any reference to the generic term *heap object* can be applied to objects in both global and local heaps.

At this point you probably are wondering why memory management is mentioned in three different chapters. This division merely reflects the fact that I wanted to organize the book in a (somewhat) object-oriented manner. That is, memory management is broken into three layers: raw, processor-implemented memory management, discussed in Chapter 2, "Processor and Memory Fundamentals"; program memory and module memory management (dynamic linking), discussed in Chapter 3, "Program and Module Fundamentals"; and finally, memory management as implemented by the Windows API, in this chapter. The intention behind separating the discussions was to make it easier for you to understand how memory is layered. When questions arise about a certain aspect of memory or memory management, the organization of the book should make targeting the desired section easier.

The Many Layers of Memory Management (Block, Heap, and Intelligent)

Only three types of memory exist when a computer is first booted: conventional, expanded, and extended. This represents memory in its rawest form—nothing can be done with it unless the services of a memory manager such as XMS, DPMI, EMS, or DOS (for the TPA) are present. To do anything truly useful with memory, however, some sort of memory management API must act as an interface to tasks wanting to allocate, access, and destroy blocks of memory. The job of this "first-level" memory manager is to organize its memory into "dumb" blocks that can be assigned to requesting tasks. At this level, absolutely no other services are provided to the task to aid in its memory management.

Windows' global and local heap manager can be thought of as a "second-level" memory manager in this scheme, because Windows merely embellishes the basic services provided by a boot-time memory manager such as DPMI, to present a better memory-management interface to tasks requiring blocks of memory. The "single" global heap provided by Windows is really a sparse collection of blocks allocated through the DPMI. These blocks are presented as one contiguous range of memory to the application. Libraries, as mentioned in Chapter 5, "Library Design Ideas," can actually bypass Windows' second layer of memory management and interface directly with DPMI if needed. In fact, this has to be done when large 16M+ allocations need to be made. This lets the developer remove barriers put forth by Windows' local and global heap manager, only being limited by the restrictions set forth by the processor and any available RAM or disk space.

Windows global and local heap mechanisms still leave much to be desired. Even with the removal of the 64K segment and 16M allocation limit, a need still exists for another (third) layer of memory management on top of the heap management services provided by Windows. See Figure 4.1 for an illustration.

This third layer could intelligently use the services provided by Windows' global heap manager to produce specialized forms of data management specially suited for handling large (or arbitrary) numbers of objects and collections of objects (known as lists). After all, most application data management requirements don't involve single objects, but rather groups of related (possibly named) objects. With Windows providing levels of indirection involving video access, messaging, memory management, and virtually every other aspect of the operating system being indirectly accessed, it makes sense to add a further layer of indirection, but to the "passed parameter line" used by functions. Instead of passing some fixed number (when using the Pascal calling convention) of parameters, a single list could be passed instead, with the list containing some undetermined number of parameter objects. Using this method, the parameter list of the function never needs to be adjusted, because the list handle that's passed to the function provides all the necessary indirection. Items from the list could then be addressed and retrieved by name, class, or some flat index value. One key requirement to establishing a list manager or any other form of specialized data manager is a good method of naming objects. Windows' atom manager is sorely insufficient in this area, because there is a severe limit on the number of atoms that can be created out of a single data segment.

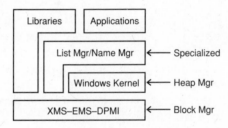

Figure 4.1. Layers of memory management.

As an example of how beneficial a list manager (and name manager) can be, take a minute or two to ponder the memory manager requirements for a custom control such as a spreadsheet. Say that every column in the spreadsheet could be represented by a list, with all those lists tied together into a single list that represents the entire spreadsheet. Now imagine that whenever rows are added to the spreadsheet, objects are added to every column/list across the board, representing a spreadsheet cell at a particular column and row intersection. Of course, just one object for a cell isn't enough, because each cell can optionally have a different font, font color, background color, read-write/read-only or hidden status, and—quite possibly—a background bitmap for the cell. Similarly, the overhead for each list that represents a column in the spreadsheet will also need to contain items like the column's width and possibly the name associated with the column ("A" or "1" or "January"). Now imagine the frequency with which columns and rows are added and deleted during the routine use of the spreadsheet. Are you scared yet? You should be, because Windows' memory managers are absolutely

minor league when compared with the major-league requirements of developing commercial applications, which require commercial, industrial-strength controls and a like memory manager.

A good list manager and name manager makes the memory-management end of developing a control like a spreadsheet much easier. Besides tackling the obvious memory management allocation problems, such as handling small or infinitely large lists of information, it also makes retrieval and access of those objects much simpler. Instead of pulling elements out of a list by some flat index value (which is still possible), one can now access elements in a list by name or class. This would make fetching the text in a spreadsheet cell (say at column 1, row 4) as simple as specifying the list for the column (1), and then saying you want the element (of class "CellText") from the list at index/occurrence 4. Getting the text color used by the cell would be as simple as specifying the list (1), class "CellColor," at index/occurrence 4. This method works wonders over using a combination of array logic and flat index values normally associated with statically allocated blocks of memory. Although Microsoft offers sample source (which is included with this book) that addresses the visual end of designing a spreadsheet, Microsoft does absolutely nothing to describe the details of the physical side of designing an appropriate memory manager. This book also cannot attempt to cover the intricacies involved with writing a name and list manager; rather, it can only bring up the existence of such forms of memory management and give ideas as to why they are needed. Writing a robust name manager is by far the easiest task, because several good algorithm books exist on the market that describe various hashing routines that can easily be implemented under Windows.

The Windows Heap Manager

A *heap* by Windows' definition is a memory space holding a series of fixed, moveable, and discardable blocks of memory. All heaps are structured similarly, with fixed objects generally residing at the bottom of the heap, moveable objects and discardable data objects in the middle, and other types of discardable objects near the top. Figure 4.2 illustrates this scheme. Unlike most memory ranges, a memory space can be composed of multiple, noncontiguous sections of memory. This low-level matter, however, is masked by the heap manager and a series of arena structures, similar to how the 80386 in enhanced mode hides the fact that the processor's "single" linear address space is really a fragmented collection of mapped and unmapped pages. Although the exact format of the arena structures is not provided by Microsoft, it's fairly easy to get an idea of what they are and how they're implemented by debugging and dumping a few heap object data structures. *Arena structures* are singly- and doubly-linked lists that map allocated memory. Each arena structure points to the block behind it, in front of it, or both. The structures are versatile enough that they can be used to map all available memory in a heap, or simply smaller ranges of memory. In addition to pinpointing the locations of related arena structures, each also uses a byte or two to name the owner of the block, or perhaps name the block itself. Additionally, the structures can also keep track of lock counts and whether they represent "live" or "dead" objects.

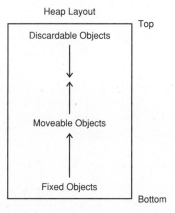

Figure 4.2. Heap organization.

In Windows' standard mode, the arena structures for global heap objects are implemented as separate segments, located just before the segment they reference in memory. This is the reason that standard-mode allocations are limited to half the amount allowed in enhanced mode. Two descriptors are required for every `GlobalAlloc()` call—one for the arena segment, and one for the actual data. In enhanced mode, paging structures are used to map available memory, and the separate arena structures are no longer required. In the case of the local heap, the arena is a four- or eight-byte structure located just before the actual data for the object. Windows' Heap Walker actually gets its information (albeit indirectly) by skimming the appropriate set of arenas when the global heap or the local heap are walked. Various ToolHelp functions provide similar arena perusing capabilities.

Technically, the global heap is a memory space used for allocating blocks of memory shareable by possibly multiple applications, and the local heap is a memory space used for allocating blocks of memory private to an application.

Intel's protected mode processors even provide two structures for this: a global descriptor table for holding shared memory segments, and a per-task local descriptor table. However, the designers of Windows didn't exactly adhere to Intel's memory and multitasking models—partly for compatibility reasons and partly for performance reasons. Under Windows 3.x, the global descriptor table is hardly used. It primarily contains descriptors used by Windows' virtual memory manager and the DPMI code. Instead, the local descriptor table is used for the "global heap." Every loaded memory object viewed in Heap Walker is composed of one or more mapped LDT descriptors. So where do local heaps come from if the LDT is no longer usable? Local heaps are actually created out of data segments in the global heap, and as such are limited to 64K. They don't break the 64K barrier like huge object allocations do. For the default local heap created out of a module's default data segment, this number is much less, usually around 45–50K.

Generally, a developer uses the local heap for multiple, small allocations, and the global heap for fewer, larger allocations, or possibly to create additional 64K local heaps. In any case, Windows treats fixed, moveable, and discardable objects in a similar fashion regardless of which heap (global or local) they're found in. It's important to understand the role of each type of object in the heap, because the wrong attributes on objects in a "busy" heap could possibly bring allocations to a standstill—even when enough memory for the allocation actually exists.

Heap objects can be moved, compacted, and discarded (unless flagged otherwise) by Windows at any time. It was previously thought that this happened only during memory allocation and compaction calls. However, any call to a Windows API function can indirectly cause memory to be moved, compacted, discarded, and even paged. This is due primarily to the movement of application segments. If a message is sent to the window of an application not entirely in memory, there's a chance that the sender's segments will be moved or discarded to make room for the code and data segments that must be loaded by Windows. This rule is similar to how a task can involuntarily relinquish processor control merely by calling certain messaging functions.

The Life Cycle of the Memory Object

Allocating memory is somewhat like checking a book out of the library. Ideally, you read the book in as quick a time as possible, and then you return it to the library so that you don't suffer any penalties and don't penalize other readers. Memory is pretty much the same, both for the local heap and for the global heap. The three big stages of memory usage are allocation, usage, and destruction. The use of Windows in real mode or protected mode alters the grouping of the memory management API functions that make up each stage. In real mode, the allocation stage consists of a single call to `GlobalAlloc()`. The usage stage consists of three steps—a call to `GlobalLock()`, the code to access the memory object, and a matching call to `GlobalUnlock()`. The destruction stage is simple—a single call to `GlobalFree()`. See Figure 4.3 for an illustration of the life cycle of a memory object.

In protected mode, however, the sandwich is altered slightly, pushing the lock and unlock commands outward into the other two layers. As a result, the only code required to access a global memory object consists of a pointer returned by the initial lock call—which has to be done only once, right after the object is created. Memory no longer needs to be locked and unlocked before and after use. In protected mode, locked segments can be moved around in memory because the actual location of the segment is never specified directly—only its selector. The only time the memory block needs to be unlocked is just before it is freed. By keeping memory access short and sweet, you eliminate many internal problems, such as sandbars in memory, and help Windows' memory manager at the same time. The function "sandwich" for local heap memory management is similar to that mentioned in the preceding paragraph, except that the lock and unlock calls are required every time the object is accessed. This is because the local heap uses subsegment allocation rather than segment allocation and has nothing comparable to the descriptor tables used by segments in protected mode.

Fixed and Moveable Memory

The first set of attributes that must be decided for any memory object is whether it's fixed or moveable in memory. This refers to whether the heap manager can relocate the block to satisfy a memory allocation that might not have been possible otherwise. Fixed memory objects are located at the bottom of a heap, growing upward, whereas moveable memory objects are located in the middle and grow outward. Whenever a fixed memory object is allocated, the arena structures are examined from the bottom of the heap upward, ensuring that the object will be located "near" other like objects.

Figure 4.3.
The life cycle of
a memory
object.

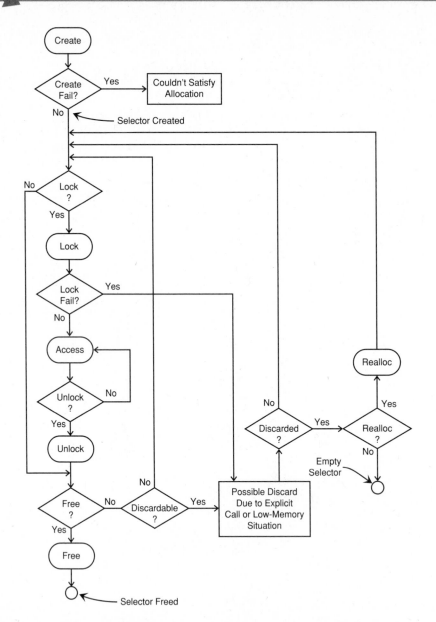

When referencing fixed memory objects, we need to put them in proper context. First, either we can be discussing fixed global heap objects, which are merely segment descriptors in a descriptor table, or we can be talking about fixed local heap objects, which are objects allocated out of the same segment. Under Windows 3.0, fixed segments presented a problem because of the possibility that Windows might be run in real mode. With the abolishment of real mode under Windows 3.1, fixed segments no longer present a problem, because all segment access is done uniformly through the use of a single descriptor table, providing a needed layer of indirection. This essentially means that under Windows 3.1, all segments can be moved in memory, yet maintain the same segmented address. Fixed local heap objects are treated the same under Windows 3.1 as they were under Windows 3.0. In a local heap, fixed objects present a sandbar to the local heap memory manager, because no method exists for moving subsegment objects without invaliding pointers to the object established by the application.

Fragmentation occurs when objects cannot be allocated in their rightful section of heap (for example, a fixed object that because of heap conditions got allocated up with discardable objects) and when fixed objects are not freed according to the order they were allocated. When memory compaction or another allocation is required, suddenly the fixed objects stand out like a sore thumb to the memory manager. Fixed objects can present a real problem for any memory manager because of the sandbars they create in memory. If an application allocates 10 fixed local heap blocks and then frees a few of them located in the middle, the space cannot be compacted and reused because the fixed objects surrounding it cannot be moved in memory. The only way the space can be reclaimed is if by chance another fixed block as large as the original allocation or smaller is required, or if the fixed objects above the free space are freed themselves. Fixed memory is required (at least in real mode) whenever a far pointer to data in the object must retain a constant value.

Fragmentation is really an issue only for local heaps and other subsegment allocators, as the global heap employs descriptor tables to permit the shuffling of fixed memory blocks. The local heap, however, has no such uniform method (as a descriptor table) to govern indirect access to moved blocks, which is also why memory locks still apply to both moveable and discardable local heap allocations.

In fact, fragmentation can be a very real and deadly issue for applications making extensive use of the local heap found in DGROUP or any other dynamically allocated task segment. The problem is a result of the manner in which moveable local heap objects are allocated. For every 20 or so moveable objects, Windows will first create a single fixed object that is used to contain pointers to any new moveable objects. Pointers returned from `LocalAlloc()` for moveable allocations actually reference a cell inside this fixed pointer block, and not the actual moveable block itself, which would be impossible because this provides no layer of indirection. The fixed pointer block is placed at the end of the current size of the heap, before the 20 or so moveable allocations that might take place.

Now say that another 20 moveable allocations are made. This means that Windows will now place yet another fixed pointer block at the "current" end of the heap, which is just after the first 20 moveable blocks we just allocated. Now, the next 20 or so allocations will "sit" directly after this second fixed memory pointer block. Repeating this test four or five times (keeping in mind the 64K limit on local heaps) will replicate the fixed memory pointer blocks throughout the local heap, sandwiched between every 20 (or so) moveable heap objects. Actually, at this point, everything's still fine and functional. The problem comes into play when the moveable heap objects are freed. Instead of determining when a fixed pointer block no longer references any moveable objects, and thus is subject to freeing itself, Windows will never remove the fixed pointer block—only reuse it! Whether the segment is compacted, shrunk, or jostled in any possible way, those fixed memory pointer blocks will always remain at the same position and represent sandbars restricting all future allocation out of that heap. The only possible recourse is a nuking of the entire segment—not pretty, especially when it involves DGROUP. In fact, in this case it's just not possible. This is why so many local heap information calls say "your mileage may vary" when returning the amount of free space in the heap. Figure 4.4 illustrates this "terminal" situation for a local heap segment.

Figure 4.4.
The local heap
fragmentation
problem.

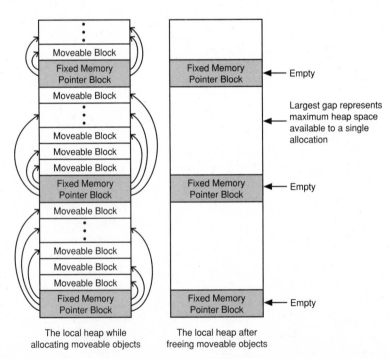

The local heap while
allocating moveable objects

The local heap after
freeing moveable objects

Like the other segment attributes, segments are designated as fixed in one of these areas:

Area	Description
Module-definition file (.DEF)	Using the SEGMENTS, CODE, or DATA statements
Resource file (.RC)	Using the FIXED resource attribute
Dynamic heap allocations	With GMEM_FIXED and LMEM_FIXED

Fixed memory segments were required with Windows 3.0 because of the possibility of running under real mode. This is because real mode had no processor-provided descriptor tables for managing the location of mapped memory segments. Instead, a more static (and private) table called the Burgermaster was used. The Burgermaster works just fine for Windows-aware applications, because all segment handles are used as an index into the Burgermaster. In special cases, Windows could manually patch segment values to reflect the current entries in the Burgermaster. An application such as a TSR or a DOS-level device driver, however, doesn't know about the Burgermaster when it's resolving addresses. As a result, the memory must be fixed so that it always stays at the same address. Plus, fixed memory blocks were guaranteed not to be banked into EMS memory. For a real-mode device driver, trying to access code that might have been banked out could be a real nightmare. In protected mode, segments are always accessed indirectly via the descriptor tables, so there's never a problem with segments moving in memory. The abolishment of real mode with Windows 3.1 removes the need for fixed memory segments.

With the advent of the 80386 processor and virtual memory paging, which operates underneath, independently of, and invisibly to segmentation, fixed memory can no longer even be called "fixed" because the paging unit can map pages out from underneath an address, retrieving them when the task owning the pages attempts to access them, causing a page fault. Creating truly fixed memory requires that it be page-locked, preventing the virtual memory manager from swapping out the locked page to disk. In enhanced mode, this kind of object truly creates a sandbar to the memory manager. Although Windows 3.1 and 3.0 allow segments to be page-locked, the call will be removed from the Windows NT API. Most applications should have no need for page-locked memory.

Fixed global and local heap objects have the "benefit" of not requiring that they be locked before use. In Windows 3.1, this applies to moveable global heap objects as well. Because of Windows' memory allocation methods, the handle is guaranteed to represent the actual address of the object, whether near or far. Because the address of the object is guaranteed not to change, the handle can continue to be used as a pointer. As shown by the following example, this applies to memory allocated by both `GlobalAlloc()` and `LocalAlloc()`:

```
HGLOBAL hMemGlobal;
LPSTR   lpGmem;

// Casting fixed global memory for immediate use. The GPTR
// flag merely stands for "GMEM_FIXED ¦ GMEM_ZEROINIT"

hMemGlobal  = GlobalAlloc(GPTR, 1024L);

lpGmem      = (LPSTR) MAKELONG(0, hMemGlobal);
lstrcpy(lpGmem, (LPSTR) "data bytes...");

GlobalFree(hMemGlobal);

...

NPWNDCLASS pWnd;

// Casting fixed local memory. Reserve enough memory for
// wndclass structure and cast it correctly. The LPTR flag
// stands for "LMEM_FIXED ¦ LMEM_ZEROINIT"


pWnd        = (NPWNDCLASS) LocalAlloc(LPTR, sizeof(WNDCLASS));
pWnd->hIcon = LoadIcon(hInst, (LPSTR) "MyIcon");
```

Discardable and Nondiscardable Memory

Discardable objects represent the most efficient kind of memory used by Windows' heap memory manager, because objects can be discarded from memory to make room for any new objects that would otherwise be unallocatable due to a lack of space in the heap. Objects are never discarded until Windows' virtual memory manager runs out of space. The most typical examples of discardable memory are the code and resource segments in an application or library. Data segments aren't designated as discardable due to the difficulty (usually) in re-creating the data. Windows treats both categories of discardable objects differently. Whereas code and resource segments are "invisibly" loaded into memory by Windows during segment-not-present faults, other forms of discardable objects must be re-created and reloaded manually by application code created by the developer. The `GlobalRealloc()` and `LocalRealloc()` functions both reuse the handles of objects that might have been discarded.

When a global heap segment is freed, the selectors associated with the memory are freed as well. Likewise for local heap objects, because a portion of the fixed memory block used to locate the moveable local heap object is zeroed out and marked as available for use by another allocation. However, when an object is discarded, its selector, in whatever form, is merely emptied and not freed. This empty selector can then be used to reallocate another block of memory using the same handle. If an application preloads or demand-loads 100 resource segments, and then through some action causes a compaction of the global heap to occur, the memory associated with the objects will be freed; however, the selectors used to represent the resources will still take up space in the local descriptor table. The selectors still exist and are allocated, but with a mapped segment length of zero, indicating that they are discarded. In fact, this is how Windows' auto-discard macros work. They reallocate the block with a length of zero, indicating that the block is discarded—nothing more special than that. When a local heap object is discarded, a similar operation is performed, except instead of zeroing the length of a selector, a word value in a fixed memory pointer block (representing the length) for the object is set to zero.

Reflecting its transient nature, discardable memory starts at the top of any local heap, growing downward toward moveable objects. Following the thinking for fixed and moveable memory objects, when a discardable object is allocated, the arena structures are scanned from the top of the heap to the bottom, ensuring that the discardable object will more than likely reside near other discardable objects. An object cannot be discarded while it is locked. Discardable memory is never fixed memory (unless locked) because the term "discardable" implies that Windows can demand-load the object (when discarded) anywhere in memory. This puts kind of a kink in being able to reference the object via a static handle.

Windows determines how to discard global heap memory based on a *Least-Recently Used (LRU) algorithm,* which basically states that the least-used object more than likely will be the first object to be discarded. The framework behind this algorithm is implemented somewhat differently in protected and real mode. In real mode, the module database contains a series of access bytes— one for each discardable segment. When a segment is accessed (via a call thunk), the access byte is tripped, informing the memory manager that it is

"recently used." In protected mode, segment descriptors include a special access bit that's automatically updated by the processor to indicate segment access. The Windows API includes two functions—`GlobalLRUOldest()` and `GlobalLRUNewest()`—to override Windows' method of determining discardability.

Sometimes, as in the case of circularly linked segments or for types of database access, the LRU algorithm doesn't apply and must be overridden. Sometimes memory access isn't predictable and orderly. Memory is discarded under possibly several conditions. Before Windows will fail a memory allocation, it will first try to compact, and then ultimately discard, memory to meet the allocation. Objects aren't discarded until the virtual memory manager runs out of room.

If both real mode and far pointers are an issue during an allocation, options exist to override the automatic compacting and discarding of memory. Memory is also discarded whenever a call is made to `LocalCompact()` or `GlobalCompact()`. Although the term "compacting" only implies "movement" of objects, objects will still be discarded one by one to meet an allocation after any moveable objects have been reshuffled in the first attempt to meet the allocation. It is strongly recommended that neither of these calls be used. The Windows NT API actually removes the calls because with efficient implementation of virtual memory, explicit compaction is no longer required. Performing any kind of compaction could possibly take an inordinate number of clock cycles to complete, and at runtime there's really no method of telling how long this will take.

The discarding of local heap objects is handled quite differently by Windows, with discardable local memory not really being as usable as discardable global heap memory. After all, how often does an application need to load its own code or resource segments? And how could it be done in a 64K segment? The only time local heap objects are discarded is during calls to `LocalAlloc()`, `LocalRealloc()`, `LocalCompact()`, `LocalDiscard()`, and `LocalShrink()`.

Compaction

Compaction refers to a process needed when "initially" no free arena exists that can satisfy a memory allocation. When the local or global heap is compacted, several steps occur: When the reshuffling and movement of objects in a heap in order to free up larger areas of space isn't enough to satisfy an allocation, objects are discarded one by one until the allocation can be met (if at all possible). Compaction does not report the "total" amount of free memory available to a program. Rather, it reports only the amount of free memory in the arena entries managed by the Windows Kernel module. It in no way reflects the amount of memory available to Windows' virtual memory manager.

Actually, the C runtime libraries have all of their memory management calls mapped to equivalent Windows local heap calls, but with a twist—all allocations are flagged as fixed and allow no compaction to occur. This is true for the data of other non-Windows applications and libraries, including DOS boxes. In fact, whenever real-mode Windows passes a far pointer to a data segment, it always references a fixed segment, ensuring that the pointer will always be valid. The offset portion of a far address referencing a fixed object won't change. The DS portion of the far address can change, however, if Windows decides to move the data segment to a spot in memory that will allow the segment to grow properly. This invalidates the segment portions of any far pointers that pointed into the local heap. Of course, this was a problem only in real mode, because in protected mode, the DS value is always referenced from the local descriptor table. The offset portion of the address will always stay the same if the object is fixed or locked.

Freeing Memory

Under Windows, memory object ownership is generally assigned on a per-task basis. Whenever memory is allocated, it belongs to the currently running task (application)—with two exceptions. For a library to "own" its own memory, the `GlobalAlloc()` GMEM_SHARE flag must be used during the allocation. In this case, Windows assigns ownership of the memory to the library's module database and not to the task database of the active application. When an application allocates memory with the GMEM_SHARE flag, ownership of the memory is assigned to the application's module database, not the task database. This ensures that the memory blocks associated with the allocation will remain in memory until the last instance of the application has itself been freed. In any case, after ownership has been determined, allocated memory stays available until its owner is terminated or when the object is explicitly freed. When the owner of any memory is terminated, its memory goes along with it—locked or not. Memory cannot be explicitly freed, however, until the lock count of the object has reached zero. At this point the block can be freed and is available for possible discarding.

Because the Windows API provides no mechanism for allocating "ownerless" memory, the only real reason to free memory is because of the impact it will

have on the program at runtime. If memory isn't conserved to be used as needed, and then freed as expediently and routinely as possible, obviously certain allocation problems might start to appear down the road. Memory should be freed as soon as the block is no longer needed.

Freed memory is quite different from discarded memory. When `GlobalFree()` or `LocalFree()` is called for a heap object, the memory associated with the handle is freed, and the handle is invalidated from further use. This contrasts with a call to `GlobalDiscard()` or `LocalDiscard()`, which frees the memory associated with the handle but leaves the handle free for further allocations. In the case of global heap objects, this means empty selectors. Actually, these latter two functions are implemented as macro calls to `GlobalRealloc()` and `LocalRealloc()`, specifying a new size of zero bytes for the block, essentially discarding it from memory.

Redefining/Reallocating Segments

A good program is one that can dynamically adjust its internal and external requirements (to a certain degree) according to the user's demands and any demands required by the operating system. This includes being flexible when it comes to allocating and freeing memory. Statically allocating a huge or far array will very easily cripple a program, in addition to wasting memory and incurring other problems, like forcing the program into large model. Fixing the size of large dynamic allocations is another bad tack to take when designing a program. The memory requirements of a program should be driven solely by the needs at hand (of the user and of the OS). To help manage and keep the global and local heaps fluid and dynamic, Windows provides two functions to resize and reflag allocated memory blocks—`GlobalRealloc()` and `LocalRealloc()`.

Reallocating a block of memory can work in one of two ways. If there's enough room in memory for the block to stay in its current position, the size of the block is merely expanded. More often than not, the block ends up moving in memory, and a different handle is returned to reference the block. This is always the case when the GMEM_MOVEABLE flag is used to move a fixed block from one location in memory to another, and when in standard or enhanced mode the block is reallocated past a multiple of 64K (64K—17 bytes in standard mode). This causes additional tiled selectors to be added to the object and usually requires that the object be moved within the LDT to accommodate the new selectors.

Not only can blocks of memory be expanded or shrunk in size, but their segment attributes can be changed as well, at least in some cases. This is done using the GMEM_MODIFY and LMEM_MODIFY flags. When these flags are used, the size value passed to the **Realloc()** function is ignored and only the attributes of the segment, not its size, are modifiable. When attributes are being changed, certain rules are enforced. Using **GlobalRealloc()**, moveable segments can be changed from discardable to nondiscardable and vice versa, and fixed segments can be changed to moveable (but not the other way around). Using **LocalRealloc()**, only the discardable and nondiscardable attributes can be changed. There is no way to change a block from moveable to fixed or vice versa with **LocalAlloc()**.

Blocks of memory that are reallocated to zero bytes with the GMEM_MOVEABLE or LMEM_MOVEABLE flag are automatically subject to discarding, because Windows considers a zero-length moveable segment as discarded. In fact, **GlobalDiscard()** and **LocalDiscard()** are implemented as macros that call these functions.

Getting Segment and Memory Manager Information

At some point the developer will need to get either information about an allocated heap object, segment, or information on the heap as a whole (global or local). Although Windows 3.0 provided a few functions for this purpose, the release of Windows 3.1 has improved the offerings dramatically, especially with the inclusion of ToolHelp, which offers functions providing information on Windows' virtual memory manager, the global heap, and the local heaps of data segments.

For global heap objects and local heap objects, the Windows API provides the functions **GlobalFlags()**, **GlobalSize()**, **LocalFlags()**, and **LocalSize()**. The **Flags** functions are used to get information about the attributes of a local or a global heap object, and the **Size** functions are used to determine the "true" size of an allocated object, which is usually larger than the amount requested due to granularity.

3.1

ToolHelp contains functions and structures for querying the virtual memory manager, the global heap, and the local heaps of any data segments. Although the structures are listed next, the functions are listed under the sections for the global heap and the local heap. Although some of the heap scanning functions and structures are used more for debugging utilities than end-user applications, they still help yield a better understanding of how Windows functions.

The function `MemManInfo()` returns a structure indicating the status of Windows' virtual memory manager, returning the following structure:

```
typedef struct tagMEMMANINFO
{
    DWORD dwSize;                    // Size of MEMMANINFO struct, used
                                     // to extend structure for future
                                     // expansion

    DWORD dwLargestFreeBlock;        // Largest free block of contiguous
                                     // linear memory

    DWORD dwMaxPagesAvailable;       // Maximum # of allocable pages

    DWORD dwMaxPagesLockable;        // Maximum # of committable pages
                                     // (that can be locked)

    DWORD dwTotalLinearSpace;        // Size of linear addr space in pages

    DWORD dwTotalUnlockedPages;      // # of unlocked and free pages in sys

    DWORD dwFreePages;               // # of free pages

    DWORD dwTotalPages;              // # of total pages, including free,
                                     // locked, and unlocked

    DWORD dwFreeLinearSpace;         // Amt of free linear mem in pages

    DWORD dwSwapFilePages;           // # of pages in system swap file

    WORD  wPageSize;                 // Size of page (in bytes)
}
MEMMANINFO;
```

The function `SysHeapInfo()` can be used to return a structure filled with information on the local heap of Windows' User and GDI modules. `SysHeapInfo()` returns the following data structure:

```
typedef struct tagSYSHEAPINFO
{
    DWORD dwSize;               // Size of SYSHEAPINFO struct, used
                               // for future expansion capabilities

    WORD wUserFreePercent;     // % free space in User local heap
    WORD wGDIFreePercent;      // % free space in GDI local heap

    HANDLE hUserSegment;       // Automatic data segment of User module
    HANDLE hGDISegment;        // Automatic data segment of GDI module
}
SYSHEAPINFO;
```

With ToolHelp, the Windows API provides functions and structures to scan entries in the global and local heaps, ala the SDK's Heap Walker utility. The `GlobalInfo()` function returns a structure containing information on the global heap, and the functions `GlobalFirst()` and `GlobalNext()` are used to return structures containing information on individual objects in the global heap. The previous functions use the following structures:

```
typedef struct tagGLOBALINFO
{
    DWORD dwSize;         // Size of GLOBALINFO struct

    WORD  wcItems;        // Count of entries in heap
    WORD  wcItemsFree;    // Count of free entries in heap
    WORD  wcItemsLRU;     // Count of LRU entries in heap
}
GLOBALINFO;


typedef struct tagGLOBALENTRY
{
    DWORD   dwSize;        // Size of GLOBALENTRY struct

    DWORD   dwAddress;     // Linear address of global heap object
    DWORD   dwBlockSize;   // Size of block in bytes
    HANDLE  hBlock;        // Handle to object

    WORD    wcLock;        // Segment lock count of object
    WORD    wcPageLock;    // Page lock count of object

    WORD    wFlags;        // Additional info about block
                          // GF_PDB_OWNER flag means that task's
                          // process data block is owner

    BOOL    wHeapPresent;  // Does object (segment) have a local heap?
```

```
       HANDLE hOwner;          // Owner of object

        WORD    wType;         // Specifies block's type:
                               // GT_UNKNOWN
                               // GT_DGROUP
                               // GT_DATA
                               // GT_CODE
                               // GT_TASK (task database)
                               // GT_RESOURCE
                               // GT_MODULE (module database)
                               // GT_FREE
                               // GT_INTERNAL
                               // GT_SENTINEL (obj is first or last in heap)
                               // GT_BURGERMASTER (block contains a table
                               //      mapping selectors to arena handles)

        WORD    wData;         // If type isn't CODE or RESOURCE, wData
                               // is zero. If wType is CODE, DATA, or DGROUP,
                               // wData contains the segment number.
                               // If type is GT_RESOURCE, wData is the
                               // following type of resource:
                               //
                               // GD_ACCELERATORS
                               // GD_BITMAP
                               // GD_CURSOR
                               // GD_CURSORCOMPONENT (data descr a cursor)
                               // GD_DIALOG
                               // GD_ERRTABLE
                               // GD_FONT
                               // GD_FONTDIR (data descr group of fonts)
                               // GD_ICON
                               // GD_ICONCOMPONENT (data descr an icon)
                               // GD_MENU
                               // GD_NAMETABLE
                               // GD_RCDATA
                               // GD_STRING
                               // GD_USERDEFINED

    DWORD   dwNext;            // Internal use
    DWORD   dwNextAlt;         // Internal use
}
GLOBALENTRY;
```

The functions `LocalInfo()`, `LocalFirst()`, and `LocalNext()` are used in a similar fashion, returning structures containing information on individual objects in the local heap of a particular data segment. ToolHelp's local heap scanning functions use the following structures:

```c
typedef struct tagLOCALINFO
{
    DWORD dwSize;      // Size of LOCALINFO struct
    WORD  wcItems;     // Total # of items in local heap
}
LOCALINFO;


typedef struct tagLOCALENTRY
{
    DWORD   dwSize;         // Size of LOCALENTRY struct

    HANDLE hHandle;         // Handle of local heap object
    WORD    wAddress;       // Address of object
    WORD    wSize;          // Size of object

    WORD    wFlags;         // Indicates object attributes, which can
                            // be LF_FIXED, LF_MOVEABLE, or LF_FREE

    WORD    wcLock;         // Lock count of object
    WORD    wType;          // Type of heap object. Valid values are:
                            // LT_FREE
                            // LT_GDI_BITMAP, LT_GDI_BRUSH, LT_GDI_DC
                            // LT_GDI_FONT, LT_GDI_METADC, LT_GDI_METAFILE
                            // LT_GDI_PALETTE, LT_GDI_PEN, LT_GDI_RGN
                            // LT_USER_ATOMS, LT_USER_CBOX, LT_USER_CLASS
                            // LT_USER_ED, LT_USER_HANDLETABLE,
                            // LT_USER_HOOKLIST, LT_USER_HOTKEYLIST,
                            // LT_USER_LBIV, LT_USER_MENU,
                            // LT_USER_OWNERDRAW, LT_USER_POPUPMENU
                            // LT_USER_PROP, LT_USER_WND
                            //
                            // Several other "internal" #defines are also
                            // available. See online help for more info.
                            // These values are for informational
                            // purposes only.

    WORD    hHeap;          // Handle to local heap
    WORD    wHeapType;      // Either NORMAL_HEAP, USER_HEAP, GDI_HEAP

    WORD    wNext;          // Internal to Windows
}
LOCALENTRY;
```

Surviving
Low-Memory Situations

Surviving low-memory situations under Windows requires a good understanding of the kinds of bottlenecks that appear with certain types of memory allocations. It's not just a matter of understanding your own module's memory requirements, but it also requires a better understanding of how memory is utilized by Windows in general. Compounding the matter is that Windows itself doesn't always handle low-memory situations gracefully. Often, when too many applications are run, or too many memory global heap allocations are made, Windows is the first to shrivel up and die.

Before a module is even loaded into memory, Windows checks the memory needs of the application and contrasts them with available memory in the global heap. Windows ensures that there is enough memory in the heap to hold all preloaded program segments and one or two dynamically created system segments (the module database and the task database). Any libraries that are implicitly (make file) or explicitly (IMPORTS) loaded by the module are checked for their memory requirements as well. If the segments of any of these modules can't fit into available memory, none are loaded into memory and the original module load request fails. Available memory doesn't refer to just the "current" amount of available memory, but to the amount of memory available after compaction, where, whenever possible, segments are moved and discarded to free up more room. One other caveat also exists: there must always be enough memory in the global heap to load the largest discardable program segment into physical RAM. If loading a particular module or modules prevents this, the module is not loaded and the request fails. This space is reserved by Heap Walker's *code fence* entry, which ensures that enough free space exists to demand-load the largest discardable segment of any running application.

Of course, these problems are trivial and the developer shouldn't worry about them, because for the most part Windows takes care of them. The real problem occurs when dynamic heap allocations (global or local) cannot be satisfied. Global heap allocation failures are the simplest to deal with, because any global heap allocations immediately stand out in a program. In contrast, local heap problems, whether on the part of your module or indirectly on the part of another module (User, GDI), are more embedded in the module and can be more difficult to spot as well as resolve. When a global allocation fails, the most likely response by a program is to create a message box explaining the error and any corrective actions that should be taken, which could include shutting down other applications if needed. In fact, the code for `MessageBox()` is stored inside a fixed and nondiscardable segment in Windows' User module, ensuring that the function will always be available in memory when called. Even in the worst of low-memory situations, `MessageBox()` will never be discarded or otherwise unavailable. In fact, if `MessageBox()` is called with the `MB_SYSTEMMODAL` and `MB_ICONHAND` flags, a single-line message box will be displayed regardless of the amount of available memory left in the system.

Do local heaps cause you problems? Welcome to the club. The 64K limitation on local heap space is one of the biggest frustrations for a developer. The funny thing is that it's not how the developer handles the local heap space, but it's how the space is handled by Windows. As you're probably well aware by now, Windows makes extensive use of the local heap space of its User, GDI, and Kernel modules, with User storing all class- and window-relevant data including menus, GDI storing all graphical object overhead and data, and Kernel storing all memory management structures and associated overhead.

Problems with available memory in User usually can be directly traced to one of three problems: too many windows/window classes, an excessive amount of extra class/window bytes per window, or the overuse of window properties. The last two problems are easily solved; unfortunately, the first isn't. Both Windows versions 3.1 and 3.0 are limited to creating about 500–700 windows, which includes top-level windows, child window controls, and MDI child windows. The reason for the big delta in window creation has more to do with determining what objects are already stored in User.

Most often this doesn't become an issue, because most users (presumably) will have at most about 15 running applications. This basically breaks down into about 45 creatable windows per application. Of course, some will create more and some less, but this is just an example. Assuming that the majority of applications create and destroy windows (and child controls) as needed, you might never bump into the window creation limit. It does become a problem for applications that pre-create many windows and dialogs, however. It's true that the window creation limit can make things simpler for the developer, because a window full of information can just be shown and hidden as needed, but the downside is that it can drain User's local heap. Other applications that encounter this problem include programs requiring large numbers of data-entry dialogs (including data-entry field windows) and MDI applications (for network management, for example) that create an unusual number of MDI child windows. The paragraph in Chapter 1 describing the User module discusses this problem in greater depth and mentions a few ways around it.

Memory problems in GDI's local heap usually are easy to fix. Instead of being caused by a flaw in Windows' design, GDI problems are usually fixed by some routine debugging on the part of the developer. It would be an odd circumstance that required a developer to create hundreds of GDI objects, thus pinching the heap for space. The only problems you're ever likely to see involving GDI's heap occur when cleanup code for a pen, brush, or bitmap hasn't been implemented. Because GDI objects are shared by Windows, creating and leaving objects lying around the heap means that they won't be cleaned up until Windows terminates.

Developers constantly run into problems with limitations of Windows' Kernel module, or rather with the limitations in Kernel imposed by the 80x86 processor. The big problem with Kernel, or rather surrounding Kernel, is the allocation of global heap objects. This is a problem because each allocated object in the global heap is made up of at least one descriptor in the LDT. The LDT, you'll remember, is limited to 8,192 descriptors in enhanced mode and 4,096 descriptors in standard mode. Any programs allocating many global heap objects quickly run out of selectors, almost guaranteeing a crash of the system. Unfortunately, there is no easy way of determining the number of free selectors available in an LDT from an application. The only solution is to use some form of subsegment allocation.

Segment allocation is the process of allocating segment descriptors out of the GDT or LDT, whereas *subsegment allocation* involves allocating small unprotected objects inside a single segment. Segment allocation should be used only for objects larger than 64K and for creating segments with a local heap. Subsegment allocation should be used for the more numerous smaller allocations that might be required by a program. Using a combination of segment and subsegment allocation is the most efficient design possible under Windows. Unlike the heap objects created using segment allocation, local heap objects are created out of a single (64K maximum) segment. No single local heap object nor the sum of all objects in the local heap can be greater than 64K. If this is the case, another segment must be allocated for an additional local heap.

With the future come promises of better memory management, and fortunately, with Windows NT that is the case. Under NT, local heaps (segments) are no longer limited to 64K, because the 4G virtual segment size is assumed. In fact, under NT all local heap API calls resolve to the same calls as do the functions in the global heap API. Taking the place of the global heap API will be APIs for other various IPC and shared-memory mechanisms. NT has improved tremendously on Windows' heap management, offering a whole new API. This new heap API makes it much easier for a library, for example, to allocate multiple local heap segments on behalf of requesting clients. The new API is much more portable and requires no assembly language code for setting up the data segment register.

Although it has not radically changed anything to do with memory management, Windows 3.1 has improved the API for determining free system resources. Under Windows 3.0, this was a hodgepodge of techniques that quite often didn't work as well as claimed. Many developers resorted to using undocumented functions. Windows 3.1, however, provides the following simple functions for determining available memory:

Function	Description
`GetFreeSpace()`	Returns the "estimated" amount of free memory in the global heap. This amount doesn't represent one contiguous allocable object. In standard mode, the return value is the number of free bytes in the heap that isn't reserved for code. In enhanced mode, the return value is an estimate of the amount of memory available to an application. This amount is not guaranteed due to the fact that memory can possibly be allocated before the task even gets a chance to perform any of its own memory manager calls.
`GetFreeSystemResources()`	Returns the "estimated" percentage of free resource space. If passed zero, value returned is free system resource space. If one, value returned is percentage of free GDI heap space. If two, value returned is percentage of free User heap space.
`MemManInfo()`	Returns information on Windows' virtual memory manager.
`SystemHeapInfo()`	Returns information on GDI and User's local heap usage.
`LocalInfo()`	Returns information on the local heap of a data segment.

continues

Function	Description
`GlobalInfo()`	Returns information on the system-wide global heap.
`GlobalCompact()`	Returns the size of the largest free entry available after the movement and discarding of heap objects. Doesn't represent the amount of memory available to the virtual memory manager, only Windows Kernel.
`LocalCompact()`	Returns the size of the largest free entry available after the movement and discarding of heap objects.

"Stress" Management

No discussion of low-memory situations would be complete without a mention of the new Stress Application and stress management library included with the 3.1 SDK. Available as an end-user (actually end-programmer) executable, or as a DLL consisting of more than eight functions, Windows' new stress-testing mechanisms are exactly what the doctor ordered when it comes to putting an application through the wringer. All too often, developers don't stress-test their code. Whether the excuse is that it wasn't necessary, or that it would take too long and wasn't worth the effort (other measures might have been prepared), there are no excuses anymore. With the new stress facilities, developers can have it "their way" when it comes to stress-testing an application under "real desktop" situations. See Figure 4.5 for a picture of the Stress Application utility.

Figure 4.5.
The main screen in Windows' Stress Application utility.

—	Stress	▼
<u>S</u>ettings <u>O</u>ptions <u>H</u>elp		

<u>Resource</u>	<u>Remaining</u>	
Global	5089.16	KB
User	88	%
GDI	83	%
Disk Space	8.43	MB
File Handles	110	

At the simplest level, the Stress application can be used alongside your own module. The application provides a convenient and easy method of allocating global memory, memory in GDI and User's local heap, available disk space, and available file handles. Allocations can be made statically at runtime, randomly, or in response to certain window messages. The stress library can also be used to tune and test an application. Comparable to embedding profiler commands into source code, the stress API can be put into certain critical code sections to test their worthiness. The stress-testing functions included with Windows 3.1 include:

Function	Description
`AllocDiskSpace()`	Allocates bytes on a specified disk storage device. The byte value indicates how many bytes are to be left remaining on the disk. Possible disk devices include EDS_WIN, which creates the file on the current Windows partition; EDS_CUR, which creates the file on the currently active partition; and EDS_TEMP, which creates the file on the partition containing the TEMP directory.
`UnAllocDiskSpace()`	Removes the file created by `AllocDiskSpace()`.
`AllocFileHandles()`	Allocates all available file handles, leaving a predetermined number of handles specified by the passed count parameter.
`UnAllocFileHandles()`	Destroys file handles created by `AllocFileHandles()`.
`AllocMem()`	Allocates global heap memory until only the specified number of bytes is available.
`FreeAllMem()`	Frees all memory allocated by `AllocMem()`.
`AllocGDIMem()`	Allocates bytes in GDI's local heap space until only the specified number of bytes is available.

continues

3.1

Function	Description
`FreeAllGDIMem()`	Frees all memory allocated by `AllocGDIMem()`.
`AllocUserMem()`	Allocates bytes in User's local heap space until only the specified number of bytes is available.
`FreeAllUserMem()`	Frees all memory allocated by `AllocUserMem()`.

Locking and Unlocking Memory

Locking an object does two things: fixes the object's address in linear memory and increments a lock count. Memory was fixed in order to not invalidate any far pointers during segment movement. The lock count was used as an indicator of whether the block could be moved in memory to help satisfy an allocation, or whether (if discardable) the block could be discarded to make an allocation succeed. The fixing of memory was an issue only in real mode (for segment allocations) and for local heap (subsegment) allocations. So under Windows 3.1, the only thing that lock counts are used for are discardable global heap objects, and for moveable and discardable local heap objects, with an object capable of having up to 255 locks. Regardless of the number of locks on a global or local heap object, it is always subject to freeing via an explicit call to `GlobalFree()` or `LocalFree()`.

Under Windows 3.0, the function `GlobalLock()` used to always increment a global heap object's lock count and return a pointer to it. Under Windows 3.1, the lock count is incremented only for discardable objects; however, a far pointer to the object is always returned. Additionally, the functions `GlobalFix()`, `GlobalWire()`, and `LockSegment()` also can increase the lock count on discardable global heap objects. The function `LocalLock()` works as usual, incrementing the lock counts for moveable and discardable local heap objects and returning a near pointer to the object.

Blocks of memory are referenced in one of two methods—via a handle or via a pointer. A handle is created when a moveable or discardable object is first created, with the handle referring to a location in memory that contains the true address of the object. Fixed memory allocations, although returning a "handle," are really returning a pointer to the object. Because the object is incapable of moving in linear memory, it requires no handle. Therefore, the "handle" value equals the address of the object. In the case of local memory, a near pointer is returned, whereas for global memory it's a segment or a selector. In both cases, the "handle" of the fixed object can be directly used to access memory without first having to lock the object. Microsoft, however, recommends that the appropriate locking mechanisms be used.

In real mode the locking and unlocking of memory was a real issue. This was because real-mode Windows employed a private segment access table (Burgermaster) unaccessible to DOS and other TSR applications. When the address of a buffer needed to be passed from a Burgermaster-aware Windows program to a non-aware TSR or network driver, the true physical address of the object needed to be passed, not a logical address like what would be generated using the Burgermaster. A logical address using descriptor tables is acceptable because in protected mode every task is forced into using descriptor tables. The passing of a memory address in real mode implies that the address passed is the "real" or physical address of the object. Because of this, in real mode, all moveable and discardable objects supported lock counts. In fact, in real mode, whenever a message is sent to a window procedure, Windows automatically locks the data segment to prevent it from moving in memory during code execution.

In protected mode, only discardable objects get their lock count incremented. In the case of discardable objects, Windows uses the lock/unlock pairing to update the LRU list for the segment. When a discardable object is locked and a null pointer is returned, the object has been discarded. This never happens with a call to `LockResource()`, because a resource handler is called first to ensure that the resource is in memory before the actual locking occurs.

Although the locking of memory is designed to prevent it from being moved and discarded, in enhanced mode, locked memory can still be paged to disk by Windows' virtual memory manager. Unless the segment is additionally page-locked, it is subject to being paged between physical RAM and disk. The page-locking count and mechanism for fixing the physical address of an object is similar to real mode's segment-locking count used for fixing the linear address of discardable objects.

Fixed, Wired, and Page-Locked Segments

Appropriate after a discussion of lock counts is a mention of the other API calls that can place lock counts on a segment. In addition to calling `GlobalLock()`, a task can also call `GlobalFix()`, `GlobalWire()` (Windows 3.0 only), and `GlobalPageLock()`. These functions are unnecessary for most Windows applications and have been dropped completely from the Windows NT API. Their continued use under Windows 3.1, however, means that they're still worth discussing.

`GlobalFix()` is similar to a regular segment lock, except that a far pointer to the block isn't returned. Unlike `GlobalLock()`, `GlobalFix()` *always* locks an object into a specific address in linear memory, regardless of its type. This is in addition to incrementing the lock count. Because this call "truly" locks a block in memory, it can potentially wreak havoc with the memory manager, unlike a call to `GlobalLock()`, which only increments the lock counts of discardable objects.

A wired block (`GlobalWire()`) is a moveable or discardable global heap object that has been moved to a location in lower memory and locked. Wired blocks, at least in real-mode Windows, were used when a segment needed to be locked for an unusually long time. This procedure was intended to help Windows' memory manager. When the block is put in a lower part of the heap, possibly with fixed objects, the block becomes somewhat removed from the "hustle and bustle" surrounding other moveable and discardable memory blocks. Although wired blocks might have been needed in real mode, it isn't a protected-mode system that utilizes virtual, paged memory.

`GlobalPageLock()` is used to lock a segment into a particular address in physical RAM, to prevent the segment from being paged to disk. Other forms of segment locking lock the segments into an address in linear memory, meaning that the segment is still subject to paging. Because the object is referred to by its "logical" or linear address, Windows is free to change the physical address of the object. This is the "lowest" level of lock that can be placed on a segment, and therefore is the one that hurts Windows' virtual memory manager the most. The only time segments need to be page-locked is when the segment needs to be accessed inside interrupt-driven code and cannot (due to the nature of its environment) be paged in from disk willy-nilly as needed.

The Global Heap

Allocating memory out of the global heap is referred to as *segment allocation,* because objects in the global heap are composed of at least one and more likely several LDT segments. This contrasts with *subsegment allocation,* used by the local heap, which consists of allocating objects inside a single LDT segment.

The Windows API provides the following global heap management functions:

Function	Description
GlobalAlloc()	Allocates a block of memory from the global heap. In standard mode, the maximum amount that can be allocated is 1M, whereas in enhanced mode the limit is increased to 16M–64K.
GlobalRealloc()	Reallocates a memory block, increasing or decreasing its size. Memory can possibly be compacted and discarded as a result. The return handle changes for fixed-to-fixed moveable reallocations, and for reallocations requiring an extra 64K segment.
GlobalFree()	Frees specified object if its reference count is zero, invalidating the handle.
LockSegment()*	Increments a lock count on the specified segment. In protected mode, the lock count is increased for discardable and automatic data segments only.
UnlockSegment()*	Decrements a lock count on the specified segment.
LockData()*	A LockSegment() macro that increments the lock count on the current data segment.

continues

189

Function	Description
UnlockData()*	An UnlockSegment() macro that decrements the lock count on the current data segment.
GlobalLock()	Returns a far pointer to the specified object. In real mode, GlobalLock() increments the lock count on an object, fixing its location in linear memory, preventing it from being moved or discarded. In protected mode, GlobalLock() increments the lock count only on discardable segments and the default data segment.
GlobalUnlock()	Decrements the lock count on an object (of the appropriate type). When the lock count is zero, the object is subject to movement and possible discarding.
GlobalFix()*	Locks the object, fixing its location in linear memory. The object is still subject to paging, which would change only its physical address.
GlobalUnFix()*	Decrements the lock count of the fixed object. When the lock count is zero, object is subject to movement and possible discarding.
GlobalWire()	Moves the object to the lowest possible position in the heap and then locks the object's location in linear memory, preventing it from being moved or discarded. The heap location is not guaranteed to be in the lower 1M of memory. Windows 3.0 only.
GlobalUnWire()	Decrements the lock count of the wired object. When the lock count is zero, the object is subject to movement and possible discarding. Windows 3.0 only.

Function	Description
GlobalPageLock()*	Unlike other functions that lock an object in linear memory, GlobalPageLock() locks a segment's address somewhere in physical RAM, so it is not subject to paging. Increments the page-lock count.
GlobalPageUnlock()*	Decrements the page-lock count on a segment. When the count reaches zero, the segment is subject to paging.
GlobalCompact()*	Moves and, if necessary, discards global heap objects to satisfy the requested allocation.
GlobalDiscard()	A macro (using GlobalRealloc()) that discards a global heap object.
GlobalNotify()*	Installs a notification procedure for the current task. Windows calls it whenever a global heap object allocated with GMEM_NOTIFY is about to be discarded. Meant for application program segments only, and should be called no more than once per instance.
GlobalLRUNewest()	Promotes the discardable object to the bottom of the discard list, making it less likely to be discarded.
GlobalLRUOldest()	Promotes the discardable object to the top of the discard list, making it the next candidate for discarding.
GlobalSize()	Returns the true size (due to granularity) of the object in bytes. Returns zero for an invalid handle or if the object has been discarded.
GlobalHandle()	Returns the handle for an object when passed its segment or selector value.

continues

Function	Description
GlobalFlags()	Returns information on whether a given memory block is shareable, EMS bankable, or discardable, or has itself been discarded. The return value also contains the lock count of the object. See the filter #defines that follow for more information.
GlobalDOSAlloc()*	Allocates an object out of the lower megabyte of conventional memory, specifically the TPA. Used for memory buffers when communicating with a TSR or other non-Windows application. Memory from this area doesn't need to be locked and should be used as little as possible because it is scarce.
GlobalDOSFree()*	Frees a DOS-based lower-megabyte object.

Not available under Windows NT

These #define values are used with calls to GlobalAlloc() and GlobalRealloc():

Global[Re]Alloc()	Description
GMEM_FIXED	Allocates fixed memory.
GMEM_MOVEABLE	Allocates moveable memory.
GMEM_NODISCARD	Allocates nondiscardable memory.
GMEM_DISCARDABLE	Allocates discardable memory. Used mostly with code and resource segments, which are demand-loaded by the operating system.
GMEM_NOCOMPACT	Indicates that memory should not be compacted or discarded to satisfy the allocation.
GMEM_ZEROINIT	Initializes memory contents to zero.
GMEM_MODIFY	Used with GlobalRealloc() to change attributes of memory without altering its size.

Global[Re]Alloc()	*Description*
GMEM_NOTBANKED	Allocates memory that is guaranteed not to be banked into EMS page frames. Cannot be used with GMEM_NOTIFY.
GMEM_LOWER	Same as GMEM_NOTBANKED.
GMEM_SHARE	Allocates the memory to be shared by multiple applications. This flag must be used for any memory to be used with DDE or the clipboard. Also used by libraries to allocate global heap memory on behalf of themselves, and not the current task.
GMEM_DDESHARE	Same as GMEM_SHARE.
GMEM_NOTIFY	Calls the developer-supplied notification routine whenever the object is to be discarded.
GHND	Used with **Global[Re]Alloc()** to create a moveable block of zero-initialized memory.
GPTR	Used with **Global[Re]Alloc()** to create a fixed block of zero-initialized global memory.

These #define values are used as a mask on the return value from Windows API's **GlobalFlags()** function, which retrieves information on a global heap object:

GlobalFlags() *Return Value Bit Mask*	*Description*
GMEM_DDESHARE	See GMEM_SHARE.
GMEM_SHARE	Indicates a shareable object.
GMEM_DISCARDABLE	Indicates a discardable object.
GMEM_DISCARDED	Indicates that an object has been discarded.

continues

193

GlobalFlags() Return Value Bit Mask	Description
GMEM_NOT_BANKED	Indicates an EMS nonbankable object.
GMEM_LOCKCOUNT	Indicates the lock count of object.

Example Use of Global Flags:

```
if(GMEM_DISCARDED & GlobalFlags(hGlobal))
{
    // Block has been discarded
}
```

The following typedefs, #defines, and messages are all related to global heap usage.

Miscellaneous	Description
HGLOBAL	A handle to a global memory block.
GLOBALHANDLE	See HGLOBAL.
WM_COMPACTING	A message sent to all top-level windows when Windows detects that too much system time is spent compacting memory. wParam contains a value indicating the percentage of time spent compacting memory over a 30–60 second interval (8000h == 50%).

The Local Heap

Any local heap API calls are referred to as subsegment allocation, because all the objects created out of the heap exist in a single segment. This contrasts with allocations from the global heap, where each allocated object is its own segment. The local heap can be quite efficient for this reason, because descriptors aren't wasted for every memory allocation. The local heap, however, suffers from the 64K segment limit and therefore doesn't see as much use as it could. Most often, the local heap is reserved for multiple small allocations consisting of anywhere from 10 bytes to several thousand bytes. Both applications and libraries can have a local heap, but with libraries it's optional. When Windows first loads an application, it automatically pre-creates several local heap entries that point to the "temp" drive and the drive used by Windows.

Every moveable local heap object actually allocates a small portion of fixed memory for the object. Actually, every 20 or so moveable local heap allocations will create a small fixed memory block, containing pointers to the moveable blocks. The local heap handles in source code actually point to these fixed heap objects and obviously don't point directly to a moveable object's data. This would provide no mechanism for moving the object, because all the handle values in the source code would need to get updated. Unfortunately, as mentioned earlier, Windows never frees these memory blocks, but only reuses them. This means that when the blocks are created, they represent a permanent sandbar that exists for the life of the data segment.

The Windows API provides the following local heap management functions:

Function	Description
LocalAlloc()	Allocates a block of memory from the local heap, which is limited to 64K, or much less in the case of a local heap located in an automatic data segment.
LocalRealloc()	Reallocates a memory block, increasing or decreasing its size. Memory can possibly be compacted and discarded as a result.
LocalFree()	Frees a specified object if its reference count is zero.
LocalLock()	Returns a near pointer to a specified object, and increments the lock count on an object, preventing it from being moved or discarded.
LocalUnlock()	Decrements the lock count on an object. When the lock count is zero, the object is subject to movement and possible discarding.
LocalCompact()*	Moves and, if necessary, discards objects to satisfy the requested allocation.

continues

195

Function	Description
LocalDiscard()	A macro (using LocalRealloc()) that discards an object.
LocalSize()	Returns the true size (due to granularity) of the object in bytes. Returns zero for an invalid handle or if the object has been discarded.
LocalShrink()*	Shrinks the size of a needlessly large data segment. The amount decreased will never infringe on existing heap, stack, or other data.
LocalHandle()	Returns the handle for an object when passed its segment or selector value.
LocalInit()*	Initializes the local heap for a specified data segment. Leaves the data segment locked. The data segment should be unlocked with a call to UnlockData().
LocalFlags()	Returns information on whether a specified memory block is discardable or has itself been discarded. The return value also contains the lock count of the object. See the #defines that follow for more information.

*Not implemented under Windows NT

The following list of #defines are used in calls to LocalAlloc() and LocalRealloc():

Local[Re]Alloc() Flag	Description
LMEM_FIXED	Allocates fixed memory.
LMEM_MOVEABLE	Allocates moveable memory.
LMEM_NODISCARD	Allocates nondiscardable memory.
LMEM_DISCARDABLE	Allocates discardable memory. Not often used for local heap objects.
LMEM_NOCOMPACT	Indicates that memory should not be compacted or discarded to satisfy the allocation.

`Local[Re]Alloc()` *Flag*	*Description*
LMEM_ZEROINIT	Initializes memory contents to zero.
LMEM_MODIFY	Used with `LocalRealloc()` to change attributes of memory, without altering its size.
LHND	Used with `Local[Re]Alloc()` to create a moveable block of zero-initialized memory.
LPTR	Used with `Local[Re]Alloc()` to create a fixed block of zero-initialized memory.

Miscellaneous	*Description*
LMEM_DISCARDABLE	"&" this `#define` value with the return value from `LocalFlags()` to tell whether the object is discardable.
LMEM_DISCARDED	"&" this `#define` value with the return value from `LocalFlags()` to tell whether the object has been discarded.
LMEM_LOCKCOUNT	"&" this value with the return value from `LocalFlags()` to determine the object's lock count.
HLOCAL	A handle to a local memory object.

Multiple Local Heaps (Subsegment Allocation)

Yet another problem with local heaps is that they were designed around the basic premise that a module will have only one. Of course, this works just fine for the majority of applications; however, a fair number will require some kind of implementation involving multiple local heaps. After all, global heap overhead is too expensive at a minimum of one selector per application. The global heap, as mentioned earlier, should be used only for the storage of larger objects, whereas the local heap is designed to be used with a larger number of smaller allocations, on the order of 10 bytes to several kilobytes.

The problem, if indeed it can be called that, is that all the local heap management API calls assume the current data segment for all heap operations. This can easily be overcome by prepping the value of DS before any local heap calls are made.

What kind of modules need this kind of functionality? Specialized memory managers are a good first choice. A second might be a library that wanted to keep a separate local heap for every client application that has attached to it. The application's local heap could be used by the library in this case; however, the local heap of an application is kind of an unknown as far as the library is concerned. How is the library supposed to know how the application will be using its local heap? It's not supposed to know, which is the reason for separate local heaps. Of course, this mechanism requires that any client modules of the library explicitly call a "Hello" and "Goodbye" function, but doing this usually isn't a problem.

The first step in dynamically creating a local heap is to allocate a global heap segment. This segment is then prepped by calling `LocalInit()`, which reserves the first 16 bytes in the data segment for a series of internal pointers. Before `LocalInit()` can be called, however, the true size of the global heap object needs to be ascertained. `LocalInit()` must know the exact size of the data segment, and due to granularity, the heap functions don't always return the exact amount asked for—sometimes the returned amount is higher. Next, the segment must be locked and the data segment register prepped for the new local heap segment. Remember, DS is already pointing to your module, and it needs to be changed to reflect the value of the global heap segment just created. Finally, any local heap routines are called and allocations are made, and then the original value of DS is restored and the function can exit.

The following code illustrates how to dynamically create a local heap:

```
HGLOBAL hGlobal;
LPSTR   lpBuffer;


BOOL RetVal;

WORD wSegment; // You say segment, I say selector!
WORD wSize;    // Size doesn't have to be a dword because
               // local heaps can't be greater than 64K

if((hGlobal = GlobalAlloc(GHND, 4096L)) == NULL)
{
    // Handle error and leave routine

    ...

}
```

```
if((lpBuffer = GlobalLock(hGlobal)) == NULL)
{
    // Free block just alloc'd

    GlobalFree(hGlobal);

    // Now handle errors and leave


    ...
}

wSegment = SELECTOROF(lpBuffer);           // Getting hi-word
wSize    = (WORD) GlobalSize(hGlobal) - 16; // Get true size

RetValue = LocalInit(wSeg, 0, wSize);      // Create the heap

GlobalUnlock(hGlobal);
GlobalUnlock(hGlobal);    // Unlock again because LocalInit leaves a
                          // lock outstanding on DS
```

Now, of course, some method must exist to establish the DS register before any local heap API calls are made. The following code does just that:

...using variables from the previous example...

```
if((lpBuffer = GlobalLock(hGlobal)) == NULL)
{
    // Handle errors and leave


    ...
}

wSegment = SELECTOROF(lpBuffer);

_asm
{
    push ds
    mov  ax, wSegment
    mov  ds, ax
}
```

...local heap API calls...

```
_asm
{
```

```
    pop ds
}
```

```
GlobalUnlock(hGlobal);
```

Of course, if the intent of the subsegment allocation is to interface with a client module, a whole "wrapper" API must be built around functions similar to the previous one, returning dword values consisting of the global heap segment in the high word and the offset of the local heap object in the low word. There's no way around this because the heap allocator is no longer working with the default data segment. As a result, all references are far.

Atoms

It's well-known that under Windows, all common code and resource segments are shared by like instances of an application. Along this line, Windows' atom management API provides a unique way to manage strings. Using atoms, a string is added to a table, and a unique ATOM handle identifier is returned for further access to the string. If the string already exists in the table, its reference count is merely incremented and a duplicate handle is returned. Windows allows only one atom table per program data segment or dynamically allocated task segment and can keep track of as many as 65,535 occurrences of a particular string for each table. Windows guarantees that for any one atom table, only one occurrence of the string is stored. Atoms are perfect for programs requiring heavy string usage. Instead of manipulating numerous variable-length strings of characters, you can use a simple atom handle or an array of atom handles to access strings, eliminating most overhead. Management of data structures of any size is greatly simplified when using atoms rather than character strings.

Windows provides two basic types of atom tables: *local atom tables,* which store atoms privately in a module's data segment, and the *global atom table,* which holds globally shared atoms that are used by DDE. A global atom table requires no special preparation because Windows is the one assuming all the overhead. Local atom tables, however, require that a local heap be established for the data segment. For the automatic data segment of an application or a library, this isn't a problem because a heap is created automatically by Windows during the execution of the module's startup code. Data segments dynamically allocated by a task, however, must make a single call to **LocalInit()** before using any of Windows' atom management (or local heap) functions. **LocalInit()** reserves the first 16 bytes of the segment for use as a task header, which contains, among other things, a pointer to the local atom table for the segment. Atom tables residing in dynamically allocated segments must also make an additional call to `InitAtomTable()`, which creates a small atom table out of a fixed local heap object in the module's data segment. In fact, every unique local atom created by an application resides in a separate (and fixed) local heap object slightly bigger than the size of the string. The extra bytes are there, because like every local heap allocation, a few bytes need to be reserved for the arena structure, which contains pointers and other bits of data. `InitAtomTable()` isn't required for the automatic data segment of a module because, like the local heap, a call to `InitAtomTable()` is automatically performed by Windows when the program makes its first call to `AddAtom()`.

The Windows API provides the following functions for atom management:

Function	Description
`InitAtomTable()`	Initializes the atom table in the current data segment. It is not needed for the default data segment because it's done automatically by Windows. The size of the table should be a prime number. The number 37 is used by default.
`AddAtom()`	Adds a string to the local atom table. If a string already exists, the reference count is merely incremented, and a duplicate atom value is returned.
`DeleteAtom()`	Decrements the reference count of a string in the atom table, removing it when the count is zero.
`FindAtom()`	Finds a specified string in the atom table, returning a handle.
`GetAtomName()`	Fills a buffer with a string representing a specified local atom handle.
`GlobalAddAtom()`	Adds a string to the global atom table, which is used by DDE. If a string already exists, the reference count is merely incremented, and a duplicate atom value is returned.

continues

Function	Description
GlobalDeleteAtom()	Decrements the reference count of a string in the global atom table, removing it when the count is zero.
GlobalFindAtom()	Finds a specified string in the global atom table, returning a handle.
GlobalGetAtomName()	Fills a buffer with a string representing a specified global atom handle.
MAKEINTATOM()	Creates an integer atom that can be added to the atom table through a call to AddAtom(). The return value is a far pointer (whose high word is zero) to the integer atom. This lets the atom-management functions know that this is an integer atom and not a string atom.
GetAtomHandle()	Returns a handle to a local heap structure for a local atom. Not recommended for Windows 3.x; provided only for compatibility with previous versions of Windows.

Resources

To the developer, resources provide an excellent means for storing any of several kinds of data. The obvious use of a resource file is for storing icons, bitmaps, cursors, and dialogs. Resource files also can be used to encapsulate entire data files, to abstract any "structural" data from program code, and as a place to put any end-user or distributor-alterable data, which can range from simple string tables to developer-defined *and* customizable graphical resources. Resources are compiled in two separate stages, somewhat comparable to the program compilation and linking process. First, resources are compiled (tokenized) into a .RES file. Second, after the executable or loadable module has been generated, the compiled resource file is attached to the module, with the .EXE module header updated to reflect the addition of all the new resources, segments, and so on. Even if no resources are going to be used by a module, an empty .RC file still needs to be created and compiled into the target module—if anything, just so Windows can put bytes in the module header indicating that no resources exist.

Objects listed in a resource file are basically in one of two formats. Either the object is defined completely, as is the case with dialogs and menus, or the object is defined via a pointer to a file name, as is the case with icons, bitmaps, and cursors. Obviously, it would be difficult to store and input binary data for these objects into a resource file by hand or otherwise (it can be done though). Some objects are definable on a single line in the resource file, and some objects require several lines to describe them, using a BEGIN and END block to sandwich the data. In either case, the line length cannot exceed 256 characters. Resources can be assigned the same attributes as program code and data segments.

The resource compiler uses the following general format:

```
rc [options] resourcefile [executable/loadable module]
```

Because resources are compiled in two stages, it takes two sets of command lines to invoke the resource compiler. Additionally, libraries must specify the module name; otherwise, .EXE will be assumed.

For compiling resources into a .RES resource file:

```
rc -r [options] resourcefile.rc
```

For linking a resource file to an executable application:

```
rc [options] resourcefile.rc [executable.exe]
```

For linking a resource file to a loadable module (library):

```
rc [options] resourcefile.rc library.dll
```

Several optional parameters can be used with the resource compiler, although most deal with real mode and as such aren't as useful anymore. Table 4.1 shows the options used by rc.

As mentioned in Chapter 3, "Program and Module Fundamentals," resources are always loaded into the global heap as moveable and discardable objects. There are only two exceptions to this rule. The first is that a select few "precious" resources are not flagged as discardable. This includes things such as the mouse's arrow cursor and Program Manager's accelerator table. (Two resources that see quite a bit of action, no?) In cases such as these, it would make absolutely no sense to discard such small objects only to have them reloaded just clock cycles later. The second exception involves dialog resources with edit windows using the DS_LOCALEDIT flag. In this case, the resource data is stored in the local heap of the instance creating the dialog. This is

always the case when the window is created dynamically in the module's source code.

Table 4.1. Resource compiler options.

Option	Description
-? or -H	Displays a list of resource compiler commands.
-d	Defines a symbol for the resource compiler preprocessor. This symbol can be used with preprocessor statements such as #ifdef and #ifndef.
-e	For libraries, it changes the default location of global memory from below the EMS bank line to above it.
-fe	Renames the executable/loadable module.
-fo	Renames the .RES compiled file.
-i	Has the resource compiler search the specified directory before searching any directories in the INCLUDE environment variable.
-k	Disables the load-optimization feature of the resource compiler. Normally, all preloaded resources are packed together in memory, regardless of their position in the resource file, allowing Windows to load the resources much faster.
-lim32	Indicates that the module uses expanded memory according to the LIM EMS specification version 3.2.
-multinst	Specifies that instances are not to share EMS banks, which is the default.
-p	Used with libraries that will be called by only a single application (but possibly multiple instances). Allows more library segments to be loaded above the bank line.
-r	Used to create a separate .RES file from the .RC file, not automatically compiling the resources into the module.
-t	Compiles a module for protected-mode use only.
-v	Verbose option for resource compilation.
-x	Tells the resource compiler not to check the INCLUDE environment variable when searching for include files and resources.

Resources get their names by their mere presence in a resource file; however, they have much in common with certain dynamically created GDI and User objects, particularly bitmaps, cursors, icons, menus, fonts, and dialogs. Each of these "resource" types shares the same data format as its equivalent resource, except that they differ in how and where they're loaded.

Note: Throughout this book (as well as in the SDK manuals) it has always been stated that resources are read-only. Well, this is and isn't true. When a resource is loaded and then locked to get a pointer to the object, the pointer actually points to read-write memory. It's quite easy to load a custom resource data structure and then twiddle a few bytes, modifying the copy of the resource as it sits in memory. In fact, any task that tries to load the same resource will get a pointer to the modified copy. Of course, when the resource is unlocked and eventually discarded, the original resource is what gets loaded. This trick is mentioned only as an aside, because I can't imagine anyone at Microsoft sanctioning the modification of resources. However, for those truly unique situations, who knows what hacks might need to be performed?

Getting Resourceful with Resources

All the custom controls presented in this book perform their initialization shortly after receiving their first WM_MOVE message. It all starts with a temporary window property that gets established during the control's WM_CREATE. During WM_MOVE this temporary property is checked for. If it doesn't exist, control is returned to `DefWindowProc()`. However, if it does exist, it is promptly removed, and the control's initialization is performed. Only as early as the first WM_MOVE message is a window guaranteed to have enough "overhead" already established by Windows that most initializations involving various window messages can be performed. This includes retrieving and setting window text and adding strings to a listbox or combobox.

All the custom controls presented in the book use a special system for customizing their appearance and performing certain initializations. Basically, it involves the presence of custom resource data structures, with the name of the structure being the ID of the control. This method works quite handily for quickly identifying the data structure for a window. For dialogs, which have no control ID, the class of the dialog is used as the name of the data

structure. Remember that all resources can be given a numeric or an alphanumeric name.

Each data structure defines various attributes of the control. Common to all control data structures is the first string of word values, which ends in a null. These words define the extended style bits of the control, specifying whether the control has a 3D appearance, among other things. The second common piece of information (which follows the ending null in the structure) is the ASCII label text associated with the control. Because static windows are no longer used for labeling controls, some means must exist for specifying the control's label. Although several functions are provided to get and set this label, it can also be established in the structure. Following the label field in the structure is data completely private to the control class. In the case of the listbox and combobox custom controls, this data specifies the listbox entries that are to be initially stuffed into the listbox at "create" time. The bitmap control uses the rest of the structure to define the bitmap to be viewed, whereas the button control uses the structure to define a series of bitmaps that are to represent the normal, pushed, focus, and disabled button states. The grab bar control uses the rest of the structure to define which windows it is to split between.

The only problem with this method is that the resource file can very quickly get busy. Some possible solutions include separating the custom control resource structures into separate #include files, combining the individual control structures into one larger structure, and finally, offloading some of the structures into raw ASCII files that must be manually parsed and processed.

Windows offers two methods of storing custom resource data structures. The developer can use the predefined RCDATA structure, for defining raw resource data, or a custom resource can be built instead. The format of a raw data resource is as follows:

```
ResourceName RCDATA [load-option] [mem-option]
BEGIN
    "Now is the time...\\0",
    0xffff,
    255
END
```

A custom resource can be in one of the following formats:

```
ResourceName ResourceClass [load-option] [mem-option]
BEGIN
    "Now is the time...\\0",
    0xffff,
```

```
    255
END
```

or

```
ResourceName ResourceClass [load-option] [mem-option] filename.ext
```

The problem with either of these types of structures is that the resource compiler is only smart enough to insert a single #define into a field in the resource. Specifying several OR'd #define values just isn't possible, generating an error. This is why the style WORDs defining extended style attributes for the custom controls aren't OR'd together in a single field, but are listed in a comma-delimited series, ending with a null value, to indicate the end of the list.

Initializing data structures and controls through a resource file makes for very clean source code. Unfortunately, because resources aren't truly read-write, and because applications and windows on the desktop can't truly be considered objects (and therefore be made persistent), the only kind of initialization that can be done here is somewhat static in nature. After all, the only way you can change the resources so that they're different the next time they're loaded by the application is by changing the .RC file and recompiling the resources into the executable again. Despite the compromises, resources still remain an excellent place to extra any kind of data possible.

The Windows API provides the following functions for manipulating resources:

Function	Description
LoadAccelerators()	Loads an accelerator table from a specified module instance. No cleanup is necessary when using this function.
LoadBitmap()	Loads bitmap from a specified module instance. If the instance is NULL, predefined "system-internal" bitmaps can be loaded. Clean up with call to DeleteObject().
LoadCursor()	Loads a cursor from a specified module instance. If the instance is NULL, predefined "system-internal" cursors can be loaded. No cleanup is necessary when using this function.

continues

Function	Description
LoadIcon()	Loads an icon from a specified module instance. If the instance is NULL, predefined Windows "system-internal" icons can be loaded. No cleanup is necessary when using this function.
LoadMenu()	Loads a menu from a specified module instance. Cleanup with a call to DestroyMenu() is required when a menu isn't associated with a window.
LoadResource()	Uses a handle from FindResource() to load a resource into the global heap, returning a global heap handle to the resource. The resource is not actually loaded until the object is locked using LockResource(). This function should not be used as a generic loader for all resource types. In those cases, a special function is provided (LoadCursor()). Cleanup is required with a call to FreeResource().
LoadString()	Loads a string from a specified module instance. The string is copied along with a terminating null. No cleanup is required.
FindResource()	Determines the location of a resource and returns the handle identifying it. This handle is used by LoadResource().
FreeResource()	Frees the resource associated with the handle returned by LoadResource(). The resource is freed only if its reference count is zero.

Function	*Description*
`LockResource()`	Locks a resource in memory and increments its reference count. A locked resource is not subject to movement or discarding. Before a discardable resource is about to be locked with this call, a resource handler routine is called. `UnlockResource()` must eventually be called.
`UnlockResource()`	Unlocks a resource and decrements the reference count. When the count is zero, the object is subject to movement and discarding. Implemented as a `GlobalUnlock()` macro.
`SizeofResource()`	Returns the size (in bytes) of a specified resource. The size might be slightly larger due to granularity. Used with `AccessResource()`.
`AccessResource()`	Opens a specified resource file as read-only, returning a DOS file handle. The resource file must be closed with a call to `_lclose()`.
`AllocResource()`	Allocates uninitialized global heap memory for a specified resource. All resources are loaded in this manner, with this function actually being called by `LoadResource()`. Cleanup is required with a call to `FreeResource()`.
`SetResourceHandler()`	Installs a "resource-loader" callback function. Windows calls this function before any call to `LockResource()`, allowing a module to process and load its own resources. The typedef `RSRCHDLRPROC` is used to specify a function callable by `SetResourceHandler()`.

continues

Function	Description
MAKEINTRESOURCE()	A macro used to convert an integer value into a long pointer to a string, with the high word of the pointer set to zero. This macro essentially converts an integer resource identifier into one that can be used by Windows' resource-management functions, and it is used in place of the normal resource string name. Referring to resources is much faster using this method.
GetFileResource()	Copies a resource from a specified file into a buffer. Windows 3.1 only.
GetFileResourceSize()	Returns from a passed file name the size of the resource specified by type and ID. Windows 3.1 only.

The following #defines are used by FindResource() to locate a specific type of resource in a module:

Resource Type	Description
RT_ACCELERATOR	Identifies an accelerator table resource.
RT_BITMAP	Identifies a bitmap resource.
RT_CURSOR	Identifies a cursor resource.
RT_DIALOG	Identifies a dialog resource.
RT_FONT	Identifies a font resource.
RT_FONTDIR	Identifies a font directory resource.
RT_ICON	Identifies an icon resource.
RT_MENU	Identifies a menu resource.
RT_RCDATA	Identifies user-defined raw resource data.
RT_STRING	Identifies a string resource.

Despite the presence of a FindResource() #define value for every type of resource, Windows just won't allow certain resources to be loaded by

`FindResource()`, and with some resources Windows just prefers that an appropriate loader function be used instead. The following list documents those resources:

Resource	Load Function
Accelerator	`LoadAccelerators()`
Bitmap	`LoadBitmap()`
Cursor*	`LoadCursor()`
Icon*	`LoadIcon()`
Menu	`LoadMenu()`
String*	`LoadString()`

*`FindResource()` *cannot be used with these resource types.*

Sometimes, though, even Windows' resource loader functions don't work quite the way they should. For example, device-independent bitmaps (that is, 256 colors) cannot be loaded by `LoadBitmap()`. Instead, the functions `FindResource()` and `LoadResource()` must be used to preserve the palette and other information, which is ignored by `LoadBitmap()`.

String Tables

String tables are used to isolate country-specific string data from executable code. A string table contains a series of country-dependent character strings (each referenced by an ID) that are loaded on demand by the developer for use in message boxes and any other kind of display requiring text/language-specific information. Locating such strings in a simple resource file allows them to be modified later by (possibly) a nonprogrammer working to port language-specific portions of the application to that of another country. Each string can be no longer than 255 characters and must occupy a single line in the resource file. Embedding a carriage return into a string is done by inserting a "\012" between the appropriate portions of text (that is, `"Line One\012Line Two"`).

Unlike other resources that generally are loaded into the global heap as a single "segment," string tables are loaded into the global heap as (possibly) a series of separate segments, each containing a group of related strings. The grouping of strings in separate segments allows related strings to be loaded and discarded at the same time. The grouping mechanism bundles 16 strings to a single segment, using the upper 12 bits of the identifier to determine which segment is used to hold the strings. Any string resource containing the same 12 bits in its identifier is bundled into the same resource segment.

Following is an example of how you might use and take advantage of string tables:

```
// module.h:

#define IDS_STOP     1
#define IDS_ERROR    2
#define IDS_INFO     3
#define IDS_WARNING 4

#define IDS_FILENOTFOUND 30
#define IDS_DIRNOTFOUND  31


// module.rc:

STRINGTABLE
BEGIN
    IDS_STOP,    "STOP"
    IDS_ERROR,   "ERROR"
    IDS_INFO,    "INFORMATION"
    IDS_WARNING, "WARNING"

    IDS_FILENOTFOUND, "File not found"
    IDS_DIRNOTFOUND,  "Directory not found"
END


// module.c:
...

// Uh-oh, we couldn't file a file, so send message via MsgBox

MessageDisplay(hInstMyApp, hDlgApp, IDS_FILENOTFOUND, IDS_ERROR);


...

int FAR PASCAL MessageDisplay
(
    HINSTANCE hInst, HWND hWnd, int nMsgID, int nCaptionID
)
```

```
{
    BYTE Cap[20];
    BYTE Msg[50];

    WORD wIconType;

    // Load MsgBox text. Checking return value really isn't necessary

    LoadString(hInst, nMsgID, (LPSTR) Msg, sizeof(Msg));

    // Load caption string

    LoadString(hInst, nCaptionID, (LPSTR) Cap, sizeof(Cap));

    // Auto-determine the icon type to use. It's very handy to have
    // the caption id auto-determine the icon type. This suffices in
    // 90% of msg cases anyway.

    switch(nCaptionID)
    {
        case IDS_STOP  :
        case IDS_ERROR :

            IconType = MB_ICONSTOP;
            break;

        case IDS_WARNING :

            IconType = MB_ICONEXCLAMATION;
            break;

        case IDS_INFO :

            IconType = MB_ICONINFORMATION;
            break;

        default :

            break;
    }

    IconType |= MB_OK;

    return(MessageBox(hWnd, (LPSTR) Msg, (LPSTR) Cap, IconType));
}
```

Basically, string tables are another form of indirection for a module. Instead of being hard-coded into an application, string constants are accessed indirectly via a single ID value. This permits the changing of the data referenced by the ID but doesn't change the ID by which the string is referenced. The use of string tables is also advantageous because the strings no longer take up space in the module's automatic data segment; rather, they are stored as discardable, demand-loaded resources.

Objects, Handles, and Indirection

Although it's probably obvious, the smooth-flowing chaos that is Windows is made possible by the power and flexibility of handle-based indirection. Every distinct, discrete object in Windows is referred to by a handle.

A handle almost always is used either as an index into some kind of "master" table, as a pointer to another pointer, or in the case of fixed objects, as a pointer to the actual data. If the handle represents an index, the handle's value usually is shifted by some predetermined amount and added to the base of the table to address a descriptor for that object. (Figure 4.6 shows an example of indirection provided by handles.) In either case, the handle indirectly references an object, allowing Windows to change the descriptor value and the "physical" address of the object without changing the handle by which the object is referenced. All objects under Windows have a unique handle associated with them, and they usually are subject to movement, discarding, and so on by Windows' memory manager. Handles are guaranteed to be unique only among the object's class. A handle to a specific window will always be unique among the pool of active window handles. Although a window handle might equal a GDI object handle—a brush, for example—the two would never be used in the same context; thus, uniqueness is still preserved. It's very important to understand the role that handles and indirection play in Windows.

Overhead for Windows objects falls into one of two places: the local heap of a module or the system-wide global heap. It really depends on how and where the object was created. If the object is a loadable resource, the data for the actual object (a bitmap, for example) is allocated out of the global heap. This even includes the child objects (windows) inside a dialog, because their storage space, too, is allocated out of the global heap. If the code required to create the object exists inside the module, overhead for the object often is placed in some module's local heap, which has a 64K limit. A call to `CreateDialog()` adds object entries to the global heap, because it references a resource structure in a module's .RES file, whereas a call to `CreateWindow()` ends up taking space in the local heap of User. All the `LoadIcon()`- and `LoadBitmap()`-type functions add entries to the global heap, because they all use pre-created resources. When a demand-loaded bitmap or icon is selected into a display context, a duplicate entry in the global heap is created by GDI to hold the object for its own purposes. This can be verified in Heap Walker by double-clicking any of the private resources owned by GDI.

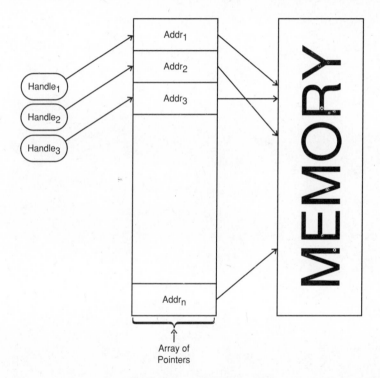

Figure 4.6. Indirection provided by handles.

If you haven't guessed by now, nothing under Windows is accessed directly— nothing. Indirection is available everywhere under Windows, because indirection is applied to function calls (thunks), memory (local and global descriptor tables), display contexts, and message queues, to name just a few things. In fact, the only programs with direct access to anything are the 32-bit flat-model virtual device drivers and Windows' virtual memory manager itself.

The following objects are all referenced via a (currently) 16-bit handle:

Object	Overhead	Cleanup	Typedef
Accelerator	Kernel	N/A	HACCEL*
Bitmap	GDI (28–?K)	`DeleteObject()`	HBITMAP
Brush	GDI (26–38 bytes)	`DeleteObject()`	HBRUSH
Control	User (60–70 bytes)	`DestroyWindow()`	WORD
Cursor	GDI	`DestroyCursor()`	HCURSOR

Device context	GDI (28–?K)	`DeleteDC()`
		`ReleaseDC()`
		`EndPaint()`
			HDC

Device driver	Kernel	N/A	HDRVR*
Dialog	User	`DestroyWindow()` `EndDialog()`	HWND
File	Kernel/DOS	N/A	HFILE*
Font	GDI (30–42 bytes)	N/A	HFONT
GDI object	GDI	`DeleteObject()`	HGDIOBJ*
Global atom	Kernel	`GlobalDeleteAtom()`	ATOM
Global memory	Kernel (24 bytes)	`GlobalFree()`	HGLOBAL*
Icon	GDI	`DestroyIcon()`	HICON
Instance	User	`PostQuitMessage()`	HINSTANCE
Library	Kernel	`FreeLibrary()`	HMODULE*
Local atom	Module	`DeleteAtom()`	ATOM
Local memory	Module (4–6 bytes)	`LocalFree()`	HLOCAL*
Menu	GDI (20 bytes +20 per item)	`DestroyMenu()`	HMENU
Metafile	GDI	`DeleteMetaFile()`	HMETAFILE*
Module	Kernel	N/A	HMODULE*
Palette	GDI (22 bytes)	N/A	HPALETTE
Pen	GDI (22 bytes)	`DeleteObject()`	HPEN

Object	Overhead	Cleanup	Typedef
Resource	Kernel (24 bytes)	`FreeResource()`	HRSRC*
Region	GDI (38–?K)	N/A	HRGN
Task	Kernel/DOS	N/A	HTASK*
WindowClass	User (40–50 bytes)	`UnregisterClass()`	N/A
Window	User (60–70 bytes)	`DestroyWindow()`	HWND

*New typedef with Windows 3.1

The amount of overhead in bytes for each object type is an approximation. The numbers generated come from using Windows' 3.1 Heap Walker and Soft-ICE/W to dump the local heaps of User and GDI. Numbers are a couple of bytes higher for Windows 3.0 objects. Remember that for certain objects, such as bitmaps and regions, the numbers can be several kilobytes higher.

Also note that for certain objects, several cleanup functions are listed. Use the function appropriate for how the object was created. For example, modal dialogs are destroyed with `EndDialog()`, whereas modeless dialogs are destroyed with `DestroyWindow()`. The same rule also applies to device contexts. Window device contexts gotten using `BeginPaint()` are destroyed with a call to `EndPaint()`, whereas window device contexts gotten using `GetDC()` or `GetWindowDC()` are destroyed with a call to `ReleaseDC()`. Memory device contexts are destroyed with a call to `DeleteDC()`.

Cleanup for handled objects depends on how and where the object was created. The vast majority must be explicitly deleted by the user after they are no longer needed. This is especially true of objects created by an application that exist in another module's local heap, such as GDI and User. Most of the GDI objects are shared by Windows among multiple modules, so they aren't automatically destroyed when a module terminates. This could change in a future version of Windows. If all the GDI and User objects were implemented via the global heap rather than the local heap, chances are that cleanup wouldn't be necessary. The same also applies to any libraries that are dynamically (via `LoadLibrary()`) loaded by a module, because they must be explicitly freed when they are no longer needed. Windows doesn't auto-destroy objects that are shared among modules.

Any objects that are "owned" or "attached" to another object usually are destroyed along with their owner. This includes the child windows of a dialog, any menus attached to a window, and allocated global and local heap entries for a module (including loaded resources). The best check that can be done to ensure that object storage is being freed correctly is to check the amount

of "Free System Resources" in Program Manager, making sure that it doesn't increase by large amounts every time your module is loaded and unloaded. A slight increase is normal; however, it shouldn't keep increasing with each unloading of the module. To help pinpoint the problem more quickly, use Heap Walker's snapshot feature to take pictures of the local heaps of GDI, and User, which helps pinpoint any leftover objects.

Heap Walker

Heap Walker is used to view the structure and contents of the system-wide global heap, which contains memory used by Windows and all its applications and libraries. Heap Walker is most commonly used by the developer to view the effects of an application's program segments on this special area. Heap Walker's screen essentially is one big listbox, with each row in the listbox representing an allocated object in the global heap. Think of Heap Walker as a heap-oriented report generator. Just like any good report generator, Heap Walker column headings, many of which can be sorted on, are used to note different object attributes, including things such as the address, handle, size, lock status, type (code, data), and additional information. Several global heap views are available, including a view of all heap entries, entries only in the Least-Recently Used list, and a view consisting solely of entries in the free list. Figure 4.7 shows a sample Heap Walker display.

In the Heap Walker display, notice that the Task Database entry is now referred to as just "Task." Code segments also include their segment number rather than just "CODE." The "Group_" series of entries, such as Group_Icon and Group_Cursor, is used to keep track of miscellaneous information about the resource.

Sorting by module name and scrolling through the rows of entries, you can fairly easily get an idea of the size, location, and presence of a module's segments. This is in addition to being able to view the effect an application has on the segments of other programs, mainly on the automatic data segments of Windows' GDI and User modules. Figure 4.8 shows a Heap Walker dump of GDI's automatic data segment. Besides allowing an object-by-object dump of the global heap, Heap Walker also is capable of displaying the local heaps of data segments that have taken the appropriate steps to create a local heap, which mainly consists of a call to `LocalInit()`. Using the function to continually monitor the size of GDI and User's local heaps ensures that your application is destroying unneeded objects and not leaving them lying around, taking up valuable memory.

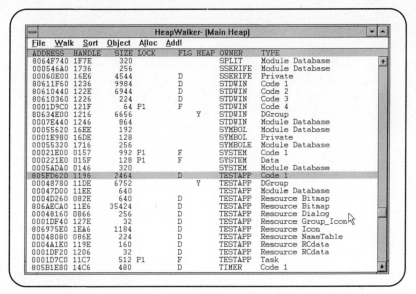

Figure 4.7.
A sample Heap Walker display.

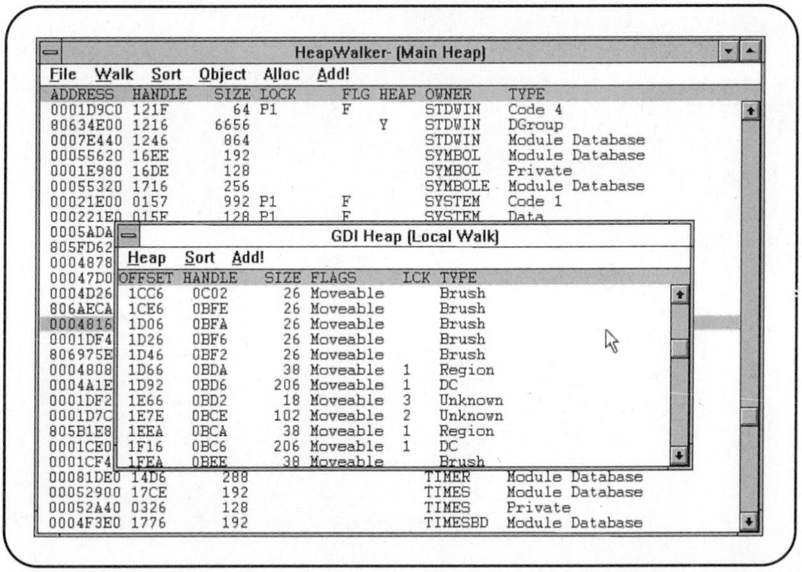

Figure 4.8.
An example of GDI's automatic data segment in Heap Walker.

To make it easier to compare what can potentially be reams of information, Heap Walker provides a "file.txt" heap-dumping routine, making it easier to get a before-and-after snapshot of the memory. It's a good idea to get a "base" reference point by taking a snapshot of the User and GDI heaps before the application is actually executed. Then, after activating and working with the module in question for several minutes and over several instances, do a final snapshot of User and GDI's local heaps. Anything larger than 10K indicates a possible problem. At the least, it should be a red flag to take a look at the module's cleanup procedures. Just like the weight-loss plans advertised on late-night cable television, the amount of normal User and GDI data segment expansion varies from application to application. To be really sure, run the application 30 to 40 times, and look for data segment deltas approaching 20K to 30K or larger. One of the nicest things about the new version of Heap Walker is that it's so flexible. The 3.0 version didn't allow local heap windows to be sorted or captured to a text file.

Heap Walker also can intelligently display certain GDI objects, including bitmaps, cursors, dialogs, icons, and menus (see Figure 4.9). At the very least, it can do a raw hex dump of the object. The Windows 3.0 version of Heap Walker was limited to dumping only 64K of raw heap object information. Heap Walker 3.1, however, breaks the 64K barrier, allowing any object in the global heap object to be viewed in its entirety. The 3.1 version of Heap Walker offers more sorting options (sort by handle and not just address), and in general has improved greatly on the readability of the display.

Figure 4.9.
An example of a GDI bitmap object in Heap Walker.

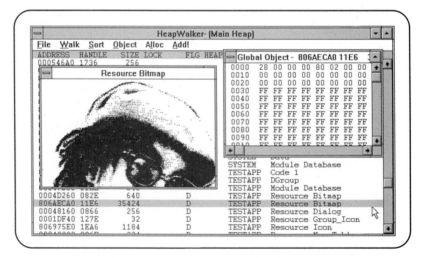

One valuable display option, especially when working with large numbers of program segments, is Heap Walker's capability to use symbol files (.SYM). If a program's symbol files are copied to the Windows system directory, Heap Walker labels segments using their assigned name rather than the more cryptic "CODE" and "DATA" labels normally used. Of course, this isn't much help unless the program consists of more than one segment and has bothered naming them in the first place.

The structure and placement of the global heap viewed by Heap Walker varies, depending on the mode that Windows is run in. In Windows 3.0 real mode, the global heap consists of memory just above DOS and any loaded TSRs and just below the start of video memory. In Windows 3.0 EMS 4.0 configuration, the global heap also includes any expanded memory that can be mapped into the lower 1M of address space. A normal walk of the heap, however, does not include banked EMS objects, only objects in the global heap that are below the bank line. Real-mode Heap Walker provides the additional capability of walking through a specific application's banked EMS objects, solving the problem.

In protected mode the global heap starts just above DOS and TSRs, as in real mode. Unlike the heap in Windows 3.0 real mode, the Windows 3.1/3.0 protected-mode global heap does not end at 1M. Rather, it's at the end of the virtual memory pool represented by physical RAM and the hard disk space allocated exclusively for implementing the paging mechanism required for supporting demand-paged virtual memory.

Heap Walker often greets its user with a fatal exit. The reason for this is simple. When an application corrupts the heap, Heap Walker ends up manipulating and navigating through invalid pointers. Carefully check all sections of source code containing global and local memory allocations, repairing sections where Kernel cleanup of the objects wasn't performed.

Predating Windows 3.1's Stress Application utility, Heap Walker provides the capability of allocating memory out of the global heap for similar stress-testing purposes. Notice what happens when the option to allocate "all of memory" is selected. Do your screen fonts come up kind of "funky"? This is a result of what happens during low-memory situations. Device contexts might not be created correctly and, almost assuredly, new objects such as fonts won't be loaded into memory. This is why the courier font or some other system stock font is shown on an application suffering from low-memory syndrome. Windows has a great method of using system objects when custom objects can't be created. This is also why certain icons, bitmaps, and other resources aren't flagged as discardable. Windows wants to ensure that these objects will always be in memory.

This chapter has covered the module's basic interface to memory allocations—the Windows heap manager, discussing both the pros and the cons of global versus local heap usage. Several "related" types of memory management have also been discussed, which build somewhat on the memory management services provided by Windows, including resources and atoms.

Whereas the memory-management discussions in chapters 2 and 3 were more of an informative nature, this chapter describes the basics of memory management that are absolutely crucial to the Windows developer. Heap management, resources, and atoms are the first in line for any developer wanting to allocate memory, not XMS, DPMI, or any knowledge of how memory is mapped. Of course, to some, these topics are just as important, which is why they are included in the book in the first place. After you've read through the first few chapters in the book, this chapter should just fall right into place. You'll find this happening quite frequently when low-level concepts are mastered, because high-level concepts do nothing but use the lower-layer concepts as building blocks.

Library
Design Ideas

"Effective library design?" you're saying. What? Perhaps you are thinking that you would rather see a chapter on effective application design. For reasons mentioned earlier, when it comes down to it, library design—not application design—is the key to creating excellent Windows programs. Whatever the amount of code reuse, if it's done halfway right, at least 50 percent of common code should already be in a library, waiting to be tapped. If this is the case, the "application" end of the design really is a lesser component when compared to designing support libraries, at least in the "ideal" sense. After all, this is the whole emphasis of this book—top-down design and heavy implementation of libraries for common code. The emphasis should be shifted to the foundation of your application, which is where most of your application should lie—in a library. An application should, in theory, consist of only glue and other "specialized" code that ties together a series of support libraries.

It is true that many aspects of library and application design have already been covered somewhat in the previous chapters. This chapter, however, is focused solely on some design ideas that can help create better, more streamlined libraries. This chapter covers the library from top to bottom, exploring why libraries are different from applications and how that can be used to the developer's advantage.

This chapter covers

☐ Types of libraries

☐ Customizing libraries

☐ Startup and termination code

How Libraries Differ from Applications

Libraries differ from applications in several respects: in how they're created, in how they're treated by Windows, in how they're loaded, and in the functions they're capable and incapable of carrying out. Most of these differences are easily explained when you uncover the details behind the inner workings of an application. An application is considered a process (or single task) under Windows. Unlike OS/2, which allows multiple threads of execution to be spun off the first thread of a process, only one thread of execution exists in an application and its loaded libraries at any point in time. This "thread" is described in part by an object called the task database, discussed more fully in Chapter 3, "Program and Module Fundamentals."

The task database (TDB) contains everything that makes an application different from a library, including a message queue, a file handle table, an environment block, and a DOS path. An application also contains a stack segment, which is key to the concept behind a thread of execution, because a stack segment (along with a code segment and instruction pointer) always pinpoints a thread. A library has none of these things and can only borrow them from its parent application. The only portions of a library shared in common with applications are code segments, resource segments, and data segments. This is why all the windows created by a DLL are always associated with the current task, which must be an application. Because it's lacking a TDB, a library contains no message queue to process messages in. Libraries additionally contain no stack segment, which yields the dilemma of SS != DS, a property that's actually assumed to be true for most functions. This means that a number of application-OK functions are restricted from use by libraries.

Standard C functions excluded from use by libraries include `fprintf()`, `fscanf()`, `sprintf()`, `sscanf()`, `vfprintf()`, `vsprintf()`, and any other similar functions. The reason is that the macros used for processing a variable number of arguments assume SS == DS, which isn't true for libraries. If needed, however, the macros can be easily rewritten to accommodate libraries. True, the Windows function **wsprintf()** accepts a variable number of parameters and can be used by both applications and libraries; however, it's a Windows function from the ground up, so it is exempt from the rule. As a side note, the reason that functions like **wsprintf()** require a full casting to LPSTR for strings is the same reason that all functions accepting a variable number of arguments require a full cast. If the compiler isn't sure of the number or type of parameters being passed, it has no means of possibly promoting values from int to long or near to far.

Syntactically, libraries differ from applications in several ways. Table 5.1 illustrates some of these differences.

Whereas an application has a central `WinMain()` loop that stays in memory, pumping out messages to all its created windows, a library has a `LibMain()` and `WEP()` entry and exit functions. There is no "heart" section of code that keeps processing and receiving input. The only sections of code inside a library guaranteed to get called are the functions LibMain() and WEP(). This contrasts with an application, which theoretically gains control whenever it has a message waiting in its queue.

Table 5.1. Application/library differences.

	Application	*Library*
Source Module	WinMain()	LibEntry(), LibMain(), WEP()
	#define _WINDOWS	#define _WINDOWS
		#define _WINDLL
Make File	Compiler=	/A[S,M,...] /A[S,M,...]w
	Linker=	?libc?w.lib ?dllc?w.lib
Module-Def File	NAME *statement*	LIBRARY *statement*
	STUB 'WINSTUB.EXE'	n/a
	STACK *statement*	n/a

At the beginning of every source module for a library, a #define _WINDLL statement must exist, because it weeds out the functions that don't apply to libraries. In the library's make file, a couple of other differences include the w associated with the compiler flag specifying the memory model. This tells Windows that SS != DS. Additionally, the library-specific C runtime import libraries must be chosen.

The module definition file is also different, with applications being named via NAME rather than LIBRARY. The STUB statement also doesn't apply to libraries because libraries aren't executable. The filename after STUB defines an application to run if Windows isn't present and the application is executed anyway. Usually this is defined as WINSTUB.EXE, which prints a message saying something like This program requires Microsoft Windows. Lastly, the STACK statement isn't required because libraries contain no stack.

Names and Ordinals

The functions in a module can be referenced by name, by ordinal (number), or by both. The advantages to referencing functions by name is that the reference "floats" with the function, regardless of where the function sits (its ordinal position) in the exported names table. Names are also slightly more

227

personable than numbers. However, names are also much slower during speedy-lookup attempts. Instead of an ordinal being used as an index into a table, a series of names in a table must be scanned and compared.

How a function is exported should be determined by how the function is intended to be used by a client module. Ordinals are really only advantageous when using `GetProcAddress()` to perform repeated lookups, and when the application is first loaded into memory. During the development phase of a software project, it might be best not to use ordinals, because any change to the ordinal position of a function affects any modules that implicitly, explicitly, or dynamically import by ordinal, making a full recompile of all associated modules necessary. Later in the development phase, this isn't as much of an issue because functions are less likely to change, and the increased speed of using ordinals would be a natural part of the fine-tuning process.

Dynamic Link, Object, and Import Libraries

Under Windows, the term *library* can get a bit confusing at times, because three different types of libraries are supported: dynamic-link libraries, object libraries, and import libraries. Each is completely different from the others, having in common only the name *library*. Actually, this helps you understand what libraries are used for. Table 5.2 illustrates some of the differences between the types of libraries.

Table 5.2. The differences between libraries.

	DLL	*Object*	*Import*
Contents	Dynamically linked code	Statically linked code	No code, only module names, function names, and ordinals
File Extensions	.exe, .dll., .drv, .fon	.lib	.lib
Examples	gdi.exe, toolhelp.dll, mouse.drv, roman.fon	mlibcew.lib, sdllcaw.lib	libw.lib
Viewer	exehdr.exe	lib.exe	lib.exe

Basically, a library is a collection of functions, references to functions, or both. In the case of a DLL, the actual addresses of the functions in the library are unresolved until runtime; only a series of names and offsets (along with the actual code) are kept until the library is loaded by Windows. At this point, all `far` address entry points are patched and dynamic links are completed. With object libraries, function addresses are known at link time, requiring no dynamic linking mechanisms to be implemented. The code for object libraries is embedded directly into the developer's code, not merely references to the code, as is the case with DLLs.

Import libraries are created to allow seamless access to DLLs, containing just enough information to resolve references to the DLL when it is first loaded into memory at program load time, just before the application is actually executed. Every function in an import library contains three items: the ordinal number and the name of the function, and the name of the module in which the function resides. Whether a name or an ordinal value ends up being used to establish the link depends on how the function was originally exported. If a function explicitly declares an ordinal value, that particular number is assigned to the function and used by the import library. If, instead, only a name is specified, the function will be implicitly imported by name when using the library. In this case, even though the function is referenced in the import library by name, the function is still assigned a "floating" ordinal. This means that the number is assigned only after the explicitly declared ordinals have been enumerated. For any kind of library, when explicit ordinal values haven't been assigned, it's always safest to link by name. For import libraries, this is done by default. For explicitly and dynamically loaded libraries, however, the "paper or plastic" choice is still available.

An example of an import library is libw.lib, which is used to dynamically link to functions in the Windows libraries User, GDI, and Kernel. Normally, a single import library is associated with a single DLL. In this case, for ease of use, they have been combined into a single import library. This trick is discussed later in this chapter.

The SDK's `implib` utility, along with a module-definition (.DEF) file, is required to generate an import library for a DLL. The contents of a library can easily be viewed through the use of the appropriate "viewer" utility. For DLLs, this utility is exehdr.exe, which, when used with the `/Verbose` switch, completely dumps the structure of any module, be it application or library. In the case of object libraries and import libraries, the lib.exe utility can be used.

Loading Libraries

A library can be loaded in one of three ways: implicitly via a make file, explicitly via a module-definition file, or dynamically in a source module. The first two forms are known as load-time dynamic linking, because all references to functions are resolved when the module is loaded into memory. Runtime dynamic linking is exhibited by a dynamically loaded library, because references are "resolved" on the fly within source code by using `GetProcAddress()` to return the entry points of desired functions. Each technique is discussed in the following sections.

Implicitly Loaded DLLs

A library (.DLL) is implicitly loaded when its import library (.LIB) is included on the linker command line for the requesting module. This is the easiest method of loading a library, because functions can just be "used" blindly, with no regard for what's in the library. If the function is present, no problem. If it's not, you get an unresolved reference error from the linker. The following linker statement (extracted from a make file) implicitly loads two dynamic link libraries:

```
module.exe: module.obj module.def
    link /align:16 /NOD module,,, libw stdwin mlibcew, module.def
```

The DLLs User, GDI, and Kernel are implicitly loaded through the use of the import library libw.lib, which, as mentioned earlier, contains all the function declarations for Windows' three primary API libraries. The second implicitly loaded library is stdwin.dll, which is one of the DLLs included in this book. Now, all the functions in both of these libraries are immediately on tap for module.exe, bearing in mind, of course, that include files declaring these functions are still required. The object library mlibcew.lib is also loaded; however, it isn't a DLL and is exempt from this discussion.

Although no guarantees are made about the load-ordering of implicitly loaded libraries, this isn't really an issue. The entry points of all affected libraries aren't called until all associated libraries have already been loaded into memory. This doesn't mean, however, that a library's entry point can be used to call functions in another "parallel" loaded library, because the other libraries haven't yet had their entry points called. This means that not only hasn't any possible initialization been done for the library, but a local heap (if specified) hasn't been created yet either. This problem is similar to the order in which implicitly linked libraries are unloaded, although the outcome isn't the same. When Windows unloads a series of implicitly loaded libraries, all associated WEP() functions are called before any library is unloaded. In this case, WEP() *can* be used to call functions in other parallel-loaded libraries, because the libraries are guaranteed to have been initialized already and won't be unloaded until the last WEP() has been called.

In any case, implicitly loaded libraries are brought into memory before the client module that references the library is itself loaded and starts executing. If the client module happens to be an application and is itself in the process of being loaded, the entry-point code for such a library cannot call any Windows function that invokes the messaging system. Because the application's queue hasn't been created yet, the results are undefined.

Assumptions can, however, be made about the linker's processing of libraries, which is done from left to right. This rule often is used with the /NOE (no extended dictionary search) linker switch, which prevents the linker from searching consecutively through the libraries listed on the linker command line.

Implicitly loaded DLLs had a number of problems under Windows 3.0 that have been fixed for release 3.1. One of the biggest problems involved circularly linked libraries. This is when several libraries are loaded that contain circular references to each other. Quite often, some of the libraries weren't automatically freed as they should have been, forcing the developer to manually free the libraries instead. Additionally, with implicitly loaded DLLs, Windows would free the application *before* calling WEP(), meaning that WEP() was incapable of calling very many functions and could do virtually nothing that required the application to be in memory. This also meant that WEP had to be in a fixed, nondiscardable segment, because since the application was no longer in memory, Windows had no means for determining how or where to load WEP().

When a library is implicitly loaded, all references to functions inside the library are done depending on how the function was originally exported. If the library exported its functions by name, references to functions in the library by a client module are done by name. If the library is changed to export functions by ordinal, and the client module (without recompiling) still loads the library, then references will obviously still be by name. After the client application is recompiled using the library's new module-definition file, function references will be done by ordinal, reflecting the new changes. When changing explicitly set ordinal values of the functions in any kind of library, it's always safest to do a full recompile of all associated modules.

A library is implicitly loaded only if the linker can find a reference to one of the library's functions in the module loading the library. Just having the library in the linker command line isn't enough. If a library is implicitly loaded merely for the use of registered window classes, the `LoadLibrary()` function must be used at the beginning of the application to force a reference to the library. The reason is simple. When the linker is resolving references to functions, it has only object modules, import libraries, and static libraries from which to resolve references. The linker has absolutely no knowledge whatsoever of the resource file and any associated window classes embedded inside DIALOG statements. The linker also has no means of scanning calls to `CreateWindow()` and similar calls in source modules to determine the window classes that are needed and in which libraries they reside. Remember that one of the properties of a library is that it is used only if a function inside it is referenced. Obviously, the use of window classes requires no functional reference, only an embedded static string of edit, listbox, or something similar.

In the case of the sample applications included in the book, this is the reason for the explicit call to `LoadLibrary()` at the beginning of the module, and conversely, `FreeLibrary()` at the end of every module. Sometimes it isn't convenient to keep track of whether any functional references to a library exist, with it being easier just to perform both an implicit and a dynamic load of the library. A call to `LoadLibrary()` forces the requested library to be included in the module's module name table, a structure discussed in Chapter 3, "Program and Module Fundamentals." One way to force a linker reference to a custom control library is to include an InitListbox(), InitBitmap(), or InitSuperControl() type of function in each library. This guarantees a reference to the module and has the added benefit of allowing the library's initialization to be done in a place other than LibMain(). It also guarantees a per-task initialization, which is something LibMain() can't currently offer.

Explicitly Loaded DLLs

Libraries are explicitly loaded by declaring them in the requesting module's module-definition file—more specifically, by specifying the desired module's name and the requested function's name or ordinal number in the IMPORTS statement of the parent module wanting to load the library. The disadvantage of this method is that every function used must be individually declared, which can get a bit tedious after a while. Updating the list for both additions and deletions, is the biggest chore of all. The advantage to explicitly loaded libraries is that the developer has control over aliasing the imported function's name and can optionally import functions by their ordinal value rather than just by name. There is no limit to the number of functions that may be imported by a module, except for a general limitation of a 64K name space. See the following example of the IMPORTS statement:

```
IMPORTS
    MODULE.FunctionName
    Alias1=MODULE.FunctionName
    Alias2=MODULE.Ordinal#
```

Like implicitly loaded libraries, references to functions in explicitly loaded libraries are resolved when the application is first loaded into memory. When Windows can't find a library that has been bound to a module, a system-modal message box is created asking the user to insert a disk containing the DLL into drive A:. The message box is created for every library that's being imported. One of the reasons that implicitly and explicitly loaded libraries are loaded before their parent module is that when Windows is unable to load any of these libraries, the application itself is not loaded.

The only disadvantage to implicitly or explicitly loading a library is when there is a chance that the library or function won't exist. In this case, the library should be dynamically loaded via LoadLibrary(), which is discussed in the next section.

Dynamically Loaded DLLs

A library is dynamically loaded via the LoadLibrary() function. This is referred to as runtime dynamic linking, which means that any links are resolved at runtime, if at all. The advantage to dynamically loaded libraries deals more with flexibility, not simplicity. A runtime dynamic link, when it fails, merely returns a null status code to the developer. When a load-time dynamic link fails, however, it informs the end user of the application, which isn't ideal. Although LoadLibrary() is one of three ways that a .DLL-type library can be loaded, it is the only way that device-driver (.DRV) libraries can be loaded.

In this example, user's MessageBeep() function is used to dynamically load and call a function in a module. The following code snippet shows two examples of how this can be done. This first example shows a runtime link established by name, and the second example shows a runtime link established by ordinal. The first example typecasts the function pointer correctly, helping to catch any parameter passing errors. Remember that because there isn't an include file, the typedef replaces what would normally be a function declaration in a header file. Both examples show the different methods of calling functions through pointers.

```
FARPROC lpProc; // The generic method of casting the funcptr

typedef void (WINAPI* MSGBEEP)(UINT); // The preferred method, as
                                      // it catches parm errors

MSGBEEP MessageBeeper;               // Declare the actual funcptr

hInst = LoadLibrary("USER.EXE");     // Set up one-half of link

//
// Get the func address from the library; this sets up other half
//

MessageBeeper = (MSGBEEP) GetProcAddress(hInst, "MessageBeep");

(*MessageBeeper)(1);  // You say pohtayto

MessageBeeper(1);     // I say pohtahto

//
// Get address again, this time using numeric ordinal value
//

lpProc = (FARPROC) GetProcAddress(hInst, MAKEINTRESOURCE(104));

(*lpProc)(1);         // You say tohmayto

lpProc(1);            // I say tohmahto

FreeLibrary(hInst);   // Free the library for cleanup
```

Of course, in this case, **GetModuleHandle()** could have been used rather than the calls to **LoadLibrary()** and **FreeLibrary()**, because obviously the library User is virtually guaranteed to be loaded in memory at all times.

Unlike implicitly and explicitly loaded libraries, which are loaded before their parent module, when a library is dynamically loaded via **LoadLibrary()**, its entry point (LibEntry) is called immediately, unless the library has already been loaded through some other means. Likewise, when **FreeLibrary()** is called for a dynamically loaded library with a reference count of one, WEP() is immediately called. This contrasts with the WEP()s of implicitly and explicitly loaded libraries, which are called just before the parent module is to be unloaded from memory.

LibEntry() **and** LibMain()

With the exception of font libraries, all loadable and executable modules under Windows should contain an entry point. Although a module can be loaded and unloaded just fine without one, to ensure future portability, an entry point should always be declared. To a programmer writing applications, this section of code is pretty much hidden by Windows, because the C runtime code declares itself as the starting point, and later automatically calls WinMain(). With DLLs, however, the opposite is true. Not only does the programmer have the source to this seldom-seen section of code, but it can be modified as well. In a DLL the startup code is contained in a single assembly file (libentry.asm). The routine LibEntry() declares itself as the entry point by putting its name along with the END statement at the end of libentry.asm. LibEntry() is the first routine to be called, and from there control is transferred to the DLL's LibMain() function, which has the following format:

```
BOOL WINAPI LibMain
(
    HINSTANCE hInst, WORD wDataSeg, WORD cbHeap, LPSTR CmdLine
);
```

Although most of the documentation for Windows specifies that a command-line string is passed to LibMain() (and LibEntry()) through ES:SI, this is not the case. A null value is always passed.

LibEntry()'s job is to initialize a library's local heap. Although the SDK includes the source to LibEntry(), there are not too many occasions when it needs to be modified. One time, however, is when the developer is creating a resource-only library. Although a resource-only library still needs code in the form of a LibEntry() entry point and a WEP() termination function, it doesn't need the full functionality that LibEntry() provides, which is one reason to modify it.

The initialization of a newly loaded library is simple. First, LibEntry() saves the registers and initializes (optionally) the library's local heap with a call to **LocalInit()**. Next, LibMain(), which generally is used by the programmer to initialize any custom control classes, is called.

Because of real-mode support under Windows 3.0, LibMain() also had to unlock its data segment (because the call to LocalInit() in LibEntry() locked it for you). Under Windows 3.1, the explicit unlock call isn't needed, because under protected mode, lock counts affect only discardable objects.

3.1

Finally, LibMain() returns a true or a false if it can initialize itself. When control is returned to LibEntry(), control is in turn handed back to Windows. The

application's thread of execution running through `LibMain()` is about the only time that a library is guaranteed to get called, other than when it is unloaded and `WEP()` is called.

> **Caution:** Not every Windows function can be called from the `LibMain()` of implicitly and explicitly loaded DLLs, including APIs involving messaging. The reason for this is that the DLL is loaded by Windows before the application is loaded and its message queue created. Although a task for the function was created by the application's startup code with a call to **InitTask()**, it takes a later call to **InitApp()** for the message queue to get created. Because a DLL uses the messaging queue of the task that is calling into it, the DLL cannot call any function that causes a message to be sent. This includes calls that yield control to a different application.

Because `LibMain()` is a one-shot kind of function, it's a perfect candidate to be in its own code segment, or lumped in with the segment `INIT_TEXT`. The segment `INIT_TEXT` is created by `LibEntry()` and traditionally is created to hold initialization and other one-shot code. Windows treats this segment as special: Just after `LibEntry()` finishes its execution, Windows promotes it to the top of the discard list with a call to **GlobalLRUOldest()**. This ensures that `INIT_TEXT` will be one of the first segments to get discarded when Windows gets pinched for memory. When code or resources are demand-loaded from disk, it's done a segment at a time, no smaller. `LibMain()` could easily end up getting swapped in with some other functions in a code segment when there's absolutely no chance of its getting used again. To put `LibMain()` in the segment `INIT_TEXT`, use a `pragma` similar to this:

```
#pragma alloc_text(INIT_TEXT, LibMain)
```

Remember that the line containing this statement and all other `alloc_text` pragmas must be placed after the function declaration (the prototype) and before the actual definition of the function, which is done in a source module. The `pragma` also must be in the same module as the function it's referencing.

Following is the format of libentry.asm:

```
PAGE,132
;;;;;;;;;;;;;;;;;;;;;;;;;;;;;;;;;;;;;;;;;;;;;;;;;;;;;;;;;;;;;;;;;;;;;;;;;;;;;;
;       LIBENTRY.ASM Windows dynamic link library entry routine        ;
;;;;;;;;;;;;;;;;;;;;;;;;;;;;;;;;;;;;;;;;;;;;;;;;;;;;;;;;;;;;;;;;;;;;;;;;;;;;;;

include cmacros.inc       ; Used for the shortcut macros you see
```

```
        externFP <LibMain>          ; The lib's C init routine to be called

        createSeg INIT_TEXT, INIT_TEXT, BYTE, PUBLIC, CODE     ; Define segment
        sBegin    INIT_TEXT         ; Start segment
        assumes   CS,INIT_TEXT      ; Set code segment register

        ?PLM=0                      ; 'C' naming
        externA  <_acrtused>        ; Ensures that Win DLL startup code is linked

        ?PLM=1                      ; 'PASCAL' naming
        externFP <LocalInit>        ; Windows heap init routine

        cProc   LibEntry, <PUBLIC,FAR>   ; Entry point into DLL

        cBegin
            push    di              ; Handle of the module instance
            push    ds              ; Library data segment
            push    cx              ; Heap size
            push    es
            push    si

            ; If you have some heap then initialize it

            jcxz    callc           ; Jump if no heap is specified

            ; Call the Windows function LocalInit() to set up the heap
            ; LocalInit((LPSTR)start, WORD cbHeap);

            xor     ax,ax           ; Quickest way to make AX = 0
            cCall   LocalInit <ds, ax, cx>
            or      ax,ax           ; Did it do it OK?
            jz      error           ; Quit if it failed

            ; Invoke the C routine to do any special initialization

        callc:
            call    LibMain         ; Invoke the 'C' routine (result in AX)
            jmp     short exit      ; LibMain does any stack cleanup

        error:
            pop     si              ; Clean up stack on a LocalInit error
            pop     es
            pop     cx
            pop     ds
            pop     di
```

```
exit:

cEnd                     ; End our little routine
sEnd INIT_TEXT           ; End INIT_TEXT segment definition
end    LibEntry          ; Designate LibEntry as DLL entry point
```

All About WEP()

Similar to LibEntry() and LibMain(), WEP() is called only once for a particular DLL, just as the library is about to be unloaded from memory. Libraries are unloaded by an explicit call to **FreeLibrary()**, implicitly via the freeing of the module that loaded the library, or by the shutdown of Windows. In all but the last case, the library's reference count must be zero for the unload to occur and for WEP() to be called.

WEP() is pitched as the place where the developer should perform shutdown-style operations on the DLL, such as freeing memory, unregistering classes, and freeing other DLLs. In reality, however, this is not the case, because WEP() cannot perform many of the functions you would expect. Although LibEntry() is called on the task and stack of the active application, WEP() isn't. WEP() uses a smaller-than-normal stack provided by Kernel. A call to **MessageBox()** is out of the question, as are calls to **LoadLibrary()**, **FreeLibrary()**, any of the global memory allocation APIs, and DOS calls. You also don't need to unregister classes in WEP(), because classes created by a DLL are automatically destroyed when the DLL is unloaded anyway.

What you really should do is create a Hello() and Goodbye() set of functions in the library that perform initialization and termination for (possibly) multiple clients. Not only does this ensure that the library's entry and exit functions are called, but they're done with a large enough stack size to eliminate most of the previously mentioned restrictions. This adds another benefit, because now the library is effectively instanced and can set up different data segments, services, or whatever for the different client modules attaching to it. Having an explicit Hello() and Goodbye() set of functions also eliminates the ambiguity involving the loading problems associated with implicitly loaded libraries. Using these two functions ensures that the library will always be linked in with the application.

A library's WEP() function has the following format:

```
int FAR PASCAL WEP(int iParam);
```

238

The parameter iParam will have a value of either WEP_FREE_DLL or WEP_SYSTEM_EXIT, depending on whether the shutdown was caused by a call to **FreeLibrary()** (if the reference count is at zero) or whether the shutdown was caused by the termination of Windows itself. In any case, WEP() should always return a one.

WEP() was engineered to be callable under very low-memory situations, when the nonresident portion of the DLL's name table might have been discarded and cannot be loaded back into memory. In this case, the name table doesn't refer to the names found in the module database, but to the thunks required for each function. This is one of the reasons WEP's name is made resident in the DLL's name table—to guarantee that the name will always be present in memory and never paged to disk.

Windows' handling of WEP() has been completely redesigned for release 3.1. Basically, now you can always count on WEP() being called when a library is about to be unloaded. Under certain circumstances with Windows 3.0, WEP() wasn't called, was called after the module itself had been freed from memory, or was called even though LibEntry() wasn't. Under Windows 3.1, if LibEntry() isn't called for some reason, neither is WEP(). Additionally, WEP() is called while the application itself is still in memory. This means that WEP() can now be placed in a discardable segment, because the application still exists in memory, and the Windows loader is able to set up the appropriate links and load the WEP() segment in from disk. Under Windows 3.0, with the application out of memory, the appropriate segment/bundle links weren't in place to allow Windows to demand-load the segment.

Also under Windows 3.1, whenever implicitly loaded DLLs are about to be freed, all associated WEP() functions are called first, allowing WEP() to call functions in parallel-loaded libraries without fear of having library code segments discarded and unavailable. Like before, references to WEP() must always be in uppercase, and the function must be exported with an ordinal value of one and its name made resident in the name table. Plus, the segment that WEP() is contained in can now be flagged as both moveable and discardable. Given that WEP() can now be in a discardable segment and is guaranteed to get called while the application is still in memory, the explicit ordinal value of one and the RESIDENTNAME flag don't make much sense. If the WEP code can be discardable, and get reloaded when the function is needed, why can't the portion of name table be reloaded as well? And why must an ordinal value of one be used when Windows is using GetProcAddress() to call WEP()? In this case, the name "WEP" could just as easily be passed by Windows to **GetProcAddress()** as the ordinal value, one.

Debugging Startup and Termination Code

Setting breakpoints in the LibEntry() or LibMain() routines of a library is quite simple, especially for dynamically loaded libraries. In this case the breakpoint can be set from the CodeView command line by typing bp LibMain or bp LibEntry. This can be done at any point before the *first* call to **LoadLibrary()**, likewise for breakpointing the library's WEP() routine.

To set breakpoints in the startup and termination code for implicitly and explicitly loaded libraries, the breakpoints must be established before the first line of code in the application is executed. Be sure to establish breakpoints before pressing any step or trace keys. If CodeView is in source-output mode, pressing either of these keys causes the application's startup code and associated library code to be called automatically, before your cursor is eventually placed on the first line of your application's source code.

Debugging an implicitly loaded library's WEP() routine from a nonresident debugger like CodeView can yield bizarre results because the breakpoint isn't hit until after CodeView thinks the application has terminated. This can cause a general protection fault and other odd errors. Fortunately, because WEP() isn't used extensively for uninitialization purposes, this isn't much of an issue. If it is, use a resident-debugger like Soft-ICE/W.

One other method of debugging startup and termination codes involves switching to the mixed-source output mode, which shows both source code and assembly. Although this mode isn't as pretty, you get a much better idea of what's going on before an application is loaded by Windows. Pressing trace or step while in mixed mode lets you watch exactly how Windows loads your application.

One of the many advantages to using a resident-debugger such as Soft-ICE/W is that it debugs with symbols. This means that instead of seeing a lot of unintelligible addresses, you can get an output similar to this:

```
#:00000043    XOR     BP,BP
#:00000045    PUSH    BP
#:00000046    CALL    KERNEL!INITTASK        ; Calls DLL LibEntry procs

#:0000004B    OR      AX,AX
#:0000004D    JZ      00AA
#:0000004F    MOV     [STKHQQ+2E(003E)],ES ; Setting up stk chk stuff
#:00000053    ADD     CX,0100
#:00000057    JB      00AA
```

```
#:00000059    MOV      [STKHQQ],CX
#:0000005D    MOV      [STKHQQ+02(0012)],SI
#:00000061    MOV      [STKHQQ+04(0014)],DI
#:00000065    MOV      [STKHQQ+06(0016)],BX
#:00000069    MOV      [STKHQQ+08(0018)],ES
#:0000006D    MOV      [STKHQQ+0A(001A)],DX
#:00000071    CALL     __cinit                ; Call C runtime things
#:00000074    CALL     __setargv
#:00000077    CALL     __setenvp

#:0000007A    XOR      AX,AX
#:0000007C    PUSH     AX
#:0000007D    CALL     KERNEL!WAITEVENT       ; App startup code
#:00000082    PUSH     WORD PTR [STKHQQ+04(0014)]
#:00000086    CALL     USER!INITAPP          ; Last step to create an app

#:0000008B    OR       AX,AX
#:0000008D    JZ       00AA
#:0000008F    PUSH     WORD PTR [STKHQQ+04(0014)]
#:00000093    PUSH     WORD PTR [STKHQQ+02(0012)]
#:00000097    PUSH     WORD PTR [STKHQQ+08(0018)]
#:0000009B    PUSH     WORD PTR [STKHQQ+06(0016)]
#:0000009F    PUSH     WORD PTR [STKHQQ+0A(001A)]
#:000000A3    CALL     WinMain               ; Call the app's WinMain

#:000000A6    PUSH     AX                    ; Cleanup C runtime and
#:000000A7    CALL     _exit                 ; Windows startup stuff
#:000000AA    MOV      AL,FF
#:000000AC    PUSH     AX
#:000000AD    CALL     __exit
```

Note how the startup code for applications differs from the startup code for libraries. For libraries, the INIT_TEXT code holding LibEntry() and LibMain() can be discarded because LibMain() doesn't sit in a tight loop processing messages. Application startup code must wait until the WinMain() "task" finishes execution.

Creating a Single Import Library for Multiple DLLs

Although import libraries normally are associated with a single DLL, it is quite easy to create an import library that can resolve references to multiple DLLs.

In fact, this is done for the functions in User, GDI, and Kernel, because they are all compiled into the single import library LIBW.LIB.

The SDK's import library builder implib is quite capable of accepting multiple module-definition files on its command line. This could be advantageous for situations involving a large number of libraries and the usual restrictions involving the linker and the length of DOS' command line. Although the linker can redirect its input from a text file, solving some problems, there still might be situations in which it would be advantageous to create a single import library.

This technique is quite simple, requiring only that references to the DLL's WEP() function be removed temporarily from the module-definition file. Although Windows requires that WEP() be exported and in the .DEF file, for the purpose of another module using the .LIB file being able to resolve references to another library, WEP() is not needed. After all, it's never called by a developer application or a library, only by Windows. To do this cleanly, a separate set of module-definition files needs to be created, with the WEP() function reference eliminated. implib is then used in the following manner:

```
implib dll1copy.def dll2copy.def dll3copy.def
```

Removing the C Runtime Functions

One of the ways a library's code size can be reduced is through the elimination of the C runtime code. The C runtime code is required for any library (or application) that calls any of the standard C functions, including strcpy(), printf(), and fgets(). In the case of applications, it is also required because of numerous internal variables that need to be accessed, including _environ, _argc, and _argv. Although it can be done for applications, removal of the C runtime code is really practical only for libraries.

The first step is to select the appropriate import library. In general, import libraries use the following format: {s,m,c,l}{dll,lib}c{e,a}w.lib. The first parameter specifies the memory model, the second specifies whether the import library is for a library or for an application, and the third parameter specifies whether floating-point emulation or the alternate math package is to be used. Eliminating the C runtime code is as simple as selecting a library of the form {s,m,c,l}nocrt[d].lib. Again, the first parameter indicates the memory model, with the second, and optional, d parameter used with DLLs.

The reason for the difference between the C runtime code for applications and libraries is that libraries contain no stack or separate environment block (no PSP), so references to those variables must be eliminated. DLLs also cannot reference the command line's `argc` and `argv` variables. A library has access to "its" environment by calling `GetDOSEnvironment()`, which returns a pointer to the environment block of the client application that loaded the library.

If the linker reports unresolved external symbols, your library is making implicit calls to the C runtime functions. Implicit calls are invoked by stack-checking routines (use `/Gs` to disable) or routines that use long division. If these implicit calls are still desired, and only explicit calls (`strcpy`, `fputs`) need to be eliminated, then the `/NOE` option can be used to prevent extended dictionary searches. By default, all external symbols from import libraries are put into a single dictionary. By using this linker switch and by placing the `?nocrt.lib` import library before (rather than instead of) any other import library, the problem can be resolved.

Although a series of different libraries is used for C, Windows, and DLL-callable functions, just a single set of include files is used to reference these functions. To help keep track of the differences in the functions between the C runtime libraries for DOS and for Windows, as well as the differences in the libraries between applications and DLLs, Windows incorporates a series of `#define` statements. If `#define _WINDOWS` is at the beginning of a source module, the Windows versions of the C runtime library function prototypes are used; otherwise, DOS is assumed. This weeds out functions relating to keyboard and screen I/O. Additionally, if `#define _WINDLL` is found, certain functions are dropped from the include files that don't apply to DLLs, which are mainly functions that assume SS == DS.

Creating a Resource-Only DLL

Chapter 3, "Program and Module Fundamentals," mentions that every module has a limit of 254 *usable* program segments. It also mentions that this limitation could easily be overcome by creating additional client libraries for the application. Obviously, libraries containing code can be built, because this is one of the primary reasons behind writing DLLs in the first place. Lesser known is that resource-only libraries can be created as well, containing no

application-callable code or even a data segment—only resources and a small code stub containing an entry point and WEP(). This can be quite handy for categorizing and unbinding resources from an application or a library, and it makes for an easy handoff to a graphics artist or other individual responsible for adding that extra finish to an application.

LibMain() is no longer needed; only a NOP entry point and WEP() are required. Although a library with no entry point and only a WEP() procedure loads, unloads, and works just fine under 3.1 and 3.0, it would be prudent to stick an entry point in anyway. The amount of code space taken up is miniscule and not worth worrying about. The third step is to declare DATA NONE in the library's module-definition file. This prevents a data segment from being created and loaded into memory when Windows loads the module.

A library's normal entry point, LibEntry(), can be abbreviated greatly, because local heap initialization routines as well as the call to LibMain() are no longer needed. The external link to the C and Windows runtime libraries can be removed as well. The resulting code stub is your library's new entry point:

```
PAGE,132
;;;;;;;;;;;;;;;;;;;;;;;;;;;;;;;;;;;;;;;;;;;;;;;;;;;;;;;;;;;;;;;;;;;;;;;;;;
;
;         LIBENTRY.ASM
;
;         Windows dynamic link library entry routine
;
;         This stub is used only to declare an entry point
;
;;;;;;;;;;;;;;;;;;;;;;;;;;;;;;;;;;;;;;;;;;;;;;;;;;;;;;;;;;;;;;;;;;;;;;;;;;

include cmacros.inc

createSeg INIT_TEXT, INIT_TEXT, BYTE, PUBLIC, CODE
sBegin    INIT_TEXT
assumes   CS,INIT_TEXT

cProc    LibEntry, <PUBLIC,FAR>    ; Entry point into DLL
cBegin
    nop
cEnd

sEnd INIT_TEXT
end  LibEntry
```

There are numerous other ways that this stub could be written, but this is one of the simplest. Another option would be to leave the normal LibEntry() stub

244

in place, and to actually include the C runtime libraries. This would be a good choice if you weren't really sure whether the resource-only library might get extended with some code at a later date, and it would eliminate unnecessary code tweaking later on.

Following is our module-definition file for a resource-only library:

```
LIBRARY  RESONLY   ; Name the library
EXETYPE  WINDOWS

CODE PRELOAD MOVEABLE DISCARDABLE
DATA NONE                          ; Create no data segment

EXPORTS
    WEP @1 RESIDENTNAME            ; Export WEP as resident
```

Following is the make file for our resource-only library:

```
all: resonly.dll                    // Used for make/nmake compatibility

resonly.res: resonly.rc resonly     // Compile the resources
    rc -r resonly.rc

libentry.obj: libentry.asm          // Compile the entry point stub
    masm -Mx libentry,libentry;

resonly.obj: resonly.c resonly      // Compile WEP code
    cl -c -Od -ASw -Gsw -Zpe resonly.c

resonly.dll: resonly.obj libentry.obj resonly.def resonly.res
    link resonly libentry,resonly.dll,,snocrtd, resonly.def
    rc resonly.res resonly.dll      // Add resources

resonly.dll: resonly.res            // In case only the .res chgd
    rc resonly.res resonly.dll      // Add resources to module
```

Creating a DLL with No Data Segment

Creating a library with no data segment may seem like an odd thing to do; after all, the resource-only library in the previous example has no data segment, so what's the difference? In this case, you still have code and (optionally) resource segments, but no data segment. This kind of module is desirable for functions assuming SS == DS. Remember that a majority of the C runtime and other DOS-style functions assume that SS == DS. In fact, some functions, such as `LocalAlloc()`, work on the current data segment. If a library calls `LocalAlloc()` on behalf of an application, the memory is allocated locally to the library and not to the application. To use the calling application's data segment on a function-by-function basis, the NODATA attribute can be used on EXPORTed functions, as in the following example:

```
EXPORTS
    WEP             @1 RESIDENTNAME   ; Export WEP as resident
    MyLocalAllocer @2 NODATA
```

This yields a greater amount of flexibility than using DATA NONE. If `LibEntry()` is still being used for the library, and it pulls in the C runtime functions via a statement similar to the following:

```
?PLM=0                    ; 'C'naming
externA <_acrtused>       ; Ensures that Win DLL startup code is linked
```

then the NODATA option must be used on every function that wants to use the client application's data segment. The reason is simple. The C runtime libraries create several default entries in a data segment, and although the library would be using the application's data segment for all other functions, any internally referenced data in the library would be relative to the application's data segment. Writes therefore would affect the DS of the application and not of the library, which has no data segment to corrupt.

Intercepting API Calls

Windows holds true to the plug-and-play, tinker-toy (in the good sense!) metaphor, providing indirection through aliases, hooks, DLLs, and various other mechanisms. One benefit that's derived from all of this is the ability to intercept the exported functions of any loaded library—including Windows User, GDI, and Kernel modules. Of course, this can be done only for modules that can link to a "trapper" import library—it doesn't affect any other loaded modules. The following example illustrates this procedure using Kernel's `GlobalAlloc()` function.

Basically, the effect is achieved by having trapper export its own `GlobalAlloc()` function, which resolves (via the alias) to a stub replacement for a `GlobalAlloc()`-clone piece of code already located in trapper, which in this case is called `NewGlobalAlloc()`. Next, the target module imports the new version of `GlobalAlloc()`

through trapper's import library. To use the new definition of `GlobalAlloc()`, the target module must link to trapper's import library before any reference to libw.lib, the import library that Windows uses to define User, GDI, and Kernel functions, which naturally includes the original declaration of `GlobalAlloc()`.

```
// (in the library source module trapdll.c)
HANDLE FAR PASCAL NewGlobalAlloc(WORD wFlags, DWORD dwSize)
{
    //
    // "Trap" processing goes here.
    //

    ...

    return(GlobalAlloc(WORD, DWORD));
}


// (in trapdll.c's module-definition file)
EXPORTS
    WEP                         @1 RESIDENTNAME
    GlobalAlloc=NewGlobalAlloc @2

// (in the target module's--in this case an application's--make file)
module.exe: module.obj module.def
    link /align:16 module,,, trapdll libw slibcew, module.def
```

As long as the import library trapdll.lib is referenced before libw.lib in the target module's make file, the function can be intercepted. Although the load order or processing order of any kind of library should never be counted on, in the case of import libraries and the linker, library functions are resolved on a first-come, first-serve basis. This is why the trapper library can still call `GlobalAlloc()` by its original name. It's using the address of `GlobalAlloc()` as found in libw.lib, unlike the target module, which is using the definition of `GlobalAlloc()` as it's exported by the trapper library.

Creating Hook/Filter Libraries

Chapter 1, "Windows Fundamentals," mentions the different uses for DLLs, one of which includes the creation of hook code for filtering mouse, keyboard, and other message events on a system-wide or task-specific basis. System-wide hook code should reside in a library, whereas task-specific hooks can reside in the application whose events are being filtered.

Basically, code is used to establish the hook, pass control to other hooks, and, finally, remove the hook. Windows 3.0 implemented this process using functions similar to window subclassing. When a hook was created, the address of the prior hook function (if any) was returned. The address of this function was saved in a global variable and was called later for any events that the current filter didn't want to process.

Windows 3.1 changes this metaphor, making it more in line with the thought behind Windows NT. All references to prior hook functions are kept internally by Windows, with the hook application totally unaware of other filter functions. Instead of returning the entry point of the prior hook function, a hook ID is returned. Windows uses this ID in its internal hook processing to know which is the next hook in the chain; when the hook is finally removed, the ID is used to determine which function in the chain is to be removed.

Windows 3.1 also changes the number and types of hooks that can be installed by applications. Under Windows 3.0, most hook code had to be in libraries. However, under Windows 3.1, almost all the hooks can be designated as system-wide (installed in libraries) or flagged as task-specific (installed in applications).

Not too many stipulations and problems are associated with hook code. As long as the code resides in the right place (library or application), and the appropriate functions are exported and designated as `far` and `pascal` (or `CALLBACK`), and the hook isn't established inside `LibMain()`, everything works fine. A hook is really no different from a window function or any other kind of callback procedure.

The only issue, which often pops up in "critical" sections of code, is that `SendMessage()` cannot be used while inside a hook procedure. This can potentially cause a deadlock situation. A deadlock occurs when the hook is invoked due to a `SendMessage()` call. If the hook yields control to another task with a call to `SendMessage()`, the original task that called `SendMessage()` will not be able to service any other messages until the original message is processed and control is returned. The hook code can use `SendMessage()` to pass a message to the current task, because this doesn't relinquish control to a different task.

As a side note, a task can determine whether it is processing a "sent" message with the `InSendMessage()` function. If this is an issue for a particular task, a combination of `InSendMessage()` and `ReplyMessage()` should be used before the task invokes any other function that yields control, such as `GetMessage()`.

To demonstrate hook functions, specifically a keyboard message filter, this book includes two files: HotKey, a DLL that services the keyboard filter code, and HotApp, a windowless application that loads hotkey.dll, installs the hook, and before termination, removes the hook. The HotKey library communicates with the application via a call to `PostAppMessage()`, which requires only a task handle and not a window handle to send a message. When the "unload" key sequence of Ctrl-Shift-X is pressed, the HotKey library posts a `WM_QUIT` message to HotApp, which lets it break out of its message loop, uninstall the keyboard filter, and finally terminate.

Unfortunately, a full-screen DOS window is exempt from messages (as if there are any!), keyboard, mouse, and all other filter functions. A windowed-DOS box receives paint and movement messages, but that's about it. Running the SDK's Spy utility or something similar on a windowed-DOS box gives you all the details you need. This has to do with the fact that DOS boxes execute inside their own virtual machine, whereas all Windows applications and libraries run under the System VM. A DOS box is, essentially, its own "canned unit," and it is pretty exempt from most rules regarding applications and libraries. This puts a bit of a kink in our HotKey program, because the hotkey won't work when a DOS window is active and has the focus. This isn't too much of a problem, but it is somewhat annoying. The only way to write a "true" hotkey program is to incorporate the services of a virtual keyboard device driver, which can be used to trap for all keystrokes or only specific hotkey combinations. VxDs, you'll remember, have access to everything in the system all the time, which includes keystrokes.

The main code for the HotKey application is as follows:

```
//
// Install the hook. This couldn't be done in the library's LibMain,
// because LibMain is called with a "girly-man" sized stack.
//

InstallHook();

//
// Spin gears waiting for a WM_QUIT from library
//

while(GetMessage(&msg, NULL, NULL, NULL))
{
```

```
        //
        // The only dispatches we need are because of the desktop window
        //

        DispatchMessage(&msg);
}

//
// Remove the hook. This call is placed in the application for parity
//

RemoveHook();
```

The hook code library (HotKey) contains the following functions:

```
static HANDLE hTaskClient;
static HHOOK  hHook;

...

LRESULT CALLBACK HotKeyProc(int nCode, WPARAM wParam, LPARAM lParam)
{
    if(nCode >= 0)
    {
        //
        // Only when code is >=0 do you want to do stuff
        //

        switch(wParam)
        {
            case 'D' :

                //
                // See if ctrl key is held down
                //

                if((GetAsyncKeyState(VK_CONTROL) & 0x8000) == 0x8000)
                {
                    //
                    // See if shift key is held down
                    //

                    if((GetAsyncKeyState(VK_SHIFT) & 0x8000) == 0x8000)
                    {
                    //
                    // Launch a windowed DOS window
                    //
```

```
                        WinExec((LPSTR) "doswnd.pif", SW_SHOWMAXIMIZED);
                }
                else
                {
                    //
                    // Launch a full-screen DOS window
                    //

                    WinExec((LPSTR) "dosfull.pif", SW_SHOWNORMAL);
                }

                //
                // Boog out of here w/o passing to deffilterfunc
                //

                return(1L);
            }

            break;

        case 'X' :

            if((GetAsyncKeyState(VK_CONTROL) & 0x8000) == 0x8000)
            {
                if((GetAsyncKeyState(VK_SHIFT) & 0x8000) == 0x8000)
                {
                    // With a press of Ctrl-Shift-X, pass a
                    // message to the client app so that it can
                    // remove itself from memory. When the app
                    // receives this message, HWND will be null
                    // to indicate a task message as opposed to a
                    // window message. GetCurrentTask can't be
                    // used here because the HotKey app probably
                    // isn't the current task.

                    PostAppMessage(hTaskClient, WM_QUIT, 0, 0L);

                    return(1L);
                }
            }

            break;

//      ...(case stmts for addn'l hotkey definitions are in here)...

        default :
```

```
                    break;
            }
    }

    //
    // Pass control to next filter in chain
    //

    return((LRESULT) CallNextHookEx(hHook, nCode, wParam, lParam));
}
```

The following library function is called by HotApp to install the keyboard hook:

```
VOID WINAPI InstallHook(VOID)
{
    //
    // Remember task handle for future call to PostAppMessage
    //

    hTaskClient = GetCurrentTask();

    //
    // Set up hook func for key trapping
    //

    hHook = SetWindowsHookEx
    (
        WH_KEYBOARD, (HOOKPROC) HotKeyProc, hInstDLL, NULL
    );
}
```

The following library function is called by HotApp to remove the keyboard hook:

```
VOID WINAPI RemoveHook(VOID)
{
    //
    // Unhook the hook
    //

    UnhookWindowsHookEx(hHook);
}
```

Table 5.3 shows the event hook functions included with Windows 3.1.

Table 5.3. Event hook functions included with Windows 3.1.

Function	Description
CallNextHookEx()	"Inheritance" function for hook code. Passes hook information to the next installed hook in the chain.
DefHookProc()	Obsolete in Windows 3.1; retained for backward compatibility. Replaced with the function CallNextHookEx().
SetWindowsHook()	Obsolete in Windows 3.1; retained for backward compatibility. Replaced with the function SetWindowsHookEx().
SetWindowsHookEx()	Installs a developer-defined hook function into (possibly) a chain of hook functions. In all cases except for journal hooks and the system message hook, the hook can be set up as global (system-wide) or local (task-specific) in scope. The following hook values can be used:

Hook Value	Description
WH_CALLWNDPROC	Installs a window function filter, trapping all calls to SendMessage(). Calls to PostMessage() aren't affected. This hook drastically affects system performance and should be used only during debugging.
WH_CBT	Installs a computer-based training filter, which is called before Windows performs any of the following operations:

- Window creation, activation, focus, destruction
- Window sizing, movement, minimization, maximization
- Completion of a system command (SC_)
- Removal of keyboard and mouse events from the system queue
- Synchronizing with the system queue (WM_QUEUESYNC)

continues

Table 5.3. continued

Function	Description	
	Hook Value	*Description*
	WH_DEBUG	Installs a debugging filter, which is used to trap calls to any hook created via **SetWindowsHookEx()**.
	WH_GETMESSAGE	Installs a message filter, trapping system-wide all calls to **GetMessage()**. The filter function is called immediately after the call to **GetMessage()**, allowing the filter to modify the message as necessary.
	WH_HARDWARE	Installs a hardware event filter to trap nonstandard hardware events. Mouse and keyboard events are not included.
	WH_JOURNALPLAYBACK	Installs a message-playback filter. Used in conjunction with WH_JOURNALRECORD.
	WH_JOURNALRECORD	Installs a message-recording filter, which can be used in conjunction with WH_JOURNALPLAYBACK to record and later play back messages a la Windows' Recorder utility. Windows calls this filter function whenever it processes a message from the event queue. The filter function shouldn't modify the message.
	WH_KEYBOARD	Installs a keyboard message filter, which is called by Windows whenever an application calls **GetMessage()** or **PeekMessage()** and a WM_KEYUP or WM_KEYDOWN keyboard event is available to be processed. This allows the keyboard event to be processed before the key character is translated and processed any further by the application.

Function	Description	
	Hook Value	*Description*
	WH_MOUSE	Installs a mouse message filter, which is called by Windows whenever `GetMessage()` or `PeekMessage()` is called and a mouse event exists in the queue.
	WH_MSGFILTER	Installs a task-specific message filter, which doesn't affect system performance like the other filters. This is the only filter that can be installed by an application and not a library. Windows calls this filter function whenever a dialog box, message box, or menu has retrieved a message, and before that message has been processed.
	WH_SHELL	Installs a shell application filter, which is called by Windows whenever a window is created, activated, or destroyed.
	WH_SYSMSGFILTER	Installs a system-wide message filter, which is called by Windows whenever a dialog box, message box, or menu has retrieved a message and before that message has been processed, allowing modification of the message.
UnhookWindowsHook()	Obsolete in Windows 3.1; retained for backward compatibility. Replaced in 3.1 with the function `UnhookWindowsHookEx()`.	
UnhookWindowsHookEx()	Removes an application-defined hook function from (possibly) a chain of hook functions.	

Using a DLL to Support Window Classes

One common use for DLLs is to create and service window classes. Although message queues and the message dispatching loop are owned only by applications, window classes can be owned by an application or a library. Remember that ownership implies simply the life of the object. When the owner of any objects is terminated, all its objects go with it, which can include windows, window classes, and globally allocated memory.

Fortunately, `LibMain()` can be used to execute almost every function associated with the creation of custom controls, including the Windows API calls `GetClassInfo()` and `RegisterClass()`. The dilemma is whether `LibMain()` should be used to register the class library and perform any related initialization calls, or whether a separate initialization function should be called to perform the same task. Because global classes need to be registered only once, `LibMain()` is the best choice, especially because it doesn't choke on the calls and issue a general protection fault. Putting the `RegisterClass()` function and related calls into a separate function would require that the library constantly check itself for a call by a client module, determining whether the initialization had already been done. Unregistering the class in `WEP()` isn't necessary, because window classes don't need to be explicitly unregistered. They're automatically removed from memory when the module that registered them has unloaded.

The custom controls included with the book fall into one of two categories—*superclassed* and *pure*. The superclassed controls include the listbox control, combobox control, edit control, and custom dialog class. They're superclassed because they depend on Windows' base classes to inherit the majority of their methods. The pure controls include the bitmap, button, and split bar controls, which are designed from the ground floor up, requiring no "real" help from Windows or any of its system control classes, other than the common window inheritance function `DefWindowProc()`. Each type of custom control (superclassed or pure) initializes itself differently.

The `LibMain()` initialization routine for the superclassed listbox control is shown as follows:

```
#pragma alloc_text(INIT_TEXT, LibMain)


int PASCAL LibMain
(
    HINSTANCE hInst, WORD DataSeg, WORD HeapSize, LPSTR CmdLine
```

```
)
{
    WNDCLASS wc;

    //
    // First, get default info for class. This is used for class info
    // tidbits that you want to keep, and to remember the original
    // class window function for the listbox.
    //

    GetClassInfo(NULL, "listbox", &wc);
    lpfnListboxWndProc = (FARPROC) wc.lpfnWndProc;

    //
    // Init custom ctrl by just "patching" over WNDCLASS values you
    // need to change. You can't muck with certain values because you
    // have no idea of how Windows is using them, like extra wnd and
    // class data. In this case, all you can do is expand the values.
    //
    // The style bit needs to be changed from "internal class" to
    // GLOBALCLASS.
    //

    wc.hInstance     = hInst;
    wc.lpszClassName = "AtomicListbox";
    wc.lpfnWndProc   = AtomicListboxWndFn;
    wc.style        |= CS_GLOBALCLASS | CS_DBLCLKS;
    wc.hbrBackground = NULL;

    //
    // Register new listbox class
    //

    if(!RegisterClass(&wc))
    {
        return(FALSE);
    }

    //
    // Remember the instance in a global var
    //

    hInstListboxDLL = hInst;

    return(TRUE);
}
```

The `LibMain()` initialization routine for the pure bitmap control is shown as follows:

```
#pragma alloc_text(INIT_TEXT, LibMain)

int WINAPI LibMain
(
    HINSTANCE hInst, WORD DataSeg, WORD HeapSize, LPSTR CmdLine
)
{
    WNDCLASS wc;

    //
    // Init button control. Because this control depends on no "base"
    // class control for its methods, you're free to set up the wndclass
    // struct however you want, including wnd & class extra data, which
    // in this case is used to keep track of where the bitmap is
    // positioned inside its "viewport" window.
    //

    wc.hInstance     = hInst;
    wc.style         = CS_DBLCLKS | CS_GLOBALCLASS;
    wc.lpszMenuName  = NULL;
    wc.lpszClassName = "AtomicBitmap";
    wc.lpfnWndProc   = AtomicBitmapWndFn;
    wc.hCursor       = LoadCursor(NULL, IDC_CROSS);
    wc.cbClsExtra    = 0;
    wc.cbWndExtra    = BITMAPWNDEXTRA;
    wc.hbrBackground = NULL;
    wc.hIcon         = NULL;

    //
    // Register your new bitmap class
    //

    if(!RegisterClass(&wc))
    {
        return(FALSE);
    }

    //
    // Remember the instance in a global var
    //
```

```
    hInstBitmapDLL = hInst;

    return(TRUE);
}
```

Other than the previous registration functions, the only other function required in a library to support a custom control is a window class procedure. Usually, extra support routines are provided to help with the window procedure's processing of its methods, and if the control is to support the dialog editor, additional interfacing functions are also needed.

The bitmap control is the only custom control in the book that has been interfaced to Windows' dialog editor, and in this case, only the "visual view" of the control has been interfaced. No style dialog or other dialog-editor interface functions have been provided, although they are easy to create.

All the custom control libraries presented in this book depend on the library STDWIN to handle a certain number of default methods for the controls. Implementing a single level of inheritance using Windows and C is no great feat. However, implementing multiple levels of inheritance, as well as "has a" relationships, is another matter altogether, and one that's best suited to a language such as C++ or even SmallTalk.

This chapter has covered several topics specific to libraries, including the startup and termination code, import libraries, and methods of dynamic linking. Given that all medium to large applications are completely library-bound, it's a good idea to fully understand the topics discussed in this and the preceding chapter. Indeed, the test application and custom controls presented in this book encompass a single application and seven libraries—and this is just for a sample application! You'll very quickly find that when you abstract code and controls into one or more libraries, your coding productivity will be greatly increased and your applications will get more and more robust with each revision.

Dialog and Custom Control Design

How important is the front end of an application? Twenty percent? Forty percent? Seventy percent? It's all a balance, really. Even though an application might blaze right along with an excellent, tight engine, if the interface is too unwieldy and cumbersome, users won't be working as swiftly as they might on a slightly slower application that might be far more intuitive. Windows programming skills, unlike generic DOS skills, are definitely broken into basic categories—interface and engine. With DOS, only the engine portion was stressed, because the interface consisted of a simple character-based system. Windows, however, adds a highly complex graphical layer, involving numerous messages that add a nightmare of complexity (but extra benefits!) to those wanting to develop a snappy and intuitive front end. Compounding this problem is the ambiguities between the different categories of windows, and the general confusion surrounding how and when messages are sent.

This chapter covers all things windowing:

- Dialogs

- Controls

- Window design

- Positioning and movement

- Client and non-client areas

- The window manager

- A couple of GDI topics related to painting and drawing text

The messaging system is also covered to a certain extent, but not in the general sense as in Chapter 1. Rather, this section discusses messages as they apply to certain categories of windows.

Categories of Windows

Basically, there are two categories of windows: top-level and child. A top-level window can be overlapped or popup (described later). This type of window is generally represented by a window with a frame or border, caption, system menu, top-level menu, and minimize and maximize buttons. None of these "widgets" is mandatory for top-level windows because they can exist on child windows too; however, they're usually found only on top-level windows. If top-level windows have a caption, they can be dragged with the mouse and, in general, positioned anywhere on the desktop.

Child windows are different from top-level windows in that they have no menu, are clipped inside their parent, and generally don't change position or size. The last point is true because they have no caption for movement or thick-framed border for sizing. Although it is possible to put these components on a child window, that usually isn't done (except for MDI child windows). Child windows must have a parent window and may themselves contain child windows.

Child windows are created using the `WS_CHILD` style attribute. Omitting this attribute implies a top-level window. The parent for a given window (which doesn't imply that the window is a child window) is passed as a parameter when the window is created, through **`CreateWindow*()`**, **`CreateDialog*()`**, or **`DialogBox*()`**.

For top-level windows, the parent is used to specify an owner for the window. An owned window is merely a window that is always visually on top of its owner. This comes in handy when a series of related windows needs to be created. One top-level window is created as the main window, and the rest are created as owned. This makes it difficult to lose track of a related group of windows on a possibly "busy" desktop. The parent of a child window is a window containing (and thus clipping) the child window within its boundaries. A child window can never be created without a parent window being specified. One extra thing that differentiates child windows from top-level windows is a control ID. This integer value is specified when the window is created and is used to reference the child window within its parent. Top-level windows use this same "slot" value as a handle to a menu. Because only top-level windows are capable of having menus, this works out well.

A parent window is also different from an owner window in that a parent window commonly receives notification messages on the activity of its children. These notifications are received through the messages `WM_PARENTNOTIFY` and `WM_COMMAND`. One thing in common for "owner" windows and parent windows is that any offspring (owned windows or child windows) are automatically destroyed, shown, hidden, minimized, or restored, along with their respective parent/owner. Additionally, top-level windows come in two flavors: overlapped and popup. The difference is that overlapped windows must have a caption and a border, whereas popup windows can have no distinguishing features whatsoever. Popup windows are often used for splash screens and other types of windows that don't require the usual non-client trappings.

To confuse you even further, take the case of MDI child windows. Here is a case of a child window that has a caption, a system menu, and minimize and maximize buttons just like top-level windows—so what's the difference? Well, in this case MDI child windows still have no top-level menu and are still clipped inside their parent window (MDI client). Their appearance throws you off at first because they have captions or borders, and they look and smell like top-level windows. However, if you run Spy you'll notice that MDI children never receive WM_ACTIVATE messages, because only top-level windows can be made active. Instead, MDI children receive WM_MDIACTIVATE, which is sent from the MDI client window. Any window with a caption will receive WM_NCACTIVATE messages, but only top-level windows will receive WM_ACTIVATE messages. Developers often complain that MDI child windows are incapable of having menus. The reason for this is that they are assigned a control identifier (because they are indeed child windows) and have no open slot for a menu handle.

Child windows can be created in various categories: stock and custom controls, top-level like MDI child windows, and even dialogs. Yes, there's nothing preventing a child window from being a dialog. Of course, a little more work is involved, but it's absolutely possible. Like MDI child windows, child window controls can be given a thick frame and caption, although it is very nonstandard and absolutely not recommended. (I see people trying it right now!) Adding the WS_CAPTION and WS_THICKFRAME styles to a listbox or edit control actually allows the control to be moved around via the mouse inside the parent window. Note that unlike MDI child windows, in this case the caption of the control is never painted as active. This is because with MDI, there's a "middleman" client window that can perform such windowing trickery. Another problem with user-moveable child controls is that Microsoft states in its manuals that there is no generic method of handling overlapping controls neatly. This doesn't mean that you can't create an edit control inside a listbox cell entry; it just means that non-neat overlapping controls might not be painted as cleanly as you would like.

Other than a system menu or pull-down menu, top-level windows generally take no input and show no output, with the exception of the minimize and maximize buttons, a thick-framed border, and possibly a painted background or client area. In contrast, the sole purpose of a child control is to provide input to the parent window, output to the user, or both. A menu, although it is a component of the window much like a control is, is considered more an integral part of the window as a whole, with the individual menu items representing and functioning as if they were individual controls. Just like controls, menu items can be created, destroyed, enabled, disabled, take input, and even show output in the form of a checkbox next to a menu item or by using owner-draw, as control windows are capable of doing. Also like controls, each menu item has a corresponding integer ID.

The Window Class

All windows, regardless of their type, are based on some common grouping of data, referred to as a class. This class structure, WNDCLASS, defines a set of common attributes that are to be shared by windows created from the class. The WNDCLASS data structure is defined as follows:

```
typedef struct WNDCLASS
{
    UINT        Style;          // Class style bits
                // CS_VREDRAW--Whole window is auto-invalidated when
                // vertical size of window changes
                // CS_HREDRAW--Whole window is auto-invalidated when
                // horizontal size of window changes
                // CS_CLASSDC--Window uses common class display context
                // for painting operations. Shared by all instances of
                // window.
                // CS_OWNDC--Gives each window its own display context.
                // Use with discretion because each DC consumes at least 800
                // bytes of GDI local heap space
                // CS_PARENTDC--All windows share parent's display
                // context for painting. Cannot be used with the window
                // style WS_CLIPCHILDREN. This means that child GDI output can
                // overlap into the client area of the parent
                // CS_BYTEALIGNCLIENT--Aligns window client area on byte
                // boundaries
                // CS_BYTEALIGNWINDOW--Aligns window on byte boundaries,
                // resulting in slightly faster window movement
                // CS_SAVEBITS--Saves portion of screen image covered by
                // window. Windows uses this to re-create display when
                // window is destroyed, not sending WM_PAINT messages to
                // underlying window. Should be used only for smaller
                // windows, because it increases the amount of time required
                // to display window when created
                // CS_DBLCLKS--Allows control to receive double-click
```

```
                              // messages. Required for any control that must interface
                              // with the SDK's Dialog Editor utility
                              // CS_NOCLOSE--Removes the 'Close' system menu option
                              // from window
                              // CS_GLOBALCLASS--Specifies an application global
                              // class, as opposed to an application local class (the
                              // default) or Windows' internal system class (edit,
                              // listbox, combobox, and so on)

        WNDPROC     lpfnWndProc;      // Class window procedure
        int         cbClsExtra;       // Programmer assoc. data words w/class
        int         cbWndExtra;       // Programmer assoc. data words w/window
        HINSTANCE   hInstance;        // Module that called RegisterClass
        HICON       hIcon;            // Default icon
        HCURSOR     hCursor;          // Default cursor
        HBRUSH      hbrBackground;    // Default bkgrd brush
        LPCSTR      lpszMenuName;     // Menu for class
        LPCSTR      lpszClassName;    // Class name
}
```

Although several class styles are possible for a given type of window, not all of them are practical, or even usable for that matter. For example, the class styles CS_HREDRAW and CS_VREDRAW are commonly used by developers for virtually every kind of custom window class. However, they're actually practical only for certain types of windows, because these styles automatically invalidate the entire client area of a window when its size changes. This has the unfortunate effect of causing a noticeable amount of on-screen painting activity, most of which is pointless. When a window is resized or somehow obscured and needs to be repainted, Windows automatically defines a clipping region and (at some point) informs the application of the portions that have changed. It's usually not necessary to do a full invalidation and redraw each time.

Another class style that has kind of gone by the wayside (and for good reason) is CS_SAVEBITS. This style was intended to be used by small windows (like dropdown menus) that aren't on-screen for long periods. The desired behavior is for the window to preserve the section of window underneath it, redisplaying this saved section of bitmap when the window is eventually destroyed or removed. This removes the painting burden from the window being covered, because it never receives a WM_PAINT message. The only problem is that this functionality isn't absolutely guaranteed, and under certain conditions, the bitmap is never saved.

The last two useless class style bits are CS_OWNDC and CS_CLASSDC. These styles cause Windows to create and maintain additional display contexts for individual windows or windows in a class, which get stored in GDI's local heap.

The problem isn't with the idea, but rather the implementation. Because local heaps (including GDI, User, and DGROUP) are basically easy to put into a terminal situation, any use of the local heap beyond what is necessary isn't recommended. This is especially true of local heaps that are used by other applications. Because local heaps are capable of automatically generating a series of "gapped" unremoveable sandbars in memory, it's not wise to place any more objects in them than is required. GDI objects aren't a problem because they tend to be created and destroyed quickly. Private and class display contexts, however, exist for the life of the window, making them more of an issue. Although the initial release of the custom controls included in the book uses private display contexts for the dialog and bitmap window classes, the second release of window classes switches back to a manually maintained display context, using DCs from the common pool of five.

After the WNDCLASS structure is filled in, the class can be registered with a call to `RegisterClass()`, which accepts a far pointer to the structure. `RegisterClass()` can be called only once for any particular class. If a class is registered twice, the second attempt fails. To remove a class, the function `UnregisterClass()` can be called. This step is unnecessary, however, because window classes are automatically unregistered when the "owning" module that initially registered the class is terminated.

A class is registered in one of three contexts:

- System global—a stock window class that can only be registered by Windows which allows all active applications use of the class (edit, listbox, static). This class is similar to an application global class, except these classes are provided when Windows is first loaded, and they aren't unregistered until Windows terminates. A developer can effectively modify stock window classes through global subclassing (`SetClassLong()`), although several problems can occur. These are discussed more fully at the end of Chapter 1.

- Application global—a developer-defined class allowing system-wide use of the class for any application that has loaded the DLL registering the class.

- Application local—a window class commonly used by applications to register top-level windows that don't need to be shared as do custom control classes.

Much in the manner of when an executable filename is typed on the DOS command line, when a program references a class, Windows performs as many as three searches to locate the class. First, Windows checks to see whether the class is registered locally. If it isn't, the application global class list is checked.

If this search also proves fruitless, the system global class list is checked. If the search still fails, the call obviously fails. This searching method allows an application to override class names without affecting other applications. All internal class lists are available via a series of ToolHelp functions. The owner of a window class is specified by the HINSTANCE field in the WNDCLASS structure. When the owner of any class is terminated, all windows based on that class must also be terminated. Of course, this is true for the owners of all objects, whether memory objects, GDI objects, or owners of other windows.

The Window

Additionally, all windows use the structure CREATESTRUCT, an "instance"-related window structure that uses its own information plus information from WNDCLASS to create an actual window. The structure CREATESTRUCT is defined as follows:

```
typedef struct
{
    LPSTR      lpCreateParams; // Used with MDI applications, it
                       // points to a CLIENTCREATESTRUCT structure. This value
                       // is referenced indirectly through WM_CREATE and lParam,
                       // where lParam points to CREATESTRUCT

    HINSTANCE hInstance;   // Identifies the instance of the application
                       // that is to service msgs for the window

    HMENU     hMenu;       // Specifies a menuID for top-level windows,
                       // or integer identifier for child controls

    HWND      hWndParent; // Specifies an owner window for top-level
                       // windows, or a parent in the case of child
                       // windows

    int    cy;    // Specifies height of window in device units,
                  // which normally are pixels
    int    cx;    // Specifies width of window in device units
    int    y;     // Specifies y coordinate of upper-left corner of
                  // window. Coordinates are relative to the screen
                  // for top-level windows, and are relative to the
                  // parent window for child windows
    int    x;     // Specifies x coordinate of upper-left corner

    long   style // Style long bits for window
           // WS_OVERLAPPED, WS_POPUP, WS_CHILD
```

```
        // WS_CLIPSIBLINGS--Specifies that child window is to
        // clip other children during paints. Normally, child
        // windows should not overlap each other. For use only
        // with windows defined via WS_CHILD
        // WS_CLIPCHILDREN--Excludes child controls from paint
        // DC used by parent. Used with parent window style only.
        // Cannot be used in conjunction with CS_PARENTDC
        // WS_VISIBLE--Specifies an initially visible window. By
        // default, windows are not visible
        // WS_DISABLED--Creates an initially disabled window
        // WS_VSCROLL--Creates a window with a vertical scroll bar
        // WS_HSCROLL--Creates a window with a horizontal scroll bar
        // WS_MINIMIZE--Creates an initially minimized window
        // WS_MAXIMIZE--Creates an initially maximized window
        // WS_BORDER--Creates a window with a thin border
        // WS_DLGFRAME--Creates a window with a double border
        // WS_THICKFRAME--Creates a window with a sizable border
        // WS_CAPTION--Creates a window with a caption and
        // border. Cannot be used with WS_DLGFRAME
        //      The following styles imply that a caption is used:
        // WS_SYSMENU--Creates a window with a system menu
        // WS_MINIMIZEBOX--Creates a window with a minimize button
        // WS_MAXIMIZEBOX--Creates a window with a maximize button
        //      The following styles are for child controls:
        // WS_GROUP--Creates a logical "group" of controls. The
        // function IsDialogMessage uses this bit to determine which
        // controls in a group are accessible via the arrow keys
        // WS_TABSTOP--Creates a control capable of receiving the
        // focus via the Tab key. Used by IsDialogMessage

    LPSTR lpszName;   // Window name/caption
    LPSTR lpszClass;  // Window class

    long  ExStyle;    // Extra style bits for window:
        // WS_EX_DLGMODALFRAME--Same as WS_DLGFRAME
        // WS_EX_NOPARENTNOTIFY--Creates a control that doesn't
        // notify its parent via WM_PARENTNOTIFY when the window is
        // created or destroyed
        // WS_EX_TOPMOST--Creates a window that is always "visually"
        // on top of other windows
        // WS_EX_ACCEPTFILES--Creates a window capable of accepting
        // file drag-and-drop messages (from FileManager, for example)
        // WS_EX_TRANSPARENT--Creates a transparent window. Any
        // windows beneath the window are painted before it
    }
CREATESTRUCT;
```

All window-creation functions (`CreateWindow()`, `CreateDialog()`, `DialogBox()`) use this structure. Usually it isn't modified directly by the developer, however, because all the fields in the structure are directly passed in the function call that creates the window. The structure can, however, be examined and modified during the `WM_CREATE` message for the window, which passes a long pointer to the structure via `lParam`. Under Windows 3.0, the structure was often modified when working with MDI child windows, because certain styles of windows were prohibited, including thin-frame windows and those with a modal dialog style of border. This behavior can easily be overridden by manually setting bits in the style field of the window structure during `WM_CREATE` and then passing control to `DefMDIChildProc()`.

Under Windows 3.1, this technique is no longer needed for MDI child windows because a new style bit has been created—`MDIS_ALLCHILDSTYLES`—that allows child windows of any style to be created. However, this modify-on-the-fly technique works quite well for other cases.

Class/Window Extra Data

Just as Windows maintains internal data for each registered window class and window by-product, so can the developer. This is made possible during the call to Windows' `RegisterClass()` function. Note the two integer values in the previously listed `WNDCLASS` structure. The first integer value, cbClsExtra, defines the number of additional per-class words you want to have allocated for storage information about the window class. The second integer value in the structure, cbWndExtra, defines the number of additional per-window words you want allocated with each created window "instance" of the class. Both values should ideally remain at a minimum, because making them too large (more than 20 or so bytes) will cause User's local heap to get cramped for space awfully quickly. Extra data is accessed similar to an array, using the functions `GetClassLong()`, `GetClassWord()`, `GetWindowLong()`, `GetWindowWord()`, `SetClassLong()`, `SetClassWord()`, `SetWindowLong()`, and `SetWindowWord()`. Like accessing an array, using stray values can cause access to parts of memory you shouldn't be dealing with. You must always take care when changing window and class values via the extra data, because all of it is lumped into one spot in User's heap. In this case, overwriting is worse than with an array. Instead accessing some random, possibly uninitialized spot in memory, you're almost guaranteed to corrupt the following structure in memory, which just happens to describe another window on the desktop. Problems related to overwrites can be very difficult and extremely frustrating to track down. The window you save may be your own!

Under Windows 3.x, any task can read and write to the extra data of another window, even a window in a totally different application. This can be restricted under Windows NT, however. All the extra data functions specify a window as a target, and an index into the window's class/window data space. Even though the quantities for both of these fields can be expressed in bytes, they are automatically rounded (up) to words by Windows. So to be safe, make sure you've defined each quantity as a multiple of two bytes (the size of a word). Under Windows NT, because just about everything is a 32-bit DWORD, extra data will be in the form of extra DWORDs. Using data associated with class and window structures is very object-oriented, because you're storing the data with the object it references—it also has the benefit of being quite fast. The use of window data (as well as window properties) helps eliminate many reentrancy issues that often plague Windows development.

Window Properties

In addition to class and window extra data, Windows also provides window properties—a simpler method of associating information with a window. Every type and class of window on the desktop is capable of associating some named property ("Font" or "3DState") with an arbitrary handle. Possible handle choices are to GDI objects (brushes, fonts, icons), an atom handle to a hashed string, a dynamically allocated memory handle pointing to memory in either the local or global heap, or possibly some simple static value. The use of window properties is simpler than extra data because properties can be dynamically added to and removed from a window, with no fear of overwriting the data of another application. Instead of manually indexing into an array, properties are accessed via a simple, hashed name. Unlike window data, properties are slightly slower to access—but not much slower relative to the whole scheme of things. This shouldn't be much of a problem for most applications and shouldn't restrict usage.

Any properties added to a window must be destroyed when the window containing them is destroyed. Likewise, any GDI or Kernel objects referenced by the property handle must be deleted. Both of these steps are usually done by the developer during a window's WM_DESTROY method. Like extra data, an application may read and write to the properties of windows owned by a different application. Under NT, this too can be optionally restricted.

The dynamic nature of window properties makes them a good candidate for holding temporary values associated with a window. In fact, properties are used in this manner by all the custom controls in the book. Almost all the control classes face the dilemma of initializing certain items and structures for every window they're in charge of. The WM_CREATE message can't always be used because certain structures related to the window haven't been created by Windows yet. For example, the custom control code associated with both the combobox and listbox classes has built-in methods that automatically load the controls at runtime. The only problem is that when ?B_ADDSTRING messages are sent during WM_CREATE, Windows crashes and burns. Attempting to process the new method after the create message had already been processed (but while still in the WM_CREATE message itself) proved to no avail either. The only solution was to process the listbox and combobox data in a later message, mainly WM_MOVE. This was done by establishing a temporary window property during WM_CREATE, which is picked off by the first WM_MOVE message received by a window. It is here that the property is removed and the control initialized. The property is removed simply because you don't want initialization to occur during the next WM_MOVE message received by the window.

One idiosyncrasy in the way properties work is the manner in which they are retrieved. The function GetProp() is passed a window handle and property name as parameters, returning the handle associated with the property, and null if the property couldn't be found. The problem occurs when the handle being stored is itself null. So now, does a null return value indicate that the property didn't exist in the first place or that it did and had a value of null? The function should really be prototyped as returning a BOOL value, indicating success or failure of the function, and as being passed a third parameter—a long pointer to the application-supplied handle value to be stuffed. Windows 3.0 had a problem in the way it handled properties containing a null value—basically, it didn't handle them! Under version 3.0, when a property handle was set to a null value, the hashed property name ended up getting stored as an atom. Thankfully, Windows 3.1 has fixed the problem, making workarounds unnecessary.

The Windows API provides the following functions for manipulating window properties:

Function	Purpose
EnumProps()	Invokes caller-supplied callback function with each window property defined for a particular window.
GetProp()	Retrieves value of passed property name.
RemoveProp()	Removes property from window.
SetProp()	Adds new property to window or changes existing property.

Window States

No matter what the type of window, each is capable of being put into one of several different input states. Top-level windows and dialogs can be created modeless, application-modal, and system-modal. In addition, they can be active, inactive, visible, hidden, enabled, and disabled. Child windows don't have a modal state associated with them; however, they can be put into several other input states. Child windows may be enabled, disabled, visible, hidden, with "focus," or without "focus." Child windows (including owned windows) always inherit the state of their parents. If a parent window is made enabled, disabled, visible, or hidden, then so are its children. Several "size" states are also associated with a window. A window can be either in its regular size or in a minimized or maximized state.

Mode

Mode refers to the input state of the window. For example, when a system-modal window is created, all mouse and keyboard activity on the desktop comes to a halt until the window is responded to and eventually destroyed. Destruction of a system-modal window is necessary before other windows and controls on the desktop can be activated and gain the input focus, or before any inter-task messages can be sent. System-modal windows are generally used for critical error handling. Application-modal windows must be responded to and destroyed before any other top-level window or dialog in the application can be made active. Other applications on the desktop are not affected by application-modal windows; only the application that created it is. The term *modeless* describes the majority of the windows on the desktop. A modeless window does not have to be destroyed before another window on the desktop is activated.

An application-modal window is automatically created by a call to `DialogBox...()`, whereas modeless dialogs and windows are created by calls to `CreateDialog...()` and `CreateWindow()`. Windows' `MessageBox()` function allows the developer to create message dialogs in all three states: system-modal, application-modal, and modeless. Application and system-modal window states can be duplicated by merely disabling certain top-level windows. This is sometimes more efficient, because a window doesn't have to be destroyed for the modal state to change. Windows even provides a function for making windows system-modal *after* they were created. This is done by merely passing a window handle to the function `SetSysModalWindow()`. If a system-modal window creates another window or dialog, the newly created window becomes system-modal. When it is destroyed, the prior system-modal window takes its place. System-modal windows should be used as infrequently as possible, because their use blocks access to other portions of the desktop. Just because your application is having a problem, it doesn't need to impact other applications on the desktop. But then again, maybe it is *that* critical a message. The call is up to the developer.

Active and Inactive Windows

There can be only one active window on the desktop. An active window is the window whose child control currently has the focus for keyboard and mouse input. Depending on your settings in the control panel, the active window usually is the one with a blue caption bar. Windows are made active and inactive by various means, including clicking on the window with the mouse, using Alt-Tab to switch between tasks, using Ctrl-Esc to bring up the task manager, or by program control.

The active window on the desktop can be any top-level window, but never a child window. A window can be made active with a call to the function `SetActiveWindow()`. When one window is activated, another is notified that it has been deactivated. Windows will then gray the inactive window's caption to signify such. A window doesn't necessarily have to be the active window to receive mouse input because Windows provides the function `SetCapture()` to redirect input to a particular window. When capturing is no longer needed, a call to `ReleaseCapture()` can be made. `SetCapture()` is generally used to trap mouse movement outside of a window's client and non-client areas.

Enabled and Disabled Windows

The enabled and disabled state apply to all windows on the desktop—regardless of their type. A window that is enabled is capable of accepting mouse and keyboard input and is painted to reflect this fact. A disabled window is not available for user-initiated input of any kind (although messages can still be sent or posted to the window). Disabled windows are usually painted grayed-out to indicate their state. Controls aren't the only thing that can be disabled; menu items and even items in a listbox can be disabled and grayed dynamically to indicate that a particular choice can longer be made. When a parent window is disabled, so are all of its child windows. When the parent window is reenabled, so are its children—unless individually disabled. When an owned modal dialog is created by a window, the window is disabled before the modal dialog is displayed.

Visible and Hidden Windows

Another state applying to all window types is visibility—is the window visible or hidden? Unless otherwise specified, all windows are initially created hidden. Hidden windows are still capable of receiving mouse and keyboard input; they just don't receive paint and other similar messages. In a resource file, if the parent dialog is specified as being visible, by default all child controls in the dialog are visible as well. Likewise, when the parent window is hidden, so are all the children of the parent. When windows are created manually, each must be specified as being visible or it will be hidden.

The Focus

The focus is obtained by only one window on the desktop, always a child window. Windows directs all mouse and keyboard input to the window with the focus. Not having the focus does not eliminate a window from receiving mouse and keyboard input from other sources though, like another task. A window or child control can always be sent keyboard and mouse messages from a task, even when it doesn't have the focus, is hidden, is disabled, or is inactive. Of course, whether the program decides to process them is another matter.

Similar to the activation of top-level windows and dialogs, most controls undergo a visual change when focus is obtained or lost. Every control class varies when it comes to indicating a focus state. Usually the rule is to decide what part of the control your eye is specifically drawn to. Is it the name of the control, an item or possibly several inside the control, or just some manipulation of the primary image inside an owner-draw button or owner-draw listbox entry? Window controls containing a label or some other section of text usually inverse the text, draw a dashed border around it, or do both.

Button class controls use a dashed box around the text of their associated label and don't bother to highlight it. For push buttons, the label is centered in the button, whereas for radio buttons and check boxes, it's the text just to the right of the circle or square graphical portion of the control. A push button that has the focus usually is used inside some kind of a dialog, which means that it usually has thickened borders as well, a visual indicator that it is the new default button. Listboxes show that they have the focus by drawing a dashed rectangle around the currently selected listbox entry. Edit controls and editable comboboxes highlight any text inside the control and place a blinking (or possibly solid) caret inside the control for editing (cursor positioning) purposes. A menu shows that it has the focus by highlighting the current top-level menu or submenu item. Although menus don't really have the focus in the sense that controls do, and more important, aren't windows, they do need a similar function.

Dialogs

Dialogs are a special form of window. Dialogs are different from windows in how (and where) they are created, destroyed, and process messages. The primary reason for dialogs is the easy creation of a window pane containing multiple child controls. Can you imagine creating a complex dialog manually? Most of the time, the answer is an emphatic no! Dialogs are much more convenient for creating a window with multiple child controls, because the entire dialog structure usually resides in a simple structure in the application's resource file. This contrasts with the many lines of code that would be required to create each window manually. All dialogs are windows, but not all windows are dialogs. Although they don't need to, dialogs usually contain at least one child control. A dialog can be an overlapped window, popup window, or even a child window.

A dialog can be defined in two ways. First, there is the dialog proper, created using the functions `CreateDialog*()` or `DialogBox*()`. When a window is created in this method, it is assumed to have several extra structures associated with it (described later) that mainly deal with the font and child controls found in the dialog. Additionally, a window (or dialog rather) created in this fashion has a series of extra window data, used to store state information for the dialog. This state information keeps track of the control with focus, the default button, and various other undocumented tidbits. Second, there is "dialog functionality," which can be added to any type of parent window (except for composite controls). All that's necessary for this is a call into `IsDialogMessage()`. What this does is add a little dialog-style keyboard functionality to the window, providing special processing for the arrow and Tab keys, and the Return key. Dialogs don't have to call `IsDialogMessage()`, and conversely, you don't have to be a dialog to call `IsDialogMessage()`.

Scrolling Dialogs

Dialogs can also be created as scrollable, which is done in one of two ways. The first, and easiest, method actually is done by the `TestApp` dialog example in this

275

book (see the appendixes) that demonstrates all the custom controls. This involves creating a thick-framed window with the WS_HSCROLL and WS_VSCROLL window attributes, to put on a vertical and a horizontal scroll bar. Then, controls are positioned inside the window without regard for the actual client size that's initially established for their parent. So if the dialog has a width of 200 dialog units and a height of 100 dialog units, you still might have controls that are positioned and effectively clipped outside of this region—but that's OK. Next, you interpret the WM_VSCROLL and WM_HSCROLL messages destined for the window. Each press or manipulation of the scroll bar is translated into a ScrollWindow() call, which automatically handles the scrolling of off-screen child windows into view. Because the client window area is being manipulated in a nonstandard fashion, it is necessary to maintain an x and y origin offset, which is used to determine when the scrolling process should begin and end. These scrolling ranges change dynamically as the window gets resized.

The other method involves using a child window dialog—that is, a dialog defined as WS_CHILD in a resource file. This method has the distinct advantage of allowing multiple child dialog panes to be embedded in a single, over-lapped parent window. To move a dialog created in this fashion, you can use SetWindowPos(), because you've embedded a whole child window into your top-level window pane. The "inner" dialogs then might be separated by a series of grab bars, or merely just scrolled around within the parent window. This is definitely not something you want to overdo, because it could end up confusing not only the user of the application but the developer too! Problems with this technique involve focus determination, because Windows expects the first child descendant of a top-level window to get the focus, not some child control embedded who-knows-how-many levels deep in your windowing scheme. Both of these dialog-creation techniques can be quite useful for creating extensive "industrial-strength" data entry screens. The IRS and the standard long form come to mind quickly.

Using dialogs as child windows poses a variety of other problems too. Part of the problem is due to the fact that an embedded child dialog never receives WM_ACTIVATE, which is used by the default dialog procedure to set and reset the control having the focus, and to tweak the default button. Because certain messages are no longer received by the dialog window procedure, the extra window data for the dialog is never set correctly. Because the dialog won't remember who had the focus or update the default button properly, it's up to the developer to handle these things manually. This means rewriting the functionality behind DM_SETDEFID, which is used to establish a default button, DM_GETDEFID, which is used to retrieve the default button, and WM_NEXTDLGCTL, which is used to set the focus and modify the default button appropriately in a dialog. This isn't difficult, just a little time-consuming. To get a head start, immediately superclass all controls, having them post WM_PARENTNOTIFY messages whenever they gain or lose the focus. This is required so the parent window will know immediately whenever control has been lost, and store the window handle in some appropriate, and most important, generic location. This means not storing it inside a dialog's extra data, but rather as a window property, which is something all windows are capable of having. Manual methods must also be implemented for handling the Return key and the default button. When handling dialog-style processing manually it's not too difficult to do a better job than what is offered by Windows. In fact, handling keyboard processing manually means that certain messages, like WM_NEXTDLGCTL and WM_GETDLGCODE, won't end up being needed. The reason WM_NEXTDLGCTL won't be needed is that **SetFocus()** can be used as a replacement, and the reason WM_GETDLGCODE won't be needed is that **IsDialogMessage()** won't be around to send the message.

Dialog Messages

Many misconceptions regarding dialogs need to be dispelled. Most developers think of dialogs as system-modal, double-bordered top-level windows. This is not the case, however, because dialogs can be created in any of a variety of flavors—overlapped, popup, or child. Generally associated with dialogs is the function **IsDialogMessage()**, which provides special keyboard processing for the dialog, including things such as the default button, control window "accelerators" (such as &Cancel and Prin&t), the Tab key (for switching back and forth between controls), and the arrow keys, which are used to switch between controls defined within a group. Actually, **IsDialogMessage()** can be used for any window that needs to provide dialog-style processing and isn't limited to dialogs.

The majority of a dialog's "keyboard" functionality is implemented via the function **IsDialogMessage()** and the message WM_GETDLGCODE. Although Microsoft documents **IsDialogMessage()** thoroughly enough, the same cannot be said for WM_GETDLGCODE, which has a confusing description to say the least. First, look at the way the **IsDialogMessage()** function is embedded into an application's message processing loop:

```
//
// This loop breaks when GetMessage returns a WM_QUIT (which is 0)
//

while(GetMessage(&msg, NULL, NULL, NULL))
{
```

```
//
// The global variable hDlgActive is used to determine
// the "active" dialog for the application. This allows the msg
// loop to process the dialog-extended functionality for any
// dialog that happens to be on the screen. This variable is
// set or reset (to NULL) in every wndproc during the window's
// WM_ACTIVATE message, similar to the following:
//
// case WM_ACTIVATE :
//
//     hDlgActive = (wParam) ? hWnd : NULL;
//     break;
//
// Here is your dialog-aware message loop:
//

    if(hDlgActive)
    {
        if(IsDialogMessage(hDlgActive, &msg))
        {
            //
            // You don't need to pass on to Translate or Dispatch
            // because IsDialogMessage handles these messages too.
            //

            continue;
        }
    }

    //
    // For an active dialog, these functions kick in only when another
    // window is activated, or when the mouse veers beyond the non-
    // client area of the dialog (off the edge).
    //

    TranslateMessage(&msg);
    DispatchMessage(&msg);
}
```

When **IsDialogMessage()** is called, it sends a series of WM_GETDLGCODE messages to all the child controls in the parent window hDlg. This message is used to determine how the controls want to respond to the "dialog-specific" keys mentioned earlier. This is needed because each control type interprets these keys differently. For an example, consider a button control, a multiline edit control, and the Tab key. When Tab is pressed on a button, the focus generally is shifted to the next WS_TABSTOP-defined control within the window, whereas when the Tab key is pressed in an MLE, a tab character is inserted into the edit control and the blinking caret moves over by some amount. Focus, however, still remains on the MLE. The same is true of buttons, listboxes, and the arrow keys. When an arrow key is pressed on a button, the focus switches to the next button (or control) in the group, whereas with the listbox, the arrow keys are used to navigate through entries in the listbox. It is because of these differences that `IsDialogMessage()` needs to continually send messages to the controls. It doesn't remember who does what, and it figures that at some point the developer might want certain behaviors to be reimplemented.

Developers are better off eliminating references to the function `IsDialogMessage()`. A better implementation method exists that is much more intuitive and object-oriented. Instead of snatching keystrokes out from applications just as they've come out of the message queue, a better idea would have been to put the `IsDialogMessage()` code somewhere inside the `WM_KEYDOWN` method found in `DefWindowProc()`. This way, if a window didn't want the keystroke, it would be available for dialog-style processing. For example, if a multiline edit control wanted to process the enter key, all it would have to do would be process the `WM_KEYDOWN` message and not return control to `DefWindowProc()`—it's that simple. If a control, say a listbox, doesn't handle the Enter key on a `WM_KEYDOWN`, then `DefWindowProc()` would be free to interpret it as a press of the default button. Instead, Microsoft implemented it the current way, causing developers grief over how to alter the Enter key, write decent custom controls, and decipher the cryptic description behind `WM_GETDLGCODE`. Because most developers don't have the source code to `DefWindowProc()`, the best solution is to rewrite the dialog functionality inside a common window procedure. All of this (with the exception of default button handling) has actually been done with the source code included for the custom controls in this book.

The controls included in this book include three "pure" custom control classes (button, bitmap, split bar), three superclassed controls (edit, combobox, listbox), and an enhanced dialog window class. The term *superclassed* means that the controls still have their root in Windows' stock control class methods. For these controls, `WM_GETDLGCODE` is simply passed on to the default class method, because no behavior modifications are needed. The pure classes, however, need to "define" their functionality. In the case of the bitmap control, this means that it needs to intercept the arrow keys, much in the manner of the listbox control, because they are used to control the scroll bars used to navigate around the bitmap. This is done in the bitmap control's window procedure via the following statement:

```
case WM_GETDLGCODE :

    return(DLGC_WANTARROWS);
```

For the pure controls, the default method handler is `DefWindowProc()`, whereas for the superclassed controls it is the original class window function, which is remembered by the DLL and called via `CallWindowProc()`. After any control-specific message processing is done, the class procedure too will eventually call `DefWindowProc()`. When `DefWindowProc()` processes the WM_GETDLGCODE message, it returns a zero, indicating that all input is to be captured and attempted to be processed. If the keystroke isn't used, it is lost. `IsDialogMessage()` processes only keystroke messages, passing all other messages through to `TranslateMessage()` and `DispatchMessage()`, which is why these functions shouldn't be called a second time in the application's message dispatching loop. When a message is posted, it enters the application's queue and eventually trickles down to `DefWindowProc()` or `DefDlgProc()`. When a message is dispatched or sent to a particular window, it first enters the "uppermost" method for the window, then possibly passing through a chain of window functions, which act as filters. Eventually, the message makes its way down to either `DefWindowProc()` or `DefDlgProc()`, when the window cannot or does not want to process the message itself.

A dialog is different from a window in that it requires additional data structures besides the WNDCLASS and CREATESTRUCT structures associated with all windows. In the case of a resource file-defined dialog, these structures are generated automatically. For dynamically allocated and created dialogs, however, the structures must be defined manually by the developer, because they don't exist in any header file.

An abbreviated form of the resource file-defined dialog used by STDWIN.DLL for printing bitmaps is shown as follows:

```
PrintOptions DIALOG LOADONCALL MOVEABLE DISCARDABLE 53, 61, 136, 121
STYLE       WS_POPUPWINDOW ¦ WS_VISIBLE ¦ WS_CAPTION ¦ DS_MODALFRAME ¦
            DS_SETFONT
CAPTION     "Print Options"
FONT        8, "Helv"
BEGIN
    CONTROL "# C&opies:" -1, "STATIC", SS_LEFT ¦ WS_CHILD, 8, 8, 33, 10

    CONTROL "1" IDC_COPIES, "edit",
        ES_LEFT ¦ WS_CHILD ¦ WS_BORDER ¦ WS_TABSTOP,
        43, 7, 20, 11

    CONTROL "Por&trait" IDC_PORTRAIT, "BUTTON",
```

```
            BS_AUTORADIOBUTTON | WS_CHILD | WS_GROUP | WS_TABSTOP,
            9, 31, 36, 11

    CONTROL "&Landscape" IDC_LANDSCAPE, "BUTTON",
            BS_AUTORADIOBUTTON | WS_CHILD | WS_TABSTOP,
            9, 43, 47, 11

    CONTROL "&Aspect" IDC_ASPECT, "BUTTON",
            BS_PUSHBUTTON | WS_CHILD | WS_TABSTOP | WS_GROUP,
            48, 81, 38, 15

    CONTROL "&Print" IDC_PRINT, "BUTTON",
            BS_PUSHBUTTON | WS_CHILD | WS_TABSTOP,
            48, 101, 38, 15
END
```

All windows have some kind of window text. This window text is in the form of a caption (for top-level windows) or a label, as it is with buttons and statics. For edit controls, the window text is in the form of alphanumerics stuffed inside the edit control. Listboxes, comboboxes, and scroll bars, however, have no label, caption, or accelerator explicitly bound to them. For these controls, the window text isn't used at all. Accelerator keys are based on some form of window text. If the control doesn't explicitly have a label, as is the case with edits, comboboxes, listboxes, and scroll bars, the accelerator of the static label (if any) that exists just prior to the created control in the dialog is used as a replacement. For the preceding dialog, this means that the static label "C&opies" will be used as an accelerator for the control existing directly below it, which is an edit.

This is also true for the functioning of the Tab and arrow keys and the default button. In the case of the arrow keys, the first control in every logical "group" of controls should be defined with the WS_GROUP style bit. This bit defines every control at this point and below as being a member of the group. This association stops as soon as another control with WS_GROUP is defined. The arrow keys are used to shift focus between items in a defined group. This behavior is primarily used only with button controls, because most other control types require the arrow keys for other purposes. The style bit WS_TABSTOP just ensures that the control is capable of accepting and losing focus via the Tab key, regardless of any established groups of controls.

When any kind of window is created, it is placed inside a special data structure known as a window list, which is kept internally by Windows. In the case of any parent window, all of its child windows are stored off of a list with the parent window as the root. Additionally, all the peer or sibling windows of a child or parent window are attached in a parallel list. These lists, kept for all top-level and child windows on the desktop, are used to determine the z-, tab-, and arrow-ordering of windows. The z-order really only applies to top-level windows and MDI child windows, because it controls the bottommost to topmost order of activation for a window, whether the window is activated by keyboard or mouse control. For child windows, the ordering of the window list determines the order in which windows are created, destroyed, and tabbed or arrowed through. See the section on window lists and z-ordering at the end of the chapter for more information.

A dialog is broken down into three basic structures, including the master structure DLGTEMPLATE, which defines the dialog's general characteristics, and the structures FONTINFO and DLGITEMTEMPLATE, which follow it immediately in memory and define the font used in the dialog and the individual controls found inside. The structure DLGTEMPLATE is defined as follows:

```
typedef struct
{
    long dtStyle;    // Can be any of the following (including WS_*):
        // DS_LOCALEDIT--Specifies DGROUP storage for edit controls
        // stored in the dialog. This permits the messages
        // EM_GETHANDLE and EM_SETHANDLE to be used, which retrieve an
        // HLOCAL handle to the edit data. Normally, edit data is stored
        // in a global segment
        // DS_SYSMODAL--Creates a system modal dialog
        // DS_MODALFRAME--Creates a thick (unsizable) dialog border,
        // commonly used with DS_SYSMODAL
        // DS_ABSALIGN--Aligns the dialog box relative to the screen
        // and not the owner window
        // DS_SETFONT--Specifies that a font other than the system
        // font is to be used with the dialog
        // DS_NOIDLEMSG--Specifies that WM_ENTERIDLE is not to be sent
        // to the owner of the dialog. WM_ENTERIDLE is sent when a menu
        // or a dialog has entered an "idle" state. For a dialog, this
        // means that no messages exist in its queue

    BYTE dtItemCount;    // This count specifies the number of items in
        // the dialog, which cannot exceed 255. This also specifies the
        // number of DLGITEMTEMPLATE structures found after FONTINFO

    int  dtX;  // Specifies the x coordinate of the upper-left corner of
                // the dialog. Units are 1/4 of the current dialog base
                // width unit, which is calculated from the dimensions
                // of the system font. The dialog unit/pixel mapping
                // can be retrieved by GetDialogBaseUnits(VOID),
                // which returns a long. The loword contains the base
```

```
                    // width in pixels and the hiword contains the base
                    // height in pixels. Both values must be scaled (that is,
                    // 1/4 or 1/8) to actual dialog units before they are used
      int  dtY;  // Specifies the y coordinate of the upper-left corner.
                    // Units are 1/8 of the current dialog base height unit

      int  dtCX; // Width of dialog in 1/4 dialog base width units
      int  dtCY; // Height of dialog in 1/8 dialog base height units

      char dtMenuName[];    // Specifies the ASCII menu name to use. The
                    // menu may also be set via RegisterClass

      char dtClassName[];   // Specifies an optional class name for the
                    // dialog. If a class name is specified, then the
                    // RegisterClass call used to register the dialog must
                    // specify DLGWINDOWEXTRA for the WNDCLASS field
                    // cbWndExtra
      char dtCaptionText[]; // Specifies the dialog caption
}
DLGTEMPLATE;
```

The structure FONTINFO, which must immediately follow DLGTEMPLATE in memory, is defined by the following simple structure:

```
typedef struct
{
    short int PointSize;     // Size of typeface in points
    char      szTypeFace[];  // ASCII typeface name. The reason this
                    // field is not a preallocated array of bytes is that
                    // the structure might not be used
}
FONTINFO;
```

Following FONTINFO in memory is the structure DLGITEMTEMPLATE, of which a copy exists for each control in the dialog. This structure is laid out as follows:

```
typedef struct
{
    int  dtilX;        // x position of ctrl in dialog units (same as dtX
                    // earlier)
    int  dtilY;        // y position of ctrl in dialog units (ditto for dtY)
    int  dtilCX;       // Width of ctrl in dialog units (same as dtCX)
    int  dtilCY;       // Height of ctrl in dialog units (same as dtCY)
    int  dtilID;       // Integer identifier for control. Must be unique
                    // for controls that accept developer messages

    long dtilStyle;    // Style bits of ctrl
```

```
    char dtilClass[]; // Class name of control
    char dtilText[];  // Window text for control
    BYTE dtilInfo;    // Number of bytes reserved for dtilData
    PTR  dtilData;    // Data passed through lpCreateParams in
                      // CREATESTRUCT data structure
}
DLGITEMTEMPLATE;
```

Several functions and messages are designed explicitly for dialog windows, including those shown in Tables 6.1 and 6.2.

Table 6.1. Dialog functions.

Function	Description
CreateDialog()	Creates a dialog located in a resource file.
CreateDialogIndirect()	Creates a dialog located in a developer-defined structure.
CreateDialogIndirectParam()	Same as CreateDialogIndirect(), except that it passes a developer-defined long value during the message WM_INITDIALOG.
CreateDialogParam()	Creates a dialog, passing a developer-defined long value during the WM_INITDIALOG message.
DefDlgProc()	Handles default message processing for dialogs. DefWindowProc() shouldn't be used for dialogs.
DialogBox()	Creates an application modal dialog box. When the line of code creating the dialog is executed, execution does not continue until the dialog box is destroyed via EndDialog().
DialogBoxIndirect()	Same as DialogBox(), except that creation is via a developer-defined structure, not via a dialog located in a resource file.
DialogBoxIndirectParam()	Same as DialogBoxIndirect(), except that it passes a long value during WM_INITDIALOG.
DialogBoxParam()	Same as DialogBox(), except that it passes a long value.
EndDialog()	Used to destroy a modal dialog. DestroyWindow() should be used only on modeless dialogs and other window types.

Function	Description
CheckDlgButton()	Changes the state of a two- (checkbox) or a three-state button.
CheckRadioButton()	Changes the state of a radio button, modifying the state of other radio buttons in the group at the same time.
IsDlgButtonChecked()	Determines the state of a two- or a three-state button.
GetDlgCtrlID()	Returns the integer ID of a control within a dialog.
GetDlgItem()	Returns the window handle when given a dialog handle and an integer control ID.
GetDlgItemInt()	Returns text from a dialog edit control as an integer value.
SetDlgItemInt()	Sets text in a dialog edit control from an integer value.
GetDlgItemText()	Returns window text from a dialog control. Comparable to the generic window form of GetWindowText().
SetDlgItemText()	Sets window text from a dialog control. Comparable to the generic window form of SetWindowText().
GetNextDlgGroupItem()	Returns the next or the previous control with the WS_GROUP style.
GetNextDlgTabItem()	Returns the next or the previous control in a group with the WS_TABSTOP style bit set.
GetDialogBaseUnits()	Returns a long value, indicating the width (low word) and height (high word) of the base units used by dialogs.
MapDialogRect()	When passed a dialog handle and a RECT structure, returns the screen coordinates in pixels (as opposed to dialog units) of the dialog.
IsDialogMessage()	Used in application's main message-processing loop to handle dialog-specific messages (default button, Tab, arrows, accelerators). Automatically translates and dispatches messages as well, making additional calls unnecessary.

continues

Table 6.1. continued

Function	Description
SendDlgItemMessage()	Same as SendMessage(), except that the window handle is specified in the form of a parent dialog window handle and child window integer control ID.

Table 6.2. Dialog messages.

Message	Description
WM_GETDLGCODE	Sent by the dialog manager whenever special dialog processing is to take place, including a check to see whether the control will process a particular keystroke (arrows, Tab, Enter), whether the control is to receive an EM_SETSEL message when it gets the focus, and to determine the type of a particular button. The application should return a value (possibly multiple ORed values) indicating its support of certain keystrokes and messages. When you are working with Windows' stock controls, the original class method should be processed first, to add or mask off certain bits before returning the new result. For pure custom controls, a flat value can be returned. The parameter wParam is not used, and lParam (if not null) is a far pointer to a message structure, containing the message (keyboard input) being sent to the control. Input for a control can be selectively processed based on the contents of the message by returning DLGC_WANTCHARS when the message is one destined for the control. Returning a zero value lets the dialog manager process the message as it sees fit. The following WM_GETDLGCODE return values are supported by the dialog manager:

DLGC_WANTALLKEYS	Control is to receive and handle all messages.
DLGC_WANTMESSAGE	Same as the preceding.
DLGC_WANTARROWS	Control is to handle arrow key processing.
DLGC_WANTTAB	Control is to handle Tab key processing.

Message	*Description*	
	DLGC_WANTCHARS	Control is to receive WM_CHAR messages.
	DLGC_HASSETSEL	Control should receive an EM_SETSEL message when getting the focus.
	DLGC_DEFPUSHBUTTON	Control is to handle default button processing.
	DLGC_UNDEFPUSHBUTTON	Used with DLGC_BUTTON to indicate that the control is a button other than the default button.
	DLGC_BUTTON	Control is a button.
	DLGC_STATIC	Control is a static.
	DLGC_RADIOBUTTON	Control is a radio button.
WM_ENTERIDLE	Sent to an application's top-level windows, informing it that a modal dialog is entering an idle state, meaning that it has no messages to process in its queue.	
WM_INITDIALOG	Sent to a dialog immediately before it is to be displayed. This message is ideal for any initialization of the dialog or any of its child controls. This message is sent only to dialogs created with a passed procedure-instance (non-null value) as a parameter. This can be done for both internal and private dialog classes, however. The message is first sent to the private dialog class (if any), where the default action of **DefDlgProc()** is to pass it to the procedure instance defined in the call that created the dialog. For dialogs using the internal dialog class, the message is sent as usual.	
WM_NEXTDLGCTL	Sent or posted to a dialog window procedure to alter the control focus. Different from SetFocus because the default button is taken into account and possibly updated.	

Controls and Child Windows

Controls are different from any other type of window. Top-level windows and dialogs are most often used as a pane, or backdrop, for a series of child windows. These child windows can take the form of either stock or custom controls, or they can even be a series of dialogs or additional child windows, which may themselves contain control windows. Controls are used to provide input and output to the user and to the application itself. Controls can be created only as child windows, and as such must always have a parent. A control can never be a top-level window. A control can be thought of as the bottom-most rung in the window chain, although there is nothing preventing a control from being a parent itself, as is the case with the combobox control.

Controls are unique because in addition to the window handle associated with all types of windows, child window controls have an additional integer ID used to reference the control within its parent pane. Even though the ID is an integer, capable of 65,535 different values, there is still a maximum of only 255 controls in a single dialog. Two of these IDs are treated specially by **IsDialogMessage()**: IDOK (with a value of one) and IDCANCEL (with a value of two). These two IDs are posted via WM_COMMAND whenever the user presses Enter or Esc in a dialog. The IDOK ID is commonly stolen by **IsDialogMessage()** to process the default button in a dialog, whereas IDCANCEL often is processed by the developer to remove a message box from the screen, as opposed to double-clicking the system menu or selecting any system menu close option.

Child controls differ from other windows in how they respond to events. It is true that they have a window procedure as do other types of windows; however, they also maintain a "dual residency," much as the president of our country does. But in this case what they're doing is "legal." Child controls keep one foot in their own window procedure and one foot in the window procedure of their parent. Child window controls have three groups of associated messages: generic window messages (WM_*); specialized window messages (EM_*, LB_*, and so on); and parent window notification messages, which are posted through WM_COMMAND (the majority) and WM_PARENTNOTIFY. The messages going to WM_PARENTNOTIFY tell the parent whenever a child window is created, destroyed, or clicked on. For this message, wParam is the message indicating the event occurring (WM_CREATE, WM_DESTROY, and so on) and lParam contains in its low word the handle of the window and in its high word the control ID of the window. The control notification messages posted to WM_COMMAND are similar in format, although the notifications are for different reasons that are specific to the control. Child-initiated WM_COMMAND messages are posted whenever the control gains or loses the focus, and when items or text in the control are selected. Basically, notifications occur for the majority of events that a parent window would like to accept without having to resort to subclassing to intercept additional messages.

Several Windows API functions and messages are designed explicitly with child windows and child controls in mind, including those shown in Tables 6.3 and 6.4.

Table 6.3. Child window functions.

Function	Description
ChildWindowFromPoint()	When passed a parent window handle and a point structure (relative to the parent), determines which child window (if any) contains the point. Unlike WindowFromPoint(), this function includes hidden and disabled windows during its search.
EnumChildWindows()	Enumerates (via a callback function) all the child windows of a specified parent. Does not enumerate top-level, owned, or popup windows.
GetDlgCtrlID()	See descriptions in the earlier dialog section.
GetDlgItem()	
GetNextDlgGroupItem()	
GetNextDlgTabItem()	
SendDlgItemMessage()	
GetChildWindowRect()	Determines the window coordinates of a specified child window in relation to its parent. This function is located in the library STDWIN.DLL.
GetWindow()	Can be used to search the window manager's list of top-level and child windows. The window manager maintains a list of all top-level windows, their child windows, and the child windows of any child windows.
GetParent()	Returns the parent window of a specified child window.
SetParent()	Sets a new parent for a specified child window.
IsChild()	Determines whether the specified window is a child of a specified parent window, or whether it exists somewhere in the chain of windows leading to the parent.

Table 6.4. Child window messages.

Message	Description
WM_CHILDACTIVATE	Sent to a child's parent window when **SetWindowPos()** is used to move the child window.
WM_COMMAND	Posted to any window containing a menu, accelerators, or child controls when any of the aforementioned items generate an event.
WM_CTLCOLOR	Sent to a parent window, allowing it to change the text color, text background color, and background brush used to draw child windows, message boxes, and the parent window itself. If passed to **DefWindowProc()**, the default system colors are used.
WM_PARENTNOTIFY	Posted to the parent of any child control, notifying the parent of creation, destruction, and mouse button clicks.
WM_SETFONT	Sent to all child controls, establishing the font.

Going with the Flow (of Messages, That Is!)

Understanding the basic flow of messages throughout the life of an application is an important concept to pick up. Per Microsoft, you cannot depend on "nitpicky" particulars regarding message flow; however, several basic message-ordering conventions can be depended on.

The first message received by a top-level window on its creation is WM_GETMINMAXINFO. Windows sends this message to a window to ascertain its minimum and maximum dimensions, passing (via lParam) the following MINMAXINFO structure:

```
typedef struct
{
    POINT ptReserved;      // Reserved for internal use

    POINT ptMaxSize;       // Maximized width (ptMaxSize.x) and maximized height
                           // (ptMaxSize.y) of window
```

```
        POINT ptMaxPosition;      // Position of left side of maximized window and
                                  // position of top side of maximized window

        POINT ptMinTrackSize;     // Minimum tracking width and minimum height of window
        POINT ptMaxTrackSize;     // Maximum tracking width and tracking height of window
}
MINMAXINFO;
```

> **Note:** The POINT structure contains two values, an x and a y integer position.

On receiving this message, the window has the opportunity to modify the values and pass them back to Windows, which allows or denies the size operation based on the returned dimensions. Normally, the values for the maximum size and maximum tracking size are equal. The values for the "maximized position" refer to the coordinates the window is anchored at when the window is itself maximized. Normally, this is a negative number for both the x and the y elements of the point structure, which explains why maximized windows never show their borders: This value places the borders (thick or thin) just off the edges of the screen. The "tracking" sizes refer to the size of the window as it is being stretched by a mouse or through keyboard movement.

The next message received by a top-level window is WM_NCCREATE, which is used to initialize the range and position of scroll bars and to allocate memory internal to the window, which includes fields for window text and other items. The window normally returns a one to indicate that the non-client area was successfully created, whereas a zero aborts the creation of the window. When WM_NCCREATE is received by a window procedure, lParam points to the window's CREATESTRUCT structure.

After WM_NCCREATE, Windows sends a WM_NCCALCSIZE message, which is used to determine how much of the window's total area is to be used for non-client items such as a border, scroll bars, and possibly a caption (for top-level windows only). For superclassed and subclassed controls, the size of the non-client area should not be altered. Two processes cannot share portions of a window's non-client area; it is an all-or-none kind of space. If a custom control is to use the non-client area to create special control "labels" or other kinds of embellishments, it cannot depend on Windows to maintain the non-client area and keep track of borders and scroll bars at the same time. Another application can paint into a non-client area maintained by Windows; it just can't exclusively have an outermost or innermost portion of this area to itself.

When WM_NCCALCSIZE is sent to a window, wParam is used as a BOOL flag to indicate whether the application is capable of modifying the dimensions of this area. wParam should be set to TRUE if this is the case, FALSE if otherwise. lParam is used as a long pointer to a structure called NCCALCSIZE_PARAMS, which has the following format:

```
typedef struct
{
    RECT            rgrc[3];  // Contains three rect structures. The first indicates
                              // the new coordinates of the window. The second rect
                              // indicates the coordinates of the window before it
                              // was moved or resized, and the third rect is used
                              // to indicate the coordinates of the client area
                              // before the window was moved. The second and third
                              // rects are valid only when wParam is true for
                              // WM_NCCALCSIZE.
                              //

    WINDOWPOS FAR *lppos;     // Points to a WINDOWPOS structure, containing
                              // information used in the call that moved or sized
                              // the window.
}
NCCALCSIZE_PARAMS;
```

Note: The RECT structure contains four integer values (left, top, right, and bottom).

If wParam is set to FALSE, the application should return zero. If it is set to TRUE, indicating that the non-client area has been altered, the application should return one or a combination of the following values:

Value	Description
WVR_ALIGNTOP WVR_ALIGNBOTTOM WVR_ALIGNRIGHT WVR_ALIGNLEFT	Aligns client area of window in one of possibly multiple positions. Values may be combined (that is, WVR_ALIGNTOP ¦ WVR_ALIGNLEFT).
WVR_HREDRAW WVR_VREDRAW WVR_REDRAW	Causes complete window redraw on horizontal or vertical size change. These styles are similar to CS_HREDRAW and CS_VREDRAW, except that they include the whole window. WVR_REDRAW is a combination of the above two values.

Value	Description
WVR_VALIDRECTS	Indicates that on return from WM_NCCALCSIZE, the second and third rects contain source and destination rects for the window. Windows combines these two rects to form a clipping rect for paint updates. This allows more elaborate client window preservation strategies.

Even with all these preparations, redrawing of the window (at least the client portion) might still occur because of the class style bit settings CS_HREDRAW and CS_VREDRAW. If wParam is set to TRUE and the application still returns a zero, the old client area is preserved and aligned with the new rect representing the moved or sized client area.

After WM_NCCALCSIZE, Windows sends a WM_CREATE, which is where an application can perform a fair amount of its initialization code. There's a limit to what can be done, however, because window messages cannot be sent at this point in the window's life. Basically, the developer is limited to setting window properties, extra class and window data, and allocating memory. Basically, the WM_CREATE method is comparable to LibMain() in the operations that may be performed. All the custom controls in this book use WM_CREATE to establish a one-time window property, which is then picked off by a later message (WM_MOVE) and removed from the window's property list. At this point the control's initialization (external to Windows' initialization) is performed. All the custom controls available in this book (dialog, edit, listbox, combobox, bitmap, button, split) have initialization code performed during the window's receipt of its first WM_MOVE message. It is then that strings are automatically put into listboxes and comboboxes, bitmaps are loaded, and other data structures are created and initialized.

Obviously, WM_CREATE is sent before the control returns from the function used to create the window and before the window is made visible. In fact, WM_CREATE and other initialization messages are always sent (as opposed to posted) because the application might not have entered its message-processing loop yet, thus hindering somewhat the flow of any messages residing in a message queue. Like WM_NCCREATE, when WM_CREATE is received by a window procedure, lParam points to the window's CREATESTRUCT structure. Unlike WM_NCCREATE, the window should return a one to abort the creation of the window and a zero to continue. In the case of a parent window, WM_CREATE is sent before the WM_CREATE messages of any children. This is another reason why WM_CREATE isn't always the best message to use for initialization of a top-level window.

After the message WM_CREATE is processed by a top-level window, the same process is started again (excluding WM_GETMINMAXINFO) for all child windows. At this point, with the exception of a few minor messages (WM_GETTEXT), no more messages are sent to the window until a call to **ShowWindow()**, at which time (you guessed it!) the message WM_SHOWWINDOW is sent to the window. The message WM_SHOWWINDOW is not sent when a main window is shown initially minimized or maximized, or when SW_SHOWNORMAL is used.

At this point, the window still is not visible. Following WM_SHOWWINDOW is the message WM_NCACTIVATE, which is used to activate (and for some windows deactivate) the non-client area of a top-level window. If an application returns TRUE for wParam, the caption is always drawn as active; with a return value of FALSE, the caption is drawn as inactive, most likely appearing grayed out. After WM_NCACTIVATE is processed, a portion of the window's caption is painted on the screen.

Following WM_NCACTIVATE is WM_ACTIVATE, which is sent both to the window being inactivated and the one being activated, in that order. This message is processed only by top-level windows. During this message, wParam can be one of the following values: WA_INACTIVE, indicating that the window is being made inactive; WA_ACTIVE, indicating an active state achieved through the keyboard or task manager; and WA_CLICKACTIVE, indicating that the window is being made active through a mouse click. The LOWORD value of lParam indicates whether the active window is minimized (if nonzero) and the HIWORD value of lParam contains the handle of the "other" window being inactivated or activated, whatever the case. This HWND may be null. In the case of a window being activated through a mouse click, WM_MOUSEACTIVATE is also sent to the window.

Following WM_ACTIVATE is a call to WM_SETFOCUS, which is used to establish the "active" control in the dialog or window. This message is received by both top-level and child windows. For this message, wParam represents the handle of the window losing the focus (possibly null), and lParam is not used. An application should return zero if it sets the focus during this message.

Caution: A window should never set the focus to itself during the processing of this message, because it's the easiest way to generate a stack fault. Of course, this is true of all "sent" messages that indirectly invoke themselves again. The window procedure will keep executing over and over until the stack limit is reached, and the application will fault.

Shortly after WM_SETFOCUS is received by a parent window, one of its child windows also receives the message.

Following WM_SETFOCUS is the message WM_NCPAINT, which is responsible for painting the borders, scroll bars, and other non-client portions of a top-level window. This message carries no parameters with it, and the only thing an application can do is return a zero if it processes the message. Following WM_NCPAINT for top-level windows are the messages WM_SIZE, WM_MOVE, and WM_PAINT. Child windows execute WM_NCPAINT before WM_PAINT.

The message WM_SIZE is sent to a window after its size has changed, although the size of the window was actually determined during WM_GETMINMAXINFO. During WM_SIZE, wParam is one of the following values: SIZE_MAXIMIZED, indicating that the window has been maximized; SIZE_MINIMIZED, indicating that the window has been minimized; SIZE_RESTORED, indicating that the window is in a "restored" state; SIZE_MAXHIDE, sent to all popup windows when another window is maximized; and SIZE_MAXSHOW, sent to all popup windows when another window has been "restored" to its former size. The loword of lParam contains the new width of the window and the hiword of lParam contains the new height.

The message WM_MOVE is sent after a window's position has moved. During this message, the loword of lParam contains the x coordinate of the upper-left corner of the window and the hiword of lParam contains the y coordinate of the upper-left corner of the window. For top-level windows these coordinates are relative to the screen, whereas for child windows they are relative to the upper-left corner of the parent's client area.

When it's time for the application to terminate, the message WM_CLOSE is sent to the main top-level window of the application. This is done either through a button press or via the system menu of the window. When Windows itself wants to shut down, it sends a WM_QUERYENDSESSION message to the window, not WM_CLOSE or WM_DESTROY. In fact, in this case WM_QUERYSESSION is the only message the application will see again. Regardless, the WM_CLOSE method's job is to destroy the main window, which in turn eventually destroys all owned and child windows. Windows and modeless dialogs are destroyed through a call to **DestroyWindow()**, whereas modal dialogs use **EndDialog()**. Either of these functions causes a WM_DESTROY to be sent to the top-level window. Before the WM_DESTROY message is received, however, the window receives WM_NCACTIVATE and WM_ACTIVATE messages to indicate that another window is replacing it in the window manager's list.

When WM_DESTROY is received by a top-level window, all its children are still valid and "live," meaning that messages and other forms of window cleanup can be performed on all child and owned windows at this point. The message WM_DESTROY is sent to a window after its image has been removed from the screen. Right after the window processes WM_DESTROY, it receives the message WM_NCDESTROY, which is used to clean up the memory originally allocated for the window. If the application itself is terminating, the last message seen is WM_QUIT. This message causes the message loop to break and the Windows termination code for the application to be executed, freeing all instance-related segments, including the program's data segment, task database, and other dynamically allocated data segments.

A Quick Review of the Order of Messages

Although you can't depend too much on the exact ordering of messages, you can trust the following rules:

- For top-level windows, WM_CREATE is sent before any child windows receive it.

- The messages WM_SIZE and WM_MOVE are guaranteed to be given before the window is painted and are an excellent place to do any initialization requiring the sending of additional messages.

- The message WM_SHOWWINDOW cannot really be depended on in a general sense.

- Cleanup for a window should be done during WM_DESTROY.

- Checking for when a window is going from an inactive to active state (or vice versa) should be done during WM_NCACTIVATE. This applies to top-level as well as MDI child windows.

- The message WM_NCCREATE is the earliest point at which the creation of a window can be aborted. A return value of zero causes CreateWindow() to fail, returning a null value.

Designing Custom Controls

Designing custom controls is an interesting but painful exercise. It truly helps the developer gain a greater appreciation and understanding of the innermost workings of Windows. Designing stand-alone code and simple subroutines is one thing, but designing a custom control library that is to be used by multiple applications is quite different.

Not only does it force an unbelievable amount of "discipline" on the developer, but it is quite difficult because it's never really clear what messages and methods will always be provided by Windows for a custom window class. The "simple" answer is that anything having to do with a window's non-client area is automatically handled by Windows. This also includes WM_* messages and WS_* window styles. Windows handles the non-client aspect of a control, because this is a "common" part of all windows.

The client area, however, is what's customized by the actual control and the developer, which is why this part must be handled explicitly. This means that if you design a dialog or a top-level window class and specify a border, thick frame, caption, or system menu, all aspects of these components will be handled by Windows. Likewise, if you specify a child window with a border or scroll bars, it too will be handled by Windows, although it is up to the developer to handle how the scroll bars interface with the client area.

Using Color in a Window

Use of color (if not overdone) can be an excellent means of attracting attention to key portions of a window. The fact that the system colors can be used can sometimes be considered a problem with a built-in answer, because the user has explicitly configured his or her system for a certain combination of colors—and might want it that way. For certain things, however, such as extra emphasis on important labels or using colors for warning conditions or (if you have artistic tendencies) a really nice interface, customizing the colors in an application can be an easy method of making your application stand out. Figures 6.1 and 6.2 illustrate the dialogs used by Windows to customize screen, window, and control colors.

Figure 6.1.
The Windows
Color dialog
box.

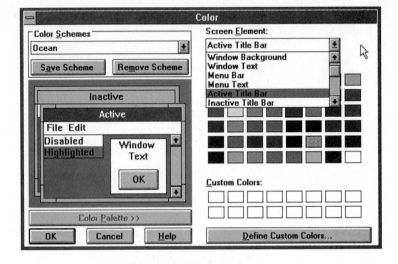

Figure 6.2.
The Windows
Custom Color
Selector dialog
box.

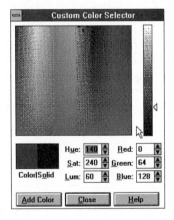

Before we discuss color in any more detail, we need to discuss the basic unit of color, a 32-bit DWORD value known as COLORREF, which specifies a red, green, and blue value that is used to generate a color. Although COLORREF can additionally be used to specify an index into a logical palette as well as a palette-relative RGB value, we're concerned only with explicit RGB values. Figure 6.3 shows the format of this 32-bit color value.

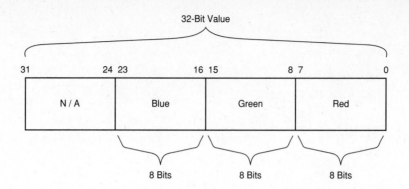

Figure 6.3.
Format of a 32-bit color value.

Because three bytes are used to generate the actual color, this provides for 24-bit color, generating more than 16 million colors. It's quite easy to generate "extreme" colors such as black (all zeros), white (all 0xff values), and pure red, green, and blue. It's more difficult is to generate all the colors in between. For this reason, stdwin.h includes a number of #defines that declare the basic 16 system colors in their "flattened" RGB format, making it easier to include them in your applications. The basic colors are defined as follows:

Color	Value
COLOR_BLACK	0x00000000L
COLOR_WHITE	0x00ffffffL
COLOR_LIGHTGRAY	0x00c0c0c0L
COLOR_DARKGRAY	0x00808080L
COLOR_RED	0x000000ffL
COLOR_DARKRED	0x00000080L
COLOR_GREEN	0x0000ff00L
COLOR_DARKGREEN	0x00008000L
COLOR_BLUE	0x00ff0000L
COLOR_DARKBLUE	0x00800000L
COLOR_MAGENTA	0x00ff00ffL
COLOR_DARKMAGENTA	0x00800080L
COLOR_CYAN	0x00ffff00L

continues

Color	Value
COLOR_DARKCYAN	0x00808000L
COLOR_YELLOW	0x0000ffffL
COLOR_BROWN	0x00008080L

The colors weren't left in their RGB "macro" form because they often are included in custom data structures inside resource files, and the resource compiler doesn't process macros or any other form of Boolean logic that's nested inside a custom resource data structure. The preprocessor for the resource files works just fine outside of custom data structures; it's just inside that only "flat" numeric values or strings can be used.

Retrieving and changing the defined system colors used for painting the different elements of the display is a trivial matter. Windows provides a message and two functions for this purpose: WM_SYSCOLORCHANGE, GetSysColor(), and SetSysColors(). The message WM_SYSCOLORCHANGE is sent to all top-level windows when a change is made to any of the system colors, whether by user input or by program control. This message is broadcast much in the manner of the WM_FONTCHANGE message, which notifies applications that the font pool has changed, and WM_WININICHANGE, which notifies applications whenever any changes are made to profile settings in WIN.INI. When the message WM_SYSCOLORCHANGE is sent to a window, Windows invalidates the window as well, indirectly causing a WM_PAINT message to be put in its queue, thus ensuring that any changes to the system colors will be reflected in a prompt fashion. Naturally, if an application has any hard-coded values, GDI objects, or other data based on the system colors, they should be recalculated to take the new color changes into account.

The function GetSysColor() is provided by the Windows API to extract the color values of various components of the display, including captions, borders, buttons, highlighted text, and various other window components. The function returns a COLORREF value when passed an integer #define representing the window component whose color you want to determine. The following 21 #defines are provided by Windows:

#define Value	Description
COLOR_ACTIVEBORDER	Active window border color
COLOR_ACTIVECAPTION	Color of the active window caption
COLOR_APPWORKSPACE	Background color of MDI client windows

#define Value	Description
COLOR_BACKGROUND	Background color of a desktop window
COLOR_BTNFACE	Color of the face of a push button
COLOR_BTNHIGHLIGHT	Color of the "light" edge of the 3-D effect for buttons
COLOR_BTNSHADOW	Color of the "dark" edge of the 3-D effect for buttons
COLOR_BTNTEXT	Color of the text in a button
COLOR_CAPTIONTEXT	Color of the active window caption text
COLOR_GRAYTEXT	Color of "dimmed" or grayed text
COLOR_HIGHLIGHT	Background color of highlighted control text
COLOR_HIGHLIGHTTEXT	Color of highlighted text within a control
COLOR_INACTIVEBORDER	Color of an inactive window's border
COLOR_INACTIVECAPTION	Color of an inactive window's caption
COLOR_INACTIVECAPTIONTEXT	Color of an inactive window's caption
COLOR_MENU	Menu background color
COLOR_MENUTEXT	Menu text color
COLOR_SCROLLBAR	Color of a scroll bar's "void" or gray area
COLOR_WINDOW	Background color of a window
COLOR_WINDOWFRAME	Color of a window frame
COLOR_WINDOWTEXT	Color of text in a window

The counterpart to `GetSysColor()` is `SetSystemColors()`, which can be used to set the colors of one or more display elements. The function accepts three parameters: an integer value specifying the number of elements that are to be changed; a `far` address to an array of integers containing the actual element `#define` values that are to be changed; and a `far` address to an array of `COLORREF` values, containing the new color values for the various window components referenced by the prior parameter.

To sum up, the following functions, macros, and messages are provided to manipulate and deal with colors on a low-level basis:

Function	Description
RGB(r, g, b)	Returns a COLORREF value when passed three bytes representing the levels of red, green, and blue making up the color.
GetBValue(rgb)	Returns a byte representing the blue component of a COLORREF value.
GetGValue(rgb)	Returns a byte representing the green component of a COLORREF value.
GetRValue(rgb)	Returns a byte representing the red component of a COLORREF value.
GetNearestColor()	Returns the nearest COLORREF value for a specified display context and color to be matched against.
GetSysColor()	Returns the color of the requested screen component (that is, caption, border, highlighted text). COLOR_ value (see above).
SetSysColors()	Allows the system colors to be changed.

Erasing and Painting Windows

There are several components to the "color" of a specified window. There is the background brush, used to erase the window and prepare it for painting. There is the background and foreground colors for text that is drawn in the window, and there is any painting or drawing done in the client area of the window. This can include **BitBlt**ed pictures and other, more manually drawn graphics (lines, circles, and so on). Each component is discussed in the following paragraphs.

First, there is the brush used to paint the background of the window, which is done during the window's WM_ERASEBKGND message and precedes any painting that is to be done in the client area of the window. The default action on this message is to erase the background of the window using the background brush color specified in the window's class structure. If this value is NULL, the developer must manually trap the message and explicitly perform the fill. The background of a window is erased during the WM_PAINT message for the window. When **BeginPaint()** is used to start the painting operation and return a valid display context to the window's display area, Windows checks the value of fErase in the following structure:

```
typedef struct
{
    HDC   hdc;              // Screen display context for window
    BOOL  fErase;          // True if background is to be erased
    RECT  rcPaint;         // Dimensions of painting clip rectangle
    BOOL  fRestore;        // Reserved
    BOOL  fIncUpdate;      // Reserved
    BYTE  rgbReserved[16]; // Reserved
}
PAINTSTRUCT;
```

If this value is true, WM_ERASEBKGND is sent to the window with the hdc value from this structure, which is sent via wParam. Just as with WM_PAINT, this is the only display context that should be used to erase the background of the window. Additional memory display contexts may be created; however, this is the only screen DC that should be used for drawing.

The InvalidateRect() function can be used to invalidate and indirectly paint a window in one of two ways. The function accepts a window handle, RECT structure, and BOOL as parameters. When null is specified for the rectangle, the entire client area of the window is added to the update region. A TRUE or FALSE value for the Boolean indicates whether the background for the window needs to be erased as well. For certain kinds of controls, such as the button and bitmap controls, the background never really needs to be erased, because the paint method takes care to completely paint the client area of the control. When InvalidateRect() is called, the portion of the window rect is invalidated and added to the update region for the window, and a WM_PAINT message is put into the window's message queue.

> **Tip:** Calling UpdateWindow() causes any WM_PAINT message possibly festering at the bottom of the queue to be pulled and sent to the window. This can be nice when an automatic redraw of a window is necessary and you don't want the lag associated with waiting for the WM_PAINT message to be processed. There is a lag time, because WM_PAINT is considered a low-priority message and isn't processed until either UpdateWindow() is called or no other messages exist in the queue. As parts of a window are covered or in some other way invalidated, Windows accumulates the invalid regions into a single WM_PAINT message that can at some point be sent to the window. This concatenation and delay process helps speed up redrawing and eliminates any superfluous paint messages.

Backgrounds are painted with a specific colored brush using the function `FillRect()`, which accepts a display context, RECT structure, and a GDI brush object as parameters. The library STDWIN.DLL, in addition to holding the dialog window class procedure, also contains the default window procedure for the custom controls used in this book. This default procedure handles all the common methods used by the custom controls. Erasing backgrounds is one of these methods, because the focus of a control is indicated by the color of its background, and implementing this series of `if()` statements would get tedious if you put it inside the window procedure of every custom control in your library. Erasing the background of a window is as simple as the following code example:

```
case WM_ERASEBKGND :

    //
    // Erase bkgrd of ctrl. If a class brush is defined, then use it.
    // Otherwise, the 3-D mechanism of parent dialog, where active
    // ctrl is white bkgrd and inactive ctrl has bkgrd brush of its
    // dialog parent. If the parent has no defined bkgrd brush color
    // (which shouldn't happen), use dkgray for lack of anything else.
    //

    if((hBrush = GetClassWord(hWnd, GCW_HBRBACKGROUND)) == NULL)
    {
        if(GetFocus() == hWnd)
        {
            hBrush = GetStockObject(WHITE_BRUSH);
        }
        else
        {
            //
            // Because you don't have focus, dim the control with the parent's
            // brush, which should always be defined.

            hBrush = GetClassWord(GetParent(hWnd), GCW_HBRBACKGROUND);
        }
    }

    GetClientRect(hWnd, &Rect);                    // Get client dimensions of window

    FillRect((HDC) wParam, &Rect, hBrush);    // Fill with a brush

    return(1);      // Indicate that background doesn't need to be erased now
```

Working with Text and Fonts

Working with text and fonts under Windows is a fairly straightforward affair. When any window is first created, it is assumed to be using the default system font. In fact, unless otherwise specified, the default font for any display context is the system font as well. Windows that don't use the system font include dialogs created with DS_SETFONT and windows that have been explicitly "told" otherwise, through the message WM_SETFONT. Using a font is as simple as not specifying any kind of font at all (in which case the default font—usually the system font—is used), or retrieving a font via WM_GETFONT or the function `CreateFont()`. The message WM_GETFONT is often sent to a window to determine the type of font it expects as a default inside its window pane. This message returns either a font handle or null (if it is using the system font). An actual handle to the system font can be obtained by calling `GetStockObject`(SYSTEM_FONT). When use of the system or default font needs to be overridden, `CreateFont()` can be used to create a particular font.

When a window is dynamically created inside a dialog created using DS_SETFONT, the message WM_SETFONT must be manually sent to the window to establish its font. The dialog attribute DS_SETFONT applies only to when the dialog is first created; it doesn't cover windows created later in the dialog's life.

Information can be retrieved for a particular font in several ways. If only a handle to the font is obtained, the function `GetObject()` can be used to obtain a filled-in LOGFONT structure for the font. This function returns only generic information about the logical font. When a font has been selected into a device context, various additional operations can be performed on the font, returning point-size-specific information that can be used for text placement and other purposes. One of these functions is `GetTextMetrics()`, which returns a TEXTMETRIC structure. The information returned in the TEXTMETRIC structure applies to the characters in the font as a whole; however, it is particular to the point size of the font as it will be used. When string-specific information is needed, the function `GetTextExtent()` can be used. This function returns a DWORD value, with the loword containing the width of the given string and the hiword containing the height of the string. The only problem with this function is that it doesn't take line feeds into account, nor does it account for characters in the string that end up being unprintable. If a string resembling "My name is &&&&&&&&Mike Klein" is passed, the returned width includes the accumulative widths of eight ampersand characters. Even if a single ampersand is passed in the string, which would be hidden upon a call to `DrawText()` or `TextOut()`, it will be included in the returned length. What's really needed is a function to take these quirks into account. Lastly, another useful function is `GetTextFace()`, which can be used to determine the ASCII typeface name of any font selected into a display context.

Three components need to be taken into account when drawing text. Not only is there the color used for text drawn inside the window, but there also is the background color for the text, and a text drawing "mode" that can be TRANSPARENT or OPAQUE. This specifies whether text is to be merely "overlaid" onto any existing graphics or whether it is to be drawn using an explicit background color. The following functions control the color and mode of drawn text:

Function	Description
`GetBkColor()`	When passed a display context, returns a COLORREF value indicating the background color used when drawing text.
`SetBkColor()`	Sets the background color for drawing text when passed a display context and a COLORREF value.
`GetTextColor()`	When passed a display context, returns a COLORREF value indicating the color used for text drawn in the DC.
`SetTextColor()`	Sets the color for drawing text when passed a display context and a COLORREF value.
`GetBkMode()`	When passed a display context, returns the drawing mode, which can be either OPAQUE or TRANSPARENT.
`SetBkMode()`	Sets the background text drawing mode when passed a display context and either the OPAQUE or the TRANSPARENT parameter.

Caution: Whenever settings are changed in a display context during any GDI operation, those settings should be restored when the operation is completed. This includes the changing of fonts, colors, mapping modes, drawing modes, selected bitmaps, and any other GDI object. Often you'll find that when you don't restore things to the way they were, bizarre occurrences will result. This is especially true when things such as a mapping mode or a drawing mode are changed.

Changing the Colors of Stock Controls

Changing the color of "pure" custom controls is simple. After all, the developer wrote the control and has easy access to class structures and paint methods, and basically is aware of what is going on at all times because the source code for all methods is available. However, changing the color of stock controls, such as edit controls, listboxes, and statics, can be a little more difficult because certain methods, including WM_PAINT, aren't implemented by the developer. This means that certain guesses must be made about how the control functions, which isn't good. The background of any control, stock or otherwise, is easily changed via the hbrBackground field in the control's WNDCLASS structure. With stock controls, however, the developer has no immediate access to the pen color and pen background color used for drawing text. After all, these are things that are embedded in the control's paint method, which is a little more complex than WM_ERASEBKGND. One easy solution to fiddling with the colors of stock controls is the message WM_CTLCOLOR, which is received by any parent window, allowing the developer to change the colors of any child controls in the window, as well as the window itself or any owned message box. When WM_CTLCOLOR is received, it is in the following format:

```
wMsg            = WM_CTLCOLOR      // The message itself
wParam          = hDC             // The display context of the window
LOWORD(lParam)  = hWnd            // The window handle
HIWORD(lParam)  = type of control // Can be one of the following:
```

Ctrl Type	Description
CTLCOLOR_BTN	Permits changes in the color of buttons.
CTLCOLOR_DLG	Permits changes in the color of the window itself.
CTLCOLOR_EDIT	Permits changes in the color of edit controls.
CTLCOLOR_LISTBOX	Permits changes in the color of listboxes.
CTLCOLOR_MSGBOX	Permits changes in the color of message boxes.
CTLCOLOR_SCROLLBAR	Permits changes in the color of scroll bars.
CTLCOLOR_STATIC	Permits changes in the color of static labels.

Normally, the colors of these controls are based on the system colors defined in Control Panel. Obviously, changing the source of these colors would be a real no-no, which is why WM_CTLCOLOR is provided. Likewise, having to manually subclass all the controls in a dialog would be too tedious if the only reason they were being tapped into was to change a color or two. The library STDWIN.DLL, which contains a custom dialog class called AtomicDialog, uses the WM_CTLCOLOR message to customize the colors of the listbox, edit control, and combobox controls provided by Windows in an attempt to provide a somewhat common color scheme along with the "pure" custom controls: AtomicBitmap, AtomicButton, and AtomicSplit. This works fine for every control except two forms of the combobox, CBS_SIMPLE and CBS_DROPDOWN, which have an embedded edit control and listbox in addition to the combobox window itself. In this case, the WM_CTLCOLOR message going to the combobox itself had to be trapped, not the WM_CTLCOLOR sent to its parent window. This is because the edit control and listbox are child windows of the combobox and not the dialog. After a little manipulation of lParam, the WM_CTLCOLOR message originally sent to the combobox is re-sent to the parent dialog, and all is handled as normal. The case statement used by AtomicDialog in its window procedure is as shown:

```
case WM_CTLCOLOR :

    //
    // Handles painting of noncustom Windows built-in controls so
    // that they still look good with your dialog. All this does is
    // to brighten the ctrl by making it white when it's got the
    // focus, or otherwise using the bkgd color when it doesn't have
    // the focus. This code is removed when nothing but "pure" custom
    // controls are implemented.
    //

    if(GetFocus() == LOWORD(lParam))
    {
        //
        // Set background color for text (leave text color the same)
        // and return a brush for the background fill, which is
        // different from the background color for text.
        //

        SetBkColor((HDC) wParam, COLOR_WHITE);
        return(GetStockObject(WHITE_BRUSH));
    }

    //
    // Set the bkgrd color for the text to be equal to the backgrd
    // COLORREF specified in the private resource structure that
```

```
// describes the dialog. At create time for the dialog, this color
// is extracted from the dialog resource struct and placed into
// a window property.
//

SetBkColor
(
    (HDC) wParam,
    MAKELONG(GetProp(hDlg, "RGBlo"), GetProp(hDlg, "RGBhi"))
);

//
// Return a background brush equal to the dialog's backgrd color
//

return(GetClassWord(hDlg, GCW_HBRBACKGROUND));
```

When WM_CTLCOLOR is received by a parent window, three basic things can be done: setting the text color, setting the text background color, and setting the window's background brush color. This background brush color is the same field that's in the WNDCLASS structure for every class of window. Setting it here overrides any class settings that might be established for the background color. Intercepting the brush color in WM_ERASEBKGND, however, overrides any setting because this is actually where the work gets done.

Adding Labels to Controls

All the custom controls in this book use a function from the library STDWIN.DLL called **DrawCtrlLabel()**, which, when given the handle to a control window, draws a 3-D graphical label positioned somewhere around the control. After a few minor preparations, **DrawCtrlLabel()** calls **DrawRectLabel()**, which uses a display context, RECT structure, and string, to actually draw the label. These functions can be used to draw labels above, in the middle, or at the bottom of a control. When a label is positioned at the top or bottom of (above or below) the control, the label can also optionally be left- or right-justified or centered. When the label is positioned in the middle of a control (as it is for a toggle button or a checkbox), the label is positioned just to the left or right of the control, not within it. Drawing control labels like this is fast and efficient and cuts down on the window overhead in User. Groupboxes also are drawn in this manner, not requiring a window handle. Groupboxes call **DrawRectLabel()** directly, after automatically determining the number of controls the groupbox is supposed to "lasso." For controls, labels are created in the private resource structure associated with every control, whereas groupboxes are defined in the single dialog structure associated with each class of dialog.

The following code snippet (from **DrawRectLabel()**) illustrates several commands used to draw colored text in a window:

```
//
// Put text on transparently and set map mode. The hDC was retrieved in the
// function DrawCtrlLabel, which used the form....hDC = GetDC(hWndParent);
//

BkgdMode = SetBkMode(hDC, TRANSPARENT); // You want your text to be "overlaid" onto
                                        // the label you're painting/filling. Because
                                        // of this you don't need to set the text
                                        // background color

MapMode = SetMapMode(hDC, MM_TEXT);     // In case it isn't set already


//
// Get font to draw with. You want the font (8 pt. helv) used by your parent window.
// This font was defined using DS_SETFONT and the FONT statement. A font will
// always be retrievable, so then immediately select it into your parent window's
// memory display context, and remember the old font in the DC, because you'll need
// to stick it back in later.
//

hFont = SelectObject(hDC, (HFONT) SendMessage(hWndParent, WM_GETFONT, 0, 0L));


//
// Get width of text to be used for the label. The function DrawCtrlLabel reads the
// window property "Label" that's associated with every control. This property
// returns a global atom containing the control's name. You couldn't use window text
// because for edit controls the window text is what's stored inside the edit, and
// it isn't a label. Groupboxes get their "label" from inside the private dialog
// resource structure, which is another reason they call the function DrawRectLabel
// directly, because there's no associated window to store the label with.
//
// The font must be selected into the DC for the width function to work properly.
//
// The string Label is being referenced starting at the third position because
// the first two characters of every label are used to determine the format of
// the label. The first character can be T, M, or B for a top-, middle-, or bottom-
// positioned label. The second character can be L, C, or R for a centered or a
// left- or right-justified label. In the case of a label positioned in the middle,
```

```
// the L and R positions are used not to left- or right-justify the label within
// the control, but rather to position the label just to the left or right of the
// control.

Extent = GetTextExtent(hDC, &Label[2], lstrlen(&Label[2]));

//
// Fill the label with your colored brush and draw a "raised" effect around the
// label's RECT. When SinkRect is called with a positive number, the RECT is
// painted as "sunken in." When it is called with a negative number, the
// RECT is painted as "popped out." Another function, SinkControl, accepts
// a window handle as a parameter. This function gets the RECT for the
// control and then calls SinkRect. The groupbox-drawing algorithm, which
// has no associated window, determines the amount of RECT to lasso all the
// controls it must manage, and calls SinkRect directly.
//

FillRect(hDC, &RectLabel, hBrush);
SinkRect(&RectLabel, hDC, -SizeLabel);

//
// Shrink in rectangle of label for your text format rect, which should
// be a tad smaller so that you don't overwrite the 3-D effect.
//

InflateRect(&RectLabel, -SizeLabel, -SizeLabel);

//
// You'll draw the text of the label using the system color for window text
//

Color = SetTextColor(hDC, GetSysColor(COLOR_WINDOWTEXT));

//
// Draw the formatted label into your RECT
//

DrawText
(
    hDC,
    &Label[2],
    -1,
    &RectLabel,
    DT_CENTER | DT_SINGLELINE | DT_VCENTER
);
```

```
//
// Here's where you restore the DC just the way you found it. The DC itself is
// actually cleaned up in the function that called this one. This function
// doesn't auto-generate a DC because sometimes this function is called from
// a window's WM_ERASEBKGND or WM_PAINT method, which already provides a DC
// for the developer, meaning that another shouldn't be generated.
//

SetTextColor(hDC, Color);
SelectObject(hDC, hFont);
SetMapMode(hDC, MapMode);
SetBkMode(hDC, BkgdMode);

...
```

Paint Messages and the Queue

Windows 3.1 has changed tremendously in the way that WM_PAINT messages are generated and processed. This is the primary reason behind the crisp and quick "snap" of windows onto the screen. A window receives WM_PAINT messages whenever it is covered by another window, changes its size, is implicitly invalidated via a drawing or a paint operation, or is explicitly invalidated via the function **InvalidateRect()**. The message WM_PAINT is unique compared to all other messages because it is continually pushed to the bottom of an application's message queue. Any other messages (except WM_TIMER) are always given a higher priority. The WM_PAINT doesn't get serviced until no other messages exist in the queue or an explicit call to **UpdateWindow()** is made. This helps eliminate superfluous screen updates and in general makes an application seem much more responsive. The update region described by a WM_PAINT message in a window's queue is "concatenated" to any existing WM_PAINT message in the queue, resulting in a (possibly) larger and larger update region for the window, and having a net effect of eliminating additional, possibly redundant paint messages. When the function **ValidateRect()** is called for a particular window, the area passed to the function is subtracted from the "cumulative" update region scheduled to be painted for the window.

Painting changes under Windows 3.1 include an elimination of the many redundant calls to `UpdateWindow()`, which often were done on focus switches and other periods when the message was better left "percolating" at the bottom of the queue.

The function `BeginPaint()` should be the only way that a display context handle is received during the WM_PAINT message for a window, and it should be used only during WM_PAINT. To paint at other times, either `GetDC()` or `GetWindowDC()` should be used. `BeginPaint()` is called with a window handle and a long pointer to a PAINTSTRUCT structure. The window handle specifies the window whose DC and update region is to be retrieved, and all this information is stuffed into the passed paint structure. Before `BeginPaint()` returns, it checks the value of fErase in PAINTSTRUCT. If the value is TRUE, Windows first sends a WM_ERASEBKGND message to the window, allowing the background to be erased. When this is done, `BeginPaint()` returns a valid display context to the WM_PAINT message, and painting can start. At this point, the entire window area is validated, and the developer must depend on the RECT structure in the PAINTSTRUCT to determine the update region. `BeginPaint()` automatically clips all output to this rectangular region, which is the smallest rectangle that encloses the area to be updated. When any client-area painting is finished, `EndPaint()` is called with the same window handle and PAINTSTRUCT pointer, and painting is officially over. `BeginPaint()` hides the caret, whereas `EndPaint()` restores the caret.

The library STDWIN.DLL uses the WM_PAINT method of the `AtomicDialog()` window class to draw all bitmap backgrounds, groupboxes, and control labels. Control labels need to be drawn during the dialog's paint message because they aren't part of the control's client or non-client area. Rather, they are painted onto the parent dialog's client area, somewhere around the control it is supposed to be labeling. If a window were to partially cover the label or the 3-D effect of a control (which is also part of the parent dialog), the control would never get any message to update itself, which is why the parent must take charge of this operation. However, in the case in which a child control is resized, moved, or zoomed (expanded into its parent area), the child does explicitly send the appropriate messages to redraw its label and 3-D effect. In this case, you don't want the parent to "blindly" redraw the labels and 3-D effects for all its child controls when only one control might have been moved or somehow altered.

Putting the Display Context in Context

A display context (DC) defines an output device and a series of GDI objects used to generate output on a particular device such as a display or a printer. Every Windows GDI function requires a handle to a display context or a device context. The display context can be thought of as a sort of small database of information, and it is used as a kind of "display" semaphore. Display contexts allow coordinated access to the screen display while providing a clipping mechanism (among other things) used to restrict display output among tasks. The display context's clipping mechanism can be compared to the spooling used by Windows' Print Manager, because both coordinate access to a device among multiple tasks. The "database" concept of a display context is useful because context values rarely are changed between drawing operations, and because it helps to promote the concept of device independence. Initially, it is set to the values shown in Table 6.5.

Table 6.5. Display context defaults.

Attribute	Default
Background color	COLOR_WHITE (see stdwin.h for #define value)
Background mode	OPAQUE
Bitmap	None
Brush	WHITE_BRUSH
Brush origin	(0, 0)
Clipping region	Client area
Color palette	DEFAULT_PALETTE
Device origin	Upper-left client area
Drawing mode	R2_COPYPEN
Font	SYSTEM_FONT
Intercharacter spacing	0
Mapping mode	MM_TEXT (pixels)

Attribute	Default
Pen	BLACK_PEN
Pen position	(0, 0)
Polygon-filling mode	ALTERNATE
Relative-absolute flag	ABSOLUTE
Stretching mode	BLACKONWHITE
Text color	COLOR_BLACK (see stdwin.h for #define value)
Viewport extent	(1, 1)
Viewport origin	(0, 0)
Window extent	(1, 1)
Window origin	(0, 0)

Internally, Windows maintains a pool of five display contexts. When a display context is given to an application, it is unavailable to other applications, and as such must be returned to the common pool as quickly as possible. Most applications absolutely depend on the retrieval of a display context and include no error-checking when none exists, thus causing the application to fail. Generally, a display context should be freed before any operation that could cause control to yield to Windows and possibly another application. Display contexts are retrieved through the functions `GetDC()`, `GetWindowDC()`, `CreateDC()`, and `BeginPaint()`, and released through the functions `ReleaseDC()` (used with `GetDC()` and `GetWindowDC()`), `DeleteDC()` (used with `CreateDC()`), and `EndPaint()` (used with `BeginPaint()`).

When display contexts from the common pool are exhausted, the system will appear to be hung, but this isn't really the case. It's just that no free DCs are available to do any painting.

A display context differs from a device context because it involves a clipping region and is specially constructed for a particular window, not an entire device, such as a display or the printer. There is no limit to the number of device contexts an application may create. Device contexts are retrieved through the function `CreateDC()`, which can create a device context for the screen or the printer. Although by default no clipping is provided for a device context, a clipping region can easily be created and passed into the device context using the function `SelectClipRgn()`, which accepts a handle to a device context and a handle to a region as parameters. A region is a polygonal or elliptical area within a window that defines a clipping space for GDI. Regions are allocated out of GDI's DGROUP and can be immediately deleted or reused as soon as they are passed to a GDI function. Basically, a region is a connected series of points similar to a simpler region—the RECT structure. Windows provides functions for creating regions of any type and for combining them and treating them much in the manner of the more widely used RECT-style of region. Although in principle, regions sound like a powerful capability, in practice, such is not the case. Windows 3.1 and 3.0 both have problems with complex regions and regions extending beyond the dimensions of a display context.

The following function snippets create and free display and device contexts:

```
HDC         hDC;
HWND        hWnd;
PAINTSTRUCT Paint;


hDC = GetWindowDC(hWnd);        // Gets display context to entire window, including
                               // its non-client area. This isn't too useful
                               // for stock controls or controls modified through
                               // subclassing and superclassing, only for pure
                               // custom controls. The clipping region is the
                               // entire window, including the non-client area.
ReleaseDC(hWnd, hDC);          // Free up the display context


...


hDC = GetDC(hWnd)              // Gets display context to client area of window.
                               // This is the most common method for painting
                               // graphics during any message other than
                               // WM_PAINT. The clipping region is the entire
                               // client area of the window.


ReleaseDC(hWnd, hDC);          // Free up the display context


...


case WM_PAINT :

    BeginPaint(hWnd, &Paint);  // Gets display context to client area of
                               // window. This is the only way a screen DC
                               // should be gotten during a WM_PAINT message.
                               // The clipping region selected is the
                               // scheduled update region for the window, as
```

```
                                    // was accumulated through various WM_PAINT
                                    // messages, until an UpdateWindow was sent.

        EndPaint(hWnd, &Paint);        // Free up the display context

...

hDC = CreateDC("DISPLAY", NULL, NULL, NULL); // Creates a screen device context,
                                             // with no automatic clipping region.
                                             // This function can be used with the
                                             // names of most .DRV device-driver
                                             // files, including printer drivers,
                                             // the DIB (DIB.DRV) driver, and any
                                             // other video drivers.

DeleteDC(hDC);
...
```

Retrieving the Device Context for a Printer

Windows' WIN.INI profile settings file contains a series of "devices" entries for each installed printer. The first one is the default. Each profile line has the following format:

```
[devices]
HP LaserJet III=hppcl5a,LPT1:
...
```

The first field in the record is the name of the printer, the second field is the name of the (.drv) driver file that supports the printer, and the third field is the printer port that the printer is attached to. The function `GetDefaultPrinterDC()` in STDWIN.DLL gets the device context for the default printer. The `CreateDC()` call that is ultimately generated is as follows:

```
hDCPrtr = CreateDC("hppcl5a", "HP LaserJet III", "LPT1:", NULL);
```

Just like any other device context, `DeleteDC()` is used to free a printer device context. A printer DC is used exactly like a display context, except that the size of the DC is limited to a single printed page. When a page's worth of graphics and text has been drawn, the page must be ejected with a NEXTFRAME or a NEXTBAND call, and DC must be used all over again for output to the second page. When Windows' Print Manager is running, the job is not sent until the ENDDOC escape is sent to the printer. Printing is fairly straightforward and almost as easy as using straight GDI functions, because the vast majority of the printer calls are merely GDI calls, and only a few `Escape()` functions are used to actually set up the printer itself. This is how Windows shows its device-independence to the extreme. Going from one type of display to another or one type of printer to another is one thing, but having screen and printer graphics drawing using the same interface is an absolute time-saver. Although `Escape()` codes can be used to directly access a specific printer's functionality, this isn't recommended.

Retrieving a Memory Display Context

A memory display context is similar to a device context or a display context in that it is used to hold the output from GDI operations. A memory DC is not directly connected to any device, however. It is merely a temporary holding tank for GDI operations. Memory DCs are commonly used to hold an intermediate series of GDI calls, after the last of which the memory DC is `BitBlt`ed to a screen or a printer DC and the image "snapped" onto the device. Unlike a display context, which contains no "default" bitmap, a memory device context contains a bitmap that is exactly one pixel by one pixel in size. A printer device context essentially contains a bitmap large enough for the entire printed page. Any time a memory display context is used for GDI operations, a compatible bitmap must be created that is large enough to hold the desired output, whether it is `BitBlt`ed to a printer or a display context. Bitmaps can be selected (using `SelectObject()`) only into a memory device context. The different bit-blitting functions (`BitBlt()`, `StretchBlt()`) should be used to transfer the bitmap image from one memory DC to another, or directly to an actual display or device context.

Using Information Contexts

An information context (IC) is just like a device context, with one very important exception—it cannot be the destination of any GDI calls, and therefore cannot be used to output data to a specific device. So what good are ICs? ICs generally are used for the very feature their name implies: information. An IC is created through the call `CreateIC()`, which accepts the same parameters as `CreateDC()`: a driver name, a device name, a DOS output device name (null), and a pointer to a DEVMODE structure, in case the device's own settings are to be overridden. Information contexts are ideal because they don't require the overhead and other limitations associated with device contexts. The following code snippet illustrates the correct usage of an information context:

```
HDC hIC;
TEXTMETRIC TextMetric;

//
// Get information context to screen display device
//

hIC = CreateIC("DISPLAY", NULL, NULL, NULL);

//
// Get metric information on font used in IC
//

GetTextMetrics(hIC, &TextMetric);

//
// Free up space used by information context
//

DeleteDC(hIC);
```

Common Device Context Functions

The following common GDI functions deal with most common device-context manipulation operations:

Function	Description
BeginPaint()*	Retrieves a display context for a window during its WM_PAINT message. This is the only time this function should be used. The clipping region of the display context is set to the smallest rectangle encompassing the range of areas needing to be updated.
EndPaint()	Frees a display context retrieved through BeginPaint().

continues

319

Function	Description
GetDC()*	Retrieves a display context clipped to the client area of a window.
GetDCEx()	Retrieves a display context for a given window. Unlike GetDC(), this function allows overrides to settings established by class and private display contexts and window styles such as WS_CLIPCHILDREN, returning DCs from the common pool.
GetWindowDC()*	Retrieves a display context whose clipping region extends to the outermost edge of the window, including the non-client area.
ReleaseDC()	Frees a display context retrieved through GetDC() or GetWindowDC().
CreateDC()	Retrieves a device context for a display or a printer device, with no clipping region selected. There is no effective limit to device contexts created in this manner. A clipping region can be selected into the device context if needed.
DeleteDC()	Frees a device context created through CreateDC(), CreateIC(), or CreateCompatibleDC().
CreateIC()	Creates an information context for a device. An IC consumes less overhead than a device context; however, it cannot be used for GDI output, only for information calls (that is, GetTextMetrics()).
CreateCompatibleDC()	Creates a memory display context compatible with a specific device. This function is used as a "middleman" when images must be transferred indirectly to another display context or device context.

Function	Description
`CreateCompatibleBitmap()`	Creates a bitmap compatible with a specific display context. This function is commonly used with `SelectObject()` to create a DC "fully" compatible with a specific device.
`DeleteObject()`	Deletes a GDI object, removing it from GDI's local heap. Objects that can be deleted include pens, brushes, bitmaps, fonts, regions, and palettes. An object should not be deleted while it is currently selected into a device context.
`GetObject()`	Returns information on a specified GDI object when passed the handle to the object, a far pointer to the object's structure, and the size of the structure to fill. This function is most commonly used to retrieve information about bitmaps.
`SelectObject()`	Selects a new object into a device context, with a handle to the prior object as a return value. The handle to the prior object normally is saved and selected back into the device context when the GDI operation is finished. At this point, the original object usually is passed to `DeleteObject()`. When a metafile is selected into a device context, cleanup need not be performed because the metafile does its own cleanup. Bitmaps can be selected only into memory display contexts.

A total of five "common" display contexts are maintained by Windows at any time.

The Non-Client Area

Although Microsoft recommends that the developer not meddle with the non-client area of a window, there are many reasons for doing so, including the creation of "truly" custom controls, adding 3-D effects to the scroll bars, caption, and system menus of a window. This is not to advocate every application's maintaining its own 3-D look, because this would be too confusing for the user. If not overdone, however, the 3-D appearance can be pleasing and easy to work with. Actually, IBM's Common User Access (CUA) Advanced Interface Guide recommends that MDI child windows place a miniature representation of the window's icon on the left side of the window's caption bar. In this manner, the "miniature" icon representation could be dragged-and-dropped onto another object without requiring that the MDI child window be in a minimized state. Customization of the non-client area is key to implementing such a feat.

Although the 3-D effect for the custom controls (as well as the control labels) listed in this book is done on the parent's client window area, ideally it should be a part of the child control's non-client area. This isn't done, because when a developer assumes "creative" control of the non-client area, he assumes complete control and must maintain all aspects of the non-client space. For instance, if a third scroll bar were to be added to the bitmap control to handle z-axis zooming, it would have to be created and maintained inside the client window area, not the non-client area. This means that all bitmap scrolling operations must be sure to exclude the client area of the window that contains the additional, third scroll bar. If the scroll bar were maintained as a part of the non-client area of the window, the client area could be used with abandon.

Normally, the non-client area is created, sized, and painted by Windows, period. Either Windows or an application, but not both, can define the size of a window's non-client area. If a developer were to assume the responsibility of creating and defining the size of the non-client area for a control, everything having to do with the non-client area would have to be handled by the developer, which could be a big hassle. Traditionally, the non-client area of any window is managed completely by Windows, and the client area of a window is managed by the developer. When scroll bars are added to a window, however, although they are handled by Windows, the developer needs to create the code to "link" them to the client area of his or her application or to some other input mechanism. Although the client area of every window maintains update regions to determine which parts of the window need to be repainted, for the non-client area of a window it's an all-or-none affair.

Non-Client Area Messages

Trapping mouse hits and checking for other events in the non-client area of a window is simple, because Windows sends the following messages any time a non-client event occurs for a window:

Message	Description
WM_NCACTIVATE	Sent when the caption of a window needs to be changed from an active to an inactive state or vice versa.
WM_NCCALCSIZE	Sent when the non-client size of a window needs to be determined, thus indirectly determining the client size of a window.
WM_NCCREATE	Sent when a window is first created. This message initializes scroll bars and allocates window text and additional memory related to per-window overhead. The parameter lParam points to the window's CREATESTRUCT parameter.
WM_NCDESTROY	Sent when the non-client area of a window is about to be destroyed. Completion of this message frees memory overhead associated per-window.
WM_NCPAINT	Sent when the non-client area of a window needs to be painted.
WM_NCHITTEST	Sent to the window containing the mouse or having the capture state whenever the mouse is moved within the window. The parameter lParam contains the x and y coordinates of the cursor in the low and high words, respectively. The return value from **DefWindowProc()**, which indicates the position of the cursor within the window, can be one of the following values:

Hit-Test Code	Description
HTTOP	Hit is in the top horizontal border of the window.
HTBOTTOM	Hit is in the lower horizontal border of the window.
HTLEFT	Hit is in the left vertical border of the window.
HTRIGHT	Hit is in the right vertical border of the window.

continues

Hit-Test Code	Description
HTTOPLEFT	Hit is in the upper-left corner of the window border.
HTTOPRIGHT	Hit is in the upper-right corner of the window border.
HTBOTTOMLEFT	Hit is in the lower-left corner of the window border.
HTBOTTOMRIGHT	Hit is in the lower-right corner of the window border.
HTSYSMENU	Hit is in the window's system menu.
HTCAPTION	Hit is in the window's caption area.
HTREDUCE	Hit is in the window's minimize box.
HTZOOM	Hit is in the window's maximize box.
HTMENU	Hit is in the window's menu area.
HTCLIENT	Hit is in the window's client area.
HTHSCROLL	Hit is in the window's horizontal scroll bar.
HTVSCROLL	Hit is in the window's vertical scroll bar.
HTGROWBOX	Hit is in the "size box" of a window, which is the "void" section of the box where a vertical and a horizontal scroll bar meet.

Hit-Test Code	Description
HTSIZE	Same as HTGROWBOX.
HTTRANSPARENT	Hit is in the section of a window currently covered by another window.
HTNOWHERE	Hit is on the desktop.
HTERROR	Same as HTNOWHERE, except that **DefWindowProc()** generates a system beep.
WM_NCMOUSEMOVE	Sent to a window whenever the mouse moves over a non-client portion of a window. The wParam value of this message contains the value returned from WM_NCHITTEST after being processed by **DefWindowProc()**.
WM_NCLBUTTONDBLCLK	Left button double-click within the non-client area of the window.
WM_NCLBUTTONDOWN	Left button pressed within the non-client area of the window.
WM_NCLBUTTONUP	Left button released within the non-client area of the window.
WM_NCMBUTTONDBLCLK	Middle button double-clicked within the non-client area of the window.

continues

Hit-Test Code	Description
WM_NCMBUTTONDOWN	Middle button pressed within the non-client area of the window.
WM_NCMBUTTONUP	Middle button released within the non-client area of the window.
WM_NCRBUTTONDBLCLK	Right button double-clicked within the non-client area of the window.
WM_NCRBUTTONDOWN	Right button pressed within the non-client area of the window.
WM_NCRBUTTONUP	Right button released within the non-client area of the window.

Note: The non-client mouse click messages generate WM_SYSCOMMAND messages to the window where applicable (that is, a double-click on a caption restores and maximizes a window). In all cases, the parameter lParam is a POINT structure containing the cursor coordinates.

Generally, the functions **DefWindowProc()** and **DefDlgProc()** do all the processing for a window's non-client area, which includes handling the series of WM_NC* messages. The return value from the message WM_NCHITTEST is bundled with other messages, including WM_SETCURSOR. When the cursor is over the client area of a window, Windows by default uses the class cursor for the window. When the cursor is over a non-client portion of the window, however, the NCHITTEST value is interpreted and the cursor possibly set to any of a variety of arrows (up/down, left/right, northeast/southwest, northwest/southeast), depending on where on a section of thick-framed border the cursor might be located. **DefWindowProc()** passes WM_SETCURSOR the parent window first, allowing it to override the class cursor established by a child window. Depending on whether a true or false value is returned, further processing of a new cursor value is halted. A returned true value indicates that the parent wants to override the child's cursor.

To change the cursor for the client portion of a window, only the class cursor needs to be changed. If multiple cursors are to be used for windows of a single class, WM_SETCURSOR must continually be trapped and processed. The application can at this point either set a new class cursor or call a combination of LoadCursor() and SetCursor(). This is in fact done for the window class AtomicBitmap, which uses a crosshair or an arrow cursor, depending on whether the bitmap is editable (supports pixel plotting). The following code fragment from BITMAP.DLL illustrates this:

```
case WM_SETCURSOR :

    //
    // Noneditable bitmaps get an arrow cursor, whereas editable
    // ones get the crosshairs. The style property will be WS_MODIFY
    // for bitmaps that can be modified.
    //

    SetCursor
    (
        LoadCursor
        (
            NULL,
            !(GetProp(hWnd, "Style") & WS_MODIFY)?
                IDC_ARROW : IDC_CROSS
        )
    );

    break;
```

If an application wants to provide a custom cursor for a section of non-client area in a window, it must intercept WM_SETCURSOR, interpret the hit-test code embedded into lParam, and set the cursor accordingly. In the dialog TestApp (found in Appendix A), which is used to demonstrate all the custom controls included in this book, several portions of the non-client area of the window are customized, including the system menu and the caption, both sporting a 3-D appearance as well as different cursor types. When the cursor is over the system menu, a box-within-a-box cursor is displayed, whereas when the cursor is over the window's caption, a hand cursor is displayed rather than the usual arrow. Unlike the client area of a window, the non-client area has no concept of a validation region. You can't just draw in the non-client area of a window and call **ValidateRect()**, because the **Validate*** functions are for only the client area of a window, not the non-client area. To alter the non-client areas of a window, an exact series of steps needs to occur. First, certain desired style bits are dynamically removed. Second, the default painting method for the window is invoked. Finally, the style bits are added back to the window. The following code snippet illustrates these principles:

```
#define WIDGETS (WS_SYSMENU ¦ WS_CAPTION ¦ WS_MINIMIZEBOX ¦ WS_MAXIMIZEBOX)

...(the dialog's window procedure)...

case WM_SETCURSOR :

    switch(LOWORD(lParam))
    {
        case HTSYSMENU :

            //
            // When you're hovering over the system menu, change the
            // cursor to a "box within a box."
            //

            SetCursor(LoadCursor(NULL, IDC_ICON));
            return(1);

        case HTCAPTION :

            //
            // When you're hovering over the caption bar, change the
            // cursor to a hand, indicating that the window can be
            // dragged
            //

            SetCursor(LoadCursor(hInstTestApp, "Hand"));
            return(1);

        default :

            break;
    }
    break;

case WM_ENTERIDLE :
```

```
    if(GetWindowLong(hDlg, GWL_STYLE) & WS_SYSMENU)
    {
        //
        // When you drop the system menu down, force the cursor into
        // an arrow. Otherwise, it tries to use the cursor used for
        // the caption. This overrides Windows behavior.
        //

        SetCursor(LoadCursor(NULL, IDC_ARROW));
    }
    break;

WM_NCPAINT :

    ...

    //
    // Remove the style bits you want to handle
    //

    SetWindowLong(hDlg, GWL_STYLE, (lStyle ^= WIDGETS) | WS_BORDER);

    //
    // Let the default method paint the non-client, and make
    // it think that certain window styles aren't invoked
    //

    lResult = DefWindowProc(hDlg, Msg, wParam, lParam);

    //
    // Now turn the style bits back on
    //

    SetWindowLong(hDlg, GWL_STYLE, lStyle |= WIDGETS);

    ...(your code for drawing in the non-client areas)...
```

Don't worry about calling **SetCursor()** repeatedly, because (as you're probably well aware) WM_SETCURSOR is called for absolutely every movement of the mouse. When **SetCursor()** is called with the same value as the prior cursor, the function returns almost immediately. In the dialog TestApp, when the cursor hovers above the system menu of the window, the cursor changes to this "box." When the mouse is pressed over the system menu, however, the cursor changes to an

arrow because you've invoked a new kind of non-client cursor—the one used for menus. (More specifically, Windows uses the cursor used for the caption.) This is the reason that the message WM_ENTERIDLE is trapped. This message is sent to a top-level window whenever a menu is displayed or a message box is created. This brings up another issue with the altering of non-client window characteristics—overriding default behaviors.

Overriding Default Behaviors

To have complete control over the system menu, including its "pressed" image, you would need to process the WM_NCLBUTTONDOWN message manually and not let DefWindowProc() handle the method. Because the system menu and other non-client components aren't separate windows, their methods must be handled manually. Although things such as the minimize box and maximize box look, feel, and smell like buttons, they aren't. This is really no great feat, because it's done for the "pure" AtomicButton button class control presented in this book.

Repainting things such as the caption is a bit trickier, because changing the caption style bit implies by default that there is no system menu or minimize and maximize buttons. This means that they must be drawn and handled manually during your processing of WM_NCPAINT, because when DefWindowProc() does this, you've stripped the style bits out from underneath it. Notice how, when you fail to process a WM_NCPAINT message, the images might not visually appear on the display; however, when the mouse is clicked in the appropriate areas, Windows still knows to display a pressed and an unpressed image. The reason for this is that during WM_NCPAINT, DefWindowProc() doesn't know about the buttons. When a press or other kind of action is performed on the "subwidget," the style bits have already been re-added, so DefWindowProc() paints the control as it normally would. In the case of the system menu, the default painting action is to merely PatBlt(), or inverse the image. In the case of the minimize and maximize arrows, a different bitmap is selected altogether. To verify this, examine the following Heap Walker dump showing GDI's storage for these system "widget" bitmaps (see Figure 6.4).

Figure 6.4.
A Heap Walker
dump showing
storage in GDI.

Notice how there is only one image for the system menu, one for the system menus of MDI children, and multiple pressed and unpressed images for minimize and maximize arrows and the like. To verify the handling of the widget/buttons, run Spy on a top-level window and check the flow of messages. Notice how a WM_NCPAINT message is received only initially, and when any of the window's "subwidget" controls such as the minimize and maximize buttons are pressed, no further paint messages are generated. If the system menu were processed this way, you would need to completely take over hit-testing for this "subcontrol." Because the image is reversed only upon "focus," however, you're OK. Because the other non-client widgets are another matter, you would need to completely take over all hit-testing to do a clean job of painting anything other than the system menu and caption.

Whenever any kind of precise window or text positioning is needed, whether for the client or non-client area of a window, it helps to know the exact dimensions of internal Windows components, including things such as the scroll bars, caption height, and so forth. Windows provides a function for determining the dimensions of various window components: `GetSystemMetrics()`. When passed a `#define` value, this function returns the associated metric (unit of measurement). The following values are predefined:

Metric	Description
SM_CXBORDER	Width of unsizable-style window border/ frame
SM_CYBORDER	Height of unsizable-style window border/ frame
SM_CXDLGFRAME	Width of unsizable-style thick dialog border/ frame
SM_CYDLGFRAME	Height of unsizable-style thick dialog border/ frame
SM_CXFRAME	Width of sizable-style thick window frame
SM_CYFRAME	Height of sizable-style thick window frame
SM_CXHSCROLL	Width of arrow bitmap on horizontal scroll bar
SM_CYHSCROLL	Height of arrow bitmap on horizontal scroll bar

continues

Metric	Description
SM_CXVSCROLL	Width of arrow bitmap on vertical scroll bar
SM_CYVSCROLL	Height of arrow bitmap on vertical scroll bar
SM_CXHTHUMB	Width of thumb box on horizontal scroll bar
SM_CYVTHUMB	Height of thumb box on vertical scroll bar
SM_CXFULLSCREEN	Width of maximized top-level window's client area
SM_CYFULLSCREEN	Height of maximized top-level window's client area
SM_CXSCREEN	Width of entire screen/display
SM_CYSCREEN	Height of entire screen/display
SM_CXICON	Width of system icon
SM_CYICON	Height of system icon
SM_CXICONSPACING	Width in pixels of system rectangle used for tiling icons
SM_CYICONSPACING	Height in pixels of system rectangle used for tiling icons
SM_CXCURSOR	Width of system cursor
SM_CYCURSOR	Height of system cursor
SM_CYCAPTION	Height of window caption
SM_CYMENU	Height of window menu bar
SM_CXSIZE	Width of system menu and minimize and maximize buttons
SM_CYSIZE	Height of system menu and minimize and maximize buttons
SM_CXMIN	Minimum width of window
SM_CYMIN	Minimum height of window
SM_CXMINTRACK	Minimum tracking width of window
SM_CYMINTRACK	Minimum tracking height of window
SM_MOUSEPRESENT	Nonzero value returned if mouse installed

Metric	Description
SM_SWAPBUTTON	Nonzero value if mouse buttons have been swapped
SM_CXDOUBLECLK	Width in pixels of system rectangle in which both clicks of a double-click must occur
SM_CYDOUBLECLK	Height in pixels of system rectangle in which both clicks of a double-click must occur
SM_CMETRICS	Number of system metrics defined
SM_DEBUG	Nonzero value if debug version of Windows is running
SM_MENUDROPALIGNMENT	Alignment of popup menu items with respect to the left- or right-most edge of its corresponding top-level menu item
SM_PENWINDOWS	Handle to Pen Windows DLL, if installed
SM_CYKANJIWINDOW	Height of Kanji window
SM_DBCSENABLED	Nonzero value if Windows is using a double-byte char set

The function `SystemParametersInfo()` can also be used to query (and set) several system-wide parameters related to the display or non-client area of a window. The function is defined as shown:

```
BOOL SystemParametersInfo(UINT uAction, UINT uParam,
                          LPVOID lpParam, UINT uWinIni);
```

The return value is nonzero if the function is successful. The parameter `uWinIni` can be either `SPIF_UPDATEINIFILE` or `SPIF_SENDWININICHANGE`, depending on whether the changes are to be written to WIN.INI and broadcast to all desktop applications. The following (partial) list of values may be used for the parameter `uAction`:

uAction	Description
SPI_GETBORDER	Retrieves the multiplying factor used to determine the width of a window border. uParam is zero, and lpParam is a pointer to an integer containing the multiplying factor.

continues

uAction	Description
SPI_SETBORDER	Sets the border multiplying factor. uParam contains the new factor; lpParam is null.
SPI_GETGRIDGRANULARITY	Gets granularity of the desktop sizing grid. uParam is zero; lpParam is a pointer to an integer to receive the granularity.
SPI_SETGRIDGRANULARITY	Sets granularity of the desktop sizing grid. uParam is zero, and lpParam is a pointer to an integer containing the granularity.
SPI_GETMENUDROPALIGNMENT	Determines whether popup menus are left- or right-aligned. uParam is zero, and lpParam is a far pointer to a BOOL indicating TRUE if menus are right-aligned and FALSE if left-aligned.
SPI_SETMENUDROPALIGNMENT	Sets alignment for popup menus. uParam is TRUE for right alignment and FALSE for left alignment. lpParam is null.
SPI_SETDESKPATTERN	Sets the pattern used for tiling the desktop. If uParam is –1 and lpParam is null, the WIN.INI setting is used.
SPI_SETDESKWALLPAPER	Sets the desktop bitmap. uParam is zero, and lpParam points to a string naming the bitmap file.
SPI_ICONHORIZONTALSPACING	Sets the width of the cell used for spacing icons. uParam is the new width (in pixels) to use if lpParam is null. Otherwise, uParam is zero, and lpParam is a far pointer to an integer to contain the current value.
SPI_ICONVERTICALSPACING	Sets the height of the cell used for spacing icons. uParam is the new height (in pixels) to use if lParam is null. Otherwise, uParam is zero, and lpParam is a far pointer to an integer to contain the current value.

uAction	Description
SPI_GETICONTITLEWRAP	Determines whether icon titles are wrapped. uParam is zero, and lParam is a far pointer to a BOOL that is to contain the wrap mode: TRUE if wrapping is on, FALSE otherwise.
SPI_SETICONTITLEWRAP	Sets whether icon titles are to be wrapped. uParam is TRUE if wrapping is to be turned on, FALSE if otherwise. lpParam is ignored.
SPI_GETICONTITLELOGFONT	Retrieves the LOGFONT structure used for drawing icon titles. uParam contains the size of the LOGFONT structure, and lpParam is a far pointer to the LOGFONT structure.
SPI_SETICONTITLELOGFONT	Sets a new LOGFONT structure for drawing icon titles. uParam contains the size of the LOGFONT structure, and lpParam is a far pointer to the LOGFONT structure.

The function **SystemParametersInfo()** allows access to numerous other system settings that can be altered. See Windows documentation for additional information.

Interface Design

Much like the buttons, dials, switches, and displays on a ham radio, multimeter, or network analyzer, controls come in numerous forms and styles. With every new release of Windows, the "artistic" design of controls is improved, with controls looking more and more like their real-world counterparts. Often, a dialog is used to simulate the appearance of a particular piece of hardware, such as a multimeter or the front panel of an audio mixing board. This yields a strong benefit for the user: "Relearning" what the controls are and how they function isn't necessary, because the user hopefully is already aware of how the real-life component functions. "Instant" recognition of the controls in a window should be a priority. Is the window too busy? Does it take forever to find out which control has the focus, or even too long to figure out how to use the control?

Figure 6.5 shows the main dialog created using the dialog class and custom controls developed in this book. Admittedly, it's a little cluttered and busy. Attention is immediately drawn to the control having the focus, however, and the functions of various components are fairly obvious. As Burger King says (no, not the Burgermaster!), you can "have it your way." Because all the 3-D mechanisms and graphics controls for the dialog are optional, you can implement as much or as little of the functionality offered by the dialog and control classes as you need. Note the 3-D system menu and caption bar, as well as the new style of "hand" cursor when the caption is dragged. All the controls sport a 3-D "self-generated" label, as well as a fully integrated 3-D appearance (including Windows' stock controls as well).

Figure 6.5.
Windows stock controls.

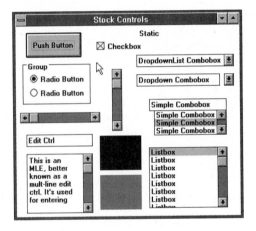

Eliminating this level of interpretation and translation associated with control images in an application is often bypassed by developers during the development stages of writing custom controls. Abuse of owner-draw is rampant in Windows 3.x applications. Hopefully this will change as the initial gush of enthusiasm over Windows and its highly graphical interface turns more to questions of speed and ease of use. This is a perfect example of a developer not doing usability studies on an application, or of a marketing person thinking that his or her toolbar must be bigger than the competition's. This is commonly referred to as "toolbar envy." Any toolbar containing more than 10 buttons is commonly known in the trade as a "toolbar from hell," or (with a nod to our boys from Desert Storm) "The Mother of all Toolboxes." People who use Windows and people who don't use Windows often complain about the speed (or lack thereof) when working with Windows applications. There is no doubt that the overly high graphical overhead might have something to do with this. One of the nice things about a bare-bones DOS application is that the user is forced to use the keyboard for most input, and the screens are primarily text-based. It is true that many DOS-based applications use a mouse; however, it doesn't seem to be relied on as much as it is under Windows. Likewise, a text-based interface is easier to navigate, requiring no extra step of interpretation as is the case with an unlabeled graphics image.

The mouse is an excellent input device, but only when the user isn't familiar with how to use the keyboard or is missing an arm or multiple fingers. The only other time a mouse is useful is for precise and quick pixel positioning in a paint or draw package or for operations similar to marking blocks of text or specifying areas on a screen. As soon as you learn the four or five window navigation keys used by Windows (Alt-Tab, Alt-Esc, Alt-Enter, Ctrl-Esc, Tab, Shift-Tab), as well as any & shortcut keys displayed on the dialog, there is no real reason, other than psychological, to keep using the mouse. A truly usable, fast application must provide easy and simple keyboard support. The mouse acts as a kind of crutch and is relied on far too much. One of the reasons the mouse can be a problem is that when you use the mouse to select an item that could have just as easily been selected with the keyboard, you must remove your hand from the mouse and place it on the keyboard for any further input.

Is the power switch difficult to find on your computer? Of course not, and neither are any other switches, buttons, or dials on any other real-life piece of hardware. Take a second to examine the reset button on your computer. Chances are, in addition to having a "lightning bolt" or some other similar picture, it also has the word *RESET* near it. Could you ever imagine the controls on a piece of hardware being labeled differently? Of course not, so try to design dialogs similarly.

All too often, however, the visual design of a control acts as a complete hindrance to its functionality. Just showing a "picture" of the control is not enough, because the user must then translate the picture into a word. It's been proven that users think first in terms of words, not images. When *house* or some other word is mentioned to a person, the first thing visualized is the spelling of the word. A large button with a picture of a big red stop sign is another matter altogether. All too often, however, the images associated with a control are not intuitive or based on images found in real life. After all, how many pictures do you see in your day-to-day life that are associated with the cut-and-paste function in a word processor? None, which is why it's so frustrating to locate this image in a toolbar with 20 or more images.

Magnifying this problem is the fact that every application shows this image differently, further confusing a user who must work with multiple applications. The problem is compounded for dynamically sizable toolboxes, because the image is never guaranteed to be in the same place. Pictures of a stop sign, a yield sign, a modem, a typewriter, a computer—these images are much more acceptable to use in the picture/toolbar metaphor. Of course, keeping the number of buttons under 10 or some other small number helps immensely. However, a common rule still holds true: Always label the control.

Designing dialogs and controls that are easy to use, identify, and navigate between is not that difficult. At the simplest level it means including & hotkeys for all controls and making sure that all controls have a label associated with them, making them easier to identify. The label for any control can easily be stored as a string resource, making it subject to future internationalization, if needed. Remember that the whole purpose of Windows is to provide for the user a common interface between applications. Realizing that this isn't always possible, the developer can still adhere to a common subset, which would mean easy identification of every control and a clear indication of focused/nonfocused and enabled/disabled states. Examining the dialogs and "widgets" of some more mature graphical user interfaces, such as those found on X-based systems, and even a newer system such as NextStep, can be a great help. Most Windows applications just don't have the same level of maturity—yet.

Following is a brief discussion of a few of the stock window classes available with Windows, including two for top-level windows—an internal window class and a dialog class—and seven for child window classes, which include the controls listed here:

Control Class	Description/Styles
Button	Push buttons, groupboxes, checkboxes, and mutually exclusive radio buttons*.
Combobox	Normal, editable, fixed, and dropdown comboboxes*.
Edit	Read-write (Windows 3.1 includes a read-only style), single and multiline edit controls.
Listbox	Normal listbox*.
Scrollbar	Both built-in (inherited) vertical and horizontal scroll bars for windows with WS_?SCROLL style bit, plus dynamic, application-created scroll bars.
Static	Used for creating labels (usually around controls) and opaque backdrops and for displaying icons. Useful for blocking or partitioning sections of screen.

Control Class	Description/Styles
MDIClient	Created inside a top-level MDI frame window. The client window is responsible for controlling MDI child windows, which can use a developer-defined class name.

*Also includes any owner-draw style.

Windows 3.1 also includes source code for two additional custom controls—a "rheostat" or dial type of control, and a microscroll control, which basically is a scroll bar without the thumb or slider mechanism. The dial control would be useful for putting a control that looked like the knob of a radio or some similar panel on a dialog, and the microscroll control could be useful if attached to an edit control, creating a sort of hybrid spin control.

The stock controls provided with Windows are a good start, and they work fine for simple applications; however, they are fairly useless for large-scale applications development. A one-person team might best be served by using as many of the built-in classes as possible, but a larger team should strongly consider rewriting most, if not all, of the controls. The problem is not in the range of offerings, but rather in how they are implemented. All have serious shortcomings, many of which cannot be corrected by subclassing or superclassing. The main problem is the lack of source code. Not source code in the sense that it can be tweaked and modified, because this can be done through subclassing or superclassing, but rather source code so that you can find out how the control's extra class and window bytes are being used. Unless existing extra data is preserved, the modified controls won't function correctly. Subclassing isn't always an option because you can't "sit in" on all of the messages received by the control.

Buttons

Like the static control, buttons come in various configurations—push buttons, two- and three-state buttons (checkboxes), and radio buttons. Buttons can also be owner-draw, which means that the developer is partially responsible for maintaining the control's state, with hints from Windows now and then in the form of various messages. The only problem with the way owner-draw is implemented for buttons is that Windows automatically assumes the button is a push button, forgetting about any radio button or checkbox style bits previously assigned. This makes owner-draw fairly useless for the stock button control class. A better idea is to completely rewrite the button class, making it more extensible in the process.

Push buttons are used to register a single state, which is when the button is pressed. Push buttons aren't queried about their current state, because the parent window usually receives a notification only when they have been pushed. Two- and three-state buttons are used for on/off and on/off/neutral types of conditions. Of the two, two-state buttons are much more common. These kinds of buttons, commonly queried for their state, can be used, for example, for turning bold, italic, and underline features in a word processor on and off and back on again.

Radio buttons are used to establish a mutually exclusive condition, such as left-, center-, and right-justification for a paragraph of text in a word processor. With radio buttons, only one button in the WS_GROUP-defined controls may be set at any one time. This rule is enforced by Windows at all times.

The groupbox is another form of button control, although it doesn't quite fit in with the rest. The job of a groupbox is to provide a visual "lassoing" of related controls. Each groupbox comes with a label, which is always positioned in the upper-left corner of the groupbox's rectangle. Basically, the groupbox doesn't have a client area paint method, other than the frame and label it draws. This is part of the reason that dynamically changing a groupbox's label doesn't work quite the way it should.

Pressing a button through program control (without knowing the name of the method) can be done in one of two ways. Either the application can be directly notified through the posting of a WM_COMMAND message, or two mouse click messages can be sent to Windows, thus indirectly notifying the application. The following code shows both techniques:

```
// Let only the application know the button has been clicked.

PostMessage(hWndButton, WM_COMMAND, nListboxID, MAKELONG(BN_CLICKED, 0));

// Let Windows know the button has been clicked. This causes a quick visual
// push of the button in addition to indirectly sending a WM_PARENTNOTIFY and
// WM_COMMAND message to the application. If desired, a small 1/4-second delay
// loop could be processed between the button clicks, making the press of the
// button more visible to the user of the application.

SendMessage(hWndButton, WM_LBUTTONDOWN, 0, 0L);
SendMessage(hWndButton, WM_LBUTTONUP, 0, 0L);
```

The Windows functions for checking buttons only change the visual state of the button; they do not notify the application that a button has been pressed. This is why sending a button-down and button-up message to the control are preferable, because they do both.

The Combobox

The combobox is an interesting control for several reasons, primarily because it is a composite control; that is, it's made up of two or more different types of windows. Before mentioning the combobox in-depth, I'll talk about some of the "core" controls that could be used in designing other composite control types. Perhaps the most common control of all is the button control, which is used in scroll bars, comboboxes, listboxes, spin controls, buttons themselves, and several of the non-client sections of a window. The scroll bar is another "core" control, being included in comboboxes, listboxes, and virtually any other window class that asks for one. Another common control is the edit control, which is used by comboboxes and spin controls. Discussing how controls can be nested in such a manner really gives one an idea of the power and flexibility that can be achieved with a "true" object-oriented environment (which Windows isn't) and language (which C isn't). Because button widgets have the potential of being so numerous, a better idea might involve not creating them as windows, but rather maintaining their image and state manually.

The relationship between the combobox and its child windows causes several problems, but none that can't be overcome with a little programming. The combobox, as mentioned earlier, is really a control composite, and it is the parent window to an edit control, a listbox control, or both. Comboboxes defined as CBS_SIMPLE consist of three windows: an edit class control, a listbox control (class of ComboLBox), and the combobox control class parent. All three windows are visible at all times, with the combobox window surrounding the first two windows.

Comboboxes defined as CBS_DROPDOWN consist of two windows: an edit class control and a ComboLBox window class as the parent, which surrounds the edit window and provides a down-arrow button. When the arrow button is pressed, another listbox appears.

Comboboxes defined as CBS_DROPDOWNLIST consist of only one window class, ComboLBox. This kind of combobox seems almost identical to the CBS_DROPDOWN style, except for a minor spacing difference between the listbox-activation arrow and the "edit" control display window. In the case of CBS_DROPDOWNLIST comboboxes, the edit control is not editable, merely displaying the currently highlighted selection in the combobox's built-in listbox.

Although the handle to the listbox for a CBS_SIMPLE style combobox can easily be retrieved by using **GetWindow()** on the combobox, to retrieve its first or second child window, the same cannot be said for the drop-down listboxes of the other two styles of combobox. This is because they aren't owned by the combobox, but rather are child windows of the desktop window. Confused? Don't worry—it all makes sense. You see, the listboxes of dropdown-style comboboxes have a special property in that they pop the listbox up and over the parent window frame and are not clipped or limited in any way by the size of their parent window. This means that you don't have to allot several inches of vertical space below a combobox in a dialog to make room for the listbox.

Because of the unique "composite" nature of comboboxes, other tricks need to be done to get them to perform in the manner of other window classes. For example, normally WM_CTLCOLOR can be used by a parent window to trap and change the colors of child control windows, including the combobox. This does absolutely nothing for the child controls of the combobox, however. For this, the WM_CTLCOLOR message going to the combobox itself needs to be trapped. Additionally, any "hotkey" or other special keystrokes cannot be processed in the WM_CHAR or WM_KEYDOWN methods for the combobox; they need to be trapped for and examined in either the edit class or listbox class child windows of the combobox. All of this is demonstrated in the superclassed combobox control included in the appendix of this book.

Like the listbox, the combobox has several new minor enhancements and tweaks in Windows 3.1. New messages include CB_GETDROPPEDCONTROLRECT and CB_GETDROPPEDSTATE, which are used to determine the dimensions and general presence of any drop-down listboxes associated with a combobox. Unfortunately, although the combobox incorporates an edit control and a listbox, only combobox messages, not edit- or listbox-specific messages, can be sent to the combobox. This isn't because they wouldn't work, because they would— but only if you sent them to the appropriate child window. Different kinds of messages can't be sent because all child controls share a common message range for control notification messages, which starts at WM_USER and goes upward from there.

The Edit Control

The edit control included with Windows comes in two basic flavors: single- and multiple-line. The single-line edit control is known simply as an *edit control,* whereas the multiple-line control is more commonly referred to as an MLE.

Edit controls are unique in that the overhead for their "window text," which in this case is the contents of the edit control, can be placed in the application's local heap (DS_LOCALEDIT) or as a global heap segment, which is the default. The other controls, including the listbox and combobox, always store their overhead as globally allocated User module segments. When the edit control's data is stored in the global heap, the only way text can be stored into and retrieved from the control is through the WM_GETTEXT and WM_SETTEXT series of window messages. When the edit overhead is stored in the application's local heap, the EM_GETHANDLE and EM_SETHANDLE messages can be used, returning a handle to the application's local heap. Using the local heap method, the developer can dynamically switch an edit control's contents on-the-fly. When this method is used, the local heap object pointed to by the original handle must be explicitly freed.

Several problems with the edit control have been fixed with the release of Windows 3.1. These fixes come in the form of window styles and window messages. The new styles include

3.1

ES_WANTRETURN, which allows the Return/Enter key to function as expected in a multiple-line edit control, which means inserting a carriage return and advancing to the next line of the control instead of activating the default button on the dialog (actually a CUA recommendation!).

ES_READONLY, permitting a simple method of creating a read-only style of edit control.

EM_GETFIRSTVISIBLELINE, which returns the index of the top-most visible line in an MLE, or zero for single-line edit controls.

EM_SETREADONLY, which can be used to dynamically alter the read-only or read-write state of a control.

Actually, many of the enhancements to stock control messages are to fix the problems involving how to determine which part of the control text was visible or had the focus. There were plenty of messages to determine what items or text had the selection, but not many to determine cursor or focus position.

Just like the listbox and combobox, edit controls can hold a maximum of 64K of text. Actually, this isn't so much a reflection of the 64K segment limit as it is a reflection on the amount of code required to support a large edit control. Initially, a single-line edit control is limited to the amount of text displayable within the edit window itself. If the style ES_AUTOHSCROLL is included, this limit is removed and whatever amount of text is typed in is scrolled across the edit control. An MLE initially is limited to 30K. After this point, both controls beep. In both cases, sending an EM_LIMITTEXT message raises the limit to 64K. Additionally, MLEs are limited to 1,024-character line lengths, 3,000-pixel width lines, and a maximum of 16,350 lines to a single MLE. All MLEs and, for that matter, all word processors employ a linked-list structure in which each line in the edit control is a separate data entry in a linked list of lines. Each line

in an MLE has 2 bytes of storage overhead, in addition to a 100-byte general overhead maintained with the control. The reason for the linked list is simple—insertions and deletions! Try to envision a 100-page document, with the user at the first character of the first page typing the letter *a*. That's one big memcpy!

The edit controls weren't designed to support large amounts of text or any other "heavy-duty" word processing features. Word-wrap and a single level of undo is as close as it gets. What Microsoft should do is provide the edit window as used by the built-in Microsoft Write utility, as a stock control for inclusion by Windows applications. While they are at it, they could include the class code for the file and directory tree windows used by File Manager, because they too are bundled with every copy of Windows. The multiple-line edit control and a good (virtual) listbox are probably two of the most difficult and tedious custom controls to implement effectively under Windows. A good custom edit control should support multiple fonts, color, and, most important, a break with the 64K storage limit.

Tip: One excellent trick, per Microsoft, involves dialogs containing tens or even hundreds of edit controls. Using an actual window for every edit control would very quickly cripple the system, which is probably why Microsoft offers this suggestion.

The trick involves the use of only one window handle and having the application manually maintain the text and auto-move the window whenever the user presses the Tab key or control mnemonic or uses the mouse to select another edit control in the dialog. Actually, the code to do such a thing is quite simple and is available along with the disk offered with this book. This code is also available from Microsoft through CompuServe.

What's needed is for the developer to allocate enough memory to contain a list of RECT structures and LMEM or GMEM handles to the data for each edit control, as well as a byte indicating the ID of the control that's "next in line" for tab/focus switching. Then, whenever the user presses the mouse on a section of client window area, this list in memory is traversed, and the developer can very quickly determine where the edit window needs to be repositioned and what text needs to be put inside it. This is one nice application for the EM_GETHANDLE and EM_SETHANDLE series of messages. This kind of dialog would best be implemented using multiple local heaps, discussed more fully in Chapter 4, "Memory Management."

The diskette offered with this book also includes a program (with source) from Microsoft that shows how to implement a simple form generator. One great idea is to combine these two ideas to create an industrial-strength data-entry forms generator. Yet another solution is to simply use the regular dialog-editor, and just before the window is created, manually skim through the resource, determining what edit controls are where, and generating the data structures in this manner. This would also require, though, that other dialog structures be loaded from the resource file and the dialog created indirectly with one of the `CreateDialogIndirect()` or `DialogBoxIndirect()` functions.

Although there is no concept of an owner-draw edit control, this point is moot for high-end word processors and the like, because by default they include multiple fonts, color, and, more frequently, embedded OLE images into their client area.

The Listbox

The listbox control is designed to enable the user to select from one or more choices in a scrolling box of entries—text or otherwise. Although it appears that the listbox is capable of holding an "infinite" number of items, again this is not the case. Because the listbox returns LB_ERR (-1) when an error occurs, it indicates that there is at most a 32K maximum number of entries. Even this number, however, is far from reality, because a listbox is limited to 64K for its storage.

Fortunately, listbox data is always stored in globally allocated segments, meaning that this maximum is not a theoretical one, as is the case with a control storing its data in a module's DBGROUP segment. Owner-draw listboxes are limited to roughly 8,160 items. This total is due to the fact that each entry in the listbox takes up 8 bytes of overhead. Four bytes of this are for the ITEMDATA values associated with each listbox entry, and 256 bytes are allocated out of the data segment for general overhead. This yields an approximate 8K of possible listbox entries.

The ideal solution for a custom listbox control is one that has been done over and over again—the virtual listbox. The key principle behind its operation is that the control asks the application what it should display. This is unlike the regular and owner-draw listboxes, which already know what they need to display because they keep track of the actual data. Using a virtual listbox implies that the listbox control is responsible only for scrolling and requesting entries from the application. It's the application's job to manage the data and (with the exception of text entries) visually display any images. As soon as you start working with mounds and mounds of data, however, you'll quickly get swamped, and Windows' memory manager will be of no real help. What's really required here is the services of a good list manager, which is discussed more in depth in Chapter 4, "Memory Management." Developing a list manager, however, is beyond the scope of this book; it would require a second book in itself. Creating a good spreadsheet or matrix/style data entry control also requires the services of a good memory/list manager.

Like the edit control, several of the listbox's shortcomings are fixed in Windows 3.1. These fixes include one new style bit and several new (rather, I should say old) messages. The style bit is LBS_DISABLENOSCROLL, which, instead of removing the vertical scroll bar when no entries exist in the listbox, merely disables that scroll bar, leaving it still in the non-client area of the control. This style bit is actually using the new scroll bar message `EnableScrollBar()`, which is mentioned in the following section. The "new" messages are LB_GETCARETINDEX and LB_SETCARETINDEX, which retrieve and set the caret for whichever item in the listbox has the "focus." Plenty of messages exist to determine what items are selected; however, until now, none has been published that works with the focused item. Actually, both of these messages existed with Windows 3.0; it's just that they have not been documented until now.

Scroll Bars

Scroll bars are one of the few stock control types that are perfect as they are. Of course, they're so simple that there's not a lot to mess up. Therefore, only one new message has been added to the 3.1 API for scroll bars: `EnableScrollBar()`.

Unlike `ShowScrollBar()`, which shows or hides the bar completely, `EnableScrollBar()` allows it to function a little more like regular windows do, allowing a disabled as well as an enabled state. Although this could always be done for scroll bars created as separate and independent windows, it couldn't be done for automatically created vertical and horizontal application window scroll bars, which don't really exist as a window but are only maintained and painted internally by Windows. Scroll bars created in this manner have no window handle to reference. In fact, the only way these kinds of scroll bars are referenced is by specifying the window they're attached to and the SB_VERT or SB_HORZ values. Remember that SB_CTL is used to reference a developer-created scroll bar, which also can be referenced via a separate window handle.

Statics

The lowly static label exists purely for graphical "labeling" purposes, providing no input and no real output. The text it contains can be changed on-the-fly by the developer, but that's about it; it doesn't send any kind of notification messages as the other control types do. This is why many static controls use a control ID number of –1, because they never get referenced by the developer. Like the variety of control types in the button class, statics come in different flavors: labels, frames, and icons. Labels are created to identify a particular control. Because buttons normally "label" themselves, statics generally are used with listboxes, edit controls, and comboboxes. However, this isn't to say that multiple static labels can be positioned by themselves on a dialog and not connected to any particular control.

"Framing" styles include SS_BLACKRECT, SS_GRAYRECT, SS_WHITERECT, SS_BLACKFRAME, SS_GRAYFRAME, and SS_WHITEFRAME, which are used to draw a filled or a hollow rectangular region around a specified area. These colors aren't black, gray, and white, as you would think; rather, they are based on the settings of the system colors for window frames (which are by default black), the desktop background (which is by default gray), and window backgrounds (which are by default white).

The style SS_ICON is used to place an icon on a window. The icon used is specified using the window text. This name doesn't specify a filename for the icon, but rather the icon's name in the resource file containing the dialog itself. The width and height associated with a static icon are ignored because the window is sized to fit the actual size of the icon. This auto-sizing feature is quite handy. The split bar, button, and bitmap control classes presented in this book also determine their own width and height when values of 0 and 0 are used by the developer. Static controls also allow simple left, right, and center justification. This is only within the actual rectangle containing the static label, however.

New messages included with Windows 3.1 for static labels include STM_SETICON and STM_GETICON, which are used to set and retrieve the current icon used in the control. Before, this was an all-or-nothing, single-shot affair, because as soon as the icon was defined, it wasn't easy to change. All this has been changed by two simple messages.

Interfacing Controls to the Dialog Editor

Although custom controls can be specifically interfaced to Windows' dialog editor, it's not always in the developer's best interests. Currently, multiple dialog editors are available from a variety of vendors, each using a different format for the inclusion of custom controls or—in some cases—using no format at all.

Although the dialog-editors used with Windows can be quite useful for simple dialogs, most have serious shortcomings that cannot be corrected. First and foremost, they break down for truly "intelligent" dialogs and custom controls. Interfacing a series of "auto-sizing" and "auto-positioning" controls in a dialog that supports custom data entry rules and logical input paths would be impossible to implement given the current crop of dialog editors. What's desperately needed are hooks into the dialog editor itself. Although simple "hits" to a dialog's buttons and implementing tab/focus control shifting are possible given the dialog-editor's demo mode, effectively demonstrating a grab bar just isn't possible.

The biggest problem with the current methods of dialog design is that the dialogs aren't truly "display-independent." It is true that Windows has a system font and uses dialog units to help mask some of the problems with different video displays; however, the design and implementation of the dialog itself is still too "static" in nature. A good head start into a more dynamic and flexible method of dialog design is to use the "auto-sizing" controls provided in this book. This allows the controls in a dialog to be aware of their parent in the sense that most stock controls aren't. All controls can "zoom" to fill the size of their parent area and optionally can float to fit vertically or horizontally with a dynamically stretched parent dialog. The grab bar offered in the library SPLIT.DLL even adjusts itself to the dimensions of the windows it is supposed to manage. See Figure 6.6 for one of the dialogs created using this system. It illustrates a resizable dialog with several float-to-fit windows. The listboxes at the bottom of the dialog dynamically resize to accommodate a lengthened parent window size, and the two MLEs and the listbox on the right of the dialog expand horizontally to accommodate any new "stretched" horizontal size for the parent dialog. In fact, even the grab bars float to fit along with the windows they're managing.

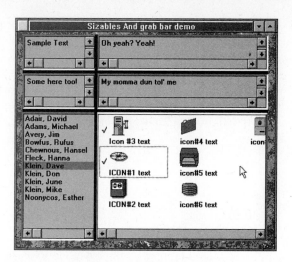

Figure 6.6.
A resizable
dialog with
float-to-fit
windows.

Groupboxes and static labels are created and positioned in such a manner as well. Neither consumes precious window handle overhead, and they are created dynamically without any positioning concerns whatsoever. For instance, the groupbox control is defined in one of the private resource structures associated with every dialog. This structure, based on the dialog's class name, contains extended style attributes, as well as specifying a background bitmap, which can be seamlessly tiled, centered, or stretched to fit. The structure also contains groupbox data. Now, instead of manually positioning a groupbox within a dialog, you merely name the groupbox in the data structure and list a series of control IDs that the groupbox is to encompass. Then, whenever the dialog is painted, this structure is scanned and the groupboxes are painted onscreen using a nice 3-D effect. Static control labels are done similarly, being named instead in the private resource data structure that can be associated with each control in a dialog. As with the groupbox, instead of dedicating a window handle and worrying about the positioning of the control, the developer merely embeds an ASCII string into the control data structure and specifies a formatting attribute. Using this system, labels can be positioned anywhere around a control: top, middle, bottom, and left-, center-, and right-justified.

Why worry about the absolute positioning of controls within a dialog when you already know "in your head" how the controls are to be positioned? This is all that should really be necessary to design a dialog, not hours of tweaking and positioning statics and groupboxes and worrying about alignment issues. Much of the structure and coding for a dialog can easily be abstracted into a series of rules and separate data structures, part of which has been done in

the controls offered in this book. The only enhancements that need to be added are a method of auto-moving the controls, so that they maintain their relative positions when a dialog is resized, and working with TrueType to ensure (in certain cases) that fonts are sized correctly when large screen displays are used or when certain controls are maximized. Although the "test" mode of the dialog editor is hyped as an important tool, it's really quite minor when you consider that another 15 minutes lets you add a window procedure and test the dialog for real.

ZoomIn

How much can really be said about ZoomIn? After all, its sole, absolute purpose is to explode sections of screen, making it easier to see the pixel layout in a particular area. ZoomIn can be quite useful when you're trying to figure out how a certain graphic was given its shading effect or 3-D look, and when you're trying to find out the colors and pixel data used for a specific pattern or special effect drawn on the screen. Although ZoomIn isn't the most crucial of utilities, it comes in handy for touch-up work and fixing minor painting details. ZoomIn was used quite extensively in generating the dialogs and custom controls for this book. Figure 6.7 shows a sample ZoomIn screen.

Figure 6.7.
The ZoomIn
utility.

Spy

Spy is a great utility for debugging the user-interface component of Windows. Even though CodeView also can be used (somewhat) for this purpose, and can trap window messages, it isn't as simple or straightforward as Spy. More important, it doesn't include a saveable, running audit trail of messages. Spy is most useful for determining what messages are going to what windows, without having to explicitly set breakpoints on the switch/case statements for a window procedure. The only shortcoming is that Spy can be used on only a single window or on all windows, not on a family tree. Spy does, however, enable the developer to run multiple instances, somewhat overcoming this barrier. Spy has three windows: an audit trail window, a message-trapping options dialog, and a target window dialog. The three windows are illustrated in Figures 6.8, 6.9, and 6.10.

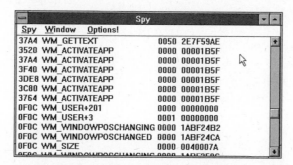

Figure 6.8. Spy's audit trail window.

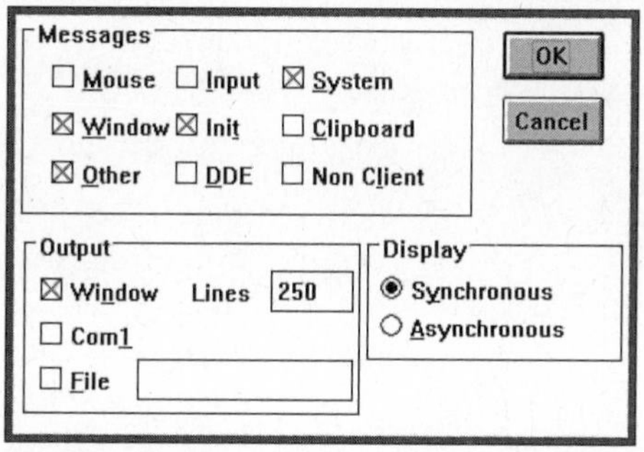

Figure 6.9. Spy's message-trapping options dialog.

Figure 6.10. Spy's target window.

Window Dimensions, Sizing, and the Coordinate System

The flow of messages going to a window during its lifetime was documented in the last couple of sections. However, there is a certain group, or cycle, of messages that are repeatedly hit that deserves a little more attention. These messages control how and where a window displays itself, and they are crucial for understanding and performing advanced window positioning and customization techniques. These messages generally are received in the following order:

Message	Description
WM_WINDOWPOSCHANGING	Sent to a window whose location, size, or z-order is about to change through a call to **MoveWindow()**, **SetWindowPos()**, or any other related window-management function. The parameter lParam points to a WINDOWPOS structure and can be modified to change positioning information.
WM_GETMINMAXINFO	Sent to a window when its maximized position and dimensions, or maximum and minimum tracking size, need to be queried. This message is the first message to be sent when a window is first created. It is then followed by the message WM_NCCALCSIZE, WM_WINDOWPOSCHANGING, and the rest in this list. If the window's state is being modified as a result of an explicit window-management function, the flow of messages is as shown in this list.
WM_NCCALCSIZE	Sent to a window when its client dimensions need to be determined. This message passes a structure (NCCALCSIZE_PARAMS) that can be modified to adjust the non-client (and thus) client dimensions of the window.

Message	Description
WM_WINDOWPOSCHANGED	Sent to a window after its location, size, or z-order position has been changed. The parameter lParam points to a WINDOWPOS structure containing the new positioning information for the window.
WM_MOVE	Sent after a window has been moved. The parameter lParam contains the new x and y position of the window. Sometimes sent after WM_SIZE and not before.
WM_SIZE	Sent after the size of a window has been changed. The parameter lParam contains the new width and height of the window. The value wParam is one of the following values: SIZEFULLSCREEN, if the window has been maximized; SIZEICONIC, if the window has been iconicized; SIZENORMAL, if the window has been resized in some other way; SIZEZOOMHIDE, sent when another window has been maximized; and SIZEZOOMSHOW, sent when another window has been restored from a maximized state.

A window is composed of both a non-client and a client area. The non-client area, as mentioned earlier, contains the scroll bars, caption, border, and other components of a window that are always processed and handled by Windows. Although they can be modified by the developer, it isn't required. Screen-based coordinates, which are relative to the main desktop window, usually refer to the upper-left portion of the non-client area of a window. However, they also can refer (if necessary) to the client portion of a window, or to child windows.

Client coordinates, which are always associated with child windows, are always relative to their parent window. Client coordinates are associated with the client area of a specified control, as well as with the coordinates of a child window within its parent. The coordinates of the client area of a window control almost always start at (0, 0) and extend either to the inside border of a window or to the beginning of the window's vertical and horizontal (if any) scroll bars. On the other hand, the client coordinates of the non-client area of a window usually don't start at (0,0); rather, they reflect the positioning of the child window within its parent. This confusion often crops up when cursor positioning, GDI functions, and child window positioning need to be performed. For example, when a child window (a listbox, for example) needs to be dynamically positioned inside its parent window, two functions must be called. First, `GetWindowRect()` is called to calculate the window's screen-based coordinates; then `ScreenToClient()` must be called to convert the window's coordinates to make them parent-window relative.

The Windows API includes the following functions for dealing with the windowing coordinate system:

Function	Description
`ChildWindowFromPoint()`	Returns the client coordinates (parent-relative) of the child window containing a specified point. Only the uppermost child window containing the point is returned.
`WindowFromPoint()`	Returns the screen coordinates of a window containing the specified point. The window cannot be hidden, disabled, or transparent. The function `ChildWindowFromPoint()` contains no such restrictions.
`GetCursorPos()`	Returns desktop-relative, screen-based coordinates of the current cursor position.
`MapWindowPoints()`	Converts points from one coordinate space to another. Can be used to convert from a child window's parent-relative coordinate space to screen units (desktop-relative) and vice versa.
`ClientToScreen()`	Converts client child window (parent-relative) coordinates to desktop-relative screen coordinates.
`ScreenToClient()`	Converts desktop-relative screen coordinates to the client coordinates of a specified parent window.
`GetWindowRect()`	Returns the desktop-based screen coordinates of a RECT structure containing the whole area of a window, non-client space included.

Function	Description
GetClientRect()	Returns the parent-based client coordinates of a RECT structure encompassing the client area of a window, which excludes scroll bars, captions, and so on.
AdjustWindowRect()	When passed a window style long, returns the RECT structure needed to encompass a window with the specified style and desired client size. The dimensions do not include borders, captions, or a second menu-line.
AdjustWindowRectEx()	Same as **AdjustWindowRect()**, except that it is passed an additional style long defining the "Ex"-tended style bits for windows created via **CreateWindowEx()**.

Window Lists and Positioning (z-ordering)

Press Ctrl-Esc to bring up Windows' Task Manager application. Notice the ordering of windows in the listbox. Now randomly select different applications (not from within Task Manager), minimizing, maximizing, and restoring them. Now press Ctrl-Esc again and notice the ordering of windows. Next, bring up any application that contains a dialog with child windows selectable via the Tab key. Notice the "premeditated" order that windows receive the focus in, every time the Tab key is pressed. The concept being illustrated is Windows' internal list of windows.

This list is used to keep track of the relationships for all top-level and child windows of applications, excluding the desktop window. All top-level windows are kept in an "upper" list, with one window essentially "on top" of all others, and every other window nested in what is known as a *z-order*, down to the bottommost top-level window in the chain. Most often, a top-level window is brought to the top of the list by a mouse click, or through Alt-Esc and Alt-Tab, which cycle through top-level windows, or through Ctrl-Esc, which brings up the task manager.

Window ordering also can be shuffled and manipulated through program control, with functions such as `BringWindowToTop()`, `ShowWindow()`, and `SetWindowPos()`. Notice how, when the minimize button is pressed on a top-level window, the window is minimized, and then the second-highest window in the z-order, not the minimized window, is the new active window. It's just assumed that when you minimize a window, it doesn't need to remain active.

Lesser known is that child windows and child controls are also based on a top-to-bottom window-ordering scheme. Child MDI windows are treated much in the manner of other top-level windows, because their position in the z-order is based on being clicked on and made active (via the user of the application), or through program control. After all, MDI child windows are, in a sense, a kind of top-level window anyway; it's just that they're nested inside another window. Child window controls (edit, listbox, and so on) are a different matter entirely. For example, when a dialog containing multiple child windows is first created, Windows allocates memory for the z-order list for the dialog's child windows and then adds windows to this list as it encounters them in the dialog resource. Then, later on, as child controls are possibly added to the dialog dynamically, they too are added to the z-order child control window list for the dialog. The z-order list for child window controls affects tab-ordering, which doesn't go off of the child control resources as they are listed in the dialog, but rather on the z-order list generated when the dialog was first created. When a child control is maximized (which isn't usually done), its position in the z-order list is lost, because it is now made the top-level child window for the dialog. When the window is then restored, it is placed at the bottom of the z-list, thus throwing off any tab-ordering scheme.

Whenever tab-aware or arrow-aware controls are added dynamically to a window, their z-order positioning must be taken into account; otherwise, the Tab and arrow keys won't function as expected. What must be done is to first acquire a handle to the window prior in the z-list to the window that is being added. If a button G is being added to a series of buttons labeled A–F, a handle to F must be acquired and a call to `SetWindowPos()` made, telling it that button G is to immediately follow F in the window manager's list. This ensures that when the right arrow or Tab key is pressed, focus will be set to the appropriate button. As a side note, one of the reasons that the function `SetParent()`, and not the function `SetWindowWord()`, is used to set the parent of a window is that it implies that Windows must perform a little processing first, which is mainly updating window manager lists to reflect the shuffling of windows from list to list.

The window lists are a greatly underutilized piece of data. All too often, manual lists of the child windows for a given parent are kept manually by the developer, instead of relying on Windows' internal management of the windows. Finding out the first, last, prior, and next sibling for a given window is as simple as a call to the function `GetWindow()`, which can also be used to determine the first child or owner for any given window.

Another group of functions that operate on the positioning, size, and z-ordering of windows are the functions `BeginDeferWindow()`, `EndDeferWindowPos()`, and `DeferWindowPos()`. They can be used to "instantly" position, size, and otherwise arrange a series of windows. These functions commonly are used to perform customized window tiling and cascading. Basically, the functions work by allocating and then filling an internally managed data structure containing various bits of information about a window.

Finally, a function is called to operation on the block of memory, and then to free it. First, `BeginDeferWindowPos()` is called to allocate the block of memory, is passed an integer value indicating the number of windows to be repositioned, and returns a special handle type (`HDWP`) that is used to refer to the internal data structure. Then, `DeferWindowPos()` is called for each window to be added to the internal list of windows and is passed parameters similar to `SetWindowPos()` that are used to identify the new position, size, and z-order location of the window. Finally, `EndDeferWindowPos()` is called to snap the windows into place and free up the data structure. The functions, which are not used very often, are affectionately referred to as "the beast" in the only sample application (DDEML/CLIENT) included with the Windows API that references them. Because there is no real way that Windows can be "simultaneously" repositioned, this series of functions is just as easily duplicated using other window-positioning functions.

Function	Description
`MoveWindow()`	Changes the position and size of a window. This function is really a masked call to `SetWindowPos()`.
`SetWindowPos()`	Changes the state, position, size, and z-ordering of a window.
`ShowWindow()`	Sets the state of a window (normal, minimized, maximized, active, visible) and indirectly sets the window's z-order. Possible state values include the following:
	SW_HIDE Hides window and makes next window in z-order active.

continues

Function	Description
SW_MINIMIZE	Minimizes window and makes next top-level peer window in z-order active.
SW_NORMAL	Activates and displays a window in its normal (restored) state. Same as SW_RESTORE and SW_SHOWNORMAL.
SW_SHOW	Activates window, displaying it in its current size and position.
SW_SHOWMAXIMIZED	Activates and maximizes window, bringing it to the top of the z-order. Same as SW_MAXIMIZE.
SW_SHOWMINIMIZED	Activates and minimizes window, bringing it to the top of the z-order.
SW_SHOWMINNOACTIVE	Minimizes window, keeping currently active window active.
SW_SHOWNA	Displays window in its normal state, keeping currently active window active. Same as SW_SHOWNOACTIVATE.

When the WM_SHOWWINDOW message is received by a window, wParam contains a value indicating whether the window is being shown (1) or hidden (0), and lParam contains a value indicating how the message was originally sent. If due to an explicit call to **ShowWindow()**, lParam is zero; otherwise, lParam is one of the following values:

SW_PARENTCLOSING	Parent window is being minimized.
SW_PARENTOPENING	Parent window is being restored or maximized.
GetDesktopWindow()	Returns a handle to the desktop window.

Function	Description
`FindWindow()`	Searches for a top-level window when given a class name, caption name, or both, returning the window's handle if successful, null if otherwise.
`GetNextWindow()`	When given a window handle, returns the handle of the next or prior top-level or child window, depending on the type of window passed. A masked call to `GetWindow()`.
`GetTopWindow()`	Returns the top z-ordered child window of a specified parent window. A masked call to `GetWindow()`.
`GetWindow()`	When given a window handle, returns an associated child or top-level window, depending on the value of the second parameter, which can be one of the following:

	`GW_CHILD`	Returns the first child window.
	`GW_HWNDFIRST`	Returns the first "peer" window, whether top-level or child. If the first parameter is a handle to a top-level window, this parameter returns the first top-level window. If the first parameter is a child window, then it returns a handle to the first child sibling.
	`GW_HWNDLAST`	Returns last "peer" window.
	`GW_HWNDNEXT`	Returns next "peer" window.
	`GW_HWNDPRIOR`	Returns prior "peer" window.
	`GW_OWNER`	Returns owner of top-level window.

Function	Description
`EnumChildWindows()`	Enumerates the child windows of a specified parent.
`EnumTaskWindows()`	Enumerates the top-level windows associated with a specified task.
`EnumWindows()`	Enumerates top-level windows on the desktop.

continues

Function	Description
`BringWindowToTop()`	Brings a popup or a child window to the top of the z-order, above all other windows.
`ShowOwnedPopups()`	Shows or hides all popup windows associated with a specified window.
`BeginDeferWindowPos()`	Allocates memory for a window-positioning structure.
`DeferWindowPos()`	Adds a window to the internal list of windows to be repositioned.
`EndDeferWindowPos()`	Repositions windows accumulated with `DeferWindowPos()`.
`GetWindowPlacement()`	Retrieves a WINDOWPLACEMENT structure for a window. This structure specifies the position of a window in its normal, minimized, and maximized states, as well as in its show state, which can be one of the following states: SW_SHOWNORMAL, SW_SHOWMINIMIZED, and SW_SHOWMAXIMIZED.
`SetWindowPlacement()`	Sets a WINDOWPLACEMENT structure for a window.

Summary

This chapter has covered a good deal of information, with most of it filling in the undescribed topics surrounding the windowing system. The windowing system, along with (naturally) Windows' message delivery mechanism, are two of the more difficult aspects of Windows to get a grip on, because the topics are so new and foreign to most DOS programmers. In fact, these capabilities represent a whole different layer of programming available under Windows. To verify this, note the number of window browsers (other than Spy) that are available for debugging under Windows. Under DOS, only a "physical" debugger was used, whereas Windows requires both a "physical" debugger, such as CodeView or Soft-Ice/W, and a "visual" debugger, such as Spy. Many times Spy can yield extremely valuable information that is otherwise unavailable under other debuggers. Mastery of both kinds of tools are needed, as well as a good understanding of this "new" interface layer of development.

PART

II

Appendixes

TestApp

Description

The dialog TestApp is merely a stub application demonstrating the features of the dialog window class and custom control window classes provided in this book. The application starts by loading the several DLLs required for supporting the custom controls used in the dialog, including

STDWIN.DLL, for the dialog window class, default handling of control class methods, and its miscellaneous support API

BITMAP.DLL (AtomicBitmap), for the bitmap control class

BUTTON.DLL (AtomicButton), for the regular and owner-draw push button class as well as the owner-draw checkbox class

COMBOBOX.DLL (AtomicCombobox), for the combobox control class

EDIT.DLL (AtomicEdit), for the edit control class

LISTBOX.DLL (AtomicListbox), for the listbox control class

SPLIT.DLL (AtomicSplit), which contains the grab-bar control class

Each of the libraries must be dynamically loaded because in most cases, the test application doesn't directly call any of the functions in the control class library. As you'll remember from Chapter 5, "Library Design Ideas," when module A contains no explicit references to library B, library B won't be automatically loaded along with the module. If the linker can find no references, the module isn't bound. When a library is being used only for a control class, the only "link" that's available is the control class name in the resource's `DIALOG` structure or a parameter to a `CreateWindow()` call. Of course, neither of these "text" references is any good for a linker that's looking for symbolic references.

After the libraries are loaded, a couple of sample dialogs are created using `CreateAndRegisterDialog()`. As the name implies, this function (optionally) registers a window class and creates a single instance of the window. This function definitely isn't the best "encapsulator" that could be developed for simplifying the window creation process; however, it's a simple start. Basically, this function accepts only a few critical parameters and auto-fills a few of the others. After the main parent dialog and single owned dialog have been created, the window is shown and painted, and the main messaging loop is entered. The only reason that calls to `ShowWindow()` and `UpdateWindow()` are needed is that the main dialog wasn't declared WS_VISIBLE, because when this style bit is set, the window is automatically shown and updated on creation. The other reason for an explicit call to these two functions is so that the dialog can be shown via the nCmdShow parameter, which is sent by Windows to the WinMain() function of an application as an indicator of how the window should be shown initially. For example, when a user runs an application from Program Manager while holding down the Shift key, Windows sends an nCmdShow code of SW_SHOWMINIMIZED, as opposed to SW_SHOWNORMAL, which is the default.

The rest of the module handles only the most "minimal" of methods for the two top-level dialogs. Messages handled by the main dialog include WM_ACTIVATE, which sets a global variable processed by IsDialogMessage() to determine whether the window should be processed as a dialog; WM_CLOSE, which destroys the main window; WM_DESTROY, which posts a WM_QUIT message to end the application; and WM_COMMAND, which is used to handle a few button methods. All other messages are routed down through AtomicDialogWndFn(), which handles the non-client painting, control resizing, scrollable client pane, and numerous other default top-level window behaviors. The second, owned dialog in the stub application doesn't process the WM_DESTROY message, because that should always be handled by the main window of the application. Nor does it handle any button methods, because there are none. It does process WM_ACTIVATE and WM_CLOSE, however.

Three of the buttons on the main dialog serve some special purpose in illustrating different features of the custom controls and STDWIN API. The button in the main dialog TestApp that resembles a light switch is a checkbox that changes the wallpaper background used by the dialog. Click the button, and while holding the mouse button down, drag the mouse outside the button's client area. Notice how the button changes states, exactly duplicating the functionality of Windows' built-in button class. Next on the list, the "Dialog" push button is used merely to activate (show) a second dialog, which demonstrates several grab bars, all separating a series of multiple-line edit controls, a regular listbox, and an owner-draw listbox. The dialog also demonstrates the "auto-resizing" of child windows within a parent window. Pressing the "Dialog" button again removes (hides) the dialog from view, acting as a sort of toggle. Another push button in TestApp is a graphical button in the image of a laser printer. This button is used to activate a sort of WYSIWYG print dialog, which can be used to print either of the two bitmaps shown in the main dialog. Which bitmap is printed depends on which wallpaper is selected.

On the right side of the dialog are examples of the AtomicEdit control and three styles of AtomicCombobox: CBS_SIMPLE, CBS_DROPDOWN, and CBS_DROPDOWNLIST.

As do all the controls, each of these supports the common 3-D style enforced by methods in STDWIN.DLL. For the edit control it was simple; however, the comboboxes required a small amount of edit control subclassing to achieve the desired effect. At the bottom of the main dialog are two AtomicBitmap controls, separated down the middle by a grab bar. The scroll bars on the bitmaps can be used to scroll around the entire client area of the bitmap, and the grab bar can be used to adjust the horizontal edges of the two bitmaps. In addition to scrolling the bitmaps to see a desired portion, Alt-Enter or a double-click of the right mouse button instantly "zooms" (maximizes) the control inside its parent's client area. Pressing Alt-Enter or double-clicking the right mouse button again restores the control to its former size.

The test dialog also includes two text-style buttons: a single checkbox and three radio buttons. Unlike the light switch, which is a bitmap-based checkbox, these two styles of buttons require no bitmap images to be defined for them. All that needs to be specified to initialize and use either control is a label. Both styles of button are three-dimensional in appearance, with the checkbox using a thick red *X* for a check state, and the radio button using a red filled-in dot. The checkbox button, when clicked, alternately displays its label to the left or right of the button, demonstrating how labels can be dynamically moved around a control. The radio buttons, when clicked, demonstrate no specific functionality other than removing and setting the check from any other radio buttons in the group.

Note that the radio buttons, like rounded push buttons and other "nonsquare" controls, bleed their parent's background through any gaps in the control. When the WS_CLIPCHILDREN style is used for the parent dialog (which is the case here), the background cannot be painted in behind the child window because it is inside the clipping region. This causes small portions of the background of the control to not match the parent's background color or bitmap background. If the parent window isn't displaying a bitmap background, the fix is a simple one, because the child control can merely fill its client area with the parent window's background brush. Additionally, if WS_CLIPCHILDREN isn't specified for the parent window, the problem never occurs, although screen updates for the window won't "snap" into place. Another possibility is if the radio buttons (or other nonsquare controls) are to be placed inside a groupbox contained in a parent window with a bitmap background. In this case, another fix is possible, which is to use the groupbox color as the background color for the control.

The main dialog TestApp is scrollable and can be used to pan around the dialog's client area, exposing different child control windows. Although the second, owned dialog isn't scrollable, its child windows are flagged as size-to-fit, meaning that they instantly resize themselves to the new size of the parent when its size is altered.

Possible Enhancements

Not applicable.

Specifications

ModuleName   TESTAPP
LibraryName   TESTAPP.EXE

Functions

`WinMain()`   Standard message-dispatching loop/
                         function for applications
`TestAppDlgProc()`   TestApp dialog window procedure
`MiscDlgProc()`   Second dialog window procedure

TestApp.c

```
/*******************************************************************************
    PROGRAM: TestApplication
    AUTHOR : Mike Klein
    FILE   : TESTAPP.EXE
    PURPOSE: Example of custom controls and API in STDWIN.DLL. Demonstrates
             not only custom controls, but customization of the nonclient
             area of a window, as well as how to create a scrollable dialog.
    *******************************************************************************/
```

```
//
// #DEFINEs
//

#define NOCOMM


//
// #INCLUDEs
//

#include <windows.h>
#include <stdlib.h>
#include "stdwin.h"
#include "bitmap.h"

#include "testapp.h"


//
// Declarations
//

LRESULT WINAPI TestAppDlgProc(HWND, UINT, WPARAM, LPARAM);
LRESULT WINAPI MiscDlgProc(HWND, UINT, WPARAM, LPARAM);

static HWND hDlgTestApp;
static HWND hDlgMisc;
static HWND hDlgActive;

static HANDLE hInstTestApp;



/*****************************************************************************
    FUNCTION: WinMain
    PURPOSE : Main message processing loop. Used for creation, initialization.
*****************************************************************************/

int PASCAL WinMain
(
    HINSTANCE hInst, HINSTANCE hPrevInst, LPSTR lpCmdLine, int nCmdShow
)
```

```
{
    MSG msg;

    HANDLE hInstSTDWIN;
    HANDLE hInstBitmap;
    HANDLE hInstButton;
    HANDLE hInstCombobox;
    HANDLE hInstEdit;
    HANDLE hInstListbox;
    HANDLE hInstSplit;

    // Load appropriate DLLs so LibMain will be activated for each and their
    // classes registered.

    hInstSTDWIN   = LoadLibrary("stdwin.dll");
    hInstBitmap   = LoadLibrary("bitmap.dll");
    hInstButton   = LoadLibrary("button.dll");
    hInstCombobox = LoadLibrary("combobox.dll");
    hInstEdit     = LoadLibrary("edit.dll");
    hInstListbox  = LoadLibrary("listbox.dll");
    hInstSplit    = LoadLibrary("split.dll");

    hInstTestApp = hInst;

    // Create the main dialog.

    if
    (
        !(hDlgTestApp = CreateAndRegisterDialog
        (
            hInst,
            "TestApp",
            NULL,
            TestAppDlgProc,
            LoadIcon(hInst, "Icon"),
            NULL,
            0,
            0,
            (hPrevInst ? FALSE : TRUE)
        ))
    )
    {
        goto EXIT;
    }
```

```
    // Create the other dialog.

    if
    (
        !(hDlgMisc = CreateAndRegisterDialog
        (
            hInst,
            "Misc",
            hDlgTestApp,
            MiscDlgProc,
            LoadIcon(hInst, "Icon"),
            NULL,
            0,
            0,
            (hPrevInst ? FALSE : TRUE)
        ))
    )
    {
        DestroyWindow(hDlgTestApp);

        goto EXIT;
    }

    // Show and paint the main dialog.

    ShowWindow(hDlgTestApp, nCmdShow);
    UpdateWindow(hDlgTestApp);

    // Acquire and dispatch messages until a WM_QUIT message is received.

    while(GetMessage(&msg, NULL, NULL, NULL))
    {
        if(hDlgActive && IsDialogMessage(hDlgActive, &msg))
        {
            continue;
        }

        TranslateMessage(&msg);
        DispatchMessage(&msg);
    }

EXIT:
```

```
        // Free stdwin & other DLLs.

        FreeLibrary(hInstSTDWIN);
        FreeLibrary(hInstBitmap);
        FreeLibrary(hInstButton);
        FreeLibrary(hInstCombobox);
        FreeLibrary(hInstEdit);
        FreeLibrary(hInstListbox);
        FreeLibrary(hInstSplit);

        return(FALSE);
    }


/****************************************************************************
    FUNCTION: TestAppDlgProc
    PURPOSE:  Processes messages for sample dialog.
****************************************************************************/

LRESULT WINAPI TestAppDlgProc(HWND hDlg, UINT Msg, WPARAM wParam, LPARAM lParam)
{
    static BYTE BitmapName[30];

    static int CtrlID;

    HWND hWnd;

    switch(Msg)
    {
        case WM_ACTIVATE :

            // Flag IsDialogMessage that this dialog is the new active one.
            // This lets it process dialog-special keystrokes accordingly.

            hDlgActive = (wParam == NULL) ? NULL : hDlg;
            break;

        case WM_CLOSE :

            DestroyWindow(hDlg);
            return(1);

        case WM_DESTROY :
```

```
        // Close up shop for the night.

        PostQuitMessage(0);
        break;

case WM_CREATE :

        // This little variable is used as a flag to determine what
        // bitmap we're currently showing. The Wallpaper switch alters
        // this value between the two other bitmaps defined for the
        // dialog as wallpaper.

        CtrlID = IDC_BITMAP;
        break;

case WM_COMMAND :

        switch(wParam)
        {
            case IDM_EXIT :

                // When escape is pressed.

                SendMessage(hDlg, WM_CLOSE, 0, 0L);

                return(1L);

            case IDC_BUTTON :

                // Just hide and show the dialog that
                // demonstrates grab bars, resizable windows, and the
                // owner-draw and regular listbox controls.

                ShowWindow
                (
                    hDlgMisc,
                    IsWindowVisible(hDlgMisc) ? SW_HIDE : SW_SHOWNORMAL
                );

                return(1L);

            case IDC_BUTTONBMP :

                // Activates WYSIWYG dialog for printing a DDB bitmap.
```

```
                        BitmapToPrinter
                        (
                            GetWindowWord(GetDlgItem(hDlg, CtrlID), BITMAPBMP),
                            hDlg,
                            "Bitmap"
                        );

                        return(1L);

                case IDC_CHECKBOX :

                        // Whenever checkbox is toggled, chg label orientation.

                        hWnd = GetDlgItem(hDlg, IDC_CHECKBOX);

                        SetLabelText
                        (
                            hWnd,
                            SendMessage(hWnd, BM_GETCHECK, 0, 0L) ?
                                "ML&Checkbox" : "MR&Checkbox"
                        );

                        return(1L);

                case IDC_CHECKBOXBMP :

                        // This button merely rotates through two predefined
                        // bitmap backgrounds for the dialog.

                        if(CtrlID == IDC_BITMAP)
                        {
                            CtrlID = IDC_BITMAP2;
                            lstrcpy(BitmapName, "Marble");
                        }
                        else
                        {
                            CtrlID = IDC_BITMAP;
                            lstrcpy(BitmapName, "Atomic");
                        }

                        // Delete old bitmap, establish new one, & force repaint.

                        DeleteObject(GetProp(hDlg, "Bitmap"));

                        SetProp
```

```
                          (
                              hDlg, "Bitmap", LoadBitmap(hInstTestApp, BitmapName)
                          );

                          InvalidateRect(hDlg, NULL, TRUE);

                          return(1L);

                  default :

                          break;
                }
            break;

        default :

            break;
    }

    // Hands default dialog message processing to STDWIN.DLL

    return(AtomicDialogWndFn(hDlg, Msg, wParam, lParam));
}


/****************************************************************************
    FUNCTION: MiscDlgProc
    PURPOSE:  Processes messages dialog containing four edits and two
              listboxes. All windows have grab bars and are resizable.
****************************************************************************/

LRESULT WINAPI MiscDlgProc(HWND hDlg, UINT Msg, WPARAM wParam, LPARAM lParam)
{
    switch(Msg)
    {
        case WM_ACTIVATE :

            // Flag IsDialogMessage that this dialog is the new active one.
            // This lets it process dialog-special keystrokes accordingly.

            hDlgActive = (wParam == NULL) ? NULL : hDlg;
            break;

        case WM_CLOSE :
```

```
            // We never close, we're open all night!! Actually, this is for
            // when the user double-clicks on the system menu. This window
            // isn't to be destroyed until the main app is closed down and
            // terminated.

            ShowWindow(hDlg, SW_HIDE);
            return(1);

        default :

            break;
    }

    // Hands default dialog message processing to STDWIN.DLL.

    return(AtomicDialogWndFn(hDlg, Msg, wParam, lParam));
}
```

B

STDWIN

Completeness of Code Listings

All the code for the custom controls and dialog class discussed and shown throughout this book is provided in its entirety, with two exceptions—the libentry.asm entry-point code and the makefiles for the custom controls. Because the custom controls use the same makefile and "make" batch file as the ones used by STDWIN.DLL, they are not reprinted. Merely duplicate the makefile and make batch file used by STDWIN and distribute it into the directories containing the rest of the source code for the other custom controls. My particular implementation involved locating the STDWIN directory at the root of a particular drive and implementing the custom controls as child directories off of the directory for STDWIN.

STDWIN.DLL

The AtomicDialog window class provides some powerful features for dialogs, including a "virtual" client area scrolling capability, top-level window non-client area customization, and an intelligent method of interacting with child controls. AtomicDialog windows automatically notify child controls whenever the size of the dialog changes, allowing them to intelligently reposition themselves. Additionally, AtomicDialog windows can have elaborate bitmap background patterns if desired, allowing tiled, centered, and stretched bitmaps that snap into place. The dialog "backdrop" of every AtomicDialog window is also used to paint any groupboxes around a related group of controls (without using window handles), and to initially paint the "inherent" graphical labels that can be automatically associated with any control. Groupboxes and control labels are auto-positioned, auto-painted (in 3-D), and otherwise completely managed by built-in methods.

This new system does have a couple of restrictions. First and foremost is that every dialog and control must have some sort of custom resource structure associated with it. This structure is used to define extended style attributes, a label, and any additional information associated with the window. The style bits and label are automatically processed by functions in STDWIN.DLL;

however, the extra data in the resource structure is passed back to the window, allowing it to perform any further initialization. Most of the controls process this information during WM_CREATE, or more likely in their first WM_MOVE message. For some controls, the resource structure is freed on first use and never loaded into memory again. For others, however, it is loaded, accessed, and freed whenever information is needed. The only data storage methods used for control and dialog overhead were window properties, extra data, and the local and global heap. These methods could be improved on quite easily, shifting storage overhead to perhaps a more intelligent memory manager. This would also have the effect of relieving User's overhead even more. Many of the possible improvements for this system are mentioned near the end of this appendix.

Like the AtomicBitmap control, the AtomicDialog window maintains a "virtual" client area. Whenever the scroll bars of either kind of window are manipulated, the origin of the window's client area is shifted to reveal a different section of client space. For the bitmap, this just means that a different part of the bitmap needs to be displayed. For the dialog client area, it actually shifts child window controls along with the dialog client area itself. How can the client area of a dialog be bigger than the dialog itself? Actually, it's not bigger. This effect is achieved by merely positioning child controls outside the dialog's known client area. Then, when the client area is scrolled (using ScrollWindow()), the child controls automatically display themselves.

Description

The library STDWIN.DLL provides a number of services. Basically, they can be broken into three areas:

- ☐ The default dialog procedure (AtomicDialogWndFn()) for windows based on the AtomicDialog class

- ☐ The default window procedure (AtomicControlWndFn()) for controls

- ☐ Miscellaneous API code for printing and clipboarding bitmaps, providing the 3-D effect used by the controls, and other support code

Each is discussed in the following sections.

AtomicDialogWndFn(), the Default Dialog Procedure

This name is a little misleading. `AtomicDialogWndFn()` really doesn't replace the need for **DefDlgProc()**; it only extends it. **DefDlgProc()** is still called to handle any method not processed by `AtomicDialogWndFn()`, which includes most of the standard window messages. The purpose of `AtomicDialogWndFn()` is to provide methods for supporting the custom dialog class and a few for the custom controls as well. What follows is a short discussion of each message it handles and how the message is handled.

Message	Description
WM_GETSIZE	This is a custom message sent to any control having a "virtual" client area, which currently includes windows using the AtomicDialog class and the AtomicBitmap class. This message implies that the control has a client area that might be above and beyond that determinable by the dimensions of the actual window itself. The message is sent in various instances, including whenever the dialog needs to paint itself and whenever the size of a dialog or bitmap control has changed, making it necessary to recalculate the scroll bar ranges. The AtomicDialog class function handles this message by first getting the client dimensions of the dialog window. Then the position of every child control within the dialog is examined, and this initial RECT value is possibly expanded during the process. In this manner a RECT structure that has effectively "lassoed" the controls within its client area is generated. The width and height of this RECT are then packaged as a DWORD return value and passed back to the sender. As an aside, the AtomicBitmap control implements this method by calling **GetObject()** on its bitmap, returning the bmWidth and bmHeight members of the returned BITMAP structure.
WM_VSCROLL	Like the AtomicBitmap control, the AtomicDialog windows pass this message WM_HSCROLL to the function ProcessScrollbars(), which scrolls the client area of the control based on the particular scroll bar message received.

WM_MEASUREITEM WM_DRAWITEM	These two messages are handled rather oddly. Normally, when an owner-draw listbox is created, its parent window receives messages allowing it to size and otherwise paint the visual appearance of the selected and unselected items contained in the listbox. However, I really wanted to isolate all the listbox code inside the listbox module itself. The solution was to reroute these messages from the listbox's parent window (which in this case is an AtomicDialog class window) to the listbox itself. This doesn't present any kind of problem, because both messages are guaranteed to be unique and aren't replicated by any listbox message. The only time this would be a problem is if the listbox were to itself create an owner-draw listbox child. The likelihood (or practicality) of this happening is pretty slim, however. It is true that any WM_PAINT messages going to the listbox could have been intercepted and handled "locally," but this would have required that a large number of listbox methods be implemented from scratch, which is something that the first solution avoids.
WM_SETCURSOR	This message is intercepted and handled to support some of the non-client customization features supported by AtomicDialog windows. Any time a dialog is defined with the style attribute WS_3D, it is assumed to have a customized system menu, a system menu cursor (a "box within a box"), a caption, and a caption cursor (a small hand). Depending on where the hit-test code points, the appropriate cursor value is returned.
WM_ENTERIDLE WM_MENUSELECT	Because of some of the workarounds required for non-client area customization, these two messages are used as a trap to set certain states required to be able to tell when and what portion of the non-client area should be painted.
WM_NCHITTEST	This message is trapped to allow a window to be dragged across the screen by clicking in the window's client area, as opposed to the normal method in which the caption bar is clicked and dragged to move the window. The message first passes control to **DefDlgProc()** and checks the hit code. If the hit code is HTCLIENT, then HTCAPTION is instead returned, leading

Windows to believe that the user is trying to drag the window via its caption bar. This has the effect, however, of causing the cursor to turn to a hand icon whenever the mouse is over a client portion of the window. This doesn't include when the cursor is over a child control, because the control's class cursor is used. The hand cursor is used because it is the default cursor for the caption bar, and Windows is now under the impression that the mouse is over the caption when it really isn't.

`WM_NCACTIVATE`
`WM_NCPAINT`

Both of these messages are trapped in order to be able to paint the custom system menu and caption bar available to AtomicDialog class windows created with the `WS_3D` custom style attribute. A message other than `WM_NCPAINT` needs to be trapped because painting methods for a window aren't always implemented during the `WM_PAINT` and `WM_NCPAINT` messages, as you would expect. Currently, the non-client area customization is an all-or-nothing affair. If the dialog doesn't have a system menu, a caption bar, and minimize and maximize buttons, the window's non-client area isn't customized. The non-client painting methods also assume a `WS_THICKFRAME` style of window.

`WM_SIZE`

This message is processed by the dialog for several reasons. First and foremost is to issue the custom window message `WM_RESIZE` to all child controls. This allows them to resize themselves within their parent, allowing them to dynamically accommodate to the size of their parent's client area. A second reason this message is trapped is to remaximize any control that currently is zoomed within its parent. A zoomed (maximized) control must always stay zoomed, either until Alt-Enter is pressed or the right mouse button is double-clicked within the client area of the control again. The third reason this message is processed is so that the dialog can call `ProcessScrollbars()`, a function that is used to dynamically adjust the range of the dialog's scroll bars, possibly removing them. Whenever the size of a scrollable dialog is changed, the scroll bar ranges must be recalculated to take into account the positions and dimensions of any child controls relative to the edges of the dialog.

WM_CREATE

This message is where most of the initialization for an AtomicDialog window takes place. All dialogs based on the AtomicDialog window class require a private data structure in the application's resource file. The name of this structure is the actual class name of the dialog, making the structure easy to locate. This structure contains style bits for the dialog and numerous other parameters ranging from colors used in the 3-D scheme, to groupbox/control associations, to the bitmap background available for every AtomicDialog. Following is the format of this structure:

```
DialogClassName RCDATA PRELOAD MOVEABLE DISCARDABLE
BEGIN
    StyleWords,        // Valid dialog styles are WS_3D, which creates a 3-D
    ...,               // dialog containing a customized non-client area, and
    ...,               // three styles indicating how (if at all) the background
                       // dialog bitmap is to be displayed. These styles include
                       // BS_TILED, BS_CENTERED, and BS_STRETCHED. They are
                       // mutually exclusive.
                       //
    0,                 // Null, indicating end of style words

    COLOR_LIGHTGRAY,   // Background brush color for dialog (can be any #defined
                       // color that's listed in stdwin.h)
    3,                 // Thickness of 3-D effect
    2,                 // Thickness of 3-D effect for labels and single-line
                       // edit ctrls
    3,                 // The gap between a control and its defined label
    0,                 // The gap between the font inside a label and the label edge
    10,                // The margin between controls and the edge of the groupbox
                       // that encompasses them
    30,                // The margin between a WS_SIZEHORZ or WS_SIZEVERT window and
                       // the border edge of its parent window
```

This is the minimum amount of data that needs to be defined for an AtomicDialog structure. The following items are required only if applicable. In any case, the structure must be terminated with a null byte.

```
    "BitmapName\0",    // The name of the bitmap resource to use for the dialog
                       // background. Its display method depends on whether
                       // BS_TILED, BS_STRETCHED, or BS_CENTERED is used.
```

```
                    // Any of a number of groupboxes can be defined at this point.
                    // The format starts with "??Groupbox Title\0", where ?? is
                    // the formatting code for the label. It can be the following
                    // code {T,M,B}{L,C,R}, indicating a top-, middle-, or bottom-
                    // positioned label, and whether it is left-, center-, or
                    // right-justified. As with all labels and resource strings
                    // in general, there must be a terminating null after the
                    // character string. This string is followed by a COLOR_ code
                    // indicating the background brush color to use for the
                    // groupbox. This is then followed by a series of CtrlIDs
                    // and finally a terminating null, indicating the end of
                    // the groupbox definition.

    "??Groupbox#1 Title\0", COLOR_*, CtrlID#1, CtrlID#2, CtrlID#3, ..., 0,
    ...
    "??Groupbox#n Title\0", COLOR_*, CtrlID#8, CtrlID#9, ..., 0,

        0                   // Terminating null for structure
END
```

The format of this structure could be greatly improved by allowing more color styles (text color, shading colors) to be stored here. System colors can be used to a certain point; however, for implementing a nice 3-D, shaded effect, it would be far better to let the user pick from predefined 3-D shading styles. To simplify things, the primary background brush color for dialogs and windows could be based on the system color for this same attribute. However, then the 3-D and shading styles could be altered around the system color choice for a window color.

WM_DESTROY

This message is used only to perform miscellaneous cleanup and remove window properties established during the life of the dialog.

WM_ERASEBKGND

This message is trapped but not processed. Windows of the class AtomicDialog have no background to erase. All drawing is done during WM_PAINT.

WM_PAINT

This message is used for a number of things. Because a fair number of painting operations can be performed here, the first thing done is to create a compatible memory display context to perform drawing operations in. In this manner, all drawing can be accumulated into an intermediate "bucket" and then BitBlted to the dialog when all drawing and painting operations are finished. Next, any dialogs that have no bitmap background or a centered background have their background erased and filled with a colored brush. This isn't needed for tiled and stretched bitmap backgrounds because there's no "background" to show through. Now, the bitmap background (if any) is tiled, centered, or stretched into place. After this, any groupboxes defined for the dialog are painted, then all child controls of the dialog have their frames and labels painted. This needs to be done during the parent's paint method because the 3-D frame and label for controls actually is a part of the parent's client area and not a part of the child. Whenever the child control processes a WM_SIZE message, however, it additionally redraws its own frame and label.

WM_CTLCOLOR

This message handles the color determination for nonpure controls, which includes the superclassed combobox, listbox, and edit controls. The combobox control actually reroutes the WM_CTLCOLOR messages it receives (for the embedded edit control and listbox control) and sends them to its parent, where they can be handled in the manner of the other noncomposite stock controls.

WM_SETDEFID

This message is sent to establish a default button for a parent window. This message is different from the message as it is handled by **DefDlgProc()**, because in this case the message can be sent to any class of parent window—dialog or otherwise. Instead of storing a handle to the default button in window extra data, a more-generic window property is used.

WM_GETDEFID

This message is sent to retrieve the default button for a parent window. Like WM_SETDEFID, this message can be sent to any class of window, not just dialogs.

AtomicControlWndFn(), the Default Control Window Procedure

Again, the name is a little misleading, because AtomicControlWndFn() really doesn't replace the need for **DefWindowProc()**; it only extends it. **DefWindowProc()** is still called to handle any method not processed by AtomicControlWndFn(), which includes most of the standard window messages. The purpose of AtomicControlWndFn() is to provide methods for supporting features found in the custom dialog class and various methods for the custom controls as well. What follows is a short discussion of each message it handles and how it handles them.

Message	Description
WM_DRAWFRAME	This is a custom message sent to a control to tell it to draw its customized frame. This differs from the non-client area of the control because this type of frame is physically located just outside the perimeter covered by the control's non-client area. The 3-D frame is "popped" in and out whenever the control loses or gains the focus; it does not blink, like labels do.
WM_DRAWLABEL	This is a custom message sent to a control to tell it to draw its label. To retrieve or set the label of a control, the functions **GetLabelText()** and **SetLabelText()** can be used.
WM_GETFOCUS	This is a custom message that can be sent to any control. It is intended, however, for composite controls such as the combobox, which can have multiple child windows that make up the control as a "whole." The default action for the message when it reaches this point is to return the hWnd that it was called with. However, the AtomicCombobox control traps this message and returns the handle to the window having the focus.

WM_WINDOWPOSCHANGING	When this message is received by a control, it invalidates its label so it may be repainted correctly when the window is finally resized or moved.
WM_RESIZE	This message is sent to a control, telling it to resize itself to accommodate the new size of its parent's client area. If the window isn't defined with the custom style attributes WS_SIZEHORZ or WS_SIZEVERT, nothing is done. Otherwise, the parent's new client area is retrieved, and the window is adjusted vertically, horizontally, or both, to accommodate the new size. The size of the margin between a control and the edge of its parent's border is defined through a value located in the dialog's custom data structure.
WM_SIZE	When this message is received by a control, it redraws its label and frame by issuing WM_DRAWLABEL and WM_DRAWFRAME messages.
WM_CANCELMODE	When this message is received, a WM_LBUTTONUP is sent to the child control, which cancels any capture mode that might be in effect.
WM_SYSKEYDOWN	This message is processed by the controls to implement certain aspects of the dialog manager that are lost when static windows aren't used to label controls. Because labels are now graphically drawn and don't consume the overhead associated with a window, the control mnemonics and hotkeys must be manually interpreted, and focus must be shifted to the correct control. This method is implemented by scanning the labels associated with every control and determining which label contains the hotkey just pressed. When it's found, focus is shifted to that control. This message is also trapped to process the Alt-Enter key, which is used to zoom and unzoom child control within its parent.
WM_DESTROY	The style and label properties are removed from the window during this message. Additionally, the string atom associated with the label property is freed.

WM_ERASEBKGND	Erases the background of the control. If no background brush is defined, any brush associated with the parent window is used.
WM_SETFOCUS WM_KILLFOCUS	These messages are used to redraw the frame and label associated with a control whenever it receives or loses the focus. Additionally, a timer is set up (or killed) to allow the label blinking effect associated with any control that has the focus.
WM_TIMER	Draws a flashed or unflashed label for a control.
WM_ENABLE	Invalidates the entire control to ensure a full paint when the control is enabled or disabled.
WM_LBUTTONDOWN WM_RBUTTONDOWN	Sets the focus to control, if focus is not already grabbed.
WM_RBUTTONDBLCLK	Responsible for zooming and unzooming a child control within its parent window. The parent window's scroll bars (if any) are removed while the child window is maximized and are restored along with the child control at a later point when the child is unzoomed. All other child controls are temporarily hidden while another control is zoomed.

Miscellaneous Support API

In addition to the default dialog and control class window procedures, STDWIN.DLL contains a number of additional functions to support the custom controls and provide other functions not necessarily related to the custom controls or dialog class. Following is a list of those functions, as well as a brief description of how they are used.

BitmapToClipboard()

Places the specified bitmap into clipboard on behalf of specified window.

BitmapToPrinter()

> Prints the specified device-dependent bitmap (DDB, not DIB) using a WYSIWYG print dialog that allows the printed image to be re-anchored and stretched anywhere within the image representing the printed page.

CalcScrollBars()

> A routine used by AtomicDialog and AtomicBitmap window classes. This function determines how much (if at all) to adjust the scroll bar ranges when the size of the window is altered. Either ranges are changed or the scroll bar is possibly removed.

CreateAndRegisterDialog()

> This function creates (and optionally) registers an AtomicDialog class of window. The passed parameters are used to specify the instance, dialog template name, parent window, window procedure, icon, background brush, class extra data, and window extra data to be associated with the window. This function is an admittedly simple attempt at encapsulating the window creation process.

DrawCtrlLabel()

> Draws a 3-D label associated with a control (if any is). The label can appear to be "sunken in" or "popped out."

DrawRectLabel()

> Draws a 3-D label positioned somewhere around a rectangular region. Label can appear to be "sunken in" or "popped out."

GetChildWindowPos()

> Returns the position/dimensions of a child window within a "virtual" dialog parent.

> The resulting RECT is client-based, returning coordinates that can be used with **SetWindowPos()** to reposition the child control. This function undoes the "shifting" done with GetChildWindowRect(), because the function **SetWindowPos()** doesn't take a window's origin into account when positioning child controls.

GetChildWindowRect()

> Returns the position/dimensions of a child window within a "virtual" dialog parent.

The resulting RECT is client-based, returning coordinates that can be used with any GDI call that requires the coordinates of a control.

GetCtrlLabelRect()

Retrieves the RECT associated with the label for a given control. After determining the RECT structure for the given control, this function calls GetLabelRect() to retrieve the coordinates of the label identifying the given area. The returned RECT structure is useful for determining label hits with the mouse and for updating control labels whenever movement or sizing of the control occurs.

GetLabelRect()

Retrieves the RECT associated with the label for a given screen region. This separate function is needed for items like the dynamically drawn groupbox, which has no window handle of its own. After determining the RECT needed to encompass a group of controls, this function is called by groupbox code inside AtomicDialogWndFn() in order to determine the RECT needed for the label associated with the groupbox.

GetLabelText()

Retrieves the text of the label associated with a given control.

GetOrigin()

Returns the "true" client origin of a given window. Implemented only for windows based on the AtomicDialog or AtomicBitmap class.

GetPrinter()

This function is used to retrieve a device context to the default Windows printer.

ProcessScrollBars()

A routine used by the AtomicDialog and AtomicBitmap window classes. This function interprets scroll bar messages destined for a window and scrolls the client area of the window accordingly.

SetAtomicClassStyle()

This function is used to read the "header" block associated with the private resource structure owned by every Atomic class of control. The beginning of the header block is common for all controls, containing a series of style words (WS_3D, WS_SIZEVERT, WS_SIZEHORZ, and so on) followed by an ending null.

The style words are then followed by an optional label for the control. This function reads in the style words, assigning an extended style word for the window as a window property, and then reads in the label for the control assigning the label to a window property as well.

The method in which style bits are handled for the dialog and control classes can seem somewhat "kluged" at times, but there was a reason for setting them up the way they are. Because the controls that are offered straddle superclassed Windows controls and custom developed pure controls, some common method was needed to establish style bits and how they are to be retrieved. Windows uses the high word of the return value from `GetWindowLong`(hWnd, GWL_STYLE) to define non-client styles common to all types of windows. The AtomicDialog class and Atomic* controls expect the same thing. It's how the control-specific styles (the low word from the return value) are stored that is different. Because custom control styles can't be cleanly intermingled with Windows control styles, a separate storage area was needed, that being the custom resource structure for each Atomic* window class. The rule is as follows: Superclassed controls define their styles the normal way, using the style parameters to `CreateWindow()` or something similar. Pure controls (including the extended style attributes for superclassed controls) are defined in the custom resource structure for the control. After the control is created, these extended style bits are accumulated into a single word value and copied to the "Style" window property. Because we aren't dealing with a large number of controls, this really doesn't present much of a problem.

Valid styles common to all windows are `WS_3D`, which provides the control with a 3-D appearance; `WS_SIZEHORZ`, which sizes the window horizontally to float with the size of its parent; and `WS_SIZEVERT`, which (you guessed it!) sizes the window vertically to float with the size of its parent. Additionally, the AtomicDialog class supports the styles `BS_CENTERED`, `BS_TILED`, and `BS_STRETCHED`, which control the positioning of the dialog's background bitmap (if any is defined). The additional control-specific extended styles are discussed with the appendix describing that particular control.

All controls have a resource associated with them whose name is actually the ID of the control itself. This function returns a far pointer to the control's custom resource structure that can be used during the initialization method of the control to perform any additional processing of the structure that is necessary. If no extra data exists after the header block, a null pointer is returned instead.

SetLabelText()

Sets the text of the label associated with a given control.

SetOrigin()

Sets the origin of the client area for a window based on the AtomicDialog or AtomicBitmap window class.

SinkControl()

When passed a window handle and a device-context handle, SinkControl() paints a "sunken" or "raised" graphical image around a control. The first integer parameter indicates the thickness of the 3-D effect, and the second integer is used to indicate the gap between the control and the start of the 3-D effect. This function calls SinkRect() when it computes the RECT of the child control it is working with.

SinkRect()

This function is called by the routine that draws groupbox perimeters and by the function SinkControl(). It attempts to draw a 3-D effect around a region by drawing a dark upper-left frame around the area and a light-colored frame around the lower-right area encompassing the region. The effect is similar to that done for push buttons.

WindowToClipboard()

This function copies to the clipboard the window image specified by the first HWND parameter. The clipboarded image is associated with the window pointed to by the second HWND parameter.

Possible Enhancements

Possible enhancements and changes to STDWIN.DLL are several. First and foremost might be to break out the code supporting the AtomicDialog class and default methods handled by the function AtomicControlWndFn(), thus separating these two pieces of code from the main support API.

In addition, several enhancements can be considered for STDWIN.DLL and for the source code of all the modules as a whole, including the following enhancements (in no particular order of importance):

☐ Adapting code to a new STRICT specification. The reason this was not done by the author is that at press time, the STRICT specification was not stable and was undergoing a number of revisions. You will find, however, that all the source code compiles with no warnings at compiler level 3. A minimal amount of effort should be involved to make it STRICT-compliant.

☐ Altering of the 3-D painting mechanism. Although the goal of a 3-D look is achieved, it is definitely not of the caliber possible by someone more graphically inclined.

☐ Interfacing controls to the dialog editor. Currently, only the bitmap control has been adapted for the dialog editor. The listbox and button controls were not interfaced because they function the same as their stock-Windows counterparts when run under the dialog editor.

☐ Changing the location of custom control structure definitions. Moving portions of the custom control data from the resource file into read-write memory when the controls are first created would be an excellent enhancement. Resources work great, but they have the drawback of being read-only. This can make certain control attributes hard to customize. Ideally, all the custom controls would support a message-based interface as well as the current resource data structure interface, allowing certain attributes (such as the windows contained by a groupbox) to be changed on-the-fly. The components of certain controls are already set up this way; however, it's not that way for all of them. Additionally, instead of using a custom data structure for each control, you could embed the different control data structures into the single data structure provided for the parent dialog window, thus concatenating all overhead into a single, self-contained resource structure. Actually, a resource structure doesn't need to be used at all; rather, the custom data for controls and dialogs can be stored in ASCII files that are referenced by resources. Some of the overhead could even be put into the WIN.INI or some other initialization file, making it even easier to customize.

☐ Changing color scheme determination. The code and colors for controlling the highlighting of a control are statically defined in certain cases. Ideally, the colors should be based on certain system colors, or they should at least be settable via a custom resource structure. Additionally, it would be nice to base the 3-D effect and shading colors on the system color used for the client area of a window. This would allow "intelligent" 3-D schemes, rather than the static method currently implemented.

☐ Changing the module and library names of the custom controls. Due to an admitted lack of hindsight by the author, all the controls are set up to use generic module names such as "listbox," "button," and so on. This could easily conflict with other libraries or module names already used by Windows. Although this isn't a problem for Windows 3.x, it could easily conflict with the libraries provided by other vendors or libraries in a future version of Windows. This problem can be remedied by simply renaming the filenames, changing the LIBRARY name in the module-definition file of each control, and changing the library names of all implicitly linked libraries in the different make files used by the various controls. Change the names to something like XBUTTON or XLISTBOX, which have a much higher probability of not being duplicated by some other library.

☐ Change the method of data storage. Much of the overhead for controls is placed in window properties and extra data, both of which take up space in User's local heap. Shifting this burden of overhead either to the library or to the client application would be ideal for truly demanding control-intensive dialogs. However, this is not to say that the current implementation isn't fairly robust, because it is. As a test, the following applications were loaded into memory to check the overall effect on User's local heap:

Microsoft Word, with six medium-sized document windows opened

Microsoft Terminal

Microsoft Paint

Windows Draw (by MicroGrafx)

TestApp (15 instances), which uses the custom controls extensively

Clock

DOS box (three instances)

Program Manager

The amount of free system resources was 37 percent after the test, indicating success. Only when this amount dips to approximately 15 to 10 percent should applications be closed down, because many applications don't respond well when system resources are at a minimum. Although using window properties isn't exactly the fastest operation in town, it works quite well under most circumstances, including this one.

■ Increasing the level of error checking. Although the error checking is in most cases sufficient, differing viewpoints definitely exist in defining how much is enough. Routines that should always succeed, such as calling `GetClientRect()` or something similar, should never be tested. However, things such as memory allocations, DC creation, and the like should always be verified. To really do error handling right, some sort of error-reporting service should be developed, possibly based around the routine `MessageBox()` and string table resources containing the caption and error text. Ideally, some sort of predefined rules would be established for determining which kind of icon should be displayed given the severity and type of error being reported.

Specifications

ModuleName   STDWIN
LibraryName   STDWIN.DLL

Functions

`LibMain()`   Standard entry point for library
`WEP()`   Standard exit procedure for library
`AtomicDialogWndFn()`   Class window procedure for dialogs
`AtomicControlWndFn()`   Default class window procedure for all controls

STDWIN.C

```
/*************************************************************************
    LIBRARY: STDWIN.DLL
    AUTHOR : Mike Klein
    PURPOSE: Handles common window functions.
 *************************************************************************/

//
// #DEFINEs, #INCLUDEs, declarations, and globals
//
```

```
#define STDWIN

#define OEMRESOURCE
#define NOCOMM
#define _WINDLL

#define WIDGETS (WS_SYSMENU ¦ WS_CAPTION ¦ WS_MINIMIZEBOX ¦ WS_MAXIMIZEBOX)

#define SCROLLAMT  8    // The scroll amount for lineup/linedown msgs.

#define PGUPPGDN   4    // The amount of scrn scrolled when pgup or pgdn
                        // on the scroll bar is pressed. The screen
                        // delta is divided by this amount.

#include <windows.h>
#include <custcntl.h>
#include <ctype.h>
#include <dos.h>
#include <print.h>
#include <stdlib.h>
#include <string.h>
#include "stdwin.h"
#include "stdprt.h"

int     PASCAL LibMain(HINSTANCE, WORD, WORD, LPSTR);
int     WINAPI WEP(int);
BOOL    WINAPI PrintOptionsDlgProc(HWND, UINT, WPARAM, LPARAM);

int     WINAPI PrintImage(HWND, LPIMAGEPARMS);
HGLOBAL WINAPI GetPrinter(VOID);
int     WINAPI UpdatePrinter(HWND);

static FARPROC lpfnComboboxWndProc;
static FARPROC lpfnEditWndProc;
static FARPROC lpfnListboxWndProc;

static UINT WM_DRAWFRAME; // Draws painted frame (in or out) around control.
static UINT WM_DRAWLABEL; // Draws 3-D label for control.

static UINT WM_GETFOCUS;  // Sent to a control to determine which window
                          // (if it is a composite control like the combobox)
                          // has the focus.
```

```
static UINT WM_GETSIZE;    // Sent to a control to determine its "true"
                           // size. For a bitmap control, it is the size of
                           // the bitmap. For a dialog, it is the "virtual"
                           // size that encompasses all scrollable controls.

static UINT WM_RESIZE;     // Sent to a window when it needs to resize itself
                           // according to the new dimensions of its parent.

static HINSTANCE hInstSTDWIN = NULL; // Instance of STDWIN.



/****************************************************************************
    FUNCTION: LibMain
    PURPOSE : Entry point for DLL.
 ****************************************************************************/

#pragma alloc_text(INIT_TEXT, LibMain)

int PASCAL LibMain(HINSTANCE hInst, WORD DataSeg, WORD HeapSize, LPSTR CmdLine)
{
    WNDCLASS wc;

    // Get wnd procs for built-in Windows ctrls: edit, combobox, and listbox.

    GetClassInfo(NULL, "combobox", &wc);
    lpfnComboboxWndProc = (FARPROC) wc.lpfnWndProc;
    GetClassInfo(NULL, "edit", &wc);
    lpfnEditWndProc = (FARPROC) wc.lpfnWndProc;
    GetClassInfo(NULL, "listbox", &wc);
    lpfnListboxWndProc = (FARPROC) wc.lpfnWndProc;

    // Register custom messages & remember the instance.

    WM_DRAWFRAME = RegisterWindowMessage("WM_DRAWFRAME");
    WM_DRAWLABEL = RegisterWindowMessage("WM_DRAWLABEL");
    WM_GETFOCUS  = RegisterWindowMessage("WM_GETFOCUS");
    WM_GETSIZE   = RegisterWindowMessage("WM_GETSIZE");
    WM_RESIZE    = RegisterWindowMessage("WM_RESIZE");

    hInstSTDWIN = hInst;

    return(TRUE);
}
```

```
/**************************************************************************
    FUNCTION: WEP
    PURPOSE : Termination function for DLL.
**************************************************************************/

int WINAPI WEP(int Parameter)
{
    return(1);
}




/**************************************************************************
    FUNCTION: BitmapToClipboard
    PURPOSE : Copies bitmap to clipboard.
**************************************************************************/

int WINAPI BitmapToClipboard(HBITMAP hBmp, HWND hWndApp)
{
    // Open clipboard, put bitmap inside, and close clipboard.

    OpenClipboard(hWndApp);
    EmptyClipboard();
    SetClipboardData(CF_BITMAP, hBmp);
    CloseClipboard();

    return(0);
}




/**************************************************************************
    FUNCTION: BitmapToPrinter
    PURPOSE : Prints copy of bitmap to printer.
**************************************************************************/

HWND WINAPI BitmapToPrinter(HBITMAP hBmp, HWND hWndApp, LPSTR Name)
{
    BITMAP        Bitmap;
    LPIMAGEPARMS  lpIP;
    HGLOBAL       hGlobal;

    // Get the default printer DEVMODE.
```

```
if(!(hGlobal = GetPrinter()))
{
    MessageBox
    (
        GetActiveWindow(), "No default printer", "ERROR", MB_OK ¦
        MB_ICONHAND
    );

    return(NULL);
}

// Get a far pointer to the IMAGEPARMS struct we'll be using for the
// life of the print dialog.

lpIP = (LPIMAGEPARMS) GlobalLock(hGlobal);

// Fill in IMAGEPARMS struct with a few basics, including a handle to
// the bitmap we're to print, as well as whether the bitmap is to be
// deleted upon finish. This part is for when Windows are printed,
// which generate an extra bitmap, which just printing a straight bitmap
// doesn't do. This extra bitmap is what was "pulled" out of the window.

lpIP->hBmp = hBmp;

// Get the size of the bitmap we're printing and stuff into the struct.

GetObject(hBmp, sizeof(BITMAP), &Bitmap);
lpIP->bmWidth  = Bitmap.bmWidth;
lpIP->bmHeight = Bitmap.bmHeight;
lstrcpy(lpIP->Name, Name);

// Bring up the print options dialog.

return
(
    DialogBoxParam
    (
        hInstSTDWIN,
        "PrintOptions",
        hWndApp,
        (FARPROC) PrintOptionsDlgProc,
        MAKELONG(hGlobal, 0)
    )
);
}
```

```
/****************************************************************************
    FUNCTION: GetChildWindowPos
    PURPOSE : UN-Offsets passed child window rect by parent ORG value.
              Used to undo the effects of a GetChildWindowRect. This call
              is needed before a control is moved with SetWindowPos.
****************************************************************************/

int WINAPI GetChildWindowPos(HWND hWndChild, LPRECT lpRect, BOOL GetRect)
{
    DWORD dwOrg;

    // Are we getting the "TRUE" rect of the window first?

    if(GetRect)
    {
        GetChildWindowRect(hWndChild, lpRect);
    }

    // Get parent window origin.

    dwOrg = GetOrigin(GetParent(hWndChild));
    OffsetRect(lpRect, -(int)LOWORD(dwOrg), -(int)HIWORD(dwOrg));

    return(0);
}



/****************************************************************************
    FUNCTION: GetChildWindowRect
    PURPOSE : Gets child window (or control) rect and converts it to the
              child coords needed to size or move it in its parent window.
              This routine also adjusts the RECT by the parent window's
              origin amt.
****************************************************************************/

int WINAPI GetChildWindowRect(HWND hWndChild, LPRECT lpRect)
{
    DWORD dwOrigin;
    HWND  hWndParent;

    hWndParent = GetParent(hWndChild);

    // First, get screen coordinates of child window/ctrl & convert to client.
```

```
    GetWindowRect(hWndChild, lpRect);
    ScreenToClient(hWndParent, (LPPOINT) &lpRect->left);
    ScreenToClient(hWndParent, (LPPOINT) &lpRect->right);

    // Now, offset it a little for "virtual" area.

    dwOrigin = GetOrigin(hWndParent);
    OffsetRect(lpRect, (int)LOWORD(dwOrigin), (int)HIWORD(dwOrigin));

    return(0);
}


/****************************************************************************

    FUNCTION: GetOrigin
    PURPOSE : Returns origin for control type. Used for "virtual" dialogs
              and bitmap controls.
****************************************************************************/

DWORD WINAPI GetOrigin(HWND hWnd)
{
    // Get window origin.

    return(MAKELONG(GetProp(hWnd, "xOrg"), GetProp(hWnd, "yOrg")));
}


/****************************************************************************

    FUNCTION: SetOrigin
    PURPOSE : Sets origin for control type. Used for "virtual" dialogs
              and bitmap controls.
****************************************************************************/

int WINAPI SetOrigin(HWND hWnd, int xOrg, int yOrg)
{
    // Set window origin.

    SetProp(hWnd, "xOrg", xOrg);
    SetProp(hWnd, "yOrg", yOrg);

    return(0);
}
```

```
/*****************************************************************************
     FUNCTION: GetPrinter
     PURPOSE : Gets DEVMODE struct for default printer & puts in IMAGEPARMS
               struct, which contains information about the image we want
               to print as well as a DEVMODE struct.
*****************************************************************************/

HGLOBAL WINAPI GetPrinter(VOID)
{
    BYTE  pPrintInfo[80];
    LPSTR lpTemp;
    LPSTR lpDevName;
    LPSTR lpDevTitle;
    LPSTR lpDevPort;
    int   SizeOfDevMode;

    HINSTANCE hInstLib;
    HGLOBAL hGlobal;
    BYTE    DevName[13];

    LPFNDEVMODE  ExtDeviceMode;  // Pointer to printer's config func.
    LPIMAGEPARMS lpIP;           // Pointer to image struct.

    // Look at win.ini for default printer setting.

    if(!GetProfileString("windows", "device", "", pPrintInfo, 80))
    {
        return(NULL);
    }

    lpTemp    = lpDevTitle = pPrintInfo;
    lpDevName = lpDevPort  = 0;

    // Now scan through and get particulars of prtr.

    while(*lpTemp)
    {
        if(*lpTemp == ',')
        {
            *lpTemp++ = 0;

            while(*lpTemp == ' ')
            {
                lpTemp = AnsiNext(lpTemp);
            }
```

```
            if(lpDevName)
            {
                lpDevPort = lpTemp;
                break;
            }

            lpDevName = lpTemp;
        }
        else
        {
            lpTemp = AnsiNext(lpTemp);
        }
    }

// Create driver file name to use LoadLibrary with (add the .drv ext).

lstrcpy(DevName, lpDevName);
lstrcat(DevName, ".drv");

if((hInstLib = LoadLibrary(DevName)) < 32)
{
    return(NULL);
}

// Get address of printer driver config func from prtr driver.

if(!(ExtDeviceMode = (LPFNDEVMODE)GetProcAddress(hInstLib, (LPCSTR)PROC_EXTDEVICEMODE)))
{
    FreeLibrary(hModule);
    return(NULL);
}

// Find out size of DEVMODE structure. This IS NOT the size of the
// struct as it's defined in print.h. So we have to find out what it is.

SizeOfDevMode = ExtDeviceMode
(
    NULL, hInstLib, NULL, lpDevTitle, lpDevPort, NULL, NULL, 0
);

// GlobalAlloc an IMAGEPARMS struct so we can start stuffing the prtr
// config struct we've got.
```

```
    if(!(hGlobal = GlobalAlloc(GHND, sizeof(IMAGEPARMS) + SizeOfDevMode * 2)))
    {
        // Couldn't alloc mem, so leave.

        return(NULL);
    }

    lpIP = (LPIMAGEPARMS) GlobalLock(hGlobal);

    lpIP->SizeOfDevMode = SizeOfDevMode;

    // Stuff our prt structure with info on the default printer.

    lstrcpy(lpIP->DevName, DevName);
    lstrcpy(lpIP->DevPort, lpDevPort);

    lpIP->hInstLib      = hInstLib;
    lpIP->ExtDeviceMode = ExtDeviceMode;

    // Get current printer configuration before we start tweaking it.

    lpIP->ExtDeviceMode
    (
        NULL,
        lpIP->hInstLib,
        lpIP->DevMode,
        lpIP->DevMode->dmDeviceName,
        lpIP->DevPort,
        NULL,
        NULL,
        DM_OUT_BUFFER
    );

    return(hGlobal);
}


/****************************************************************************
    FUNCTION: PrintImage
    PURPOSE : Prints image on printer.
****************************************************************************/
```

```
int WINAPI PrintImage(HWND hDlg, LPIMAGEPARMS lpIP)
{
    HDC     hDCPrtr;
    HDC     hDCMemory;
    BOOL    bAbort;
    POINT   Anchor;
    BOOL    Translated;
    int     Width;
    int     Height;
    RECT    Rect;
    HBITMAP hBmpOld;

    // Get RECT dimensions of page control in prt dialog.

    GetChildWindowRect(GetDlgItem(hDlg, IDC_PAGE), &Rect);

    // Change print options based on what's in the print dialog.

    lpIP->DevMode->dmCopies = GetDlgItemInt
    (
        hDlg, IDC_COPIES, (BOOL FAR *) &Translated, FALSE
    );

    if((lpIP->DevMode->dmCopies <= 0) ¦¦ (lpIP->DevMode->dmCopies > 255))
    {
        lpIP->DevMode->dmCopies = 1;
    }

    lpIP->DevMode->dmOrientation =
        IsDlgButtonChecked(hDlg, IDC_PORTRAIT) ? DMORIENT_PORTRAIT :
        DMORIENT_LANDSCAPE;

    // Establish new printer settings with ExtDevMode.

    lpIP->DevMode->dmFields ¦= (DM_ORIENTATION ¦ DM_COPIES);

    lpIP->ExtDeviceMode
    (
        NULL,
        lpIP->hInstLib,
        lpIP->DevMode,
        lpIP->DevMode->dmDeviceName,
        lpIP->DevPort,
        lpIP->DevMode,
        NULL,
        DM_IN_BUFFER ¦ DM_OUT_BUFFER
```

```
    );

    // Get a printer DC.

    if
    (
        !(hDCPrtr = CreateDC
        (
            lpIP->DevName, lpIP->DevMode->dmDeviceName, lpIP->DevPort,
            lpIP->DevMode
        ))
    )
    {
        MessageBox
        (
            GetActiveWindow(), "No default printer", "ERROR", MB_OK |
            MB_ICONHAND
        );

        return(1);
    }

    // Get page size of prtr.

    lpIP->Page.x = GetDeviceCaps(hDCPrtr, HORZRES);
    lpIP->Page.y = GetDeviceCaps(hDCPrtr, VERTRES);

    DPtoLP(hDCPrtr, &lpIP->Page, 1);

    // Fix. all coords for printer page size.

    Anchor.x = (WORD)
    (
        (float) lpIP->Anchor.x * (float) lpIP->Page.x / (float) (Rect.right - Rect.left)
    );

    Anchor.y = (WORD)
    (
        (float) lpIP->Anchor.y * (float) lpIP->Page.y / (float) (Rect.bottom - Rect.top)
    );

    Width = (WORD)
    (
        (float) lpIP->Width * (float) lpIP->Page.x / (float)
        (Rect.right - Rect.left)
    );
```

```
Height = (WORD)
(
    (float) lpIP->Height * (float) lpIP->Page.y / (float)
    (Rect.bottom - Rect.top)
);

SetCursor(LoadCursor(NULL, IDC_WAIT));

// We're printing a bitmap. First create a compatible prtr dc
// and put our bitmap into it.

hDCMemory = CreateCompatibleDC(hDCPrtr);
hBmpOld   = SelectObject(hDCMemory, lpIP->hBmp);

// Start the whole printing mechanism.

if(Escape(hDCPrtr, STARTDOC, lstrlen(lpIP->Name), lpIP->Name, NULL) < 0)
{
    MessageBox(NULL, "Unable to start print job", "ERROR", MB_OK |
               MB_ICONHAND);

    SelectObject(hDCMemory, hBmpOld);
    DeleteDC(hDCMemory);

    DeleteDC(hDCPrtr);
    return(1);
}

// Get first rect to start printing into & then keep going until we
// hit an empty rect or get an error.

Escape(hDCPrtr, NEXTBAND, NULL, NULL, &Rect);

bAbort = FALSE;

while(!IsRectEmpty(&Rect))
{
    // Make sure our coords are in sync & then blt the image.

    DPtoLP(hDCPrtr, (LPPOINT) &Rect, 2);

    StretchBlt
```

```
        (
            hDCPrtr,
            Anchor.x,
            Anchor.y,
            Width,
            Height,
            hDCMemory,
            0,
            0,
            lpIP->bmWidth,
            lpIP->bmHeight,
            SRCCOPY
        );

        if(Escape(hDCPrtr, NEXTBAND, NULL, NULL, &Rect) < 0)
        {
            bAbort = TRUE;
            break;
        }
    }

    // Did we encounter any errors? Did we have to abort? If an abort
    // happened, it would've taken care of the ENDDOC for us.

    if(!bAbort)
    {
        Escape(hDCPrtr, ENDDOC, NULL, NULL, NULL);
    }

    SelectObject(hDCMemory, hBmpOld);
    DeleteDC(hDCMemory);

    DeleteDC(hDCPrtr);
    return(0);
}


/*******************************************************************************
    FUNCTION: PrintOptionsDlgProc
    PURPOSE:  Processes messages for printer abort dialog box.
*******************************************************************************/

BOOL WINAPI PrintOptionsDlgProc(HWND hDlg, UINT uMsg, WPARAM wParam,
                                LPARAM lParam)
```

```
{
    RECT          RectPg;
    RECT          Rect;
    HGLOBAL       hGlobal;
    LPIMAGEPARMS  lpIP;
    LPDEVMODE     lpDevMode;
    PAINTSTRUCT   Paint;
    HBRUSH        hBrush;

    switch(uMsg)
    {
        case WM_INITDIALOG :

            lpIP = (LPIMAGEPARMS) GlobalLock((HGLOBAL) lParam);

            // Remember the handle to our prtr image struct.

            SetProp(hDlg, "Data", (HGLOBAL) lParam);

            // Hide the static page control.

            ShowWindow(GetDlgItem(hDlg, IDC_PAGE), SW_HIDE);

            // Update prt dialog based on printer settings.

            if(UpdatePrinter(hDlg))
            {
                // A problem, so abort.

                SendMessage(hDlg, WM_CLOSE, 0, 0L);
                return(FALSE);
            }

            SendMessage(hDlg, WM_NEXTDLGCTL, GetDlgItem(hDlg, IDCANCEL), 1L);

            return(TRUE);

        case WM_LBUTTONDOWN :

            lpIP = (LPIMAGEPARMS) GlobalLock(GetProp(hDlg, "Data"));

            GetChildWindowRect(GetDlgItem(hDlg, IDC_PAGE), &RectPg);

            // Changes anchor position of window in page control.
```

```
        if
        (
            ((int) LOWORD(lParam) > RectPg.left + 1) &&
            ((int) LOWORD(lParam) < RectPg.right - 1) &&
            ((int) HIWORD(lParam) > RectPg.top + 1) &&
            ((int) HIWORD(lParam) < RectPg.bottom - 1)
        )
        {
            // A click was made in the page control, so tell paint to
            // update.

            if(IsDlgButtonChecked(hDlg, IDC_PORTRAIT))
            {
                lpIP->Anchor.x = LOWORD(lParam) - RectPg.left - 1;
                lpIP->Anchor.y = HIWORD(lParam) - RectPg.top - 1;
            }
            else
            {
                lpIP->Anchor.x = RectPg.bottom - 1 - HIWORD(lParam);
                lpIP->Anchor.y = LOWORD(lParam) - (RectPg.left + 1);
            }

            InvalidateRect(hDlg, &RectPg, TRUE);
        }
        return(TRUE);

    case WM_RBUTTONDOWN :

        lpIP = (LPIMAGEPARMS) GlobalLock(GetProp(hDlg, "Data"));

        GetChildWindowRect(GetDlgItem(hDlg, IDC_PAGE), &RectPg);

        // Changes size of window in page control.

        if
        (
            ((int) LOWORD(lParam) > RectPg.left) &&
            ((int) LOWORD(lParam) < RectPg.right) &&
            ((int) HIWORD(lParam) > RectPg.top) &&
            ((int) HIWORD(lParam) < RectPg.bottom)
        )
        {
            // A click was made in the page control, so tell paint to
            // update.
```

```
        if(IsDlgButtonChecked(hDlg, IDC_PORTRAIT))
        {
            lpIP->Width =
                LOWORD(lParam) - (lpIP->Anchor.x + RectPg.left + 1);

            lpIP->Height =
                HIWORD(lParam) - (lpIP->Anchor.y + RectPg.top + 1);
        }
        else
        {
            lpIP->Width =
                RectPg.bottom - 1 - lpIP->Anchor.x - HIWORD(lParam);

            lpIP->Height =
                LOWORD(lParam) - (RectPg.left + 1 + lpIP->Anchor.y);
        }

        InvalidateRect(hDlg, &RectPg, TRUE);

        return(TRUE);
    }
    break;

case WM_PAINT :

    lpIP = (LPIMAGEPARMS) GlobalLock(GetProp(hDlg, "Data"));

    BeginPaint(hDlg, &Paint);

    // First, erase the static "page" picture.

    GetChildWindowRect(GetDlgItem(hDlg, IDC_PAGE), &RectPg);

    Rectangle
    (
        Paint.hdc, RectPg.left, RectPg.top, RectPg.right, RectPg.bottom
    );

    // Adjust coordinates depending on orientation.

    if(IsDlgButtonChecked(hDlg, IDC_PORTRAIT))
    {
        Rect.left   = RectPg.left + 1 + lpIP->Anchor.x;
        Rect.top    = RectPg.top  + 1 + lpIP->Anchor.y;
```

```
        Rect.right  = RectPg.left + 1 + lpIP->Anchor.x + lpIP->Width;
        Rect.bottom = RectPg.top  + 1 + lpIP->Anchor.y + lpIP->Height;
    }
    else
    {
        Rect.left   = RectPg.left   + 1 + lpIP->Anchor.y;
        Rect.top    = RectPg.bottom - 1 - lpIP->Anchor.x - lpIP->Width;
        Rect.right  = RectPg.left   + 1 + lpIP->Anchor.y + lpIP->Height;
        Rect.bottom = RectPg.bottom - 1 - lpIP->Anchor.x;
    }

    // Draw image representation, validate rect, and clean up

    hBrush = SelectObject(Paint.hdc, CreateSolidBrush(COLOR_MAGENTA));
    Rectangle(Paint.hdc, Rect.left, Rect.top, Rect.right, Rect.bottom);
    DeleteObject(SelectObject(Paint.hdc, hBrush));

    ValidateRect(hDlg, &RectPg);
    EndPaint(hDlg, &Paint);

    return(TRUE);

case WM_COMMAND :

    if(!(hGlobal = GetProp(hDlg, "Data")))
    {
        break;
    }

    lpIP = (LPIMAGEPARMS) GlobalLock(hGlobal);

    GetChildWindowRect(GetDlgItem(hDlg, IDC_PAGE), &RectPg);

    switch(wParam)
    {
        case IDCANCEL :

            if(IsWindowEnabled(GetDlgItem(hDlg, IDC_PRINT)))
            {
                SendMessage(hDlg, WM_CLOSE, 0, 0L);
            }

            return(TRUE);
```

```
case IDC_SETUP :

    // Display the printer's setup dialog box. We'll use our
    // second devmode structure to hold any possible chgd
    // values from the prt setup dialog. The only changes
    // we track are to orientation and #copies.
    // First, let's disable the print dialog so it can't
    // be closed while the printer setup dialog is displayed.

    EnableWindow(hDlg, FALSE);

    lpDevMode = (LPDEVMODE)
    (
        (LPSTR) lpIP->DevMode + lpIP->SizeOfDevMode
    );

    if
    (
        lpIP->ExtDeviceMode
        (
            hDlg,
            lpIP->hInstLib,
            lpDevMode,
            lpIP->DevMode->dmDeviceName,
            lpIP->DevPort,
            NULL,
            NULL,
            DM_IN_PROMPT ¦ DM_OUT_BUFFER
        ) == IDOK
    )
    {
        // Something was changed (at least OK was clicked).
        // Flag what might've been altered.

        lpDevMode->dmFields ¦= (DM_ORIENTATION ¦ DM_COPIES);

        // So update the printer.

        lpIP->ExtDeviceMode
        (
            NULL,
            lpIP->hInstLib,
            lpIP->DevMode,
            lpIP->DevMode->dmDeviceName,
            lpIP->DevPort,
```

```
                lpDevMode,
                NULL,
                DM_IN_BUFFER | DM_OUT_BUFFER
            );

            // Now update the printer dialog.

            UpdatePrinter(hDlg);
        }

        // Re-enable the print dialog and make it active. Since
        // the print dialog wasn't linked to the printer
        // setup dialog, another window could accidentally
        // be on top.

        EnableWindow(hDlg, TRUE);

        return(TRUE);

    case IDC_ASPECT :

        // Adjust image's aspect ratio & cause a repaint.

        lpIP->Height = (WORD)
        (
            (float) lpIP->Width *
            (float) lpIP->bmHeight /
            (float) lpIP->bmWidth
        );

        InvalidateRect(hDlg, &RectPg, TRUE);

        return(TRUE);

    case IDC_PORTRAIT  :
    case IDC_LANDSCAPE :

        // Cause a paint to occur when the orientation changes.

        InvalidateRect(hDlg, &RectPg, TRUE);

        return(TRUE);

    case IDC_PRINT :

        // Before we print the image, set the focus to the
```

```
                    // cancel button and disable the print button.

                    SendMessage(hDlg, WM_NEXTDLGCTL, GetDlgItem(hDlg, IDCANCEL), 1L);
                    UpdateWindow(hDlg);

                    EnableWindow(GetDlgItem(hDlg, IDC_PRINT), FALSE);
                    PrintImage(hDlg, lpIP);
                    EnableWindow(GetDlgItem(hDlg, IDC_PRINT), TRUE);

                    return(TRUE);

                case IDC_RESET :

                    // Set page size back to default of 1:1 & cause a paint.

                    lpIP->Anchor.x = lpIP->Anchor.y = 0;

                    lpIP->Width = (WORD)
                    (
                        (float) lpIP->bmWidth *
                        (float) (RectPg.right - RectPg.left) /
                        (float) lpIP->Page.x
                    );

                    lpIP->Height = (WORD)
                    (
                        (float) lpIP->bmHeight *
                        (float) (RectPg.bottom - RectPg.top) /
                        (float) lpIP->Page.y
                    );

                    InvalidateRect(hDlg, &RectPg, TRUE);

                    return(TRUE);

                default :

                    break;
            }
            break;

        case WM_CLOSE :

            // Free our printer driver, the image data structure, and destroy
            // the dialog.
```

```
            hGlobal = RemoveProp(hDlg, "Data");
            lpIP    = (LPIMAGEPARMS) GlobalLock(hGlobal);

            FreeLibrary(lpIP->hInstLib);
            GlobalFree(hGlobal);

            EndDialog(hDlg, TRUE);

            return(TRUE);

        default :

            break;
    }

    return(FALSE);
}


/*****************************************************************************
    FUNCTION: UpdatePrinter
    PURPOSE : Gets new printer config, and changes prt dialog based on info.
*****************************************************************************/

int WINAPI UpdatePrinter(HWND hDlg)
{
    HDC           hDCPrtr;
    RECT          RectPage;
    LPIMAGEPARMS  lpIP;

    // Get a pointer to our IMAGEPARMS struct (which contains a DEVMODE
    // struct). It's available via a handle stored in a print dialog window
    // property.

    lpIP = (LPIMAGEPARMS) GlobalLock(GetProp(hDlg, "Data"));

    if
    (
        !(hDCPrtr = CreateDC
        (
            lpIP->DevName,
            lpIP->DevMode->dmDeviceName,
            lpIP->DevPort,
            lpIP->DevMode
```

```
        ))
    )
    {
        MessageBox
        (
            GetActiveWindow(), "No default printer", "ERROR", MB_OK ¦ MB_ICONHAND
        );

        return(1);
    }

    // Get page size of prtr & delete the dc since we no longer need it.

    lpIP->Page.x = GetDeviceCaps(hDCPrtr, HORZRES);
    lpIP->Page.y = GetDeviceCaps(hDCPrtr, VERTRES);

    DPtoLP(hDCPrtr, &lpIP->Page, 1);

    DeleteDC(hDCPrtr);

    // Get dimensions of our "page" window representation in the prt dialog.

    GetChildWindowRect(GetDlgItem(hDlg, IDC_PAGE), &RectPage);

    // Anchor the image to print and set up its default size based on
    // the printer page size.

    lpIP->Anchor.x = lpIP->Anchor.y = 0;

    lpIP->Width = (WORD)
    (
        (float) lpIP->bmWidth *
        (float) (RectPage.right - RectPage.left) /
        (float) lpIP->Page.x
    );

    lpIP->Height = (WORD)
    (
        (float) lpIP->bmHeight *
        (float) (RectPage.bottom - RectPage.top) /
        (float) lpIP->Page.y
    );

    // Update the portrait/landscape orientation with what the prtr thinks
    // and adjust the # of copies too.
```

```
    if(lpIP->DevMode->dmOrientation == DMORIENT_PORTRAIT)
    {
        PostMessage(GetDlgItem(hDlg, IDC_PORTRAIT), WM_LBUTTONDOWN, 0, 0L);
        PostMessage(GetDlgItem(hDlg, IDC_PORTRAIT), WM_LBUTTONUP, 0, 0L);
    }
    else
    {
        PostMessage(GetDlgItem(hDlg, IDC_LANDSCAPE), WM_LBUTTONDOWN, 0, 0L);
        PostMessage(GetDlgItem(hDlg, IDC_LANDSCAPE), WM_LBUTTONUP, 0, 0L);
    }

    SetDlgItemInt(hDlg, IDC_COPIES, lpIP->DevMode->dmCopies, FALSE);

    return(0);
}


/*****************************************************************************
    FUNCTION: SinkControl
    PURPOSE : Paints control as if it's sunken down into the dialog.
 *****************************************************************************/

int WINAPI SinkControl(HWND hWnd, HDC hDC, int Thick, int Gap)
{
    RECT Rect;
    HDC  hDCToUse;
    HWND hWndParent;
    DWORD dwOrg;

    hWndParent = GetParent(hWnd);

    // If they didn't supply a DC, create one, and set origin.

    hDCToUse = (hDC) ? hDC : GetDC(hWndParent);
    dwOrg = GetOrigin(hWndParent);
    SetWindowOrg(hDCToUse, (int) LOWORD(dwOrg), (int) HIWORD(dwOrg));

    // Get dimensions of child & space 3-D effect around it accordingly.

    GetChildWindowRect(hWnd, &Rect);
    InflateRect(&Rect, Gap, Gap);
    SinkRect(&Rect, hDCToUse, Thick);

    // Free temp dc if one was created.
```

```
    if(!hDC)
    {
        ReleaseDC(hWndParent, hDCToUse);
    }

    return(0);
}


/*****************************************************************************
   FUNCTION: SinkRect
   PURPOSE : Visually "sinks" region of window "in" or "out."
*****************************************************************************/

int WINAPI SinkRect(LPRECT lpRect, HDC hDC, int Thick)
{
    HPEN hPen;
    int  i;

    // Select shading color for "light" portion of 3-D effect.

    hPen = SelectObject
    (
        hDC,
        CreatePen
        (
            PS_SOLID,
            1,
            GetSysColor((Thick > 0) ? COLOR_BTNSHADOW : COLOR_BTNHIGHLIGHT)
        )
    );

    // Draw one L-shaped portion of frame.

    for(i = 1; i <= abs(Thick); ++i)
    {
        MoveTo(hDC, lpRect->left - i, lpRect->bottom + i - 1);
        LineTo(hDC, lpRect->left - i, lpRect->top - i);
        LineTo(hDC, lpRect->right + i - 1, lpRect->top - i);
    }

    // Select another shading color.

    DeleteObject
```

```
        (
            SelectObject
            (
                hDC,
                CreatePen
                (
                    PS_SOLID,
                    1,
                    GetSysColor((Thick > 0) ? COLOR_BTNHIGHLIGHT : COLOR_BTNSHADOW)
                )
            )
        );

        // Draw other L-shaped portion of frame.

        for(i = 1; i <= abs(Thick); ++i)
        {
            MoveTo(hDC, lpRect->right + i - 1, lpRect->top - i);
            LineTo(hDC, lpRect->right + i - 1, lpRect->bottom + i - 1);
            LineTo(hDC, lpRect->left - i, lpRect->bottom + i - 1);
        }

        // Cleanup time!

        DeleteObject(SelectObject(hDC, hPen));

        return(0);
}


/*****************************************************************************
    FUNCTION: WindowToClipboard
    PURPOSE : Copies window to clipboard.
*****************************************************************************/

int WINAPI WindowToClipboard(HWND hWnd, HWND hWndApp)
{
    HDC     hDC;
    HDC     hDCMemory;
    RECT    Rect;
    HBITMAP hBmpOld;
    HBITMAP hBmpClipboard;
    BOOL    WasIconic;
    int     Width, Height;
```

```
    // If iconic, make normal.

    if(IsIconic(hWnd))
    {
        WasIconic = TRUE;
        ShowWindow(hWnd, SW_RESTORE);
    }
    else
    {
        WasIconic = FALSE;
    }

    // Bring window to forefront and pos it at 0,0 before we
    // copy it to the clipboard. Then move it back to where
    // it was.

    GetWindowRect(hWnd, &Rect);

    Width  = Rect.right - Rect.left;
    Height = Rect.bottom - Rect.top;

    if(!IsZoomed(hWnd))
    {
        SetWindowPos(hWnd, NULL, 0, 0, 0, 0, SWP_NOZORDER | SWP_NOSIZE);
    }

    SetActiveWindow(hWnd);
    UpdateWindow(hWnd);

    // Create DC and copy window to it & hBmp.

    hDC       = GetWindowDC(hWnd);
    hDCMemory = CreateCompatibleDC(hDC);

    hBmpClipboard = CreateCompatibleBitmap(hDC, Width, Height);

    hBmpOld = SelectObject(hDCMemory, hBmpClipboard);

    BitBlt(hDCMemory, 0, 0, Width, Height, hDC, 0, 0, SRCCOPY);

    // Open clipboard and put bitmap inside, then do cleanup.

    BitmapToClipboard(hBmpClipboard, hWndApp);

    SelectObject(hDCMemory, hBmpOld);
```

```
    DeleteDC(hDCMemory);
    ReleaseDC(hWnd, hDC);

    // Reposition window.

    if(!IsZoomed(hWnd))
    {
        SetWindowPos(hWnd, NULL, Rect.left, Rect.top, 0, 0, SWP_NOZORDER | SWP_NOSIZE);
    }

    if(WasIconic)
    {
        ShowWindow(hWnd, SW_MINIMIZE);
    }

    UpdateWindow(hWnd);

    return(0);
}


/*****************************************************************************
    FUNCTION: CreateAndRegisterDialog
    PURPOSE : Creates a dialog used by STDWIN.
*****************************************************************************/

HWND WINAPI CreateAndRegisterDialog
(
    HINSTANCE hInst,
    LPSTR     Template,
    HWND      hWndParent,
    WNDPROC   lpProc,
    HICON     hIcon,
    HBRUSH    hBrush,
    WORD      ClassExtra,
    WORD      WndExtra,
    BOOL      RegisterTheClass
)
{
    // Register my dialog class.

    if(RegisterTheClass)
    {
        WNDCLASS wc;
```

```
        wc.hInstance     = hInst;
        wc.style         = CS_DBLCLKS | CS_GLOBALCLASS;
        wc.lpszMenuName  = NULL;
        wc.lpszClassName = Template;
        wc.lpfnWndProc   = lpProc;
        wc.hCursor       = LoadCursor(NULL, IDC_ARROW);
        wc.cbClsExtra    = ClassExtra;
        wc.cbWndExtra    = DLGWINDOWEXTRA + WndExtra;
        wc.hbrBackground = hBrush;
        wc.hIcon         = hIcon;

        if(!RegisterClass(&wc))
        {
            return(NULL);
        }
    }

    return(CreateDialogParam(hInst, Template, hWndParent, 0L, 0L));
}


/****************************************************************************
    FUNCTION: AtomicDialogWndFn
    PURPOSE : Wnd proc for special dialog.
****************************************************************************/

LRESULT WINAPI AtomicDialogWndFn(HWND hDlg, UINT uMsg, WPARAM wParam,
                                 LPARAM lParam)
{
    RECT Rect;
    RECT RectWnd;
    RECT GroupBox;

    HINSTANCE hInstDlg;

    HBITMAP hBmp;
    HBITMAP hBmpOld;
    HBITMAP hBmpCaption;
    HBRUSH   hBrush;
    HBRUSH hBrushSys;
    HBRUSH hBrushCap;
    HPEN    hPen;
    HDC     hDCMemory;
    HDC     hDC;
    HDC     hDCCaption;
```

```
    LONG lResult;
    LONG lStyle;

    int Size3D;
    int OldBkMode;
    int Margin;
    int SizeLabel;
    int Width, Height;
    int FrameWidth;
    int FrameHeight;
    int BorderWidth;
    int BorderHeight;
    int WidgetWidth;
    int WidgetHeight;
    int CaptionHeight;

    int CtrlID;

    PAINTSTRUCT Paint;

    COLORREF TextColor;

    DWORD dwOrg;
    DWORD dwSize;

    BOOL IsActive;

    WORD Style;

    BYTE WndText[60];

    HANDLE hResInfo;
    static HANDLE hResData;

    LONG HitCode;

    BYTE Class[20];

    HWND hWnd;
    HWND hWndTemp;

    LPSTR lpBuffer;
    LPSTR lpszString;

    POINT Pt;
```

```
// Process custom messages.

if(uMsg == WM_GETSIZE)
{
    // Determine the "virtual" size of the dialog. This size includes
    // the "lasso'd" size of all the controls on the dialog. At a
    // minimum it is the current size of the dialog plus the scrolled
    // off client portion.

    GetClientRect(hDlg, &RectWnd);

    Pt.x = RectWnd.right;
    Pt.y = RectWnd.bottom;
    hWnd = GetWindow(hDlg, GW_CHILD);

    while(hWnd)
    {
        // If a window is hidden, don't include it in our
        // determination of how to set the scroll bar ranges.

        if(IsWindowVisible(hWnd))
        {
            // The coordinates returned by GetChildWindowRect are
            // "virtual" coordinates, with respect to the hDlg's DC origin.

            GetChildWindowRect(hWnd, &Rect);

            if(Rect.right > Pt.x)
            {
                Pt.x = Rect.right;
            }

            if(Rect.bottom > Pt.y)
            {
                Pt.y = Rect.bottom;
            }
        }

        hWnd = GetWindow(hWnd, GW_HWNDNEXT);
    }

    if(Pt.x != RectWnd.right || Pt.y != RectWnd.bottom)
    {
```

```
        // A 5-pixel slop amount is added for scrollable dialogs. The
        // dialog is assumed to be scrollable if one of the controls
        // extends past the edge of the dialog. Dialogs that have
        // controls that are VERT or HORZ size-to-fit will never have
        // controls extending past the edge of the dialog. If we just
        // went and added this +5 slop to a size-to-fit dialog, it
        // would add scroll bars to the dialog, which isn't needed
        // when the controls are size-to-fit.

        Pt.x += 5;
        Pt.y += 5;
    }


    return(MAKELONG(Pt.x, Pt.y));
}


// Process messages.

switch(uMsg)
{
    case DM_SETDEFID :

        if(CtrlID = (int) GetProp(hDlg, "Default"))
        {
            // Undefault any old default button

            SendDlgItemMessage
            (
                hDlg, CtrlID, BM_SETSTYLE, LOWORD(BS_PUSHBUTTON), 1L
            );
        }

        // Set new default button ctrl for dialog & inform it of new style.

        SetProp(hDlg, "Default", wParam);

        SendDlgItemMessage
        (
            hDlg, wParam, BM_SETSTYLE, LOWORD(BS_DEFPUSHBUTTON), 1L
        );

        return(0L);
```

```
                    case DM_GETDEFID :
                        if(CtrlID = (int) GetProp(hDlg, "Default"))
                        {
                            return(MAKELONG(CtrlID, DC_HASDEFID));
                        }

                        return(0L);

                case WM_VSCROLL :
                case WM_HSCROLL :

                        ProcessScrollBars(hDlg, uMsg, wParam, lParam);
                        return(0);

                case WM_MEASUREITEM :

                        return
                        (
                            SendMessage
                            (
                                GetDlgItem(hDlg, ((LPMEASUREITEMSTRUCT) lParam)->CtlID),
                                uMsg,
                                wParam,
                                lParam
                            )
                        );

                        break;

                case WM_DRAWITEM :

                        return
                        (
                            SendMessage
                            (
                                ((LPDRAWITEMSTRUCT) lParam)->hwndItem,
                                uMsg,
                                wParam,
                                lParam
                            )
                        );

                        break;
```

```
case WM_NCHITTEST :

    // Let the client area drag the window as the caption does.

    if((HitCode = DefDlgProc(hDlg, uMsg, wParam, lParam)) == HTCLIENT)
    {
        HitCode = HTCAPTION;
    }

    return(HitCode);

case WM_SETCURSOR :

    // We don't alter the cursor for non-3-D dialogs.

    if(!(GetProp(hDlg, "Style") & WS_3D))
    {
        break;
    }

    switch(LOWORD(lParam))
    {
        case HTSYSMENU :

            // When we're hovering over the system menu, change the
            // cursor to a "box within a box."

            SetCursor(LoadCursor(NULL, IDC_ICON));
            return(1);

        case HTCAPTION :

            // When we're hovering over the caption bar, change the
            // cursor to a hand, indicating that the window can be
            // dragged. The only exception is when the window is
            // maximized, in which case we don't use a hand, and
            // leave the cursor as an arrow.

            if(!IsZoomed(hDlg) && !IsIconic(hDlg))
            {
                SetCursor(LoadCursor(hInstSTDWIN, "Hand"));
                return(1);
            }
            break;
```

```
        default :

            break;
    }
    break;

case WM_ENTERIDLE :

    // We don't do 3-D for non-3-D dialogs.

    if(!(GetProp(hDlg, "Style") & WS_3D))
    {
        break;
    }

    if
    (
        (GetWindowLong(hDlg, GWL_STYLE) & WS_SYSMENU) &&
        wParam != MSGF_DIALOGBOX
    )
    {
        // When we drop the system menu down, force the cursor into
        // an arrow. Otherwise it tries to use the cursor used for
        // the caption. This overrides Windows behavior.

        SetCursor(LoadCursor(NULL, IDC_ARROW));

        // In addition, set a property indicating that we won't need
        // to perform a paint when we get a WM_NCPAINT, since the
        // default behavior by Windows for the system menu is to
        // do a PatBlt or InvertRect, which would invalidate any
        // painting we were to do. If we were managing the system
        // menu COMPLETELY by ourselves, testing the NCHITS and stuff,
        // then this step would be unnecessary.

        SetProp(hDlg, "HitTest", 1);
    }
    break;

case WM_MENUSELECT :

    // We don't do 3-D for non-3-D dialogs

    if(!(GetProp(hDlg, "Style") & WS_3D))
    {
        break;
    }
```

```
    if(GetWindowLong(hDlg, GWL_STYLE) & WS_SYSMENU)
    {
        if(((int) LOWORD(lParam) == -1) && !wParam)
        {
            // If the menu was cleared by an ESC or wayward mouse
            // press, then remove our temporary window property.

            RemoveProp(hDlg, "HitTest");
        }
    }
    break;

case WM_NCPAINT    :
case WM_NCACTIVATE :

    // We do no painting when the window is iconized or for non-3-D
    // dialogs. We also don't do it when the window doesn't have a
    // system menu or caption.

    if
    (
        IsIconic(hDlg) || !(GetProp(hDlg, "Style") & WS_3D) ||
        !((lStyle = GetWindowLong(hDlg, GWL_STYLE)) & WIDGETS)
    )
    {
        break;
    }

    if(uMsg == WM_NCPAINT && RemoveProp(hDlg, "HitTest"))
    {
        // When the system menu is ready to unactivate itself,
        // we don't want to intercept the NCPAINT message, since
        // it will PatBlt or whatever, and re-inverse whatever
        // color we end up painting. This is the reason
        // for the inclusion of the WM_MENUSELECT and WM_ENTERIDLE
        // message traps.

        break;
    }

    if
    (
        (uMsg == WM_NCACTIVATE && wParam) ||
        (uMsg == WM_NCPAINT && GetActiveWindow() == hDlg)
    )
```

```
{
    IsActive = TRUE;

    // Window is being made active, so select appropriate colors.

    hBrushSys = CreateSolidBrush(COLOR_YELLOW);
    hBrushCap = CreateSolidBrush(GetSysColor(COLOR_ACTIVECAPTION));
    TextColor = GetSysColor(COLOR_CAPTIONTEXT);

    hPen = CreatePen(PS_SOLID, 1, GetSysColor(COLOR_WINDOWFRAME));
}
else
{
    IsActive = FALSE;

    // Window is being made inactive.

    hBrushSys = CreateSolidBrush(COLOR_BROWN);
    hBrushCap = CreateSolidBrush(GetSysColor(COLOR_INACTIVECAPTION));
    TextColor = GetSysColor(COLOR_INACTIVECAPTIONTEXT);

    hPen = CreatePen(PS_SOLID, 1, GetSysColor(COLOR_WINDOWFRAME));
}

// Temporarily turn off the style bits for the system menu
// and for the caption, so the default window procedure doesn't
// attempt to draw them itself. This is the only way that
// painting methods can be inhibited for the non-client areas
// of a window, since only client areas have regions that can
// be validated. Re-adding the border bit ensures that a black
// line is drawn around the window's frame.

SetWindowLong(hDlg, GWL_STYLE, (lStyle ^= WIDGETS) | WS_BORDER);

lResult = DefWindowProc(hDlg, uMsg, wParam, lParam);

SetWindowLong(hDlg, GWL_STYLE, lStyle |= WIDGETS);

// Get dimensions of various window widgets.

BorderWidth   = GetSystemMetrics(SM_CXBORDER);
BorderHeight  = GetSystemMetrics(SM_CYBORDER);
FrameWidth    = GetSystemMetrics(SM_CXFRAME);
```

```
FrameHeight   = GetSystemMetrics(SM_CYFRAME);
WidgetWidth   = GetSystemMetrics(SM_CXSIZE);
WidgetHeight  = GetSystemMetrics(SM_CYSIZE);
CaptionHeight = GetSystemMetrics(SM_CYCAPTION);

// If the dialog is 3-D, then use a small 3-D effect for caption
// and system menu.

Size3D = (GetProp(hDlg, "Style") & WS_3D) ? 2 : 0;

// Get a Window DC and start drawing stuff.

GetWindowRect(hDlg, &RectWnd);

hDC          = GetWindowDC(hDlg);
hDCCaption   = CreateCompatibleDC(hDC);
hBmpCaption  = CreateCompatibleBitmap
(
    hDC,
    (RectWnd.right - RectWnd.left) - FrameWidth * 2,
    CaptionHeight
);
hBmpCaption = SelectObject(hDCCaption, hBmpCaption);

// Draw a black single-pixel RECT frame around our window widgets,
// which includes the system menu, caption, and min/max btns.
// Since we're handling the non-client drawing ourself, we need
// to do this. All Windows does for us is draw the outer frame.

SetRect
(
    &Rect, 0, 0, (RectWnd.right - RectWnd.left) - 1, CaptionHeight - 1
);

hPen = SelectObject(hDCCaption, hPen);

Rectangle
(
    hDCCaption, Rect.left, Rect.top, Rect.right, Rect.bottom
);

// Additionally, draw a single-pixel separator line between the
// system menu and the caption.
```

```
MoveTo(hDCCaption, WidgetWidth, 0);
LineTo(hDCCaption, WidgetWidth, WidgetHeight);
DeleteObject(SelectObject(hDCCaption, hPen));

// Draw a new system menu.

SetRect(&Rect, 0, 0, WidgetWidth, WidgetHeight);
FillRect(hDCCaption, &Rect, hBrushSys);
DeleteObject(hBrushSys);
InflateRect(&Rect, -Size3D, -Size3D);
SinkRect(&Rect, hDCCaption, (IsActive) ? -Size3D : Size3D);

// Draw a new-style caption. First, determine the caption's
// dimensions and fill it with a color and sink it 3-D style.
// The "algorithm" used to determine the caption width could
// be MUCH improved by dynamically checking window style bits,
// and altering things accordingly. This example assumes a
// thick-framed window with sysmenu, caption, min and max buttons.

SetRect
(
    &Rect,
    WidgetWidth + BorderWidth,
    0,
    (RectWnd.right - RectWnd.left) -
        2 * (WidgetWidth + BorderWidth + FrameWidth),
    CaptionHeight - BorderHeight * 2
);

FillRect(hDCCaption, &Rect, hBrushCap);
DeleteObject(hBrushCap);
InflateRect(&Rect, -Size3D, -Size3D);
SinkRect(&Rect, hDCCaption, (IsActive) ? -Size3D : Size3D);
InflateRect(&Rect, Size3D, Size3D);

// Draw the caption text.

GetWindowText(hDlg, WndText, sizeof(WndText));

OldBkMode = SetBkMode(hDCCaption, TRANSPARENT);
TextColor = SetTextColor(hDCCaption, TextColor);

DrawText
```

```
(
    hDCCaption,
    WndText,
    -1,
    &Rect,
    DT_SINGLELINE ¦ DT_CENTER ¦ DT_VCENTER
);

SetTextColor(hDCCaption, TextColor);
SetBkMode(hDCCaption, OldBkMode);

// Manually draw the minimize and maxmimize buttons.

hDCMemory = CreateCompatibleDC(hDCCaption);

hBmp = SelectObject
(
    hDCMemory,
    LoadBitmap(NULL, MAKEINTRESOURCE(OBM_REDUCE))
);

Rect.left  = Rect.right;
Rect.right = Rect.left + WidgetWidth;

// Transfer the minimize arrow to the window DC. I had to add
// a one here since GetSystemMetrics returned a value one less
// than the actual arrow bitmap did through GetObject. Then move
// rect over for next button.

BitBlt
(
    hDCCaption,
    Rect.left,
    Rect.top,
    WidgetWidth + 1,
    WidgetHeight,
    hDCMemory,
    0,
    0,
    SRCCOPY
);

Rect.left  = Rect.right + BorderWidth;
Rect.right = Rect.left + WidgetWidth;
```

```
// Delete the old bitmap and load the approp. new one.

DeleteObject
(
    SelectObject
    (
        hDCMemory,
        LoadBitmap
        (
            NULL,
            MAKEINTRESOURCE(IsZoomed(hDlg) ? OBM_RESTORE : OBM_ZOOM)
        )
    )
);

// Transfer it to the screen. By the way...similar to how the
// background is erased for the main dialog, you might want
// to collect all the drawing output into a single hMemDC and
// then BitBlt it in one operation to the screen DC.

BitBlt
(
    hDCCaption,
    Rect.left,
    Rect.top,
    WidgetWidth + 1,
    WidgetHeight,
    hDCMemory,
    0,
    0,
    SRCCOPY
);

// Now copy everything accumulated in hDCMemory to the screen.

BitBlt
(
    hDC,
    FrameWidth,
    FrameHeight,
    (RectWnd.right - RectWnd.left) - FrameWidth * 2,
    CaptionHeight - 1,
    hDCCaption,
    0,
    0,
```

```
        SRCCOPY
    );

    // Free everything up and leave!

    DeleteObject(SelectObject(hDCMemory, hBmp));
    DeleteDC(hDCMemory);
    DeleteObject(SelectObject(hDCCaption, hBmpCaption));
    DeleteDC(hDCCaption);
    ReleaseDC(hDlg, hDC);

    return(lResult);

case WM_SIZE :

    // If the top-level window has scroll bars, then every time the
    // window is resized, we need to compute new scroll bar extents
    // for scrolling around the child controls inside the window.
    // NOTE: Never, never do any function that will cause the parent
    // window to change sizes. This includes the obvious things like
    // calling SetWindowPos and MoveWindow from this method, and
    // it also includes things like enabling/disabling the scroll
    // bars. Doing any of these functions will cause a stack fault.

    Width  = LOWORD(lParam);
    Height = HIWORD(lParam);

    if(hWndTemp = GetProp(hDlg, "Zoomed"))
    {
        hWnd = GetWindow(hDlg, GW_CHILD);

        while(hWnd)
        {
            if(hWnd == hWndTemp)
            {
                // If we resize the parent window and there's a child
                // that's zoomed, we need to rezoom it.

                SetWindowPos(hWnd, NULL, 0, 0, Width, Height, SWP_NOZORDER);
                break;
            }

            hWnd = GetWindow(hWnd, GW_HWNDNEXT);
        }

        break;
```

```
        }

        // Whenever a parent dialog is sized, we need to reposition any
        // controls defined with the SIZEHORZ or SIZEVERT attributes, as
        // well as rezoom any control that happens to be the zoomed one.

        hWnd = GetWindow(hDlg, GW_CHILD);

        while(hWnd)
        {
            // Tell controls to resize themselves & redraw their label.

            SendMessage(hWnd, WM_RESIZE, 0, 0L);

            // Get next child in dialog, and loop through them all...

            hWnd = GetWindow(hWnd, GW_HWNDNEXT);
        }

        // Adjust scroll bar ranges when dialog is resized, possibly
        // changing the client area's origin too.

        CalcScrollBars(hDlg);

        break;

    case WM_CREATE :

        hInstDlg = GetWindowWord(hDlg, GWW_HINSTANCE);

        GetClassName(hDlg, Class, sizeof(Class));

        // Get a ptr to dialog's special resource data. This data is what
        // customizes the dialog. The ID of the private definition
        // struct for the dialog is the dialog class name, unlike for
        // controls, where the struct is id'd by the CtrlID itself.

        if(!(hResInfo = FindResource(hInstDlg, Class, RT_RCDATA)))
        {
            break;
        }

        if(!(hResData = LoadResource(hInstDlg, hResInfo)))
        {
            break;
```

```
    }

    if(!(lpBuffer = LockResource(hResData)))
    {
        FreeResource(hResData);
        break;
    }

    // Add ext style stuff from cust res for ctrl. This is the only
    // way that parasited ctrls can be extended.

    Style = 0;

    while(*((LPWORD) lpBuffer))
    {
        Style |= *((LPWORD) lpBuffer);

        lpBuffer += sizeof(WORD);
    }

    lpBuffer += sizeof(WORD);
    SetProp(hDlg, "Style", Style);

    // Set dialog's bkgrd brush color, and adv ptr.

    if(!GetClassWord(hDlg, GCW_HBRBACKGROUND))
    {
        SetClassWord
        (
            hDlg,
            GCW_HBRBACKGROUND,
            CreateSolidBrush(*((LPDWORD) lpBuffer))
        );
    }

    SetProp(hDlg, "RGBlo", LOWORD(*((LPDWORD) lpBuffer)));
    SetProp(hDlg, "RGBhi", HIWORD(*((LPDWORD) lpBuffer)));
    lpBuffer += sizeof(DWORD);

    // Set size of the following items: thickness of 3-D effect,
    // label thickness, label gap, font gap, groupbox gap,
    // resizable window/parent margin.

    SetProp(hDlg, "Size3D",    *((LPWORD) lpBuffer));
    lpBuffer += sizeof(WORD);
    SetProp(hDlg, "SizeLabel", *((LPWORD) lpBuffer));
```

```
            lpBuffer += sizeof(WORD);
            SetProp(hDlg, "LabelGap",  *((LPWORD) lpBuffer));
            lpBuffer += sizeof(WORD);
            SetProp(hDlg, "FontGap",   *((LPWORD) lpBuffer));
            lpBuffer += sizeof(WORD);
            SetProp(hDlg, "GrpGap",    *((LPWORD) lpBuffer));
            lpBuffer += sizeof(WORD);
            SetProp(hDlg, "SizingGap", *((LPWORD) lpBuffer));
            lpBuffer += sizeof(WORD);

            // Establish bkgrd bitmap, if any.

            if(*lpBuffer)
            {
                SetProp(hDlg, "Bitmap", LoadBitmap(hInstDlg, lpBuffer));
                lpBuffer += lstrlen(lpBuffer) + 1;
            }

            // Free up stuff.

            UnlockResource(hResData);
            FreeResource(hResData);

            break;

        case WM_DESTROY :

            // Clean up dialog tidbits.

            RemoveProp(hDlg, "xOrg");
            RemoveProp(hDlg, "yOrg");
            RemoveProp(hDlg, "Default");
            RemoveProp(hDlg, "HitTest");
            RemoveProp(hDlg, "Style");
            RemoveProp(hDlg, "RGBlo");
            RemoveProp(hDlg, "RGBhi");
            RemoveProp(hDlg, "Size3D");
            RemoveProp(hDlg, "SizeLabel");
            RemoveProp(hDlg, "LabelGap");
            RemoveProp(hDlg, "FontGap");
            RemoveProp(hDlg, "GrpGap");
            RemoveProp(hDlg, "SizingGap");
            RemoveProp(hDlg, "Zoomed");

            if((hBmp = RemoveProp(hDlg, "Bitmap")) != NULL)
            {
```

```
            DeleteObject(hBmp);
    }

    break;

case WM_ERASEBKGND :

    return(1);

case WM_PAINT :

    BeginPaint(hDlg, &Paint);

    // Determine "true" size of dialog client area, and create
    // appropriate bitmaps & origin settings.

    dwSize = SendMessage(hDlg, WM_GETSIZE, 0, 0L);
    SetRect(&RectWnd, 0, 0, LOWORD(dwSize), HIWORD(dwSize));

    hDC     = CreateCompatibleDC(Paint.hdc);
    hBmpOld = SelectObject
    (
        hDC,
        CreateCompatibleBitmap
        (
            Paint.hdc, RectWnd.right - RectWnd.left,
            RectWnd.bottom - RectWnd.top
        )
    );

    dwOrg = GetOrigin(hDlg);
    SetWindowOrg(Paint.hdc, LOWORD(dwOrg), HIWORD(dwOrg));
    SetWindowOrg(hDC, (int)LOWORD(dwOrg), (int)HIWORD(dwOrg));
    OffsetRect(&Paint.rcPaint, (int)LOWORD(dwOrg), (int)HIWORD(dwOrg));

    // Paint the stretched, centered, or tiled bitmap bkgrd.

    PaintBitmap(hDlg, hDC, &RectWnd);

    // Get a ptr to dialog's special resource data. This data is what
    // customizes the dialog. Use it to get to groupbox information.

    hInstDlg = GetWindowWord(hDlg, GWW_HINSTANCE);
    GetClassName(hDlg, Class, sizeof(Class));

    if
    (
```

```
        !(hResInfo = FindResource(hInstDlg, Class, RT_RCDATA)) ¦¦
        !(hResData = LoadResource(hInstDlg, hResInfo))
)
{
    goto DOLABELS;
}


lpBuffer = LockResource(hResData);

// Advance ptr to group info through a series of steps.

while(*((LPWORD) lpBuffer))
{
    lpBuffer += sizeof(WORD);
}


lpBuffer += sizeof(WORD);      // Skip past last style null word

// Skip past colorref dwords & other word items.
// NOTE:!!!! This is very position dependent. If any extra bytes,
// words, or other tidbits are to be added to the custom res
// structure for a dialog, the bytes must be accounted for
// and skipped in this section. A series of #defines would
// make this section of code much less treacherous.

lpBuffer += sizeof(DWORD) + sizeof(WORD) * 6;
lpBuffer += lstrlen(lpBuffer) + 1;
Margin   = GetProp(hDlg, "GrpGap");
SizeLabel = GetProp(hDlg, "SizeLabel");


while(TRUE)
{
    if(!*lpBuffer)
    {
        break;
    }

    // Get groupbox title & brush.

    lpszString = lpBuffer;
    lpBuffer   += lstrlen(lpBuffer) + 1;
    hBrush      = CreateSolidBrush(*((LPDWORD) lpBuffer));
    lpBuffer   += sizeof(DWORD);

    // This loop determines how big our groupbox needs to be
    // in order to surround all its accompanying controls. It
```

```
// skims the CtrlIDs of every ctrl listed in the private
// groupbox res struct.

GroupBox.left = 0;

while(*((LPWORD) lpBuffer))
{
    RECT RectLabel;

    hWnd = GetDlgItem(hDlg, *((LPWORD) lpBuffer));

    // Get coords of ctrl and its label. Then use the
    // two RECTs to get an all-encompassing rect that covers
    // both areas.

    GetChildWindowRect(hWnd, &RectWnd);

    if(!GetCtrlLabelRect(hWnd, &RectLabel))
    {
        UnionRect(&Rect, &RectWnd, &RectLabel);
    }

    if(!GroupBox.left)
    {
        // Initialize groupbox rect to coords of first ctrl.

        CopyRect(&GroupBox, &Rect);
    }
    else
    {
        // Enlarge the groupbox rect whenever we encounter
        // a ctrl with coords outside the current groupbox
        // rect.

        if(Rect.left < GroupBox.left)
        {
            GroupBox.left = Rect.left;
        }

        if(Rect.top < GroupBox.top)
        {
            GroupBox.top = Rect.top;
        }

        if(Rect.right > GroupBox.right)
        {
```

```
                            GroupBox.right = Rect.right;
                    }

                    if(Rect.bottom > GroupBox.bottom)
                    {
                            GroupBox.bottom = Rect.bottom;
                    }
            }

            lpBuffer += sizeof(WORD);
        }

        // Expand groupbox around lasso'd ctrls by margin amts &
        // then fill with class bkgrd color brush.

        InflateRect(&GroupBox, Margin, Margin);
        FillRect(hDC, &GroupBox, hBrush);
        DeleteObject(hBrush);

        // 3-D the groupbox now.

        DrawRectLabel
        (
            hDlg,
            hDC,
            &GroupBox,
            lpszString,
            TRUE,
            GetClassWord(hDlg, GCW_HBRBACKGROUND)
        );

        SinkRect(&GroupBox, hDC, -SizeLabel);
        InflateRect(&GroupBox, -SizeLabel, -SizeLabel);

        lpBuffer += sizeof(WORD);
    }

    // Free up resource stuff.

    UnlockResource(hResData);
    FreeResource(hResData);

DOLABELS:
    // Do painting for 3-D effect of ctrls as well as for ctrl labels.
```

```
// This needs to be done here, in addition to during the WM_SIZE
// message for the control itself, since the 3-D effect and the
// ctrl's label are not actually a part of the control. Thus,
// if the label portion of a control were to be covered, and
// the control never gets a paint or update message, it would
// never be painted. However, in this case, the dialog always
// gets a paint message when some part of the dialog is covered
// up, which is why we paint labels and frames here too.

hWnd = GetWindow(hDlg, GW_CHILD);

while(hWnd)
{
    // Draw the 3-D frame around a ctrl (if WS_3D is set), and
    // draw the control's label if one is defined.

    SendMessage(hWnd, WM_DRAWFRAME, hDC, 0L);
    SendMessage(hWnd, WM_DRAWLABEL, hDC, 1L);

    hWnd = GetWindow(hWnd, GW_HWNDNEXT);
}

// Transfer our accumulated images onto the screen in a single
// BitBlt operation. This gives a nice "snap" effect. Then
// do cleanup.

BitBlt
(
    Paint.hdc,
    Paint.rcPaint.left,
    Paint.rcPaint.top,
    Paint.rcPaint.right - Paint.rcPaint.left,
    Paint.rcPaint.bottom - Paint.rcPaint.top,
    hDC,
    Paint.rcPaint.left,
    Paint.rcPaint.top,
    SRCCOPY
);

DeleteObject(SelectObject(hDC, hBmpOld));
DeleteDC(hDC);
EndPaint(hDlg, &Paint);

break;
```

```
        case WM_CTLCOLOR :

            // Handles painting of non-custom Windows built-in controls so
            // they still look good with our dialog. All this does is
            // brighten the ctrl by making it white when it's got the focus,
            // or otherwise using the bkgd color when it doesn't have the
            // focus. This could be removed when ALL custom controls are
            // used. However, using it adds a little flexibility.

            if(GetFocus() == (HWND) SendMessage(LOWORD(lParam), WM_GETFOCUS, 0, 0L))
            {
                SetBkColor((HDC) wParam, COLOR_WHITE);
                return(GetStockObject(WHITE_BRUSH));
            }

            SetBkColor
            (
                (HDC) wParam,
                MAKELONG(GetProp(hDlg, "RGBlo"), GetProp(hDlg, "RGBhi"))
            );

            return(GetClassWord(hDlg, GCW_HBRBACKGROUND));

        default :

            break;
    }

    return(DefDlgProc(hDlg, uMsg, wParam, lParam));
}


/*****************************************************************************
    FUNCTION: PaintBitmap
    PURPOSE : Paints bitmap into based on its style (tiled, etc.).
*****************************************************************************/

int WINAPI PaintBitmap(HWND hWnd, HDC hDC, LPRECT lpRect)
{
    BITMAP  Bmp;
    HBITMAP hBmp;
    HDC     hDCMem;
    WORD    Style;
    int     i, j;

    Style = GetProp(hWnd, "Style");
```

```
if(!(Style & (BS_TILED ¦ BS_STRETCHED)))
{
    // We have to fill in the background since a centered
    // bitmap doesn't cover the whole parent client area.
    // We also need to fill it when no bitmap bkgrds have
    // been defined at all.

    FillRect(hDC, lpRect, GetClassWord(hWnd, GCW_HBRBACKGROUND));
}

if(Style & (BS_TILED ¦ BS_CENTERED ¦ BS_STRETCHED))
{
    // We're painting a bitmap into the dialog client area.

    hBmp    = GetProp(hWnd, "Bitmap");
    GetObject(hBmp, sizeof(Bmp), &Bmp);
    hDCMem = CreateCompatibleDC(hDC);
    hBmp    = SelectObject(hDCMem, hBmp);

    switch(Style & (BS_TILED ¦ BS_CENTERED ¦ BS_STRETCHED))
    {
        case BS_TILED :

            for
            (
                i = lpRect->left; i <= lpRect->right; i += Bmp.bmWidth
            )
            {
                for
                (
                    j = lpRect->top; j <= lpRect->bottom; j += Bmp.bmHeight
                )
                {
                    BitBlt
                    (
                        hDC,
                        i,
                        j,
                        Bmp.bmWidth,
                        Bmp.bmHeight,
                        hDCMem,
                        0,
                        0,
                        SRCCOPY
                    );
                }
```

```
        }

        break;

    case BS_CENTERED :

        // Center the bitmap.

        BitBlt
        (
            hDC,
            (lpRect->right - lpRect->left) / 2 - Bmp.bmWidth / 2,
            (lpRect->bottom - lpRect->top) / 2 - Bmp.bmHeight / 2,
            Bmp.bmWidth,
            Bmp.bmHeight,
            hDCMem,
            0,
            0,
            SRCCOPY
        );

        break;

    case BS_STRETCHED :

        // Stretch the bitmap into the client area.

        StretchBlt
        (
            hDC,
            0,
            0,
            lpRect->right - lpRect->left,
            lpRect->bottom - lpRect->top,
            hDCMem,
            0,
            0,
            Bmp.bmWidth,
            Bmp.bmHeight,
            SRCCOPY
        );

        break;
    }
```

```
        SelectObject(hDCMem, hBmp);
        DeleteDC(hDCMem);
    }

    return(0);
}


/****************************************************************************
    FUNCTION: AtomicControlWndFn
    PURPOSE : Wnd proc for all Atomic controls.
****************************************************************************/

LRESULT WINAPI AtomicControlWndFn(HWND hWnd, UINT uMsg, WPARAM wParam,
                                  LPARAM lParam)
{
    BYTE Class[30];

    HWND hWndParent;
    HWND hWndChild;

    RECT Rect;
    RECT RectChild;

    static BYTE Text[40];

    BYTE *ptr;

    BOOL Resize;

    ATOM hAtom;

    int Width, Height;
    int Amt;
    int Margin;
    int Size3D;

    WORD AtomicStyle;
    LONG Style;

    MSG msg;

    HBRUSH hBrush;
```

```
        static RECT RectCtrl;

        // Process custom messages.

        if(uMsg == WM_GETFOCUS)
        {
            // This message determines which window in a composite control
            // (like the combobox) has the focus. This isn't always the main
            // window. However, for any windows letting the message fall down
            // to here it is. The combobox, for example, intercepts this message
            // and returns the appropriate hWndFocus.

            return((LRESULT) hWnd);
        }


        if(uMsg == WM_DRAWLABEL)
        {
            DrawCtrlLabel(hWnd, (HDC) wParam, (BOOL) lParam);
            return(0);
        }


        if(uMsg == WM_RESIZE)
        {
            // The amount of margin between a size control and the
            // parent dialog is determined here. Normally the amt
            // is defined by Margin, except for grab bars, which are
            // often sized along with other windows when the parent
            // dialog is stretched outward. The grab bar should
            // extend just a little more since it never has a 3-D
            // non-client area.

            AtomicStyle = GetProp(hWnd, "Style");

            if(!(AtomicStyle & WS_SIZEHORZ) && !(AtomicStyle & WS_SIZEVERT))
            {
                return(0);
            }

            hWndParent = GetParent(hWnd);

            Margin = GetProp(hWndParent, "SizingGap");
            Size3D = GetProp(hWndParent, "Size3D");

            Margin -= lParam;
```

```
// Invalidate around ctrl so 3-D effect gets removed in the cases
// where the ctrl is shrunk in a little...

GetClientRect(hWndParent, &Rect);
GetChildWindowRect(hWnd, &RectChild);

Width  = RectChild.right - RectChild.left;
Height = RectChild.bottom - RectChild.top;

Resize = FALSE;

if(AtomicStyle & WS_SIZEHORZ)
{
    Amt = Rect.right - RectChild.right;

    Resize = TRUE;

    if(Amt < Margin)
    {
        RectChild.right  += Amt;
        RectChild.top    -= Size3D;
        RectChild.bottom += Size3D;

        InvalidateRect(hWndParent, &RectChild, FALSE);

        RectChild.right  -= Amt;
        RectChild.top    += Size3D;
        RectChild.bottom -= Size3D;

        ValidateRect(hWndParent, &RectChild);
    }

    Width = Rect.right - RectChild.left - Margin;
}

// Possibly resize child window.

if(AtomicStyle & WS_SIZEVERT)
{
    Amt = Rect.bottom - RectChild.bottom;

    Resize = TRUE;

    if(Amt < Margin)
    {
```

```
            RectChild.bottom += Amt;
            RectChild.left    -= Size3D;
            RectChild.right   += Size3D;
            InvalidateRect(hWndParent, &RectChild, FALSE);

            RectChild.bottom -= Amt;
            RectChild.left    += Size3D;
            RectChild.right   -= Size3D;
            ValidateRect(hWndParent, &RectChild);
        }

        Height = Rect.bottom - RectChild.top - Margin;
    }

    // Window got resized, so move it.

    if(Resize)
    {
        SetWindowPos
        (
            hWnd, NULL, 0, 0, Width, Height, SWP_NOZORDER ¦ SWP_NOMOVE
        );
    }

    return(0);
}

if(uMsg == WM_DRAWFRAME)
{
    if(GetProp(hWnd, "Style") & WS_3D)
    {
        Size3D = GetProp(GetParent(hWnd), "Size3D");

        SinkControl
        (
            hWnd,
            (HDC) wParam,
            GetFocus() == (HWND) SendMessage(hWnd, WM_GETFOCUS, 0, 0L) ?
                -Size3D : Size3D,
            0
        );
    }

    return(0);
}
```

```
// Process default messages.

switch(uMsg)
{
    case WM_WINDOWPOSCHANGING :

        // Whenever a window moves or is sized, cause a repaint of
        // its label.

        if(!GetCtrlLabelRect(hWnd, &Rect))
        {
            DWORD dwOrg = GetOrigin(GetParent(hWnd));

            OffsetRect(&Rect, -(int)LOWORD(dwOrg), -(int)HIWORD(dwOrg));
            InvalidateRect(GetParent(hWnd), &Rect, FALSE);
        }

        break;

    case WM_SIZE :

        // Whenever a child control is moved, repaint the frame & label.

        SendMessage(hWnd, WM_DRAWLABEL, 0, 1L);
        SendMessage(hWnd, WM_DRAWFRAME, 0, 0L);
        break;

    case WM_CANCELMODE :

        PostMessage(hWnd, WM_LBUTTONUP, 0, 0L);
        return(1);

    case WM_SYSKEYDOWN :

        switch(wParam)
        {
            case VK_MENU :

                break;

            case VK_RETURN :

                PostMessage(hWnd, WM_RBUTTONDBLCLK, 0, 0L);
```

```
        while(PeekMessage(&msg, NULL, WM_KEYFIRST, WM_KEYLAST, PM_REMOVE))
        {
            ;
        }

        return(1);

    default :

        // Loop and get all children in parent window, deciding
        // if any label accelerator has been pressed.

        hWndParent = GetParent(hWnd);
        hWndChild  = GetWindow(hWndParent, GW_CHILD);

        while(hWndChild)
        {
            if
            (
                !GetLabelText(hWndChild, Text, sizeof(Text)) &&
                (ptr = strchr(Text, '&'))
            )
            {
                if(wParam == (WORD) toupper((int) ptr[1]))
                {
                    // Switch focus when hotkey for label is pushed.

                    if(GetFocus() != hWndChild)
                    {
                        SetFocus(hWndChild);
                    }

                    // Eat keybd messages waiting in queue,
                    // to eliminate any beeps

                    while
                    (
                        PeekMessage
                        (
                            &msg, NULL, WM_KEYFIRST, WM_KEYLAST, PM_REMOVE
                        )
                    )
                    {
                        ;
                    }
```

```
                            return(1);
                    }
            }

                hWndChild = GetWindow(hWndChild, GW_HWNDNEXT);
        }

            break;
    }

    break;

case WM_DESTROY :

    RemoveProp(hWnd, "xOrg");
    RemoveProp(hWnd, "yOrg");
    RemoveProp(hWnd, "Style");

    if(hAtom = RemoveProp(hWnd, "Label"))
    {
        GlobalDeleteAtom(hAtom);
    }

    break;

case WM_ERASEBKGND :

    // Erase bkgrd of ctrl. If a class brush is defined, then use it.
    // Otherwise, the 3-D mechanism of parent dialog, where active
    // ctrl is white bkgrd, and inactive ctrl has bkgrd brush of its
    // dialog parent.

    if(!(hBrush = GetClassWord(hWnd, GCW_HBRBACKGROUND)))
    {
        if(GetFocus() == hWnd)
        {
            hBrush = GetStockObject(WHITE_BRUSH);
        }
        else
        {
            hBrush = GetClassWord(GetParent(hWnd), GCW_HBRBACKGROUND);
        }
    }

    GetClientRect(hWnd, &Rect);
```

```
        FillRect((HDC) wParam, &Rect, hBrush);

        return(1);

    case WM_SETFOCUS  :
    case WM_KILLFOCUS :

        // Draw a new label and frame on control focus change.

        SendMessage(hWnd, WM_DRAWLABEL, 0, (uMsg == WM_SETFOCUS) ? 0L : 1L);
        SendMessage(hWnd, WM_DRAWFRAME, 0, 0L);

        if(uMsg == WM_KILLFOCUS)
        {
            // Kill the timer that makes the ctrl labels blink.

            KillTimer(hWnd, 1);
            RemoveProp(hWnd, "Flash");
        }
        else
        {
            // Create a timer to make the label blink.

            SetTimer(hWnd, 1, GetCaretBlinkTime(), NULL);
            SetProp(hWnd, "Flash", 1);
        }

        // Send Set/Kill focus notify messages to parent window.
        // This helps aid in multi-dialog embedded window panes.

        SendMessage
        (
            GetParent(hWnd), WM_PARENTNOTIFY, uMsg, MAKELONG(hWnd, wParam)
        );

        break;

    case WM_TIMER :

        if(GetProp(hWnd, "Flash"))
        {
            SendMessage(hWnd, WM_DRAWLABEL, 0, 1L);
            SetProp(hWnd, "Flash", 0);
        }
        else
        {
```

```
                SendMessage(hWnd, WM_DRAWLABEL, 0, 0L);
                SetProp(hWnd, "Flash", 1);
            }
        break;

    case WM_ENABLE :

        // Make sure a paint happens when window is enabled or disabled.

        InvalidateRect(hWnd, NULL, TRUE);
        break;

    case WM_LBUTTONDOWN :
    case WM_RBUTTONDOWN :

        // If focus not already set, then set it.

        if(GetFocus() != hWnd)
        {
            SetFocus(hWnd);
        }

        break;

    case WM_RBUTTONDBLCLK :

        hWndParent = GetParent(hWnd);
        hWndChild  = GetWindow(hWndParent, GW_CHILD);
        Style      = GetWindowLong(hWndParent, GWL_STYLE);

        // Are we zooming or restoring a control?

        if(!GetProp(hWndParent, "Zoomed"))
        {
            RedrawOff(hWndParent);

            // Hide all children except for blowup window.

            while(hWndChild)
            {
                if(hWndChild != hWnd)
                {
                    ShowWindow(hWndChild, SW_HIDE);
                }
```

```
                    hWndChild = GetWindow(hWndChild, GW_HWNDNEXT);
        }

        RedrawOn(hWndParent);

        GetChildWindowPos(hWnd, &RectCtrl, TRUE);
        SetProp(hWndParent, "Zoomed", hWnd);
        SetScrollRange(hWndParent, SB_VERT, 0, 0, TRUE);
        SetScrollRange(hWndParent, SB_HORZ, 0, 0, TRUE);
    }
    else
    {
        RemoveProp(hWndParent, "Zoomed");

        // Show all children again...

        while(hWndChild)
        {
            if(hWndChild != hWnd)
            {
                ShowWindow(hWndChild, SW_SHOW);
            }

            hWndChild = GetWindow(hWndChild, GW_HWNDNEXT);
        }

        SetWindowPos
        (
            hWnd,
            NULL,
            RectCtrl.left,
            RectCtrl.top,
            RectCtrl.right - RectCtrl.left,
            RectCtrl.bottom - RectCtrl.top,
            SWP_NOZORDER
        );
    }

    // Cause parent window to "snap," causing a zoomed window
    // to fill the screen, or reset and show the scroll bars when
    // the child window is unzoomed.

    GetClientRect(hWndParent, &Rect);

    SendMessage
    (
```

```
            hWndParent,
            WM_SIZE,
            0,
            MAKELONG(Rect.right - Rect.left, Rect.bottom - Rect.top)
        );

        UpdateWindow(hWndParent);

        return(0);

    default :

        break;
    }

    // Return control back to default window proc for dialog ctrl.

    GetClassName(hWnd, Class, sizeof(Class));

    if(!lstrcmpi(Class, "AtomicCombobox"))
    {
        return(CallWindowProc(lpfnComboboxWndProc, hWnd, uMsg, wParam, lParam));
    }

    if(!lstrcmpi(Class, "AtomicListbox"))
    {
        return(CallWindowProc(lpfnListboxWndProc, hWnd, uMsg, wParam, lParam));
    }

    if(!lstrcmpi(Class, "AtomicEdit"))
    {
        return(CallWindowProc(lpfnEditWndProc, hWnd, uMsg, wParam, lParam));
    }

    return(DefWindowProc(hWnd, uMsg, wParam, lParam));
}


/****************************************************************************
    FUNCTION: ProcessScrollBars
    PURPOSE : Processes the vert and horz scroll bars for dialogs and any
              "pure" (non-Windows) controls that have them.
****************************************************************************/
```

```
LRESULT WINAPI ProcessScrollBars(HWND hWnd, UINT uMsg, WPARAM wParam,
                                 LPARAM lParam)
{
    DWORD dwOrg;
    RECT  Rect;
    int   xOrg;
    int   yOrg;
    int   Amt;
    int   Min, Max;
    int   Width, Height;

    switch(uMsg)
    {
        case WM_VSCROLL :

            GetScrollRange(hWnd, SB_VERT, &Min, &Max);
            GetClientRect(hWnd, &Rect);

            dwOrg  = GetOrigin(hWnd);
            yOrg   = HIWORD(dwOrg);
            Height = Rect.bottom - Rect.top;

            // Process messages for vert. scroll bar hit.

            switch(wParam)
            {
                case SB_TOP :

                    Amt = -yOrg;
                    break;

                case SB_BOTTOM :

                    Amt = Max - yOrg;
                    break;

                case SB_PAGEUP :

                    if(yOrg == Min)
                    {
                        // The user is already at the top, so leave. This
                        // shouldn't really ever get hit, since there should
                        // be no space on the scroll bar to perform a pgup
                        // when the viewport is already at the top.

                        return(0);
```

```
    }

if((yOrg - (Height / PGUPPGDN)) < Min)
{
    // We don't want to shoot past the top, so make
    // our delta just the right amount.

    Amt = -yOrg;
}
else
{
    // We aren't that close to the top, so move up some.

    Amt = -(Height / PGUPPGDN);
}

break;

case SB_PAGEDOWN :

    if(yOrg == Max)
    {
        // The user is already at the bottom, so leave. This
        // shouldn't really ever get hit, since there should
        // be no space on the scroll bar to perform a pgdown
        // when the viewport is already at the bottom.

        return(0);
    }

    if(yOrg + (Height / PGUPPGDN) > Max)
    {
        Amt = Max - yOrg;
    }
    else
    {
        Amt = (Height / PGUPPGDN);
    }

    break;

case SB_LINEUP :

    if(yOrg == Min)
    {
```

```
                // Scroll thumb already at top, so leave.

                return(0);
            }

            if(yOrg - SCROLLAMT < Min)
            {
                Amt = -yOrg;
            }
            else
            {
                Amt = -SCROLLAMT;
            }

            break;

        case SB_LINEDOWN :

            if(yOrg == Max)
            {
                // Thumb already at bottom of range.

                return(0);
            }

            if(yOrg + SCROLLAMT > Max)
            {
                Amt = Max - yOrg;
            }
            else
            {
                Amt = SCROLLAMT;
            }

            break;

        case SB_THUMBTRACK :

            Amt = LOWORD(lParam) - yOrg;

            break;

        default :

            return(0);
    }
```

```
        SetOrigin(hWnd, LOWORD(dwOrg), yOrg += Amt);
        ScrollWindow(hWnd, 0, -Amt, NULL, &Rect);
        SetScrollPos(hWnd, SB_VERT, yOrg, TRUE);
        UpdateWindow(hWnd);

        break;

    case WM_HSCROLL :

        GetScrollRange(hWnd, SB_HORZ, &Min, &Max);
        GetClientRect(hWnd, &Rect);

        dwOrg = GetOrigin(hWnd);
        xOrg  = LOWORD(dwOrg);
        Width = Rect.right - Rect.left;

        // Process messages for horiz. scroll bar hit.

        switch(wParam)
        {
            case SB_TOP :

                Amt = -xOrg;
                break;

            case SB_BOTTOM :

                Amt = Max - xOrg;
                break;

            case SB_PAGEUP :

                if(xOrg == Min)
                {
                    // The user is already at the top, so leave. This
                    // shouldn't really ever get hit, since there should
                    // be no space on the scroll bar to perform a pgup
                    // when the viewport is already at the top.

                    return(0);
                }

                if((xOrg - (Width / PGUPPGDN)) < Min)
                {
                    // We don't want to shoot past the top, so make
                    // our delta just the right amount.
```

```
            Amt = -xOrg;
        }
        else
        {
            // We aren't that close to the top, so move up some.

            Amt = -(Width / PGUPPGDN);
        }

        break;

    case SB_PAGEDOWN :

        if(xOrg == Max)
        {
            // The user is already at the bottom, so leave. This
            // shouldn't really ever get hit, since there should
            // be no space on the scroll bar to perform a pgdown
            // when the viewport is already at the bottom.

            return(0);
        }

        if(xOrg + (Width / PGUPPGDN) > Max)
        {
            Amt = Max - xOrg;
        }
        else
        {
            Amt = (Width / PGUPPGDN);
        }

        break;

    case SB_LINEUP :

        if(xOrg == Min)
        {
            // Scroll thumb already at top, so leave.

            return(0);
        }

        if(xOrg - SCROLLAMT < Min)
        {
            Amt = -xOrg;
```

```
            }
            else
            {
                Amt = -SCROLLAMT;
            }

            break;

        case SB_LINEDOWN :

            if(xOrg == Max)
            {
                // Thumb already at bottom of range.

                return(0);
            }

            if(xOrg + SCROLLAMT > Max)
            {
                Amt = Max - xOrg;
            }
            else
            {
                Amt = SCROLLAMT;
            }

            break;

        case SB_THUMBTRACK :

            Amt = LOWORD(lParam) - xOrg;

            break;

        default :

            return(0);
    }

    SetOrigin(hWnd, xOrg += Amt, HIWORD(dwOrg));
    ScrollWindow(hWnd, -Amt, 0, NULL, &Rect);
    SetScrollPos(hWnd, SB_HORZ, xOrg, TRUE);
    UpdateWindow(hWnd);

    break;
```

```
            default :

                break;
    }

    return(0);
}


/****************************************************************************
    FUNCTION: CalcScrollBars
    PURPOSE : Determines scroll bar stuff based on window size and
              size of "virtual" client area.
****************************************************************************/

int WINAPI CalcScrollBars(HWND hWnd)
{
    RECT  Rect;
    DWORD dwSize;
    DWORD dwOrg;
    int   xOrg;
    int   yOrg;
    int   xMargin, yMargin;
    int   Min, Max;
    int   Width, Height;
    int   ClientWidth, ClientHeight;


    // Get viewport dimensions and "true" dimensions of window client area.

    GetClientRect(hWnd, &Rect);
    dwSize = (DWORD) SendMessage(hWnd, WM_GETSIZE, 0, 0L);

    Width        = Rect.right - Rect.left;
    Height       = Rect.bottom - Rect.top;
    ClientWidth  = LOWORD(dwSize);
    ClientHeight = HIWORD(dwSize);

    // Determine things for the horiz scroll bar.

    GetScrollRange(hWnd, SB_HORZ, &Min, &Max);

    if(ClientWidth > Width)
    {
```

```
        SetScrollRange(hWnd, SB_HORZ, 0, ClientWidth - Width, TRUE);

        if(!Min && !Max)
        {
            // If there didn't used to be a horz scroll bar, then don't
            // let the following SB_VERT stuff get determined. Let this
            // function (as it's called a second time) do the determination.

            return(0);
        }
    }
    else
    {
        // Get rid of scroll bar, since it's no longer needed.
        // However, if they've already been set to zero, then don't do
        // it again. The function SetScrollRange to 0,0 causes another
        // WM_SIZE to be sent, since the scroll bars have been removed.
        // This causes this function to be hit again, which is why we
        // need this flag. The reason that we return(0), is because
        // we don't want the vert stuff to be processed twice. Only
        // let it be processed the second time around, after the horz bar
        // has been removed.

        if(Min || Max)
        {
            SetScrollRange(hWnd, SB_HORZ, 0, 0, TRUE);
            return(0);
        }
    }


// Determine things for the vertical scroll bar.

if(ClientHeight > Height)
{
    SetScrollRange(hWnd, SB_VERT, 0, ClientHeight - Height, TRUE);
}
else
{
    // Get rid of scroll bar, since it's no longer needed.

    SetScrollRange(hWnd, SB_VERT, 0, 0, TRUE);
}


// When the size of a window changes and its scroll bar ranges have
// to be redetermined, see whether the origin of the window client area
// needs to be adjusted.
```

```
dwOrg = GetOrigin(hWnd);
xOrg  = LOWORD(dwOrg);
yOrg  = HIWORD(dwOrg);

xMargin = yMargin = 0;

if(Width - (ClientWidth - xOrg))
{
    xMargin = Width - (ClientWidth - xOrg);

    if(xMargin > 0)
    {
        if(xOrg - xMargin < 0)
        {
            xMargin = xOrg;
        }

        xOrg -= xMargin;
    }
    else
    {
        xMargin = 0;
    }
}

if(Height - (ClientHeight - yOrg))
{
    yMargin = Height - (ClientHeight - yOrg);

    if(yMargin > 0)
    {
        if(yOrg - yMargin < 0)
        {
            yMargin = yOrg;
        }

        yOrg -= yMargin;
    }
    else
    {
        yMargin = 0;
    }
}

if(xMargin > 0 || yMargin > 0)
{
```

```
        ScrollWindow(hWnd, xMargin, yMargin, NULL, NULL);
        SetOrigin(hWnd, xOrg, yOrg);
        InvalidateRect(hWnd, NULL, TRUE);
    }


    return(0);
}



/******************************************************************************
    FUNCTION: SetAtomicClassStyle
    PURPOSE : Loops and reads style settings from first words in cust ctrl
              resource. When done, writes style as a property. Also reads
              the ctrl's label (if not null) and sets it too.
******************************************************************************/

LPSTR WINAPI SetAtomicClassStyle(HWND hWnd, HINSTANCE hInst,
                                 LPHANDLE pHandle)
{
    HANDLE hResInfo;
    HANDLE hResData;
    LPSTR  lpBuffer   = NULL;
    WORD   AtomicStyle = 0;

    // Lock down & get a ptr to start of resource data. The first words
    // are all style words. Read them in until a null is encountered,
    // and then store the custom style word in a wnd prop.

    if
    (
        !(hResInfo = FindResource
        (
            hInst, (LPSTR) MAKELONG(GetDlgCtrlID(hWnd), 0), RT_RCDATA
        )
        ) ||
        !(hResData = LoadResource(hInst, hResInfo))
    )
    {
        return(NULL);
    }

    if(!(lpBuffer = LockResource(hResData)))
    {
        FreeResource(hResData);
        return(NULL);
    }
```

```
    // Read and OR the style words.

    while(*((LPWORD) lpBuffer))
    {
        AtomicStyle |= *((LPWORD) lpBuffer);
        lpBuffer    += sizeof(WORD);
    }

    lpBuffer += sizeof(WORD);

    // See if a label has been defined for the control.

    if(*lpBuffer)
    {
        // One has, so add it as a global atom.

        SetProp(hWnd, "Label", GlobalAddAtom(lpBuffer));
        lpBuffer += lstrlen(lpBuffer);
    }

    ++lpBuffer;

    // Stuff the res handle so the ctrl can cleanup on its own & set style
    // bits we've been accumulating.

    *pHandle = hResData;
    SetProp(hWnd, "Style", AtomicStyle);

    if(*lpBuffer)
    {
        // Return a pointer indicating that more information follows.

        return(lpBuffer);
    }

    // If all the private res struct was used for was to define some
    // style words and a label, then don't return a pointer that indicates
    // that there is more information to be had. Just do cleanup.

    UnlockResource(hResData);
    FreeResource(hResData);

    return(NULL);
}
```

```
/******************************************************************************
    FUNCTION: DrawCtrlLabel
    PURPOSE : Paints a label around a ctrl window.
******************************************************************************/

int WINAPI DrawCtrlLabel(HWND hWnd, HDC hDC, BOOL PushIn)
{
    BYTE Label[50];
    HWND hWndParent;
    RECT RectCtrl;
    HDC  hDCToUse = NULL;
    DWORD dwOrg

    // Get some properties of parent dialog.

    hWndParent = GetParent(hWnd);
    hDCToUse   = (hDC) ? hDC : GetDC(hWndParent);

    dwOrg = GetOrigin(hWndParent);
    SetWindowOrg(hDCToUse, (int) LOWORD(dwOrg), (int) HIWORD(dwOrg));
    GetChildWindowRect(hWnd, &RectCtrl);

    if(!GetLabelText(hWnd, Label, sizeof(Label)))
    {
        DrawRectLabel
        (
            hWndParent,
            hDCToUse,
            &RectCtrl,
            Label,
            PushIn,
            GetClassWord(hWndParent, GCW_HBRBACKGROUND)
        );
    }

    if(!hDC)
    {
        ReleaseDC(hWndParent, hDCToUse);
    }

    return(0);
}
```

```
/*****************************************************************************
    FUNCTION: DrawRectLabel
    PURPOSE : Paints a label positioned somewhere around a rect.
*****************************************************************************/

int WINAPI DrawRectLabel
(
    HWND hWndParent, HDC hDC, LPRECT lprCtrl, LPSTR Label, BOOL PushIn,
        HBRUSH hBrush
)
{
    int      BkgdMode;
    int      MapMode;
    int      SizeLabel;
    RECT     RectLabel;
    HFONT    hFont;
    COLORREF Color;

    // Establish correct font for label and set text mode.

    hFont = SelectObject
    (
        hDC, (HFONT) SendMessage(hWndParent, WM_GETFONT, 0, 0L)
    );

    BkgdMode = SetBkMode(hDC, TRANSPARENT);
    MapMode  = SetMapMode(hDC, MM_TEXT);

    GetLabelRect(hWndParent, Label, lprCtrl, &RectLabel);

    // Fill the rectangular region for our 3-D label and use SinkRect to
    // make the region around the label appear "popped out."
    // The label is drawn in 3-D only if the parent window is defined as
    // having the 3-D style. The 3-D frame is drawn for controls (done in the
    // WM_DRAWFRAME method) only if the 3-D style is applied to the ctrl
    // itself.

    if(GetProp(hWndParent, "Style") & WS_3D)
    {
        FillRect(hDC, &RectLabel, hBrush);
        SizeLabel = GetProp(hWndParent, "SizeLabel");
        InflateRect(&RectLabel, -SizeLabel, -SizeLabel);
        SinkRect(&RectLabel, hDC, PushIn ? -SizeLabel : SizeLabel);
    }
```

```
// Get the system color used for drawing text in a window, draw the text,
// and then do cleanup.

Color = SetTextColor(hDC, GetSysColor(COLOR_WINDOWTEXT));

DrawText
(
    hDC, &Label[2], -1, &RectLabel, DT_SINGLELINE | DT_CENTER | DT_VCENTER
);

SetTextColor(hDC, Color);
SelectObject(hDC, hFont);
SetMapMode(hDC, MapMode);
SetBkMode(hDC, BkgdMode);

return(0);
}


/*****************************************************************************
    FUNCTION: GetLabelText
    PURPOSE : Gets text of label assoc. w/ctrl.
*****************************************************************************/

int WINAPI GetLabelText(HWND hWnd, LPSTR Label, int Size)
{
    ATOM hAtom;

    if
    (
        !(hAtom = GetProp(hWnd, "Label")) ||
        !GlobalGetAtomName(hAtom, Label, Size)
    )
    {
        return(1);
    }

    return(0);
}
```

```
/**********************************************************************
    FUNCTION: SetLabelText
    PURPOSE : Sets text of label assoc. w/ctrl.
 **********************************************************************/

int WINAPI SetLabelText(HWND hWnd, LPSTR Label)
{
    ATOM  hAtom;
    HWND  hWndParent;
    DWORD dwOrg;
    RECT  Rect;

    // Invalidate hWndParent rect where old label size is.

    if(GetCtrlLabelRect(hWnd, &Rect))
    {
        return(1);
    }

    dwOrg = GetOrigin(hWndParent = GetParent(hWnd));
    OffsetRect(&Rect, -(int)LOWORD(dwOrg), -(int)HIWORD(dwOrg));
    InvalidateRect(hWndParent, &Rect, FALSE);

    // Remove old label & delete assoc. atom.

    if(hAtom = RemoveProp(hWnd, "Label"))
    {
        GlobalDeleteAtom(hAtom);
    }

    // Set new label & ensure that it is drawn.

     SetProp(hWnd, "Label", GlobalAddAtom(Label));

    if(GetCtrlLabelRect(hWnd, &Rect))
    {
        return(1);
    }

    InvalidateRect(hWndParent, &Rect, FALSE);

    return(0);
}
```

```
/******************************************************************************
    FUNCTION: GetLabelRect
    PURPOSE : Determines label rect for given screen rect.
******************************************************************************/

int WINAPI GetLabelRect
(
    HWND hWndParent, LPSTR Label, LPRECT lprCtrl, LPRECT lprLabel
)
{
    HDC   hDC;
    DWORD Extent;
    int   CtrlHeight, CtrlWidth;
    int   LabelHeight, LabelWidth;
    int   Size3D;
    int   SizeLabel;
    int   LabelGap;
    int   FontGap;
    int   Margin;
    HFONT hFont;

    // Get some properties of parent dialog.

    Size3D    = GetProp(hWndParent, "Size3D");
    SizeLabel = GetProp(hWndParent, "SizeLabel");
    FontGap   = GetProp(hWndParent, "FontGap");
    LabelGap  = GetProp(hWndParent, "LabelGap");

    if(GetProp(hWndParent , "Style") & WS_3D)
    {
        // Adjust the positioning of the label over a little when there
        // is a 3-D border around the ctrl.

        LabelGap += Size3D;
    }

    // Get font to draw with & determine dimensions of label.

    hDC   = GetDC(hWndParent);
    hFont = SelectObject
    (
        hDC, (HFONT) SendMessage(hWndParent, WM_GETFONT, 0, 0L)
    );
    Extent = GetTextExtent(hDC, &Label[2], lstrlen(&Label[2]));
    ReleaseDC(hWndParent, hDC);
```

```
// Get ctrl dimensions & determine dimensions of label. Labels consist
// of a font surrounded by a 'FontGap' margin amt, plus a 'SizeLabel'
// 3-D thickness.

CtrlHeight  = lprCtrl->bottom - lprCtrl->top;
CtrlWidth   = lprCtrl->right - lprCtrl->left;
Margin      = (SizeLabel + FontGap) * 2;
LabelHeight = Margin + HIWORD(Extent);
LabelWidth  = Margin + LOWORD(Extent);

// Parse the ctrl title to see how we're supposed to position the label.
// These case statements manipulate the RECT for the label.

switch(toupper(Label[0]))
{
    case 'T' :

        lprLabel->top    = lprCtrl->top - (LabelHeight + LabelGap);
        lprLabel->bottom = lprLabel->top + LabelHeight;

        break;

    case 'M' :

        lprLabel->top    = lprCtrl->top + (CtrlHeight - LabelHeight) / 2;
        lprLabel->bottom = lprLabel->top + LabelHeight;

        break;

    case 'B' :

        lprLabel->top    = lprCtrl->bottom + LabelGap;
        lprLabel->bottom = lprLabel->top + LabelHeight;
        break;

    default :

        return(1);
}

switch(toupper(Label[1]))
{
    case 'L' :
```

```
        if(toupper(Label[0]) == 'M')
        {
            lprLabel->left  = lprCtrl->left - (LabelWidth + LabelGap);
            lprLabel->right = lprLabel->left + LabelWidth;
        }
        else
        {
            lprLabel->left  = lprCtrl->left - Size3D;
            lprLabel->right = lprLabel->left + LabelWidth;
        }
        break;

    case 'C' :

        lprLabel->left  = lprCtrl->left + (CtrlWidth - LabelWidth) / 2;
        lprLabel->right = lprLabel->left + LabelWidth;

        break;

    case 'R' :

        if(toupper(Label[0]) == 'M')
        {
            lprLabel->left  = lprCtrl->right + LabelGap;
            lprLabel->right = lprLabel->left + LabelWidth;
        }
        else
        {
            lprLabel->left  = lprCtrl->right - LabelWidth + Size3D;
            lprLabel->right = lprLabel->left + LabelWidth;
        }

        break;

    default :

        break;
    }

    return(0);
}
```

```
/*****************************************************************************
     FUNCTION: GetCtrlLabelRect
     PURPOSE : Determines label rect for control.
 *****************************************************************************/

int WINAPI GetCtrlLabelRect(HWND hWnd, LPRECT lprLabel)
{
    BYTE Label[50];
    RECT RectCtrl;

    // Get defined label text for ctrl (if any).

    if(GetLabelText(hWnd, Label, sizeof(Label)))
    {
        return(1);
    }

    GetChildWindowRect(hWnd, &RectCtrl);
    GetLabelRect(GetParent(hWnd), Label, &RectCtrl, lprLabel);

    return(0);
}
```

BITMAP

Description

Like the AtomicSplit and AtomicButton control classes, the AtomicBitmap control class is implemented from scratch and requires no additional method handler other than `DefWindowProc()`. This should be obvious because Windows has no stock method of displaying bitmaps, only icons. Icons, you'll remember, can be displayed via the `SS_ICON` static window style. Similar to this style, the AtomicBitmap auto-sizes itself when a width and a height of zero are given. The AtomicBitmap control is capable of displaying a device-dependent bitmap and uses vertical and horizontal scroll bars to scroll through the bitmap. The AtomicBitmap window class also supports simple pixel-plotting. Several functions are also available in STDWIN.DLL that allow DDBs to be printed and clipboarded.

Using the AtomicBitmap control class is very simple. As with the other control types, a custom data structure is required for each bitmap. This structure specifies three things: extended style bits, any label associated with the bitmap control, and the name of the bitmap to be displayed. The only style bits that are valid with AtomicBitmap controls are `WS_3D`, `WS_SIZEHORZ`, `WS_SIZEVERT`, and `BS_MODIFY`. The `BS_MODIFY` style flag indicates that the bitmap should allow pixel plotting. This flag is used to determine whether a cross hair or an arrow cursor should be used for the bitmap control. The `WS_` styles are described more fully in Appendix B, "STDWIN," which describes STDWIN.DLL and the features it provides in more depth.

The following resource code shows the DIALOG structure and custom data structures used to add an AtomicBitmap control to a dialog. The additional custom dialog structure required for all dialogs isn't shown here. It can be found, however, in the code listing for the TestApp application, and it is defined in Appendix B.

Following is the resource code used to create an AtomicBitmap control:

```
Tosh BITMAP    PRELOAD MOVEABLE DISCARDABLE TOSH.BMP

// Custom resource data structure for a bitmap control

BitmapCtrlID# RCDATA PRELOAD MOVEABLE DISCARDABLE
BEGIN
    WS_3D,                    // Valid styles include WS_3D, WS_SIZEHORZ,
    0,                        // WS_SIZEVERT, and BS_MODIFY.
    "TLPicture O' &Tosh\0",   // Label to be used with ctrl. Top, left-justified
```

```
        "Tosh\0",                    // Name of bitmap resource to use
        0
END

DialogTemplateName DIALOG DISCARDABLE LOADONCALL PURE MOVEABLE 10, 10, 350, 240
BEGIN
    CONTROL "" BitmapCtrlID#, "AtomicBitmap",
        WS_CHILD ¦ WS_BORDER ¦ WS_VSCROLL ¦ WS_HSCROLL ¦ WS_TABSTOP,
        141, 130, 110, 120
    ...(other controls)...
END
```

As with the other controls, when the bitmap control is first created, its custom data structure is scanned for window style bits and to store the control's label. The only information left in the structure is the name of the bitmap resource to display. This name is processed by BITMAP.DLL, the bitmap is loaded, and a handle to it is stored in extra window data associated with the control. If no picture is defined, as would be the case with a bitmap control created through the dialog editor, a "stub" bitmap is loaded instead, consisting of a framed picture of a house with green grass, the sun shining, and so on. The source code then checks the width and height of the new control. If either is zero, the size of the control is adjusted to the actual width and height of the loaded bitmap, similar to the ss_ICON style used by Windows for static icon controls.

Interesting to note are the methods shared by the AtomicDialog window class and the AtomicBitmap control type. Both share common methods for handling the vertical and horizontal scroll bars, as well as the method for calculating new scroll bar ranges whenever the sizes of the windows are changed. The following code snippet is used unchanged by both AtomicDialog and AtomicBitmap:

```
case WM_VSCROLL :
case WM_HSCROLL :

    // Determine amount to scroll window client area, offsetting ORG of window.

    ProcessScrollBars(hWnd, uMsg, wParam, lParam);
    break;

case WM_SIZE :

    // Only for "pure" controls where YOU maintain the scroll bars
    // do you need to reprocess the scroll bars when a window is sized.
    // Windows does this automatically for MLEs and listboxes.

    CalcScrollBars(hWnd);
    break;
```

Unlike most dialogs, where the controls never move and usually don't change size, all the Atomic* series of controls and dialogs move and resize themselves quite frequently, depending on the user of the application. Although this flexibility is quite addictive and extremely useful, it brings new headaches and problems for the developer—at least when the code was being created. The first interesting problem involved the processing of the WM_SIZE message, which calls CalcScrollBars(). The job of this function is to send a WM_GETSIZE message to the application and then determine whether scroll bars are still needed for the window. The custom message WM_GETSIZE is used for "virtual" client-area windows, such as AtomicDialog and AtomicBitmap, that have a client area possibly larger than the window itself. The AtomicBitmap control interprets and processes this message by snatching the bitmap handle from its extra window data and calling **GetObject()**, which returns information on a specified bitmap. The width and height values are then returned to the caller as a DWORD return value. This size is then used by CalcScrollBars() and compared with the actual window viewport size to determine whether scroll bars are still needed, and if so, how their ranges should be set.

The problem involved the removal of scroll bars, which indirectly causes another WM_SIZE to be sent to the window because a scroll bar is being removed, effectively increasing the size of its client area. The first problem involved the STACKSIZE setting in the application's module-definition file, which initially was set at 5K. However, this proved to be too small for a window procedure that recursively called itself one time, and changing this setting to 8K proved an excellent remedy. In fact, to use the common dialogs provided by Windows 3.1, 8K is a recommended minimum. Checking through the sample sources included with Windows 3.1 showed that about half of the examples used an 8K stack, so this doesn't seem too out of the ordinary.

The next problem was related to the fact that the function CalcScrollBars() was being recursively called at least once, although it didn't have anything to do with a problem as physical as a stack overflow. Rather, it was more logic-related. Under CalcScrollBars(), the range of the horizontal scroll bar is calculated and set first; then the vertical scroll bar is processed. If the horizontal scroll bar were to be removed (a range of zero), the function would end up getting called again indirectly because of Windows firing off another WM_SIZE message. The second time around in CalcScrollBars(), the vertical scroll bar range is set, thinking that there is no horizontal scroll bar, which is true. However, when the level of recursion "pops" and the original instance of the function is allowed to complete, the vertical scroll bar range is recalculated. Of course, this time it thinks that the window is still in its original state when the function was first called, which may or may not have included a horizontal scroll bar. The fix was to check to see whether the horizontal scroll bar was being added or removed, and if so, do an immediate return, figuring that the second, recursed call would indicate that the horizontal scroll bar wasn't changing states (visible to hidden or vice versa). This allows the thread of execution to flow down to the calculation methods for the vertical scroll bar.

Whenever keystrokes (arrows, PgUp, PgDn, Ctrl-key accelerator) are encountered in an AtomicBitmap control, they are processed and possibly used as navigation keys in lieu of using the mouse and the scroll bars. When a predefined navigation key is encountered (during WM_KEYDOWN), an appropriate scroll bar message is fired off to the window. Although a function could just as easily have been called, it is much cleaner to implement the functional interface via messaging. After the message is fired off, the following keyboard messages in the queue (WM_KEYUP) are eaten, keeping the keystroke messages in context. Ideally, this keyboard processing method should be abstracted and placed into STDWIN.DLL instead of being located in BITMAP.DLL. It could then be used for any other "pure" controls that have scroll bars and a navigable client area. The reason it wasn't used for dialog windows is that in this case the keystrokes probably are going to need to go to whatever control has the focus, and they shouldn't be trapped and used to scroll the dialog client area.

The drawing mode for editable bitmap controls is set and released via clicks of the left mouse button. Whenever the left mouse button is pressed, drawing mode is set and WM_MOUSEMOVE messages are interpreted and pixels are drawn. When the left mouse button is released, drawing mode is turned off and WM_MOUSEMOVE messages aren't interpreted. Pixels are plotted into two display-contexts—the screen DC and a memory DC containing a copy of the bitmap. When the bitmap control is first initialized, it calls **LoadBitmap()** to load a bitmap resource contained in the application into memory. The net result of this function is to add the bitmap to the global heap as a "GDI Private Bitmap." At this point, memory can be compacted and the application's copy of the bitmap lost—lost, that is, until **LoadBitmap()** is called again to bring the bitmap back in from disk. It is necessary to twice invoke **SetPixel()**, because you need to plot the points not only in the bitmap itself, but into the screen's representation of the bitmap, which normally displays only a small, clipped portion of the entire image. The only other option here would be to plot the pixels into the bitmap, invalidate the pixel, and then send a paint message to the control. This would be very costly indeed for a single pixel!

Painting the bitmap itself is fairly simple. Whenever the message WM_PAINT is received, the bitmap handle is retrieved from the control's extra data, and the image is BitBlted into the display context returned by the call to **BeginPaint()**. Before control is returned to Windows, however, any uncovered "void" areas of the bitmap control need to be painted with the class background brush. The reason for these "void" areas is twofold. Normally, the bitmap would be allowed to be scrolled only through valid areas—that is, through the bitmap itself. The bitmap is not a normal control, however. Because it can be "zoomed"—effectively maximized within its parent's client area—certain bitmaps won't be big enough to fill this entire space. The only options at this point are to shrink the parent size around the control (yuck!) or just fill the extra space with a colored background brush.

Additionally, whenever the bitmaps are sized via the split bars, there is a chance that portions of the bitmap control that have no corresponding section of bitmap will be uncovered. The grab bars cannot use WM_GETMINMAXINFO when sizing the controls because they could be managing multiple controls, each possibly returning different values. This could lead to a condition in which certain bitmaps are so small that the split bar couldn't fit symmetrically between all the controls it is supposed to manage. For this reason, controls can be sized an unlimited amount. This really never is a problem because the background area always gets erased, resulting in a clean and nondistracting effect.

Like other controls, including the AtomicButton and AtomicSplit grab bar, the AtomicBitmap control doesn't erase its background (at least not portions covered by a bitmap). Certain controls just don't have a background that needs to be erased, and eliminating this step can remove much of the flicker during a screen update.

Possible Enhancements

The AtomicBitmap control can be enhanced in several ways. Depending on the needs, the wish list goes from two items to two hundred. At a minimum, support for device-independent bitmaps should be included. As the control now stands, support is limited to device-dependent bitmaps, which are limited to 20 or so system colors. Because Windows works primarily (actually exclusively) with DIBs, this is a logical step. To replicate the simple scrolling and pixel-plotting methods already provided, adding DIB support would involve a minimal amount of effort, requiring only a few functions provided by the DIB.DRV device driver. If DIB support is to be added, however, all the bitmap functions provided by STDWIN.DLL, including BitmapToClipboard() and BitmapToPrinter(), would also need to be upgraded from working with DDBs to DIBs. DIBs are ideal for printers, because output can be translated to gray scale infinitely better when the printer, not GDI, is doing the dirty work. Printing a 256-color DIB with a LaserJetIII laser printer results in a fantastic-looking gray-scale image, as opposed to a somewhat choppy-looking black-and-white dithered image.

Other enhancements and methods that would be nice to implement for the bitmap control involve the creation of "splash" screens and other special effects. The bitmap control could be used to permanently or temporarily display a bitmap on the screen in some position, doing a "fade in," "zoom in," or some other vertical or horizontal wipe. One of the easiest methods for implementing these kinds of special effects is through extensive use of clipping regions. A clipping region, you'll remember, can be as simple as a RECT structure or as complex as multiple, compound, and arbitrarily connected points. Regions can be square, circular, elliptical, polygonal, and compound. A sparkle-in and sparkle-out effect for a bitmap could easily be achieved by first duplicating the bitmap and then using the second copied pattern as a mask for which pixels have been "sparkled" in or out of the control. By symmetrically (or randomly) cruising through the mask, you could easily achieve the desired sparkle effect.

Although this book de-emphasizes the importance of the dialog editor, especially when you are creating truly complex and custom dialogs and interfaces, the AtomicBitmap control has been partially interfaced to it. Although no style dialog is provided, the bitmap visually displays itself when it is selected as a custom control and placed into a dialog.

Specifications

ClassName   AtomicBitmap
ModuleName   BITMAP
LibraryName   BITMAP.DLL

Functions

LibMain()   Standard entry point for library
WEP()   Standard exit procedure for library
AtomicBitmapWndFn()   Class window procedure

486

BITMAP.C

```c
/*****************************************************************************
    LIBRARY: BITMAP.DLL
    AUTHOR : Mike Klein
    PURPOSE: Bitmap custom control for STDWIN.DLL.
*****************************************************************************/

//
// #DEFINEs, #INCLUDEs, declarations, and globals
//

#define OEMRESOURCE
#define NOCOMM
#define _WINDLL

#include <windows.h>
#include <custcntl.h>
#include <stdlib.h>
#include "stdwin.h"
#include "bitmap.h"


int     PASCAL LibMain(HINSTANCE, WORD, WORD, LPSTR);
int     WINAPI WEP(int);
LRESULT WINAPI AtomicBitmapWndFn(HWND, UINT, WPARAM, LPARAM);
LRESULT WINAPI BITMAPWndFn(HWND, UINT, WPARAM, LPARAM);

static HINSTANCE hInstBitmapDLL = NULL;

static UINT WM_GETSIZE;



/*****************************************************************************
    FUNCTION: LibMain
    PURPOSE : Entry point for DLL.
*****************************************************************************/

#pragma alloc_text(INIT_TEXT, LibMain)

int PASCAL LibMain(HINSTANCE hInst, WORD DataSeg, WORD HeapSize, LPSTR CmdLine)
{
    WNDCLASS wc;
```

```
        // Init bitmap control.

        wc.hInstance     = hInst;
        wc.style         = CS_DBLCLKS ¦ CS_GLOBALCLASS ¦ CS_PARENTDC;
        wc.lpszMenuName  = NULL;
        wc.lpszClassName = "AtomicBitmap";
        wc.lpfnWndProc   = AtomicBitmapWndFn;
        wc.hCursor       = NULL;
        wc.cbClsExtra    = 0;
        wc.cbWndExtra    = BITMAPWNDEXTRA;
        wc.hbrBackground = NULL;
        wc.hIcon         = NULL;

        if(!RegisterClass(&wc))
        {
            return(FALSE);
        }

        // Register any custom messages & remember the instance.

        WM_GETSIZE = RegisterWindowMessage("WM_GETSIZE");

        hInstBitmapDLL = hInst;

        return(TRUE);
}


/*****************************************************************************
    FUNCTION: WEP
    PURPOSE : Termination function for DLL.
*****************************************************************************/

int WINAPI WEP(int Parameter)
{
    return(1);
}


/*****************************************************************************
    FUNCTION: AtomicBitmapWndFn
    PURPOSE : Wnd proc for bitmap ctrl.
*****************************************************************************/

LRESULT WINAPI AtomicBitmapWndFn(HWND hWnd, UINT uMsg, WPARAM wParam, LPARAM lParam)
{
```

```
    RECT Rect;

    PAINTSTRUCT Paint;

    MSG msg;

    HBITMAP hBmp;
    HBITMAP hBmpOld;

    HINSTANCE hInst;

    DWORD dwOrg;

    int xOrg, yOrg;

    int xMargin, yMargin;

    WORD Data;

    LPSTR lpBuffer;

    HDC hDC;
    HDC hDCMemory;

    HBRUSH hBrush;

    BITMAP Bitmap;

    static HANDLE hResData;

    // Process custom messages.

    if(uMsg == WM_GETSIZE)
    {
        if(!(hBmp = GetWindowWord(hWnd, BITMAPBMP)))
        {
            return(0);
        }

        GetObject(hBmp, sizeof(BITMAP), &Bitmap);

        return(MAKELONG(Bitmap.bmWidth, Bitmap.bmHeight));
    }

    // Do normal processing of window messages.
```

```
switch(uMsg)
{
    case WM_VSCROLL :
    case WM_HSCROLL :

        ProcessScrollBars(hWnd, uMsg, wParam, lParam);
        break;

    case WM_SIZE :

        // Only for "pure" controls where WE maintain the scroll bars
        // do we need to reprocess the scroll bars when a window is sized.
        // Windows does this automatically for edit controls and listboxes
        // and overlapped windows.

        CalcScrollBars(hWnd);
        break;

    case WM_GETDLGCODE :

        return(DLGC_WANTARROWS);

    case WM_KEYDOWN :

        // These KEYDOWN msgs are used to let the keyboard work
        // the scroll bars.

        switch(wParam)
        {
            case VK_HOME :

                if(GetKeyState(VK_CONTROL) & 0x8000)
                {
                    SendMessage(hWnd, WM_VSCROLL, SB_TOP, 0L);
                }
                else
                {
                    SendMessage(hWnd, WM_HSCROLL, SB_TOP, 0L);
                }

                break;

            case VK_END :

                if(GetKeyState(VK_CONTROL) & 0x8000)
                {
```

```
        SendMessage(hWnd, WM_VSCROLL, SB_BOTTOM, 0L);
    }
    else
    {
        SendMessage(hWnd, WM_HSCROLL, SB_BOTTOM, 0L);
    }

    break;

case VK_LEFT :

    if(GetKeyState(VK_CONTROL) & 0x8000)
    {
        SendMessage(hWnd, WM_HSCROLL, SB_PAGEUP, 0L);
    }
    else
    {
        SendMessage(hWnd, WM_HSCROLL, SB_LINEUP, 0L);
    }

    break;

case VK_RIGHT :

    if(GetKeyState(VK_CONTROL) & 0x8000)
    {
        SendMessage(hWnd, WM_HSCROLL, SB_PAGEDOWN, 0L);
    }
    else
    {
        SendMessage(hWnd, WM_HSCROLL, SB_LINEDOWN, 0L);
    }

    break;

case VK_UP :

    if(GetKeyState(VK_CONTROL) & 0x8000)
    {
        SendMessage(hWnd, WM_VSCROLL, SB_PAGEUP, 0L);
    }
    else
    {
        SendMessage(hWnd, WM_VSCROLL, SB_LINEUP, 0L);
    }
```

```
            break;

        case VK_DOWN :

            if(GetKeyState(VK_CONTROL) & 0x8000)
            {
                SendMessage(hWnd, WM_VSCROLL, SB_PAGEDOWN, 0L);
            }
            else
            {
                SendMessage(hWnd, WM_VSCROLL, SB_LINEDOWN, 0L);
            }

            break;

        case VK_PRIOR :

            SendMessage(hWnd, WM_VSCROLL, SB_PAGEUP, 0L);
            break;

        case VK_NEXT :

            SendMessage(hWnd, WM_VSCROLL, SB_PAGEDOWN, 0L);
            break;

        default :

            return(0L);
    }

    // Eat following keystrokes in queue.

    while(PeekMessage(&msg, NULL, WM_KEYFIRST, WM_KEYLAST, PM_REMOVE))
    {
        ;
    }

    break;

case WM_SETCURSOR :

    // Non-editable bitmaps get an arrow cursor, while editable
    // ones get the crosshairs.

    if(LOWORD(lParam) != HTCLIENT)
    {
```

```
            break;
        }

        SetCursor
        (
            LoadCursor
            (
                NULL,
                (GetProp(hWnd, "Style") & BS_MODIFY) ? IDC_CROSS : IDC_ARROW
            )
        );

        break;

case WM_CREATE :

    SetProp(hWnd, "Atomic", 1);
    break;

case WM_MOVE :

    if(!RemoveProp(hWnd, "Atomic"))
    {
        break;
    }

    // Initialize color to black & turn off drawing mode.

    SetWindowWord(hWnd, 0, 0);

    // Get bitmap to use for control.

    hInst = GetWindowWord(hWnd, GWW_HINSTANCE);
    lpBuffer = SetAtomicClassStyle(hWnd, hInst, &hResData);

    if(!lpBuffer)
    {
        // Not bitmap specified, so use the default "picture."

        hBmp = LoadBitmap(hInstBitmapDLL, "Picture");
    }
    else
    {
        if(!(hBmp = LoadBitmap(hInst, lpBuffer)))
        {
            // Uh-oh, picture name specified, but no can do on the
```

```
                            // loading thing!

                            hBmp = LoadBitmap(hInstBitmapDLL, "Picture");
                    }

                    UnlockResource(hResData);
                    FreeResource(hResData);
            }

            // Get info on displayed bitmap & possibly adjust wnd rect.

            GetObject(hBmp, sizeof(BITMAP), &Bitmap);
            GetChildWindowPos(hWnd, &Rect, TRUE);

            if(!(Rect.right - Rect.left))
            {
                    // First, we must size the window around the bmp since
                    // a zero width and zero height was spec'd.

                    SetWindowPos
                    (
                        hWnd,
                        NULL,
                        0,
                        0,
                        Bitmap.bmWidth,
                        Bitmap.bmHeight,
                        SWP_NOZORDER | SWP_NOMOVE
                    );
            }

            // Remember bitmap by storing in extra data.

            SetWindowWord(hWnd, BITMAPBMP, hBmp);

            break;

    case WM_LBUTTONDOWN :
    case WM_LBUTTONUP   :

            // Turn draw mode on/off for BS_MODIFYable bitmap ctrls.

            if(!(GetProp(hWnd, "Style") & BS_MODIFY))
            {
                break;
```

```
    }

    Data = GetWindowWord(hWnd, 0);

    if(uMsg == WM_LBUTTONDOWN)
    {
        Data |= 0x00ff;     // Set low byte to on.
    }
    else
    {
        Data &= 0xff00;     // Set low byte to off.
    }

    SetWindowWord(hWnd, 0, Data);

    break;

case WM_MOUSEMOVE :

    if
    (
        !(GetProp(hWnd, "Style") & BS_MODIFY) ||
        (!GetWindowWord(hWnd, 0) & 0x00ff)
    )
    {
        // Either the bitmap isn't editable, or the drawing mode is
        // off. In either case, we're outta here.

        break;
    }

    // Plot the pixel in the window dc and the bitmap dc. This saves
    // us from doing it in just the bitmap and re-bitblt'g the whole
    // image again...

    hDC       = GetDC(hWnd);
    dwOrg     = GetOrigin(hWnd);
    hDCMemory = CreateCompatibleDC(hDC);
    hBmpOld   = SelectObject(hDCMemory, GetWindowWord(hWnd, BITMAPBMP));

    SetPixel(hDC, LOWORD(lParam), HIWORD(lParam), RGB(0, 0, 0));
    SetPixel
    (
        hDCMemory,
        LOWORD(lParam) + LOWORD(dwOrg),
        HIWORD(lParam) + HIWORD(dwOrg),
```

```
        RGB(0, 0, 0)
    );

    SelectObject(hDCMemory, hBmpOld);
    DeleteDC(hDCMemory);
    ReleaseDC(hWnd, hDC);

    break;

case WM_DESTROY :

    // Was a bitmap selected into ctrl?

    if(hBmp = GetWindowWord(hWnd, BITMAPBMP))
    {
        DeleteObject(hBmp);
    }

    break;

case WM_ERASEBKGND :

    // We don't do any erasing of the bitmap's background here.
    // It's only done when the scroll bar ranges are computed.

    return(1L);

case WM_PAINT :

    if(!(hBmp = GetWindowWord(hWnd, BITMAPBMP)))
    {
        break;
    }

    // Get info on bitmap & some DCs.

    GetObject(GetWindowWord(hWnd, BITMAPBMP), sizeof(BITMAP), &Bitmap);
    GetClientRect(hWnd, &Rect);

    BeginPaint(hWnd, &Paint);

    hDCMemory = CreateCompatibleDC(Paint.hdc);
    hBmpOld   = SelectObject(hDCMemory, hBmp);
    dwOrg     = GetOrigin(hWnd);
    xOrg      = LOWORD(dwOrg);
    yOrg      = HIWORD(dwOrg);
```

```
// Paint normal bitmap image.

BitBlt
(
    Paint.hdc,
    0,
    0,
    Rect.right - Rect.left,
    Rect.bottom - Rect.top,
    hDCMemory,
    xOrg,
    yOrg,
    SRCCOPY
);

SelectObject(hDCMemory, hBmpOld);
DeleteDC(hDCMemory);

// Erase background showing through. But first, determine how
// much of a gap exists (if any) between the right and bottom
// edge of the bitmap and the edge of the viewport window.

GetClientRect(hWnd, &Rect);

xMargin = (Rect.right - Rect.left) - (Bitmap.bmWidth - xOrg);
yMargin = (Rect.bottom - Rect.top) - (Bitmap.bmHeight - yOrg);

if(!(hBrush = GetClassWord(hWnd, GCW_HBRBACKGROUND)))
{
    hBrush = GetClassWord(GetParent(hWnd), GCW_HBRBACKGROUND);
}

if(xMargin > 0)
{
    // There's a gap between the right of the bitmap and
    // the viewport.

    Rect.left = Rect.right - xMargin;

    FillRect(Paint.hdc, &Rect, hBrush);
}

if(yMargin > 0)
{
    // There's a gap between the bottom of the bitmap and
    // the viewport.
```

```
                    GetClientRect(hWnd, &Rect);

                    Rect.top = Rect.bottom - yMargin;

                    FillRect(Paint.hdc, &Rect, hBrush);
                }

                EndPaint(hWnd, &Paint);

                break;

           default :

                break;
        }

    return(AtomicControlWndFn(hWnd, uMsg, wParam, lParam));
}


/****************************************************************************
    FUNCTION: BITMAPInfo
    PURPOSE : Dialog editor information function.
 ****************************************************************************/

HANDLE WINAPI BITMAPInfo(VOID)
{
    HANDLE hMem;

    LPCTLINFO lpCtrlInfo;

    // Allocate GMEM for ctrl struct.

    if(!(hMem = GlobalAlloc(GMEM_MOVEABLE, sizeof(CTLINFO))))
    {
        return(NULL);
    }

    if(!(lpCtrlInfo = (LPCTLINFO) GlobalLock(hMem)))
    {
        GlobalFree(hMem);
        return(NULL);
    }

    // Fill it in with some basic info.
```

```
        lpCtrlInfo->wVersion  = 1;
        lpCtrlInfo->wCtlTypes = 1;
        lstrcpy(lpCtrlInfo->szClass, "AtomicBitmap");
        lstrcpy(lpCtrlInfo->szTitle, "by Atomic Software, Inc.");

        lpCtrlInfo->Type[0].wType   = 0;
        lpCtrlInfo->Type[0].wWidth  = 70;
        lpCtrlInfo->Type[0].wHeight = 60;
        lpCtrlInfo->Type[0].dwStyle = WS_CHILD | WS_VSCROLL | WS_HSCROLL | WS_BORDER;

        lstrcpy(lpCtrlInfo->Type[0].szDescr, "AtomicBitmap");

        GlobalUnlock(hMem);

        return(hMem);
    }



/*****************************************************************************
    FUNCTION: BITMAPStyle
    PURPOSE : Dialog editor style-dialog invocation function.
*****************************************************************************/

BOOL WINAPI BITMAPStyle(HWND hWnd, HANDLE hCtlStyle, LPFNSTRTOID lpfnStrToId,
                        LPFNIDTOSTR lpfnIdToStr)
{
    // Since the bitmap control has only one style (BS_MODIFY) the
    // ctrl style dialog isn't used.

    return(FALSE);
}



/*****************************************************************************
    FUNCTION: BITMAPDlgFn
    PURPOSE : Dialog editor wndproc for style dialog.
*****************************************************************************/

BOOL WINAPI BITMAPDlgFn(HWND hDlg, UINT uMsg, WPARAM wParam, LPARAM lParam)
{
    return(FALSE);
}
```

```
/*****************************************************************************
    FUNCTION: BITMAPWndFn
    PURPOSE : wndproc for bitmap ctrl while in DLGEDITOR.
*****************************************************************************/

LRESULT WINAPI BITMAPWndFn(HWND hWnd, UINT uMsg, WPARAM wParam, LPARAM lParam)
{
    return(AtomicBitmapWndFn(hWnd, uMsg, wParam, lParam));
}



/*****************************************************************************
    FUNCTION: BITMAPFlags
    PURPOSE : Dialog editor function for xlating style flags.
*****************************************************************************/

WORD WINAPI BITMAPFlags(DWORD dwFlags, LPSTR Style, WORD wMaxString)
{
    return(0);
}
```

D

BUTTON

Description

Like the AtomicBitmap and AtomicSplit control classes, the AtomicButton control class is implemented from scratch, requiring no support methods from Windows' stock button control class. The only default processing required for the control is that provided by `DefWindowProc()`, which all windows require in some form. The styles of button supported by AtomicButton class methods include both graphical and text-style push buttons, and a graphical two-state checkbox style of button. The AtomicButton control class provides several enhancements over the stock button control, including a 3-D look similar to the other presented controls, and an easier method of creating graphical bitmap buttons. The 3-D look is for the regular, text-based button type, and it isn't used for graphical buttons, which are assumed to provide their own look and style. However, they too can take advantage of the 3-D interface if desired.

Defining a graphical AtomicButton control is as simple as specifying the names of four bitmaps in a private resource structure, similar to the following section of pseudo-resource code:

```
// The names of your bitmap buttons to use

Normal   BITMAP PRELOAD    MOVEABLE DISCARDABLE normal.bmp
Pushed   BITMAP PRELOAD    MOVEABLE DISCARDABLE pushed.bmp
Focus    BITMAP PRELOAD    MOVEABLE DISCARDABLE focus.bmp
Disabled BITMAP LOADONCALL MOVEABLE DISCARDABLE disabled.bmp
...


// Note here that the ID of the priv resource struct is the same
// as the ID of the control. Makes things much easier for lookup.

ButtonControlID# RCDATA PRELOAD MOVEABLE DISCARDABLE
BEGIN
    BS_PUSHBTN,     // Defines a graphical push button
    BS_BMPBTN,
    0
    "\0",           // No label for this button
    "Normal\0",     // Names of bitmaps for buttons
    "Pushed\0",
    "Focus\0",
    "Disabled\0",
    0               // Terminating null byte
END

...
```

```
// Here is a snippet of dialog code, for an example.

DialogTemplateName DIALOG ...
...
BEGIN
    CONTROL "" ButtonControlID#, "AtomicButton", ...
    ...(additional controls here)...
END
```

Possible Enhancements

The only button style left that needs to be implemented is a graphical radio button. Much of this functionality already exists inside the current button library code, so creating such a button shouldn't be a difficult feat.

Specifications

ClassName   AtomicButton
ModuleName   BUTTON
LibraryName   BUTTON.DLL

Functions

LibMain()   Standard entry point for library
WEP()   Standard exit procedure for library
AtomicButtonWndFn()   Class window procedure

BUTTON.C

```
/******************************************************************************
    LIBRARY: BUTTON.DLL
    AUTHOR : Mike Klein
    PURPOSE: Button custom control for STDWIN.DLL.
******************************************************************************/

//
// #DEFINEs, #INCLUDEs, declarations, and globals
//

#define OEMRESOURCE
#define NOCOMM
#define _WINDLL

#include <windows.h>
#include <ctype.h>
#include <string.h>
#include "stdwin.h"
#include "button.h"

int     PASCAL LibMain(HANDLE, WORD, WORD, LPSTR);
int     WINAPI WEP(int);
LRESULT WINAPI AtomicButtonWndFn(HWND, UINT, WPARAM, LPARAM);
int     PASCAL DrawButton(HWND, HDC, HDC, WORD, WORD);

static UINT WM_DRAWLABEL;


/******************************************************************************
    FUNCTION: LibMain
    PURPOSE : Entry point for DLL.
******************************************************************************/

#pragma alloc_text(INIT_TEXT, LibMain)

int PASCAL LibMain(HINSTANCE hInst, WORD DataSeg, WORD HeapSize, LPSTR CmdLine)
{
    WNDCLASS wc;
```

```
        // Register custom control class.

        GetClassInfo(NULL, "button", &wc);

        wc.hInstance    = hInst;
        wc.style        = CS_DBLCLKS | CS_GLOBALCLASS | CS_PARENTDC;
        wc.lpszMenuName = NULL;
        wc.lpszClassName = "AtomicButton";
        wc.lpfnWndProc  = AtomicButtonWndFn;
        wc.hCursor      = LoadCursor(NULL, IDC_ARROW);
        wc.cbClsExtra   = 0;
        wc.cbWndExtra   = BUTTONWNDEXTRA;
        wc.hbrBackground = NULL;
        wc.hIcon        = NULL;

        if(!RegisterClass(&wc))
        {
            return(FALSE);
        }

        // Register custom messages.

        WM_DRAWLABEL = RegisterWindowMessage("WM_DRAWLABEL");

        return(TRUE);
}


/****************************************************************************
    FUNCTION: WEP
    PURPOSE : Termination function for DLL.
****************************************************************************/

int WINAPI WEP(int Parameter)
{
    return(1);
}


/****************************************************************************
    FUNCTION: AtomicButtonWndFn
    PURPOSE : Wnd proc for dialog-smart buttons.
****************************************************************************/
```

```
LRESULT WINAPI AtomicButtonWndFn(HWND hWnd, UINT uMsg, WPARAM wParam,
                                 LPARAM lParam)
{
    HINSTANCE hInst;

    static HANDLE hResData;

    LPSTR lpBuffer;

    int BtnID;

    static WORD OldState;

    WORD State;

    BYTE *ptr;

    HBITMAP hBmp;

    WORD Style;

    BITMAP Bitmap;

    HWND hWndParent;

    RECT Rect;

    static BYTE Text[30];

    HDC hDC;

    PAINTSTRUCT Paint;

    int i, j, x, y;

    MSG msg;

    static BOOL MouseCapture = FALSE;

    // Process custom messages here.

    if(uMsg == WM_DRAWLABEL)
    {
```

```
    if((GetProp(hWnd, "Style") & (BS_BMPBTN ¦ BS_PUSHBTN)) == BS_PUSHBTN)
    {
        // Nongraphical push buttons draw their own labels.

        return(0L);
    }

    // Other buttons have a label drawn (if one is defined).

    return(AtomicControlWndFn(hWnd, uMsg, wParam, lParam));
}

// Process regular messages here.

switch(uMsg)
{
    case WM_GETDLGCODE :

        if(!lParam)
        {
            break;
        }

        if
        (
            (((LPMSG) lParam)->message == WM_KEYDOWN) &&
            (((LPMSG) lParam)->wParam == VK_RETURN)
        )
        {
            if(GetProp(hWnd, "Style") & BS_DEFAULT)
            {
                return(DLGC_WANTALLKEYS);
            }
        }

        break;

    case WM_KEYDOWN :

        if((wParam == VK_SPACE) ¦¦ (wParam == VK_RETURN))
        {
            // Send a press to the button.

            SendMessage(hWnd, WM_LBUTTONDOWN, 0, 0L);
```

```
                while(PeekMessage(&msg, NULL, WM_KEYFIRST, WM_KEYLAST,
                            PM_REMOVE))
                {
                    ;
                }

                return(0L);
            }

        break;

    case WM_KEYUP :

        if((wParam == VK_SPACE) || (wParam == VK_RETURN))
        {
            // Release the button.

            SendMessage(hWnd, WM_LBUTTONUP, 0, 0L);
            return(0L);
        }

        break;

    case WM_SYSKEYDOWN :

        if(GetLabelText(hWnd, Text, sizeof(Text)))
        {
            break;
        }

        if(ptr = strchr(Text, '&'))
        {
            // Button has a label, and includes a "&Label" hotkey '&'
            // accelerator for it too, so see if it was pressed.

            if(wParam == (WORD) toupper((int) ptr[1]))
            {
                // Switch focus when button mnemonic is pressed.

                while(PeekMessage(&msg, NULL, WM_KEYFIRST, WM_KEYLAST,
                            PM_REMOVE))
                {
                    ;
                }
```

```
                    PostMessage(hWnd, WM_LBUTTONDOWN, 0, 0L);
                    PostMessage(hWnd, WM_LBUTTONUP, 0, 0L);

                    return(0L);
                }
            }

        break;

    case BM_GETSTATE :
    case BM_GETCHECK :

        // Return button's state (pushed or normal).

        return(GetWindowWord(hWnd, BTNSTATE));

    case BM_SETCHECK :

        // Set the button's state (pushed or normal) & cause a paint.

        SetWindowWord(hWnd, BTNSTATE, (wParam) ? PUSHED : NORMAL);
        InvalidateRect(hWnd, NULL, TRUE);
        return(0L);

    case BM_SETSTYLE :

        Style = GetProp(hWnd, "Style");

        if(wParam == BS_PUSHBUTTON)
        {
            if(Style & BS_DEFAULT)
            {
                Style ^= BS_DEFAULT;
            }

            SetProp(hWnd, "Style", Style |= BS_PUSHBTN);
            InvalidateRect(hWnd, NULL, (BOOL) lParam);
        }
        else
        {
            if(wParam == BS_DEFPUSHBUTTON)
            {
                SetProp(hWnd, "Style", Style |= BS_DEFAULT);
                InvalidateRect(hWnd, NULL, (BOOL) lParam);
            }
```

```
        }

        return(0L);

    case WM_RBUTTONDBLCLK :

        // We don't want button controls to be zoomable, now do we?

        return(0L);

    case WM_LBUTTONDOWN :

        Style = GetProp(hWnd, "Style");

        // Set new button state.

        if(Style & (BS_TOGGLEBTN | BS_RADIOBTN))
        {
            // With checkboxes, it's a toggle-type action.

            OldState = GetWindowWord(hWnd, BTNSTATE);

            SendMessage(hWnd, BM_SETCHECK, OldState ? 0 : 1, 0L);
        }
        else
        {
            // With push buttons, just push them.

            SendMessage(hWnd, BM_SETCHECK, 1, 0L);
        }

        // Capture input until mouse is released & send a WM_PAINT.

        SetCapture(hWnd);
        MouseCapture = TRUE;
        UpdateWindow(hWnd);

        break;

    case WM_LBUTTONUP :

        // Button capturing is over, so release capture & determine if
        // hWndButton was pushed down when left mouse button was released.
```

```
    ReleaseCapture();
    MouseCapture = FALSE;

    Style = GetProp(hWnd, "Style");

    if(Style & BS_PUSHBTN)
    {
        if(GetWindowWord(hWnd, BTNSTATE) == PUSHED)
        {
            // Notify parent with a click message.

            PostMessage
            (
                GetParent(hWnd),
                WM_COMMAND,
                GetDlgCtrlID(hWnd),
                MAKELONG(hWnd, BN_CLICKED)
            );
        }

        SendMessage(hWnd, BM_SETCHECK, 0, 0L);
    }
    else
    {
        if(GetWindowWord(hWnd, BTNSTATE) != OldState)
        {
            if(Style & BS_RADIOBTN)
            {
                HWND hWndBtn;

                hWndParent = GetParent(hWnd);

                // For radio buttons, we need to unsel any other
                // button in the group.

                hWndBtn = hWnd;

                while
                (
                    hWndBtn = GetNextDlgGroupItem(hWndParent,
                                                  hWndBtn, 0)
                )
                {
                    if(hWndBtn == hWnd)
                    {
```

```
                                break;
                        }

                        SendMessage(hWndBtn, BM_SETCHECK, 0, 0L);
                    }
                }

                // Notify parent with a click message.

                PostMessage
                (
                    GetParent(hWnd),
                    WM_COMMAND,
                    GetDlgCtrlID(hWnd),
                    MAKELONG(hWnd, BN_CLICKED)
                );
            }
        }

        // Cause an immediate paint.

        InvalidateRect(hWnd, NULL, TRUE);
        UpdateWindow(hWnd);

        break;

    case WM_MOUSEMOVE :

        // If the left mouse button hasn't been pressed and we aren't
        // monitoring/capturing the mouse, then leave.

        if(MouseCapture == FALSE)
        {
            break;
        }

        GetClientRect(hWnd, &Rect);

        Style = GetProp(hWnd, "Style");
        x     = LOWORD(lParam);
        y     = HIWORD(lParam);

        // See if mouse pointer is being moved inside hWndButton while
        // the left mouse button is pressed down.
```

```
State = GetWindowWord(hWnd, BTNSTATE);

switch(Style & (BS_PUSHBTN | BS_TOGGLEBTN | BS_RADIOBTN))
{
    case BS_PUSHBTN :

        if(PtInRect(&Rect, MAKEPOINT(lParam)))
        {
            // It was, so if the button isn't already "visually"
            // pushed, paint it as such.

            if(State != PUSHED)
            {
                SendMessage(hWnd, BM_SETCHECK, 1, 0L);
            }
        }
        else
        {
            // It wasn't, so paint the button as if it were
            // released.

            if(State != NORMAL)
            {
                SendMessage(hWnd, BM_SETCHECK, 0, 0L);
            }
        }

        break;

    case BS_TOGGLEBTN :
    case BS_RADIOBTN  :

        if(PtInRect(&Rect, MAKEPOINT(lParam)))
        {
            // It was, so if the button isn't already "visually"
            // pushed, paint it as such.

            if(State == OldState)
            {
                State = OldState ? 0 : 1;

                SendMessage(hWnd, BM_SETCHECK, State, 0L);
            }
```

```
                }
            else
            {
                // It wasn't, so paint the button as if it were
                // released.

                if(State != OldState)
                {
                    SendMessage(hWnd, BM_SETCHECK, OldState, 0L);
                }
            }

            break;

        default :

            break;
        }

    break;

case WM_CREATE :

    // Set temporary property.

    SetProp(hWnd, "Atomic", 1);
    break;

case WM_MOVE :

    if(!RemoveProp(hWnd, "Atomic"))
    {
        break;
    }

    // Init button state.

    SetWindowWord(hWnd, BTNSTATE, NORMAL);
    GetChildWindowPos(hWnd, &Rect, TRUE);

    hInst = GetWindowWord(hWnd, GWW_HINSTANCE);

    if(lpBuffer = SetAtomicClassStyle(hWnd, hInst,
                                (PHANDLE) &hResData))
    {
```

```
                    // Get the bitmaps to be used with the buttons.

                    for
                    (
                        i = j = 0;
                        (WORD) lpBuffer[i];
                        i += (lstrlen(&lpBuffer[i]) + 1), ++j
                    )
                    {
                        SetWindowWord
                        (
                            hWnd,
                            BTNNORMAL + j * sizeof(HBITMAP),
                            LoadBitmap(hInst, &lpBuffer[i])
                        );
                    }

                    if(!(Rect.right - Rect.left))
                    {
                        // If a button size of 0 is spec'd for bitmap buttons, then
                        // size the window around the bitmap button actual size.

                        GetObject
                        (
                            GetWindowWord(hWnd, BTNNORMAL),
                            sizeof(BITMAP),
                            &Bitmap
                        );

                        if((GetWindowLong(hWnd, GWL_STYLE) & WS_BORDER))
                        {
                            Bitmap.bmWidth += GetSystemMetrics(SM_CXBORDER) * 2;
                            Bitmap.bmHeight += GetSystemMetrics(SM_CYBORDER) * 2;
                        }

                        SetWindowPos
                        (
                            hWnd,
                            NULL,
                            0,
                            0,
                            Bitmap.bmWidth,
                            Bitmap.bmHeight,
                            SWP_NOZORDER | SWP_NOMOVE
                        );
```

```
        }

    UnlockResource(hResData);
    FreeResource(hResData);
}
else
{
    int Width, Height;

    DWORD Extent;

    // If a button size of 0 is spec'd for a button, then
    // resize the button depending on the type.

    if
    (
        !(Rect.right - Rect.left) &&
        !GetLabelText(hWnd, Text, sizeof(Text))
    )
    {
        hDC    = GetDC(hWnd);
        Extent = GetTextExtent(hDC, Text, lstrlen(Text));
        ReleaseDC(hWnd, hDC);

        if(GetProp(hWnd, "Style") & BS_PUSHBTN)
        {
            // For pushbuttons, compute height and width of
            // button based on button text.

            Width  = LOWORD(Extent) + 10;
            Height = HIWORD(Extent) + 10;
        }
        else
        {
            Height = HIWORD(Extent);
            Width  = HIWORD(Extent);
        }

        SetWindowPos
        (
            hWnd,
            NULL,
            0,
```

```
                    0,
                    Width,
                    Height,
                    SWP_NOZORDER ¦ SWP_NOMOVE
                );
            }
        }

        if(GetProp(hWnd, "Style") & BS_DEFAULT)
        {
            SendMessage
            (
                GetParent(hWnd), DM_SETDEFID, GetDlgCtrlID(hWnd), 0L
            );
        }

        break;

    case WM_KILLFOCUS :

        // Turn off thick border when focus is lost on button.

        Style = GetProp(hWnd, "Style");

        if(Style & (BS_PUSHBTN ¦ BS_DEFAULT))
        {
            SendMessage(hWnd, BM_SETSTYLE, LOWORD(BS_PUSHBUTTON), 1L);
        }

        if(wParam)
        {
            BYTE Class[20];

            hWndParent = GetParent(hWnd);

            GetClassName((HWND) wParam, Class, sizeof(Class));

            if
            (
                lstrcmpi(Class, "AtomicButton") ¦¦
                (!(GetProp((HWND) wParam, "Style") & BS_PUSHBTN))
            )
            {
                // Window getting focus isn't a button, so make
                // dialog-stored def button the new default.
```

```
            if
            (
                BtnID = LOWORD
                (
                    SendMessage(hWndParent, DM_GETDEFID, 0, 0L)
                )
            )
            {
                SendDlgItemMessage
                (
                    hWndParent, BtnID, BM_SETSTYLE,
                    LOWORD(BS_DEFPUSHBUTTON), 1L
                );
            }
        }
    }

    // Just put a WM_PAINT in the queue when focus is lost.

    InvalidateRect(hWnd, NULL, TRUE);

    break;

case WM_SETFOCUS :

    // When we get the focus, check to see if the Alt key is held
    // down. This means that somebody pressed our "hotkey" '&'
    // and we want to press the button.

    if(GetAsyncKeyState(VK_MENU) & 0x8000)
    {
        if(!GetLabelText(hWnd, Text, sizeof(Text)))
        {
            if(ptr = strchr(Text, '&'))
            {
                if(GetAsyncKeyState(ptr[1]) & 0x8000)
                {
                    // Press my button.

                    PostMessage(hWnd, WM_LBUTTONDOWN, 0, 0L);
                    PostMessage(hWnd, WM_LBUTTONUP, 0, 0L);
                }
            }
        }
    }
```

```
    }

    // Make thick border for button w/focus.

    Style = GetProp(hWnd, "Style");

    if((Style & BS_PUSHBTN))
    {
        hWndParent = GetParent(hWnd);

        if
        (
            BtnID = LOWORD(SendMessage(hWndParent, DM_GETDEFID, 0, 0L))
        )
        {
            SendDlgItemMessage
            (
                hWndParent, BtnID, BM_SETSTYLE,
                LOWORD(BS_PUSHBUTTON), 1L
            );
        }

        SendMessage(hWnd, BM_SETSTYLE, LOWORD(BS_DEFPUSHBUTTON), 1L);
    }

    // Cause a WM_PAINT to fester in the application queue.

    InvalidateRect(hWnd, NULL, TRUE);
    break;

case WM_ERASEBKGND :

    // Buttons never need to paint their background, as it never
    // shows through.

    return(1L);

case WM_PAINT :

    BeginPaint(hWnd, &Paint);

    hDC = CreateCompatibleDC(Paint.hdc);

    State = GetWindowWord(hWnd, BTNSTATE);
```

```
if(!(((Style = GetProp(hWnd, "Style")) & BS_BMPBTN)))
{
    // Draw button type -- push, toggle, or radio.

    DrawButton(hWnd, Paint.hdc, hDC, Style, State);
}
else
{
    // Get button state & approp. bitmap for it.

    if(State == PUSHED)
    {
        hBmp = GetWindowWord(hWnd, BTNPUSHED);
    }
    else
    {
        if(IsWindowEnabled(hWnd) == FALSE)
        {
            hBmp = GetWindowWord(hWnd, BTNDISABLED);
        }
        else
        {
            hBmp = NULL;

            if(GetFocus() == hWnd)
            {
                hBmp = GetWindowWord(hWnd, BTNFOCUS);
            }

            if(!hBmp)
            {
                hBmp = GetWindowWord(hWnd, BTNNORMAL);
            }
        }
    }

    // We're painting an owner-draw button, so draw the bitmap.

    GetObject(hBmp, sizeof(BITMAP), &Bitmap);
    hBmp = SelectObject(hDC, hBmp);

    BitBlt
    (
        Paint.hdc,
        Paint.rcPaint.left,
```

```
                    Paint.rcPaint.top,
                    Bitmap.bmWidth,
                    Bitmap.bmHeight,
                    hDC,
                    Paint.rcPaint.left,
                    Paint.rcPaint.top,
                    SRCCOPY
                );

                SelectObject(hDC, hBmp);
            }

            DeleteDC(hDC);
            EndPaint(hWnd, &Paint);

            return(0L);

        case WM_DESTROY :

            if(GetProp(hWnd, "Style") & BS_BMPBTN)
            {
                // Delete the bitmap buttons from memory.

                DeleteObject(GetWindowWord(hWnd, BTNNORMAL));
                DeleteObject(GetWindowWord(hWnd, BTNPUSHED));

                if(hBmp = GetWindowWord(hWnd, BTNFOCUS))
                {
                    DeleteObject(hBmp);
                }

                DeleteObject(GetWindowWord(hWnd, BTNDISABLED));
            }

            break;

        default :

            break;
    }

    // Let STDWIN.DLL handle default methods for button.

    return(AtomicControlWndFn(hWnd, uMsg, wParam, lParam));
}
```

```
/****************************************************************************
    FUNCTION: DrawButton
    PURPOSE : Draws a nongraphical button.
****************************************************************************/

int PASCAL DrawButton(HWND hWnd, HDC hDCPaint, HDC hDC, WORD Style,
                      WORD State)
{
    HBRUSH hBrush;

    RECT RectTemp;
    RECT Rect;

    DWORD Extent;

    HWND hWndParent;

    HFONT hFont;

    HPEN hPen;

    HBITMAP hBmp;

    COLORREF OldColor;

    int BkgdMode;

    BYTE Text[30];

    // Get button text for push buttons.

    if(Style & BS_PUSHBTN)
    {
        if(GetLabelText(hWnd, Text, sizeof(Text)))
        {
            return(1);
        }
    }

    hWndParent = GetParent(hWnd);

    GetClientRect(hWnd, &Rect);

    // Get font to draw with & width of button text, & set draw mode.
```

```
hFont    = SelectObject(hDC, (HFONT) SendMessage(hWndParent, WM_GETFONT,
                        0, 0L));
Extent   = GetTextExtent(hDC, Text, lstrlen(Text));
BkgdMode = SetBkMode(hDC, TRANSPARENT);

// Create a compat. bitmap, and select into cloned DC.

hBmp = SelectObject
(
    hDC,
    CreateCompatibleBitmap
    (
        hDCPaint, Rect.right - Rect.left, Rect.bottom - Rect.top
    )
);

switch(Style & (BS_PUSHBTN | BS_TOGGLEBTN | BS_RADIOBTN))
{
    case BS_PUSHBTN :

        // Draw a rectangular style button. First, thicken the border
        // up by a pixel if the button is the default.

        hBrush = CreateSolidBrush(GetSysColor(COLOR_BTNFACE));

        if(Style & BS_DEFAULT)
        {
            hPen = SelectObject
            (
                hDC,
                CreatePen(PS_SOLID, 1, GetSysColor(COLOR_WINDOWFRAME))
            );

            hBrush = SelectObject(hDC, hBrush);
            Rectangle(hDC, Rect.left, Rect.top, Rect.right, Rect.bottom);
            hBrush = SelectObject(hDC, hBrush);
            DeleteObject(SelectObject(hDC, hPen));
            InflateRect(&Rect, -1, -1);
        }
        else
        {
            FillRect(hDC, &Rect, hBrush);
        }
```

```
    DeleteObject(hBrush);

    // Now draw 3-D effect for button. Thickness is assumed to be 2.

    InflateRect(&Rect, -2, -2);
    SinkRect(&Rect, hDC, (State == NORMAL) ? -2 : 2);
    InflateRect(&Rect, 2, 2);

    OldColor = SetTextColor(hDC, GetSysColor(COLOR_BTNTEXT));

    if(State == PUSHED)
    {
        OffsetRect(&Rect, 2, 2);
    }

    // Draw text for nonpushed button.

    DrawText
    (
        hDC, Text, -1, &Rect, DT_CENTER | DT_SINGLELINE | DT_VCENTER
    );

    if(State == PUSHED)
    {
        OffsetRect(&Rect, -2, -2);
    }

    if(GetFocus() == hWnd)
    {
        RectTemp.left =
            ((Rect.right - Rect.left) - LOWORD(Extent)) / 2 - 1;
        RectTemp.right = RectTemp.left + LOWORD(Extent) + 1 + 3;
        RectTemp.top =
            ((Rect.bottom - Rect.top) - HIWORD(Extent)) / 2 - 1;
        RectTemp.bottom = RectTemp.top + HIWORD(Extent) + 1 + 3;

        if(State == PUSHED)
        {
            OffsetRect(&RectTemp, 2, 2);
        }

        DrawFocusRect(hDC, &RectTemp);
    }

    SetTextColor(hDC, OldColor);
```

```
    if(Style & BS_DEFAULT)
    {
        InflateRect(&Rect, 1, 1);
    }

    break;

case BS_TOGGLEBTN :

    // For toggle buttons, draw a square, to be filled in
    // with an X, check, or block.

    if(!(hBrush = GetClassWord(hWnd, GCW_HBRBACKGROUND)))
    {
        hBrush = GetClassWord(hWndParent, GCW_HBRBACKGROUND);
    }

    hBrush = SelectObject(hDC, hBrush);
    hPen   = SelectObject
    (
        hDC,
        CreatePen(PS_SOLID, 1, GetSysColor(COLOR_BTNTEXT))
    );

    Rectangle
    (
        hDC,
        Rect.left,
        Rect.top,
        Rect.left + (Rect.bottom - Rect.top),
        Rect.bottom
    );

    SelectObject(hDC, hBrush);
    DeleteObject(SelectObject(hDC, hPen));
    InflateRect(&Rect, -1, -1);
    SinkRect(&Rect, hDC, 1);
    InflateRect(&Rect, 1, 1);

    if(State == PUSHED)
    {
        hPen = SelectObject(hDC, CreatePen(PS_SOLID, 2, COLOR_RED));
```

```
        MoveTo(hDC, Rect.left + 3, Rect.top + 3);
        LineTo(hDC, Rect.right - 3, Rect.bottom - 3);
        MoveTo(hDC, Rect.right - 3, Rect.top + 3);
        LineTo(hDC, Rect.left + 3, Rect.bottom - 3);

        DeleteObject(SelectObject(hDC, hPen));
    }

    break;

case BS_RADIOBTN  :

    // For radio buttons, we need to copy a part of the dialog parent
    // background.

    if(!(hBrush = GetClassWord(hWnd, GCW_HBRBACKGROUND)))
    {
        hBrush = GetClassWord(hWndParent, GCW_HBRBACKGROUND);
    }

    FillRect(hDC, &Rect, hBrush);

    hBrush = SelectObject(hDC, hBrush);
    hPen   = SelectObject
    (
        hDC,
        CreatePen(PS_SOLID, 1, GetSysColor(COLOR_BTNTEXT))
    );

    Ellipse
    (
        hDC,
        Rect.left,
        Rect.top,
        Rect.left + (Rect.bottom - Rect.top),
        Rect.bottom
    );

    SelectObject(hDC, hBrush);
    DeleteObject(SelectObject(hDC, hPen));

    if(State == PUSHED)
    {
```

```
                InflateRect(&Rect, -3, -3);

                hBrush = SelectObject(hDC, CreateSolidBrush(COLOR_RED));

                Ellipse
                (
                    hDC,
                    Rect.left,
                    Rect.top,
                    Rect.left + (Rect.bottom - Rect.top),
                    Rect.bottom
                );

                DeleteObject(SelectObject(hDC, hBrush));

                InflateRect(&Rect, 3, 3);
            }

            break;

        default :

            break;
    }

    // BitBlt the new image into the window and clean up.

    BitBlt
    (
        hDCPaint,
        0,
        0,
        Rect.right - Rect.left,
        Rect.bottom - Rect.top,
        hDC,
        0,
        0,
        SRCCOPY
    );

    DeleteObject(SelectObject(hDC, hBmp));
    SetBkMode(hDC, BkgdMode);
    SelectObject(hDC, hFont);

    return(0);
}
```

E

COMBOBOX

Description

Similar to the AtomicEdit and AtomicListbox controls, the AtomicCombobox control is superclassed and depends on functionality provided by Windows' stock combobox control. The AtomicCombobox class provided here differs from the stock combobox control in several ways. Because it depends on STDWIN.DLL for much of its functionality, it gets a 3-D appearance and 3-D label similar to the other presented controls. In addition, whenever focus is gotten or lost, the control's label "blinks" by popping in and out of the parent dialog, and the background color of the control switches from dim to bright. Unlike other controls, the AtomicCombobox control is not zoomable.

Methods provided inside COMBOBOX.DLL itself include mostly routines to manipulate messages destined for the combobox. Any message that causes a routine based on focus activation to occur needs to be rerouted and pointed to the correct window handle inside the combobox, which usually is the embedded edit control. In addition, the control mnemonic and hotkey-processing routines need to trap keystrokes occurring inside the edit control, not the combobox. Also, any WM_CTLCOLOR messages destined for the combobox (they're really for the combobox's embedded edit control and listbox) are rerouted to the parent window of the combobox. These messages are manipulated such that they are treated as if the combobox itself, not the controls inside, were sending the messages. This kind of switcheroo messaging is done frequently and works quite well.

The following sample resource file structure is used to initialize an AtomicCombobox control:

```
// Note here (as in all cases) that the ID of the private resource
// struct is the same as the ID of the control. Makes things much
// easier for lookup.


ComboboxCtrlID# RCDATA PRELOAD MOVEABLE DISCARDABLE
BEGIN
    WS_3D,              // Control is to have 3-D appearance.
    0,                  // End of style bits.
    "TL&Things\0",      // Label is on top of control and is left-justified.
    "apple\0",          // First string to stuff in box upon initialization.
    "bear\0",
    "@cat\0",           // The entry with the leading "@" is made the default.
    "dog\0",
```

```
    ...
    0                    // Null word, indicating end of strings to stuff.
END

...

// Here is a snippet of dialog code, for an example.

DialogTemplateName DIALOG ...
...
BEGIN
    CONTROL "" ComboboxCtrlID#, "AtomicCombobox", ...

    ...(additional controls here)...
END
```

Possible Enhancements

There aren't many ways that the AtomicCombobox control can be enhanced. A virtual-size capability is a definite no-no. Comboboxes are meant to hold only a limited number of items, so creating one with hundreds of entries would be absurd. However, like the "stuffing" of the AtomicListbox control, the AtomicCombobox control could also be enhanced by letting the private resource structure list a series of string IDs, instead of just using a series of null-terminated character strings, which is how it's currently done. Although plain ASCII strings in this structure can just as easily be customized the same way string tables can, they don't have the benefit of being reused, like strings in a table do.

Specifications

ClassName	AtomicCombobox
ModuleName	COMBOBOX
LibraryName	COMBOBOX.DLL

Functions

LibMain()	Standard entry point for library
WEP()	Standard exit procedure for library
AtomicComboboxWndFn()	Class window procedure
EditWndFn()	Window procedure for comboboxes with embedded edit control

COMBOBOX.C

```
/*****************************************************************************
    LIBRARY: COMBOBOX.DLL
    AUTHOR : Mike Klein
    PURPOSE: Combobox custom control for use with STDWIN.DLL.
******************************************************************************/

//
// #DEFINEs, #INCLUDEs, declarations, and globals
//

#define OEMRESOURCE
#define NOCOMM
#define _WINDLL

#include <windows.h>
#include "stdwin.h"
#include "combobox.h"

int     PASCAL LibMain(HINSTANCE, WORD, WORD, LPSTR);
int     WINAPI WEP(int);
LRESULT WINAPI AtomicComboboxWndFn(HWND, UINT, WPARAM, LPARAM);
LRESULT WINAPI EditWndFn(HWND, UINT, WPARAM, LPARAM);

static FARPROC lpfnComboboxWndProc;
static FARPROC lpfnEditWndProc;

static UINT WM_GETFOCUS;
```

```
/*****************************************************************************
    FUNCTION: LibMain
    PURPOSE : Entry point for DLL.
*****************************************************************************/

#pragma alloc_text(INIT_TEXT, LibMain)

int FAR PASCAL LibMain(HINSTANCE hInst, WORD DataSeg, WORD HeapSize, LPSTR CmdLine)
{
    WNDCLASS wc;

    // Get built-in class info first.

    GetClassInfo(NULL, "combobox", &wc);
    lpfnComboboxWndProc = (FARPROC) wc.lpfnWndProc;

    // Init our "ripoff" combobox custom control. Only chg class parms
    // necessary for new ctrl.

    wc.hInstance      = hInst;
    wc.lpszClassName  = "AtomicCombobox";
    wc.lpfnWndProc    = AtomicComboboxWndFn;
    wc.style         |= CS_GLOBALCLASS;

    if(!RegisterClass(&wc))
    {
        return(FALSE);
    }

    // Register custom messages.

    WM_GETFOCUS = RegisterWindowMessage("WM_GETFOCUS");

    return(TRUE);
}


/*****************************************************************************
    FUNCTION: WEP
    PURPOSE : Termination function for DLL.
*****************************************************************************/

int WINAPI WEP(int Parameter)
{
    return(1);
}
```

```
/****************************************************************************
    FUNCTION: AtomicComboboxWndFn
    PURPOSE : Wnd proc for custom combobox ctrl.
****************************************************************************/

LRESULT WINAPI AtomicComboboxWndFn(HWND hWnd, UINT uMsg, WPARAM wParam,
                                    LPARAM lParam)
{
    LPSTR lpBuffer;

    HINSTANCE hInst;

    static HANDLE hResData;

    LONG Style;

    int Index;

    // Process custom window messages.

    if(uMsg == WM_GETFOCUS)
    {
        BYTE ClassName[10];
        HWND hWndChild;

        // First, determine the type of combobox.

        Style = GetWindowLong(hWnd, GWL_STYLE);

        if((Style & CBS_DROPDOWNLIST) == CBS_DROPDOWNLIST)
        {
            // No trickery here with this kind of combobox!

            hWndChild = hWnd;
        }
        else
        {
            // Get handle to nested edit window, since it is what gets the
            // focus.

            hWndChild = GetWindow(hWnd, GW_CHILD);

            GetClassName(hWndChild, ClassName, sizeof(ClassName));

            if(lstrcmpi(ClassName, "edit"))
            {
```

```
                    hWndChild = GetWindow(hWndChild, GW_HWNDNEXT);
            }
        }

        // Return the correct focus window for combobox.

        return((LRESULT) hWndChild);
    }

    // Process window messages.

    switch(uMsg)
    {
        case WM_RBUTTONDBLCLK :

            // We don't want to zoom combobox controls--too ugly!

            return(0L);

        case WM_CREATE :

            // Set one-time initialization property.

            SetProp(hWnd, "Atomic", 1);
            break;

        case WM_MOVE :

            // Check for one-time init property.

            if(!RemoveProp(hWnd, "Atomic"))
            {
                SendMessage(hWnd, CB_SHOWDROPDOWN, 0, 0L);
                break;
            }

            // Read in style words from priv resource structure and
            // assign to STYLE window property.

            hInst = GetWindowWord(hWnd, GWW_HINSTANCE);

            if(lpBuffer = SetAtomicClassStyle(hWnd, hInst, (LPHANDLE) &hResData))
            {
                // lstrlen() through resource memory block, adding combobox
                // strings as we go along--until we hit an extra null.
```

```
        for(; *lpBuffer != '\0'; lpBuffer += (lstrlen(lpBuffer) + 1))
        {
            if(*lpBuffer == '@')
            {
                Index = (int) SendMessage(hWnd, CB_ADDSTRING, 0,
                                            (LONG) &lpBuffer[1]);
                SendMessage(hWnd, CB_SETCURSEL, Index, 0L);
            }
            else
            {
                SendMessage(hWnd, CB_ADDSTRING, 0, (LONG) lpBuffer);
            }
        }

        // Free up resource stuff.

        UnlockResource(hResData);
        FreeResource(hResData);
    }

    // We need to subclass the edit control for CBS_SIMPLE and
    // CBS_DROPDOWN. CBS_DROPDOWNLIST uses no embedded window.

    Style = GetWindowLong(hWnd, GWL_STYLE);

    if((Style & CBS_DROPDOWNLIST) != CBS_DROPDOWNLIST)
    {
        lpfnEditWndProc = (FARPROC) SetWindowLong
        (
            (HWND) SendMessage(hWnd, WM_GETFOCUS, 0, 0L),
            GWL_WNDPROC,
            (DWORD) EditWndFn
        );
    }

    break;

case WM_CTLCOLOR :

    // We'll reroute the CTLCOLOR message to AtomicDialogWndFn,
    // which is where the other "normal" controls go to get painted.
    // First, we need to fiddle with the destination window handle,
    // as well as the window that's supposed to have to focus.

    return
    (
```

```
                SendMessage
                (
                    GetParent(hWnd),
                    WM_CTLCOLOR,
                    wParam,
                    MAKELPARAM(hWnd, HIWORD(lParam))
                )
            );

        default :

            break;
    }

    // Activate default behaviors for ctrls.

    return(AtomicControlWndFn(hWnd, uMsg, wParam, lParam));
}



/****************************************************************************
    FUNCTION: EditWndFn
    PURPOSE : Wnd proc for snagging some edit messages that are hidden
              inside the combobox. These methods get rerouted to their
              combobox parent, pretending like the edit control isn't really
              nested.
****************************************************************************/

LRESULT WINAPI EditWndFn(HWND hWnd, UINT uMsg, WPARAM wParam, LPARAM lParam)
{
    switch(uMsg)
    {
        case WM_SYSKEYDOWN :
        case WM_TIMER      :

            // Again, becuase of the way that comboboxes use nested windows,
            // we need to reroute this message to the combobox, pretending
            // like there isn't a nested window.

            SendMessage(GetParent(hWnd), uMsg, wParam, lParam);
            return(0L);

        case WM_KILLFOCUS  :
        case WM_SETFOCUS   :
```

```
            // Again, becuase of the way that comboboxes use nested windows,
            // we need to reroute this message to the combobox, pretending
            // like there isn't a nested window.
            // First, though, let's force a whole paint of the control
            // when focus is received or lost.

            InvalidateRect(GetParent(hWnd), NULL, TRUE);

            SendMessage(GetParent(hWnd), uMsg, wParam, lParam);

            break;

        default :

            break;
    }

    // Activate default behaviors for combobox's "built-in" edit ctrl.

    return(CallWindowProc(lpfnEditWndProc, hWnd, uMsg, wParam, lParam));
}
```

EDIT

Description

Similar to the AtomicListbox and AtomicCombobox controls, the AtomicEdit control is superclassed, and it depends on methods provided by Windows' stock edit control class. The control as provided doesn't do anything too special. Most of the enhanced features are provided for by the default method-handling procedure `AtomicControlWndFn()`, which is housed in STDWIN.DLL. One unique feature it does provide can be found embedded in its custom resource data structure. In addition to the window style words, and auto-generated control label provided by methods in STDWIN.DLL, it includes an extra word value used to limit the amount of text typeable in the control. This value is used with the message `EM_LIMITTEXT` and is sent during the control's create method. This is just a handy way of extracting this line of code from your source module. Remember that this limit is in effect only for user-issued keystrokes and has no effect on text placed into the control through the commands `EM_SETHANDLE`, **`SetWindowText()`**, or **`SetDlgItemText()`**.

Features provided by the default methods in STDWIN include a 3-D effect, zooming of multiple-line edit controls, automatic label generation, and auto-resizing of the control's parent window. All the window procedure for the AtomicEdit control really does is restrict some of the default methods provided by `AtomicControlWndFn()`. One such restriction is with single-line edit controls, which are not allowed to process the `WM_RBUTTONDBLCLK` message that zooms a control. This feature is allowed only for multiple-line edit controls. Another change is during `WM_SETFOCUS` and `WM_KILLFOCUS` messages. Normally, this message is passed as is to `AtomicControlWndFn()`, which is responsible for changing the 3-D appearance of the frame of the control, pushing the frame in when focus is lost and popping it out when the focus is obtained. The AtomicEdit control additionally performs a full client-area invalidation before control is passed to STDWIN.DLL for default processing. The edit control does a full repaint on focus changes so that the background can go from bright to dim. Controls like the bitmap have only their frame and label highlighted and unhighlighted, because dimming a bitmap is not "cost-effective." The AtomicListbox and AtomicCombobox controls also do a full client area invalidation on focus changes.

The following resource data structure is used to initialize an AtomicEdit control:

```
EditCtrlID# RCDATA PRELOAD MOVEABLE DISCARDABLE
BEGIN
    WS_3D,      // Define any style bits here, and terminate with a null.
    0
    "{T,M,B}{L,C,R}&Label Name\0", // Specify ctrl label and format code.
    10,         // Limit edit control to 10 characters.
    0           // Terminate the ctrl resource structure.
END

// Here is a snippet of dialog code, for an example.

DialogTemplateName DIALOG ...
...
BEGIN
    CONTROL "" EditCtrlID#, "AtomicEdit", ...
    ...(additional controls here)...
END
```

Possible Enhancements

There are several ways that the custom edit control class can be enhanced. First and foremost (and the easiest) is to give it some of the features provided by the other controls, which means auto-initialization of MLE text through a custom data structure. Although custom data structures are provided for edit controls to establish label names, initialize special control style bits, and limit the text length of the control, they are not used to "prestuff" a multiple-line edit control. Single-line edit controls can be stuffed in the manner of their Windows counterparts, which means including the text in the CONTROL statement defined in the dialog containing the control. Being able to specify the name of a file resource would be another excellent modification.

A second enhancement would be to override Windows' placement of the control in the application's local heap. The current placement works just fine for single-line edit controls, but for MLEs it can very quickly eat up available DGROUP space. Even though writing a "pure" edit control class might sound like a good idea, it really isn't. This is kind of the epitome of the Not-Invented-Here Syndrome. When you start looking at requirements for fonts, color, graphics, and the like, it might be best to consider using OLE or some other means to satisfy the requirement. Many other controls would be much more valuable to spend development time on.

Using Window's stock edit control class (without superclassing), makes the global heap the default recipient for edit control text, unless DS_LOCALEDIT is supplied for the dialog. However, when the control is superclassed, DGROUP is automatically used as the storage area, whether DS_LOCALEDIT is defined for the dialog or not. The reason for this is simple—hardcoded values. Windows internally codes the classnames of several control types, making it impossible to superclass certain Windows controls. In the case of the scrollbar, superclassing can't be done at all. For widgets like the edit control, there are just some minor inconveniences. One possible workaround is to just subclass the standard edit control; however, this makes it more difficult to implement certain behaviors.

Developing a picture-template format for the AtomicEdit control is another must-have feature. Instead of developing specific picture formats (that is, SSN#, phone #), use one of the many public-domain grep pattern-matching algorithms that are available to validate the control before focus is lost. Although the pattern can be checked for character-by-character, it is much more efficient to attempt validation on receipt of a WM_KILLFOCUS message. Although implementing specific picture-filtering templates may be more appealing, in the long run using a general-case pattern-matching algorithm is best, because it solves all types of validation needs.

Another simple enhancement for the AtomicEdit control is a form of automatic focus-shifting. This could be especially useful on data-entry dialogs containing many fixed-length single-line edit controls. The only "magic" being done here is checking to see whether the last character of the edit control has been typed. If so, focus is shifted to the next control in the group. Likewise, when Backspace or the left arrow key is pressed at a caret position of zero, control is shifted to the prior control in the group. The up (prior control) and down (next control) arrow keys could be processed similarly, as they are for buttons.

Specifications

ClassName	AtomicEdit
ModuleName	EDIT
LibraryName	EDIT.DLL

Functions

LibMain()	Standard entry point for library
WEP()	Standard exit procedure for library
AtomicEditWndFn()	Class window procedure

EDIT.C

```c
/****************************************************************************
    LIBRARY: EDIT.DLL
    AUTHOR : Mike Klein
    PURPOSE: Custom edit control for use with STDWIN.DLL.
****************************************************************************/

//
// #DEFINEs, #INCLUDEs, declarations, and globals
//

#define OEMRESOURCE
#define NOCOMM
#define _WINDLL

#include <windows.h>
#include "stdwin.h"
#include "edit.h"

int     PASCAL LibMain(HINSTANCE, WORD, WORD, LPSTR);
int     WINAPI WEP(int);
LRESULT WINAPI AtomicEditWndFn(HWND, UINT, WPARAM, LPARAM);

static UINT WM_DRAWFRAME;


/****************************************************************************
    FUNCTION: LibMain
    PURPOSE : Entry point for DLL.
****************************************************************************/

#pragma alloc_text(INIT_TEXT, LibMain)

int PASCAL LibMain(HINSTANCE hInst, WORD DataSeg, WORD HeapSize, LPSTR CmdLine)
{
    WNDCLASS wc;
    FARPROC  lpfnEditWndProc;

    // Get info on Windows' ctrl first and snitch some stuff.

    GetClassInfo(NULL, "edit", &wc);

    lpfnEditWndProc = (FARPROC) wc.lpfnWndProc;
```

```
    // Init our custom ctrl.

    wc.hInstance     = hInst;
    wc.lpszClassName = "AtomicEdit";
    wc.lpfnWndProc   = AtomicEditWndFn;
    wc.style        |= CS_GLOBALCLASS;

    if(!RegisterClass(&wc))
    {
        return(FALSE);
    }

    // Register common message.

    WM_DRAWFRAME = RegisterWindowMessage("WM_DRAWFRAME");

    return(TRUE);
}


/*****************************************************************************
    FUNCTION: WEP
    PURPOSE : Termination function for DLL.
*****************************************************************************/

int WINAPI WEP(int Parameter)
{
    return(1);
}


/*****************************************************************************
    FUNCTION: AtomicEditWndFn
    PURPOSE : Wnd proc for alpha numeric-style edit ctrls.
*****************************************************************************/

LRESULT WINAPI AtomicEditWndFn(HWND hWnd, UINT uMsg, WPARAM wParam, LPARAM lParam)
{
    LPSTR lpBuffer;

    HANDLE hResData;

    // Handle custom messages.

    if(uMsg == WM_DRAWFRAME)
    {
```

```
                if
                (
                    (GetProp(hWnd, "Style") & WS_3D) &&
                    !(GetWindowLong(hWnd, GWL_STYLE) & ES_MULTILINE)
                )
                {
                    SinkControl(hWnd, (HDC) wParam, GetProp(GetParent(hWnd), "Size3D"), 0);
                    return(0L);
                }
            }

            // Handle regular messages.

            switch(uMsg)
            {
                case WM_CREATE :

                    SetProp(hWnd, "Atomic", 1);
                    break;

                case WM_MOVE :

                    if(!RemoveProp(hWnd, "Atomic"))
                    {
                        break;
                    }

                    // Set extended style for ctrl from data in priv res struct.

                    if
                    (
                        lpBuffer = SetAtomicClassStyle
                        (
                            hWnd,
                            GetWindowWord(hWnd, GWW_HINSTANCE),
                            (LPHANDLE) &hResData
                        )
                    )
                    {
                        // If they entered an integer after the style words, and
                        // the label name, which are processed by the above
                        // function, then use it in conjunction with EM_LIMITTEXT
                        // to restrict the length of the edit control.

                        SendMessage(hWnd, EM_LIMITTEXT, *((LPWORD) lpBuffer), 0L);
```

```
                // Free stuff up.

                UnlockResource(hResData);
                FreeResource(hResData);
            }

            break;

        case WM_RBUTTONDBLCLK :

            // We shouldn't need to ZOOM a single line edit ctrl.

            if((GetWindowLong(hWnd, GWL_STYLE) & ES_MULTILINE) != ES_MULTILINE)
            {
                return(0L);
            }

            break;

        case WM_KILLFOCUS :
        case WM_SETFOCUS  :

            // Do a full paint when focus changes on an edit ctrl. This is
            // what lets the edit ctrl go from white (focus) to light gray,
            // indicating that it has lost the focus.

            InvalidateRect(hWnd, NULL, TRUE);

            break;

        default :

            break;
    }

    // Pass to STDWIN.DLL to handle any common control methods.

    return(AtomicControlWndFn(hWnd, uMsg, wParam, lParam));
}
```

LISTBOX

Description

Similar to the AtomicEdit and AtomicCombobox controls, the AtomicListbox control is superclassed, and it depends on functionality provided by Windows' stock listbox control class. The AtomicListbox class provided here differs from the stock listbox control in several ways. Because it depends on STDWIN.DLL for much of its functionality, it gets a 3-D appearance and a 3-D label similar to the other presented controls. In addition, whenever focus is obtained, the control's label "blinks" by popping in and out of the parent dialog, and the background color of the control switches from dim to bright. When the focus is lost, the label stops blinking and the frame of the control is painted as "pushed in." The AtomicListbox control is zoomable, meaning that whenever Alt-Enter or a right mouse button double-click occurs in the listbox, it is immediately zoomed to fill up the parent window's client area. This works great for file pick boxes that always seem too small. The way that zooming is enabled is to allow the WM_RBUTTONDBLCLK message to filter down to where it can be processed by AtomicControlWndFn().

Methods provided inside LISTBOX.DLL itself include entry deletion support and a graphical owner-draw capability. The deletion support means that whenever the Delete key on the keyboard is pressed, the listbox deletes the currently selected entry, always being careful to maintain a default highlighted selection. The listbox also supports a simple multikey search, unlike Windows' single-key lookup. Pressing the Backspace key or pressing any of the mouse buttons on the listbox resets the search key, which holds as many as 30 characters. The owner-draw capabilities are provided via a check mark for showing a selected state (as opposed to inversing text) and via support for the embedding of icons as well as text inside each listbox cell. If the control is defined in the resource file as LBS_OWNERDRAW, it acquires the check-mark method of entry selection, as opposed to the "InverseRect" method that normally is used. Additionally, if the private style bit LS_HASICO is specified for the control, each listbox cell is assumed to have a combination of an icon and associated text label. Like the other custom controls, the control can be auto-initialized at runtime via a custom resource structure. The AtomicListbox control also can be easily fitted with a horizontal scroll bar, merely by specifying the WS_HSCROLL style when the listbox is created.

Following is a sample resource file structure used to initialize a listbox control:

```
// Note here (as in all cases) that the ID of the private resource
// struct is the same as the id of the control. Makes things much easier
// for lookup.

ListboxCtrlID# RCDATA PRELOAD MOVEABLE DISCARDABLE
BEGIN
    WS_3D,                          // Control is to have 3-D appearance.
    WS_SIZEVERT,                    // Control is to scale vertically along with parent.
    WS_SIZEHORZ,                    // Control is to scale horizontally along with parent.
    0,                              // End of style bits.
    "TL&People\0",                  // Label is on top of control and is left-justified.
    "WWWWWWWWWWWWWWWWWWWWWW\0",      // Max size of entry. Used for horz extent and
                                    // HSCROLL.
    "Adair, David\0",               // First string to stuff in box upon initialization.
    "Fleck, Hanna\0",
    "@Klein, Dave\0",               // The entry with the leading "@" is made the default.
    "Noonycos, Esther\0",
    ...
    0                               // Null word, indicating end of strings to stuff.
END

...


// Here is a snippet of dialog code, for an example.

DialogTemplateName DIALOG ...
...
BEGIN
    CONTROL "" ListboxCtrlID#, "AtomicListbox", ...

    ...(additional controls here)...
END
```

Here is another example, showing how an owner-draw listbox (with icons) is created:

```
ICON1     ICON LOADONCALL MOVEABLE DISCARDABLE ICON1.ICO
ICON2     ICON LOADONCALL MOVEABLE DISCARDABLE ICON2.ICO
ICON3     ICON LOADONCALL MOVEABLE DISCARDABLE ICON3.ICO


ListboxCtrlID# RCDATA PRELOAD MOVEABLE DISCARDABLE
BEGIN
    WS_3D,
    LS_HASICO,
    0,
    "\0",                 // No label defined for control.
    "WWWWWWWWWWWWWWW\0",
    "ICON#1 text\0",      // Text for first listbox cell.
```

```
        "ICON1\0",            // Icon to use with first listbox cell.
        "ICON#2 text\0",      // Ditto...
        "ICON2\0",
        "Icon #3 text\0",
        "ICON3\0",
        0
    END

    // Here is a different snippet of dialog code, for your new example.

    DialogTemplateName DIALOG ...
    BEGIN
        CONTROL "" ListboxCtrlID#, "AtomicListbox",
            WS_CHILD ¦ WS_BORDER ¦ WS_VSCROLL ¦ WS_HSCROLL ¦ WS_TABSTOP ¦
            LBS_NOINTEGRALHEIGHT ¦ LBS_SORT ¦ LBS_NOTIFY ¦ LBS_HASSTRINGS ¦
            LBS_OWNERDRAWFIXED ¦ LBS_MULTIPLESEL ¦ LBS_MULTICOLUMN,
            79, 80, 68, 36

        ...(additional controls here)...
    END
```

Possible Enhancements

The AtomicListbox control can be enhanced in several ways. First and foremost is through the addition of a "virtual" size capability, allowing an "infinite" number of items to be stored in the listbox. A good memory manager is an absolute must for a powerful virtual listbox. In this case, instead of having the listbox manage the data, you are putting the brunt of data management and data display on the application that owns the listbox. This isn't to say that the majority of this doesn't reside in another library, it's just that the "core" listbox code will be invoking a callback function of the application, telling the application the index of the cell that needs to be displayed. It is then up to the application to determine where in memory the string is, and to display it into a specified display context appropriately. Extending the listbox's owner-draw capabilities to include bitmaps (in addition to the icon support already provided) and for a combination of variable-height bitmaps and icon entries would also be a good fit. Currently, the AtomicListbox supports only text, text with check-mark selectors, and text with icons and check-mark selectors. Only listboxes with the style LBS_OWNERDRAWFIXED have been tested; listboxes using the style LBS_OWNERDRAWVARIABLE haven't.

Adding an "edit" capability for items in the listbox, activated by pressing Enter or some other key while on a selected item, would also be a nice feature. This is easily provided by creating a child edit control inside the listbox itself, stuffing it with the text contained in the selected listbox cell. Then, when Enter is pressed or the mouse kills the focus on the edit control, the edit window is destroyed, and the text gotten from the edit control (before it was destroyed!) is added to the listbox entry. Unfortunately, regular listboxes support no method of "edit in place." The cell must be deleted and then readded. For a virtual listbox this wouldn't be an issue.

A "cosmetic" enhancement for the listbox, when performing deletions, is to eliminate the flicker associated with every LB_DELETESTRING message sent to the listbox. This simple fix could easily be performed. Turn off redrawing of the listbox while the deletion is being performed. Next, determine whether the item to be deleted is visible (LB_GETITEMRECT in conjunction with `GetClientRect()`). If it is, then when redrawing is turned back on, validate the area above the new selected entry, leaving the area below the selected entry invalidated, making it subject to a repaint by Windows. If the item to be deleted isn't visible, redrawing can be turned back on with no other operation needing to be performed.

The "stuffing" of the listbox could also be enhanced by letting the private resource structure list a series of string IDs, instead of just using a series of null-terminated character strings, which is how it's currently done. Although plain ASCII strings in this structure can just as easily be customized the same way that string tables can, they don't have the benefit of being reused, like strings in a table do.

Specifications

ClassName	AtomicListbox
ModuleName	LISTBOX
LibraryName	LISTBOX.DLL

Functions

LibMain()	Standard entry point for library
WEP()	Standard exit procedure for library
AtomicListboxWndFn()	Class window procedure
DelLBSel()	Deletes currently selected item in listbox

LISTBOX.C

```
/******************************************************************************
    LIBRARY: LISTBOX.DLL
    AUTHOR : Mike Klein
    PURPOSE: Superclassed listbox custom control to be used w/STDWIN.DLL.
******************************************************************************/


//
// #DEFINEs, #INCLUDEs, declarations, and globals
//

#define OEMRESOURCE
#define NOCOMM
#define _WINDLL

#include <windows.h>
#include "stdwin.h"
#include "listbox.h"

int     PASCAL LibMain(HINSTANCE, WORD, WORD, LPSTR);
int     WINAPI WEP(int);
LRESULT WINAPI AtomicListboxWndFn(HWND, UINT, WPARAM, LPARAM);

static FARPROC lpfnListboxWndProc;


/******************************************************************************
    FUNCTION: LibMain
    PURPOSE : Entry point for DLL.
******************************************************************************/
```

```
#pragma alloc_text(INIT_TEXT, LibMain)

int PASCAL LibMain(HINSTANCE hInst, WORD DataSeg, WORD HeapSize, LPSTR CmdLine)
{
    WNDCLASS wc;

    // First, get default info for class.

    GetClassInfo(NULL, "listbox", &wc);
    lpfnListboxWndProc = (FARPROC) wc.lpfnWndProc;

    // Init custom ctrl.

    wc.hInstance      = hInst;
    wc.lpszClassName  = "AtomicListbox";
    wc.lpfnWndProc    = AtomicListboxWndFn;
    wc.style         |= CS_GLOBALCLASS;

    if(!RegisterClass(&wc))
    {
        return(FALSE);
    }

    return(TRUE);
}


/*****************************************************************************
    FUNCTION: WEP
    PURPOSE : Termination function for DLL.
*****************************************************************************/

int WINAPI WEP(int Parameter)
{
    return(1);
}


/*****************************************************************************
    FUNCTION: AtomicListboxWndFn
    PURPOSE : Wnd proc for custom listbox ctrl.
*****************************************************************************/

LRESULT WINAPI AtomicListboxWndFn(HWND hWnd, UINT uMsg, WPARAM wParam, LPARAM
lParam)
{
```

```
        LPSTR lpBuffer;

        HINSTANCE hInst;

        HANDLE hResInfo;

        static HANDLE hResData;

        int Index;

        LONG Style;

        WORD AtomicStyle;

        HDC hDCMemory;

        HWND hWndParent;

        BITMAP Bitmap;

        HBITMAP hBmp;
        HBITMAP hBmpCheck;

        HBRUSH hBrush;
        HFONT  hFont;

        BYTE String[100];

        // This modal "search key" stuff should be safe in a static. It should
        // be safe since I can hardly see two sets of fingers working two
        // different listbox controls.

        static BYTE SearchKey[30];

        static int KeyLen = 0;

        LPDRAWITEMSTRUCT    lpDIS;
        LPMEASUREITEMSTRUCT lpMIS;

        // Process window messages.

        switch(uMsg)
        {
            case WM_MEASUREITEM :

                    lpMIS = (LPMEASUREITEMSTRUCT) lParam;
```

```
if(GetProp(hWnd, "Style") & LS_HASICO)
{
    // If we're including icon images, then make enough room
    // in the height for the icon and a two-pixel border on the
    // top and bottom. WM_MEASUREITEM comes in with the height
    // already set for a line of text (if LBS_HASSTRINGS is used).

    lpMIS->itemHeight += GetSystemMetrics(SM_CYICON) + 4;
    break;
}

break;

case WM_DRAWITEM :

    lpDIS = (LPDRAWITEMSTRUCT) lParam;

    hBmpCheck = LoadBitmap(NULL, MAKEINTRESOURCE(OBM_CHECK));

    GetObject(hBmpCheck, sizeof(Bitmap), &Bitmap);

    hWndParent = GetParent(hWnd);

    hBrush = (HBRUSH) SendMessage
    (
        hWndParent, WM_CTLCOLOR, lpDIS->hDC, MAKELONG(hWnd,
                                                CTLCOLOR_LISTBOX)
    );

    hFont = SelectObject
    (
        lpDIS->hDC,
        (HFONT) SendMessage(hWndParent, WM_GETFONT, 0, 0L)
    );

    // Get text we're drawing. There should always be some form
    // of text label in a listbox, button, or whatever. Never rely
    // solely on images.

    SendMessage(hWnd, LB_GETTEXT, lpDIS->itemID, (LONG) (LPSTR) String);

    switch(lpDIS->itemAction)
    {
        case ODA_DRAWENTIRE :
```

```
// Erase the background of the cell entry. This removes
// any focus rect or overlapping text. Then draw item.

FillRect(lpDIS->hDC, &lpDIS->rcItem, hBrush);

lpDIS->rcItem.left += Bitmap.bmWidth + 2;

if(GetProp(hWnd, "Style") & LS_HASICO)
{
    // We're drawing an icon and some text.

    lpDIS->rcItem.top += 2;
    lpDIS->rcItem.bottom -= 2;

    DrawIcon
    (
        lpDIS->hDC,
        lpDIS->rcItem.left,
        lpDIS->rcItem.top,
        (HICON) lpDIS->itemData
    );

    DrawText
    (
        lpDIS->hDC,
        String,
        -1,
        &lpDIS->rcItem,
        DT_SINGLELINE | DT_BOTTOM
    );
}
else
{
    // We're drawing text only.

    DrawText
    (
        lpDIS->hDC,
        String,
        -1,
        &lpDIS->rcItem,
        DT_SINGLELINE | DT_VCENTER
    );
}

lpDIS->rcItem.left -= Bitmap.bmWidth + 2;
```

```
                    // Fall through to next case.

            case ODA_SELECT :

                if(lpDIS->itemState == ODS_SELECTED)
                {
                    // Item is selected, so blt a checkbox in there!

                    hDCMemory = CreateCompatibleDC(lpDIS->hDC);
                    hBmp      = SelectObject(hDCMemory, hBmpCheck);

                    BitBlt
                    (
                        lpDIS->hDC,
                        lpDIS->rcItem.left,
                        lpDIS->rcItem.top + ((lpDIS->rcItem.bottom -
                            lpDIS->rcItem.top) - Bitmap.bmHeight) / 2,
                        Bitmap.bmWidth,
                        Bitmap.bmHeight,
                        hDCMemory,
                        0,
                        0,
                        SRCCOPY
                    );

                    SelectObject(hDCMemory, hBmp);
                    DeleteDC(hDCMemory);
                }
                else
                {
                    // Item isn't selected, so blank out the space
                    // where the checkbox would be.

                    lpDIS->rcItem.right = lpDIS->rcItem.left +
                        Bitmap.bmWidth + 2;

                    FillRect(lpDIS->hDC, &lpDIS->rcItem, hBrush);
                }

                break;

            case ODA_FOCUS :

                // Draw your basic, boring focus rect.

                DrawFocusRect(lpDIS->hDC, &lpDIS->rcItem);
```

```
                    break;
            }

        SelectObject(lpDIS->hDC, hFont);
        DeleteObject(hBmpCheck);

        return(1);

case WM_LBUTTONDOWN :
case WM_MBUTTONDOWN :
case WM_RBUTTONDOWN :

    // Reset search key when an item is clicked in the listbox.

    SearchKey[KeyLen = 0] = '\0';
    break;

case WM_RBUTTONDBLCLK :

    // On a zoom, we need to reset the horizontal scroll bar to
    // a position of zero, to eliminate some painting quirks.

    if(GetWindowLong(hWnd, GWL_STYLE) & WS_HSCROLL)
    {
        SendMessage(hWnd, WM_HSCROLL, SB_THUMBPOSITION, 0L);
    }

    break;

case WM_KEYDOWN :

    if(wParam == VK_DELETE)
    {
        // Delete current listbox entry.

        DelLBSel(hWnd);
        return(0L);
    }

    break;

case WM_CHAR :

    switch(wParam)
    {
        case VK_BACK :
```

```
                    // Reset search key when the backspace key is pressed.

                    SearchKey[KeyLen = 0] = '\0';
                    return(0L);

              default :

                    if(KeyLen < 29)
                    {
                        // Increase size of search key.

                        SearchKey[KeyLen] = (BYTE) wParam;
                        ++KeyLen;
                        SearchKey[KeyLen] = '\0';

                        // Try to find string.

                        Index = (int) SendMessage
                        (
                            hWnd,
                            LB_FINDSTRING,
                            (WPARAM)-1,
                            (LPARAM) (LPSTR) SearchKey
                        );

                        if(Index != LB_ERR)
                        {
                            SendMessage(hWnd, LB_SETCURSEL, Index, 0L);
                        }
                    }

                    return(0L);
        }

        break;

    case WM_SETFOCUS  :
    case WM_KILLFOCUS :

        // We need a full paint to occur for this ctrl on a focus chg.

        InvalidateRect(hWnd, NULL, TRUE);

        break;
```

```
case WM_CREATE :

    // We call SetAtomicClassStyle here instead of during WM_MOVE,
    // since the style word must be set before the call to
    // WM_MEASUREITEM. If we wait until WM_MOVE to do this, the
    // message will already have been called.

    if
    (
        SetAtomicClassStyle
        (
            hWnd, GetWindowWord(hWnd, GWW_HINSTANCE), (LPHANDLE) &hResData
        )
    )
    {
        UnlockResource(hResData);
        FreeResource(hResData);
    }

    // Set a temporary flag so we can know to add strings and
    // icos/bmps during WM_MOVE. These kinds of things can't be done
    // during WM_CREATE because structs aren't initialized for this
    // kind of thing yet.

    SetProp(hWnd, "Atomic", 1);
    break;

case WM_MOVE :

    // Check for one-time flag.

    if(!RemoveProp(hWnd, "Atomic"))
    {
        break;
    }

    Style      = GetWindowLong(hWnd, GWL_STYLE);
    AtomicStyle = GetProp(hWnd, "Style");
    hInst      = GetWindowWord(hWnd, GWW_HINSTANCE);

    // Lock down & get a ptr to start of resource data. The first words
    // are all style words. Read them in until a null is encountered,
    // and then store the custom style word in a wnd prop.

    if
```

```
(
    !(hResInfo = FindResource
    (
        hInst, (LPSTR) MAKELONG(GetDlgCtrlID(hWnd), 0), RT_RCDATA
    ))
)
{
    break;
}

hResData = LoadResource(hInst, hResInfo);
lpBuffer = LockResource(hResData);

// Skip past the style words & any label text.

while(*((LPWORD) lpBuffer))
{
    lpBuffer += sizeof(WORD);
}

lpBuffer += sizeof(WORD);

if(*lpBuffer)
{
    lpBuffer += lstrlen(lpBuffer);
}

++lpBuffer;    // Skip past null byte for string label.

// Set horiz scroll bar the cheap way! Use first string
// entry as a dummy to determine max length. First check
// and see if they even want a horiz scroll bar!

if(Style & WS_HSCROLL)
{
    HDC hDC = GetDC(hWnd);

    Index = lstrlen(lpBuffer);

    SendMessage
    (
        hWnd,
        LB_SETHORIZONTALEXTENT,
        LOWORD(GetTextExtent(hDC, lpBuffer, Index)),
        0L
    );
```

```
        ReleaseDC(hWnd, hDC);

        lpBuffer += Index + 1;
    }


    // Skim through strings in memory, adding them to the listbox.

    for(; *lpBuffer != '\0'; lpBuffer += (lstrlen(lpBuffer) + 1))
    {
        if(*lpBuffer == '@')
        {
            Index = (int) SendMessage(hWnd, LB_ADDSTRING, 0,
                                      (LONG) &lpBuffer[1]);

            if(Style & (LBS_MULTIPLESEL ¦ LBS_EXTENDEDSEL))
            {
                SendMessage(hWnd, LB_SETSEL, TRUE, MAKELONG(Index, 0));
            }
            else
            {
                SendMessage(hWnd, LB_SETCURSEL, Index, 0L);
            }
        }
        else
        {
            Index = (int) SendMessage(hWnd, LB_ADDSTRING, 0,
                                      (LONG) lpBuffer);
        }

        // If listbox style is LS_HASICO, then load ico image
        // as ITEMDATA. Listboxes can be both LBS_HASSTRINGS and
        // LS_HASICO.

        if(AtomicStyle & LS_HASICO)
        {
            lpBuffer += lstrlen(lpBuffer) + 1;

            SendMessage
            (
                hWnd,
                LB_SETITEMDATA,
                Index,
                (LONG) LoadIcon(hInst, lpBuffer)
            );
        }
    }
}
```

```
            UnlockResource(hResData);
            FreeResource(hResData);

            break;

        default :

            break;
    }

    // Let STDWIN.DLL handle the common control behaviors.

    return(AtomicControlWndFn(hWnd, uMsg, wParam, lParam));
}


/****************************************************************************
    FUNCTION: DelLBSel
    PURPOSE : Deletes current listbox selection, while maintaining sel state.
 ****************************************************************************/

int WINAPI DelLBSel(HWND hWnd)
{
    int Index;
    int NewIndex;

    // Get currently selected listbox entry.

    Index = (int) SendMessage(hWnd, LB_GETCURSEL, 0, 0L);

    if(Index == LB_ERR)
    {
        return(LB_ERR);
    }

    // Determine which listbox cell will be the new default.

    if
    (
        Index && (Index == (int) (SendMessage(hWnd, LB_GETCOUNT, 0, 0L) - 1))
    )
    {
        // We're at the end of the listbox, so set prior entry as default.

        NewIndex = Index - 1;
```

```
    }
    else
    {
        NewIndex = Index;
    }

    // Delete the specified string & make new default sel entry.

    SendMessage(hWnd, LB_DELETESTRING, Index, 0L);
    SendMessage(hWnd, LB_SETCURSEL, NewIndex, 0L);

    return(0);
}
```

H

SPLIT

Description

Like the AtomicBitmap and AtomicButton control classes, the AtomicSplit control class is implemented from scratch. This should be obvious, because Windows has no stock window split bar class. It is true that several stock Windows applications such as File Manager have grab bars, but they aren't available to developers. The only default processing required for the control is that provided by `DefWindowProc()`, which all windows require in some form. Both vertical and horizontal grab bars are supported by the AtomicSplit control class. The purpose of a "split" or grab bar is to resize the two or more windows that are connected on the left and right or top and bottom sides of the bar. The current grab-bar implementation allows as many as 20 connected windows; however, this limit can easily be circumvented.

The sample application TestApp uses four split bars. A single vertical split bar is used in the main dialog to adjust the horizontal size of two connected AtomicBitmap controls. In addition, the second dialog uses a series of grab bars to divide its client area into two columns and three rows. Each row contains two controls. The first row contains two multiple-line edit controls, the second row contains another two MLEs, and the third row contains a text-style and graphical-style listbox. Each control is separated by three grab bars—one going down the middle dividing the controls into two columns, and two others dividing the controls into three rows.

Using the AtomicSplit control is simple. As with the other control types, a custom data structure is required for each grab bar. Unlike with the other controls, the split bar's data structure specifies only two things: extended style bits and a list of the windows to be initially managed by the grab bar. The only valid style values for grab bars are `WS_SIZEHORZ` and `WS_SIZEVERT`, which allow the grab bar to "float" its length along with other windows when the parent dialog is resized. Only one of these styles can be chosen for a split bar. After a "null" string for the split bar's label (they are assumed to have no label), the rest of the data structure is used to define the windows on the left and right or top and bottom of the split bar. Defining the bar is as simple as listing the control IDs of the windows to be managed.

The following resource code shows the DIALOG structure and custom data structures used to create the second dialog included with the sample application, which includes four MLEs and two listboxes. The additional custom dialog structure isn't printed but is available on the disk included with the book.

APPENDIX

H

Following is the resource code used to create the second dialog:

```
// Custom resource data structures for dialog

IDC_EDITUL RCDATA PRELOAD MOVEABLE DISCARDABLE
BEGIN
     WS_3D,
     0
END

IDC_EDITUR RCDATA PRELOAD MOVEABLE DISCARDABLE
BEGIN
     WS_3D,
     WS_SIZEHORZ,
     0
END

IDC_EDITLL RCDATA PRELOAD MOVEABLE DISCARDABLE
BEGIN
     WS_3D,
     0
END

IDC_EDITLR RCDATA PRELOAD MOVEABLE DISCARDABLE
BEGIN
     WS_3D,
     WS_SIZEHORZ,
     0
END


IDC_GRABBARHORZ1 RCDATA PRELOAD MOVEABLE DISCARDABLE
BEGIN
    WS_SIZEHORZ,
    0,
    "\0",                        // No title, obviously
    IDC_EDITUL, IDC_EDITUR, 0, // Wnds on top of bar
    IDC_EDITLL, IDC_EDITLR, 0  // Wnds on bottom of bar
    0
END

IDC_GRABBARHORZ2 RCDATA PRELOAD MOVEABLE DISCARDABLE
BEGIN
    WS_SIZEHORZ,
    0,
    "\0",                        // No title, obviously
```

```
        IDC_EDITLL, IDC_EDITLR, 0,  // Wnds on left of bar
        IDC_LBLEFT, IDC_LBRIGHT, 0, // Wnds on right of bar
        0
    END


    IDC_GRABBARVERT RCDATA PRELOAD MOVEABLE DISCARDABLE
    BEGIN
        WS_SIZEVERT,
        0,
        "\0",                                  // No title, obviously
        IDC_EDITUL, IDC_EDITLL, IDC_LBLEFT, 0, // Wnds on left of bar
        IDC_EDITUR, IDC_EDITLR, IDC_LBRIGHT,0  // Wnds on right of bar
        0
    END


    IDC_LBLEFT      RCDATA PRELOAD MOVEABLE DISCARDABLE
    BEGIN
        WS_3D,
        WS_SIZEVERT,
        0,
        "\0",
        "WWWWWWWWWWWWWWWWWWWW\0",
        "Chewnous, Hansel\0",
        "@Klein, Dave\0",
        0
    END


    IDC_LBRIGHT     RCDATA PRELOAD MOVEABLE DISCARDABLE
    BEGIN
        WS_3D,
        WS_SIZEHORZ,
        WS_SIZEVERT,
        LS_HASICO,
        0,
        "\0",
        "WWWWWWWWWWWWWWWW\0",
        "ICON#1 text\0",
        "ICON1\0",
        ...
        0
    END


    // The dialog structure

    MISC DIALOG LOADONCALL MOVEABLE DISCARDABLE 17, 54, 250, 219
    STYLE     WS_OVERLAPPEDWINDOW ¦ DS_SETFONT ¦ WS_CLIPCHILDREN
```

```
CAPTION        "Sizables And grab bar demo"
CLASS      "MISC"
FONT       8, "Helv"
BEGIN
    CONTROL "Sample Text" IDC_EDITUL, "AtomicEdit",
        WS_CHILD ¦ ES_MULTILINE ¦ WS_VSCROLL ¦ WS_HSCROLL ¦
        WS_BORDER ¦ ES_WANTRETURN ¦ WS_TABSTOP,
        7, 4, 68, 33

    CONTROL "Some here too!" IDC_EDITLL, "AtomicEdit",
        WS_CHILD ¦ ES_MULTILINE ¦ WS_VSCROLL ¦ WS_HSCROLL ¦
        WS_BORDER ¦ ES_WANTRETURN ¦ WS_TABSTOP,
        7, 42, 68, 33

    CONTROL "" IDC_LBLEFT, "AtomicListbox",
        WS_CHILD ¦ WS_BORDER ¦ WS_VSCROLL ¦ WS_HSCROLL ¦
        WS_TABSTOP ¦ LBS_NOINTEGRALHEIGHT ¦ LBS_SORT ¦ LBS_NOTIFY ¦
        LBS_HASSTRINGS,
        7, 80, 68, 36

    CONTROL "Oh yeah? Yeah!" IDC_EDITUR, "AtomicEdit",
        WS_CHILD ¦ ES_MULTILINE ¦ WS_VSCROLL ¦ WS_HSCROLL ¦
        WS_BORDER ¦ ES_WANTRETURN ¦ WS_TABSTOP,
        79, 4, 68, 33

    CONTROL "My momma dun tol' me" IDC_EDITLR, "AtomicEdit",
        WS_CHILD ¦ ES_MULTILINE ¦ WS_VSCROLL ¦ WS_HSCROLL ¦
        WS_BORDER ¦ ES_WANTRETURN ¦ WS_TABSTOP,
        79, 42, 68, 33

    CONTROL "" IDC_LBRIGHT, "AtomicListbox",
        WS_CHILD ¦ WS_BORDER ¦ WS_VSCROLL ¦ WS_HSCROLL ¦
        WS_TABSTOP ¦
        LBS_NOINTEGRALHEIGHT ¦ LBS_SORT ¦ LBS_NOTIFY ¦
        LBS_HASSTRINGS ¦
        LBS_OWNERDRAWFIXED ¦ LBS_MULTIPLESEL ¦
        LBS_MULTICOLUMN,
        79, 80, 68, 36

    CONTROL "" IDC_GRABBARHORZ1, "AtomicSplit", WS_CHILD, 7, 39, 140, 3

    CONTROL "" IDC_GRABBARHORZ2, "AtomicSplit", WS_CHILD, 7, 78, 140, 3

    CONTROL "" IDC_GRABBARVERT, "AtomicSplit", WS_CHILD, 75, 4, 3, 100
END
```

When the split bar is first created, it scans its private resource structure to determine the windows it is supposed to manage. Each control ID is accumulated and stored as an array of words in SPLIT.DLL's local heap. Enough memory is allocated for managing a total of as many as 20 windows, although this limit can easily be changed. When all the control IDs have been read in, the grab bar determines whether it is supposed to be a vertical or a hortizontal grab bar. If any of the windows being managed is defined as 3-D, it is assumed that all are, and the size of the grab bar is extended just enough in the right directions to make it come up flush with the windows it is managing. This is required because the 3-D effect is not a part of the window, but rather a part of the window's parent client area. When the grab bar is defined, there is no simple way of having its horizontal or vertical size come up flush with the other windows, so it is done automatically. In fact, the windows are instantly "snapped" into place after the grab bar is created, making their respective widths or heights in the dialog irrelevant, because they are automatically sized so that they touch the grab bar.

When a grab bar is clicked on, it immediately determines the positioning and dimensions of the windows it is supposed to manage. This rectangular region is then manipulated, capturing is turned on, and a cursor-clipping rectangle is established to restrict the movement of the grab bar, keeping it within valid coordinates. When the mouse is moved, an inversed bar is displayed on the screen to show where the grab bar is being dragged. The actual split bar window isn't being moved, only an inversed image of it. This effect wasn't achieved as easily as it should have been, because the regular display context for the dialog couldn't be used. Because the dialog was initially created with the style bit WS_CLIPCHILDREN, any display context you try to retrieve from the common pool (with the exclusion of a window display context) would enforce the WS_CLIPCHILDREN setting. Dynamically flipping the clipping style bit for the dialog when calling GetDC() will work, as will a call to the function GetDCEx(). This function allows the settings of any kind of display-context to be overridden.

When the left mouse button is released, capturing is turned off and the cursor-clipping rectangle is removed. Then the grab bar checks to see whether it was moved. If it was not moved, control is returned to Windows. If it was moved, the grab bar is reinversed to remove it from the display, and the windows it is responsible for managing are moved to their new positions. Additionally, depending on whether the mouse cursor is over a vertical or a horizontal grab bar, the cursor is changed to an east-west or north-south arrow cursor, indicating the presence of a grab bar waiting to be tugged.

Possible Enhancements

The AtomicSplit control can be enhanced in several ways. First and foremost is a change in how the memory keeping track of managed windows is kept. Ideally, rather than the local heap, some other (more flexible) memory manager could be used, allowing the managed-window array to dynamically resize itself to any number of managed windows. In practice, it isn't too often that grab bars are added on-the-fly; however, for word processors and other MDI-style applications, it could end up being a fairly frequent occurrence.

A second enhancement would be to allow the grab bar to get the focus. Admittedly, this isn't a standard behavior for grab bars, which usually are just dragged with the mouse. However, there's nothing wrong with having the grab bar blink, indicating focus. Then the keyboard arrow keys could be trapped by `AtomicSplitWndFn()`. Whenever the left, right, up, or down arrow keys are pressed (for the appropriate type of split bar, of course), the grab bar could be dragged across the screen. Unlike when the mouse is used, with the keyboard it might be a better idea to move the managed windows on every press of an arrow key. Otherwise, the Shift key or some other key would need to be held down to indicate a grab state, similar to how the mouse functions when the button is held down while the mouse is moved. Either kind of behavior would be simple to implement.

Most of the controls indicate their focus state by using the default method provided in STDWIN.DLL, which incorporates a blinking label. Because grab bars have no label, two options are available. The first option is to completely incorporate the `WM_SETFOCUS`, `WM_KILLFOCUS`, and `WM_TIMER` methods inside the grab bar. This is also the worst way. A better option would be to have each control respond to a `WM_BLINK` message. By default, the `WM_BLINK` would be handled in STDWIN.DLL, which means a blinking label. However, the grab bar could implement this method itself, by inversing itself each time the `WM_BLINK` message is received. This is a much cleaner way of implementing this kind of behavior, because you aren't assuming anything about the "blink method" of a control.

Another nice enhancement would be to auto-create the grab bar, eliminating the need for defining it in the resource's DIALOG statement. Because the the windows to be managed are already listed in the grab bar's custom data structure, their dimensions could be retrieved and the split bar control created automatically.

Specifications

ClassName	AtomicSplit
ModuleName	SPLIT
LibraryName	SPLIT.DLL

Functions

LibMain()	Standard entry point for library
WEP()	Standard exit procedure for library
AtomicSplitWndFn()	Class window procedure

SPLIT.C

```
/*****************************************************************************
    LIBRARY: SPLIT.DLL
    AUTHOR : Mike Klein
    PURPOSE: Split bar custom control used with STDWIN.DLL.
 *****************************************************************************/

//
// #DEFINEs, #INCLUDEs, declarations and globals
//

#define OEMRESOURCE
#define NOCOMM
#define _WINDLL

#include <windows.h>
#include "stdwin.h"
#include "split.h"

int     PASCAL LibMain(HINSTANCE, WORD, WORD, LPSTR);
int     WINAPI WEP(int);
LRESULT WINAPI AtomicSplitWndFn(HWND, UINT, WPARAM, LPARAM);

static UINT WM_RESIZE;
```

```
/*****************************************************************************
    FUNCTION: LibMain
    PURPOSE : Entry point for DLL.
*****************************************************************************/

#pragma alloc_text(INIT_TEXT, LibMain)

int PASCAL LibMain(HINSTANCE hInstance, WORD wDataSeg, WORD cbHeapSize,
                   LPSTR lpszCmdLine)
{
    WNDCLASS wc;

    // Init Split bar custom control.

    wc.hInstance     = hInstance;
    wc.style         = CS_DBLCLKS | CS_GLOBALCLASS | CS_PARENTDC;
    wc.lpszMenuName  = NULL;
    wc.lpszClassName = "AtomicSplit";
    wc.lpfnWndProc   = AtomicSplitWndFn;
    wc.hCursor       = NULL;
    wc.cbClsExtra    = 0;
    wc.cbWndExtra    = SPLITWNDEXTRA;
    wc.hbrBackground = GetStockObject(BLACK_BRUSH);
    wc.hIcon         = NULL;

    if(!RegisterClass(&wc))
    {
        return(FALSE);
    }

    // Register custom window message.

    WM_RESIZE = RegisterWindowMessage("WM_RESIZE");

    return(TRUE);
}


/*****************************************************************************
    FUNCTION: WEP
    PURPOSE : Termination function for DLL.
*****************************************************************************/

int WINAPI WEP(int nParameter)
{
```

```
        return(1);
    }


/*******************************************************************************
    FUNCTION: AtomicSplitWndFn
    PURPOSE : Wnd proc for grab-bar custom control.
*******************************************************************************/

LRESULT WINAPI AtomicSplitWndFn(HWND hWnd, UINT uMsg, WPARAM wParam, LPARAM lParam)
{
    RECT Rect;
    RECT Bar;
    RECT Wnd;

    static RECT BarOld;

    HINSTANCE hInst;

    static HANDLE hResData;

    HWND hWndParent;
    HWND hWndChild;

    int Size3D;
    int Width, Height;
    int x, y;
    int SplitMargin;
    int i;

    BOOL VertBar;

    DWORD dwOrg;

    HDC hDC;

    LPINT lpInt;
    PINT  pInt;

    // Process custom messages.

    if(uMsg == WM_RESIZE)
    {
        // Split bars have no 3-D effect to them, so when we're
        // resizing them alongside other windows which may have a 3-D
        // effect, we need to extend them just a bit farther.
```

```
            lParam = GetProp(GetParent(hWnd), "Size3D");

            return(AtomicControlWndFn(hWnd, uMsg, wParam, lParam));
        }

        // Process normal messages.

        switch(uMsg)
        {
            case WM_RBUTTONDBLCLK :

                // Inhibit the inheriting of the zoom feature, where a window
                // expands to fill its parent client space.

                return(0L);

            case WM_LBUTTONDOWN :

                // Set capturing and turn on the grab mode.

                SetCapture(hWnd);
                pInt = (PINT) GetProp(hWnd, "Grab");
                hWndParent = GetParent(hWnd);

                // This sets up an approx. min. size for windows that get sized
                // by the split bar. It uses a min. width (or height) of
                // the following...2xSCROLLBARWIDTH + 2x3D + 2xBorderWidth
                // It's an approx. but it works great and is less filling!

                SplitMargin = 2 *
                (
                    GetSystemMetrics(SM_CXVSCROLL) +
                    GetSystemMetrics(SM_CXBORDER) +
                    GetProp(hWndParent, "Size3D")
                );

                // What we're doing here is determining an area to clip the
                // cursor in. First get the SCREEN-based window rects of the
                // dialog window and the grab bar. Then get a sample window
                // RECT from each side of the grab bar, and then adjust the
                // dialog RECT so it frames the valid clipping region for
                // allowable grab-bar positioning.

                GetWindowRect(hWndParent, &Rect);
                GetWindowRect(hWnd, &Bar);
                GetWindowRect(GetDlgItem(hWndParent, pInt[0]), &Wnd);
```

```
i = 0;

while(pInt[i])
{
    ++i;
}

++i;

// Determine our type of grab bar--horiz or vert?

if((Bar.right - Bar.left) < (Bar.bottom - Bar.top))
{
    // It's a vertical grab bar. Now adjust the clipping area
    // that the grab bar is allowed to move within.

    if(Wnd.left + SplitMargin > Rect.left)
    {
        Rect.left = Wnd.left + SplitMargin;
    }

    GetWindowRect(GetDlgItem(hWndParent, pInt[i]), &Wnd);

    if(Wnd.right - SplitMargin < Rect.right)
    {
        Rect.right = Wnd.right - SplitMargin;
    }

    if(Bar.top > Rect.top)
    {
        Rect.top = Bar.top;
    }

    if(Bar.bottom < Rect.bottom)
    {
        Rect.bottom    = Bar.bottom;
    }
}
else
{
    // It's a horizontal grab bar. Now adjust the clipping area
    // that the grab bar is allowed to move within.

    if(Wnd.top + SplitMargin > Rect.top)
    {
        Rect.top = Wnd.top + SplitMargin;
```

```
                }

                GetWindowRect(GetDlgItem(hWndParent, pInt[i]), &Wnd);

                if(Wnd.bottom - SplitMargin < Rect.bottom)
                {
                    Rect.bottom = Wnd.bottom - SplitMargin;
                }

                if(Bar.left > Rect.left)
                {
                    Rect.left = Bar.left;
                }

                if(Bar.right < Rect.right)
                {
                    Rect.right = Bar.right;
                }
            }

            // Set a cursor clipping rectangle & set grab mode.

            ClipCursor(&Rect);
            SetWindowWord(hWnd, 0, 1);
            return(0L);

        case WM_LBUTTONUP :

            // Turn off the grab mode & cursor clipping.

            ReleaseCapture();
            ClipCursor(NULL);

            // Turn off grab flag, and see if bar moved. If not, then leave.

            if(SetWindowWord(hWnd, 0, 0) != 2)
            {
                break;
            }

            Size3D = GetProp(hWndParent = GetParent(hWnd), "Size3D");

            if(!IsRectEmpty(&BarOld))
            {
                // Inverse old position of grab bar, erasing it from display.
```

```
        hDC = GetDCEx(hWndParent, NULL, DCX_PARENTCLIP);

        // Explicitly set the window origin.

        SetWindowOrg
        (
            hDC,
            LOWORD(GetOrigin(hWndParent)),
            HIWORD(GetOrigin(hWndParent))
        );

        InvertRect(hDC, &BarOld);
        ReleaseDC(hWndParent, hDC);
    }

    // Get grab-bar coords. This function differs from
    // GetChildWindowRect, as it undoes the offset normally done
    // by the hdc origin. This is needed for RECTs that will be used
    // with SetWindowPos.

    GetChildWindowPos(hWnd, &Rect, TRUE);

    // Determine our type of grab bar--horiz or vert? Then adjust
    // the RECT of the grab bar so it matches where the mouse cursor
    // currently is, which is determined via lParam. When capturing
    // is turned on, lParam (low and high values) can contain negative
    // values, as they are now relative to the window doing the
    // capturing.

    if((Rect.right - Rect.left) < (Rect.bottom - Rect.top))
    {
        VertBar     = TRUE;
        Rect.right  = (Rect.right - Rect.left) +
                        (Rect.left + LOWORD(lParam));
        Rect.left  += LOWORD(lParam);
    }
    else
    {
        VertBar     = FALSE;
        Rect.bottom = (Rect.bottom - Rect.top) +
                        (Rect.top + HIWORD(lParam));
        Rect.top   += HIWORD(lParam);
    }

    // Move windows on left (or top) of grab bar to new positions.
```

```
pInt = (PINT) GetProp(hWnd, "Grab");
i    = 0;

while(pInt[i])
{
    hWndChild = GetDlgItem(hWndParent, pInt[i]);
    GetChildWindowPos(hWndChild, &Wnd, TRUE);

    if(VertBar)
    {
        Width  = Rect.left - Wnd.left - Size3D;
        Height = Wnd.bottom - Wnd.top;
    }
    else
    {
        Width  = Wnd.right - Wnd.left;
        Height = Rect.top - Wnd.top - Size3D;
    }

    SetWindowPos
    (
        hWndChild,
        NULL,
        0,
        0,
        Width,
        Height,
        SWP_NOZORDER | SWP_NOMOVE
    );

    ++i;
}

++i;

// Move windows on the right (or underneath) grab bar to new pos.

while(pInt[i])
{
    hWndChild = GetDlgItem(hWndParent, pInt[i]);
    GetChildWindowPos(hWndChild, &Wnd, TRUE);

    if(VertBar)
    {
        x      = Rect.right + Size3D;
        y      = Wnd.top;
```

```
            Width  = Wnd.right - Rect.right - Size3D;
            Height = Wnd.bottom - Wnd.top;
        }
        else
        {
            x      = Wnd.left;
            y      = Rect.bottom + Size3D;
            Width  = Wnd.right - Wnd.left;
            Height = Wnd.bottom - Rect.bottom - Size3D;
        }

        SetWindowPos(hWndChild, NULL, x, y, Width, Height, SWP_NOZORDER);
        ++i;
    }

    // Move the grab bar & reset old bar position.

    SetWindowPos
    (
        hWnd, NULL, Rect.left, Rect.top, 0, 0, SWP_NOZORDER | SWP_NOSIZE
    );

    InvalidateRect(hWnd, NULL, TRUE);
    SetRectEmpty(&BarOld);

    return(0L);

case WM_MOUSEMOVE :

    if(!GetWindowWord(hWnd, 0))
    {
        return(0L);
    }

    GetChildWindowRect(hWnd, &Bar);
    GetClientRect(hWndParent = GetParent(hWnd), &Wnd);

    dwOrg = GetOrigin(hWndParent);
    OffsetRect(&Wnd, LOWORD(dwOrg), HIWORD(dwOrg));

    // Determine our type of grab bar--horiz or vert?

    if((Bar.right - Bar.left) < (Bar.bottom - Bar.top))
    {
        VertBar   = TRUE;
        Bar.right = (Bar.right - Bar.left) + (Bar.left + LOWORD(lParam));
```

```
        Bar.left   += LOWORD(lParam);

        if(Bar.bottom > Wnd.bottom)
        {
            Bar.bottom = Wnd.bottom;
        }

        if(Bar.top < Wnd.top)
        {
            Bar.top = Wnd.top;
        }
    }
    else
    {
        VertBar     = FALSE;
        Bar.bottom  = (Bar.bottom - Bar.top) + (Bar.top + HIWORD(lParam));
        Bar.top    += HIWORD(lParam);

        if(Bar.right > Wnd.right)
        {
            Bar.right = Wnd.right;
        }

        if(Bar.left < Wnd.left)
        {
            Bar.left = Wnd.left;
        }
    }

    // Now do a check to see if the position of our inversed bar
    // is any different from the split bar window position. If not,
    // then leave.

    if(EqualRect(&Bar, &BarOld))
    {
        break;
    }

    // Indicate that the inversed grab bar has made a valid move and
    // inverse old bar position (if one exists) and inverse new bar
    // position.

    SetWindowWord(hWnd, 0, 2);

    hDC = GetDCEx(hWndParent, NULL, DCX_PARENTCLIP | DCX_CACHE);
```

```
    SetWindowOrg
    (
        hDC,
        LOWORD(GetOrigin(hWndParent)),
        HIWORD(GetOrigin(hWndParent))
    );

    if(!IsRectEmpty(&BarOld))
    {
        InvertRect(hDC, &BarOld);
    }

    InvertRect(hDC, &Bar);
    ReleaseDC(hWndParent, hDC);
    CopyRect(&BarOld, &Bar);
    return(0L);

case WM_SETCURSOR :

    // Use dimens of grab bar to determine our type of grab bar--
    // vert or horiz?--and set appropriate cursor.

    GetClientRect(hWnd, &Bar);

    SetCursor
    (
        LoadCursor
        (
            NULL,
            (Bar.right - Bar.left) < (Bar.bottom - Bar.top) ?
                IDC_SIZEWE : IDC_SIZENS
        )
    );

    return(0L);

case WM_SETFOCUS  :
case WM_KILLFOCUS :

    // The split bar doesn't process these messages the way that
    // the other Atomic controls do, so let DefWindowProc handle
    // them however it needs to.

    return(DefWindowProc(hWnd, uMsg, wParam, lParam));
```

```
        case WM_CREATE :

            // Set our temporary window property.

            SetProp(hWnd, "Atomic", 1);
            break;

    case WM_MOVE :

        if(!RemoveProp(hWnd, "Atomic"))
        {
            break;
        }

        // We need to do our initialization for the grab bar during
        // WM_MOVE because we depend on the windows attached to
        // the grab bar to be created already.

        hWndParent = GetParent(hWnd);

        // Set extended style for ctrl from data in priv res struct.

        hInst = GetWindowWord(hWnd, GWW_HINSTANCE);

        if(lpInt = (LPINT) SetAtomicClassStyle(hWnd, hInst,
                                            (LPHANDLE) &hResData))
        {
            if(pInt = (PINT) LocalAlloc(LPTR, 22 * sizeof(int)))
            {
                // Get windows on left and right (or top and bottom) of
                // grab bar and store inside SPLIT.DLL's local heap.

                i = 0;

                while(lpInt[i])
                {
                    pInt[i] = lpInt[i];
                    ++i;
                }

                pInt[i] = 0;

                if(i)
                {
```

584

```
RECT RectFirst;
RECT RectLast;
WORD Style;

hWndChild = GetDlgItem(hWndParent, pInt[0]);
Style     = GetProp(hWndChild, "Style");
Size3D    = (Style & WS_3D) ?
    GetProp(hWndParent, "Size3D") : 0;

GetChildWindowPos(hWnd, &Bar, TRUE);
GetChildWindowPos(hWndChild, &RectFirst, TRUE);

GetChildWindowPos
(
    GetDlgItem(hWndParent, pInt[i - 1]),
    &RectLast,
    TRUE
);

if((Bar.right - Bar.left) < (Bar.bottom - Bar.top))
{
    // It's a vertical grab bar, so make it as tall
    // as the first window.

    SetWindowPos
    (
        hWnd,
        NULL,
        RectFirst.right,
        RectFirst.top - Size3D,
        Bar.right - Bar.left,
        RectLast.bottom - RectFirst.top + Size3D * 2,
        SWP_NOZORDER
    );
}
else
{
    // It's a horiz. grab bar.

    SetWindowPos
    (
        hWnd,
        NULL,
        RectFirst.left - Size3D,
        RectFirst.bottom,
        RectLast.right - RectFirst.left + Size3D * 2,
```

```
                            Bar.bottom - Bar.top,
                            SWP_NOZORDER
                    );
                }
            }

            ++i;

            while(lpInt[i])
            {
                pInt[i] = lpInt[i];
                ++i;
            }

            pInt[i] = 0;
            SetProp(hWnd, "Grab", (WORD) pInt);
        }

        UnlockResource(hResData);
        FreeResource(hResData);
    }

    // Snap the windows into place. Set the status so the split
    // bar thinks that a drag has occurred. This initial "snap" is
    // for "auto" placement of the grab bar between windows.

    SetWindowWord(hWnd, 0, 2);
    PostMessage(hWnd, WM_LBUTTONUP, 0, 0L);

    break;

case WM_DESTROY :

    // Remove grab windows property & delete assoc. lmem.

    LocalFree(RemoveProp(hWnd, "Grab"));
    break;

default :

    break;
}

return(AtomicControlWndFn(hWnd, uMsg, wParam, lParam));
}
```

HotApp/HotKey

Description

The modules HotApp and HotKey provide a unique method of dynamically spawning applications. When you use the HotApp loader module and the HotKey keyboard hook library, applications are instantly "on-tap." By pressing a predefined series of keystrokes, you can instantly spawn any of a number of applications. This method is superior to that provided by Windows' Program Manager in several ways. First, Program Manager's method always switches to the same instance of desktop application and doesn't keep spawning new copies. Second, Program Manager doesn't allow a simple method of determining whether the application should run full-screen. Third, this version comes complete with source code that can be modified to achieve whatever is desired. Two additional features include a spawning hotkey and an uninstall hotkey. The spawning hotkey (Ctrl-Shift-Alt-Z) runs another instance of the currently active application. Of course, any applications that disallow this (such as Program Manager) won't be respawned. Most applications do allow this, however, and you probably will find this feature quite useful. The uninstall hotkey (Ctrl-Shift-Alt-X) completely unloads the HotApp application and the HotKey library from memory.

It is highly recommended that both the application and the library (HOTAPP.EXE, HOTKEY.DLL) be copied into Windows' system directory, and that HOTAPP.EXE be placed in win.ini's load= profile line. It can just as easily be installed through a Program Manager icon, however, as are most other applications.

HotApp and HotKey are an application and a library providing a demonstration of parasiting into the system keyboard message chain used by all Windows applications and libraries. The program is initialized by the application HotApp, whose first tasks are to check for any previously running copies (which isn't allowed) and then calling the function InstallHook(), which resides in HOTKEY.DLL. The first thing the function InstallHook() does is remember the handle of the current task. This handle is used later when the application wants to uninstall the hook. The handle is needed because the Ctrl-Shift-Alt-X keystroke combination can come when the application isn't the currently running task, which is almost always the case. A window handle can't be used by the hotkey library because the application creates no windows. Regardless, after this point, a new keyboard hook is registered, and the ID of the hook is remembered in a global variable. A global variable is also

used to remember the application's task handle. This presents no problem because multiple copies of the hotkey application aren't allowed. After the hook is installed, a MessageBox is presented confirming the installation, and control is returned to the application.

HotApp is different from most applications because, as stated previously, it creates no windows. This means that it will keep spinning its gears endlessly in a `GetMessage()` loop. The only messages it responds to are messages destined for the desktop window. Every active application is responsible for processing messages sent to the desktop. The only time the `GetMessage()` loop is broken is when the key combination Ctrl-Shift-Alt-X is pressed, which causes the hook library to post a `WM_QUIT` message to the application using `PostTaskMessage()`. This function is unique because it accepts a handle to a task and not a window as a destination for the message. After the application's message-retrieval loop is broken, a call is made to `RemoveHook()`, removing the keyboard filter entry from the chain. Then the library is unloaded and the application terminates.

Keystrokes are monitored by the filtering code character-by-character. That is, when a certain known character (x, z, w, m, n, and so on) is pressed, the current state of the keyboard is polled to determine what additional system keys (Shift, Control, Alt) also are pressed. The function `GetAsyncKeyState()` is used to determine whether a key is currently being held down. Normally, messages and keystrokes are processed on a synchronous basis, meaning that keys are interpreted and processed as they are fed into an application's message queue and sent to an application. Keystrokes are processed by an application only in a serial, or synchronous, basis, with the application's not being allowed to jump ahead of messages in the queue. They must be serviced in a first-in-first-out basis.

The function `GetAsyncKeyState()` can be compared to the function `GetKeyState()`, which returns the state of a specified key only during the processing of another keystroke message (`WM_CHAR` and so on), essentially pulling the state of a specified key from a master key-state table. This table is accessible via `GetKeyboardState()`, which when called during the processing of a keystroke message copies the state of all 256 virtual-keyboard keys to a buffer. The "yang" function to `GetKeyboardState()` is `SetKeyboardState()`, which can be used to alter the state of the keyboard. Additionally, the function `GetInputState()` can be used to determine whether any mouse, keyboard, or timer messages are in the queue, needing to be processed.

When a known keystroke combination has been pressed, the appropriate program is spawned or some other action is taken, and then any following keystrokes are eaten. When part of a keystroke message is processed (`WM_KEYDOWN`, `WM_SYSKEYDOWN`), any following keystroke messages should be gobbled up, because they would be out of context when fed to another window. Rule: When you process a keystroke message, process the whole message, downs, ups, and any translations. After a valid hotkey has been processed, control is returned to Windows and is not passed to the next keyboard filtering function in the chain of functions. Windows 3.1 has substantially changed the hooking process, because now integer identifiers, not the address of the next filtering function in the chain, are used by an application during all hooking mechanisms. This helps eliminate the knowledge about one module from another. The only time a module should ever be aware of another is when the function `LoadLibrary()` has been used to explicitly bind one module's segments to another's. This is the first of many barriers that will be more rigidly enforced under Windows NT.

Possible Enhancements

Unfortunately, because any hooks established by a Windows application or library affect only the system virtual machine, HotApp's functionality is restricted inside other virtual machines, which means DOS boxes. This means that Ctrl-Esc, Alt-Tab, or Alt-Esc must be used from within the DOS box to re-enable the keystroke trapping. The solution to this problem is to create a virtual keyboard driver, which could trap keystrokes going to all virtual machines—system or otherwise. Writing virtual device drivers of any kind is no trivial task; however, this one is simplified because a completely new driver doesn't need to be written. All that is needed is for the keyboard message chain to be sat on and filtered. The keyboard VxD could read a profile statement for HotApp, telling it what keystrokes to filter and trap on. Then, to communicate with HotApp, the VxD could use `PostMessage()` to redirect any valid keystrokes to the keyboard filter function residing in HOTKEY.DLL. Of course, the entire hot-keying program could be written completely as a VxD, but this would greatly increase the amount of work the developer would need to do.

A second suggestion to increase the functionality of HotApp is to have it create a working window. As the program stands now, it is windowless. Creating a "stub" application with an always-iconized window could add benefits, including a mechanism for adding hot-key combinations on-the-fly, as well as a means for installing and uninstalling the hook without having to reload the application each time.

HotApp.c

```
/****************************************************************************
    PROGRAM: HOTAPP
    AUTHOR : Mike Klein
    PURPOSE: Hotkey program that activates HOTKEY.DLL. This app provides
             a better hotkey mechanism than Windows' program manager since
             the same app isn't always re-activated, rather a new copy of
             the app is started on every hotkey press. See HotKey.c for more.
****************************************************************************/


#define NOCOMM

#include <windows.h>

#include "hotapp.h"
#include "hotkey.h"


/****************************************************************************
    FUNCTION: WinMain
    PURPOSE : Calls initialization function, processes message loop, waiting
              for a signal from the library that it should terminate.
****************************************************************************/

int PASCAL WinMain
(
    HINSTANCE hInstance, HINSTANCE hPrevInstance, LPSTR lpCmdLine, int nCmdShow
)
{
    MSG msg;

    // Check for other instances, which is a no-no.

    if(hPrevInstance)
    {
        MessageBox
        (
            NULL,
            "Cannot run more than one instance",
            "INFORMATION",
            MB_OK | MB_ICONINFORMATION
        );
```

```
    return(FALSE);
}


// Install the hook. This couldn't be done in the library's LibMain,
// because LibMain is called with a "girly-man" sized stack.

InstallHook();

// Spin gears waiting for a WM_QUIT from library.

while(GetMessage(&msg, NULL, NULL, NULL))
{
    TranslateMessage(&msg);
    DispatchMessage(&msg);
}

// Remove the hook. This call is placed in the application for parity.

RemoveHook();

// Good byte!

return(FALSE);
}
```

HotKey.c

```
/******************************************************************************
    LIBRARY: HOTKEY.DLL
    AUTHOR : Mike Klein
    PURPOSE: Keyboard filter library. Installed hotkeys for activating
             programs include:

             Ctrl-Shift-D.........Windowed DOS box (doswnd.pif)
             Ctrl-Alt-D..........Full-screen DOS box (dosfull.pif)

             Ctrl-Shift-C.........Control panel
             Ctrl-Shift-F.........File manager
             Ctrl-Shift-H.........HeapWalker
             Ctrl-Shift-M.........MS-DOS Executive
             Ctrl-Shift-N.........Notepad
             Ctrl-Shift-P.........Print Manager
             Ctrl-Shift-W.........Microsoft Write
```

```
              Note: Ctrl-Alt of the above provides a maximum sized window.

              Ctrl-Alt-Shift-Z.....Spawn copy of currently active application

              Ctrl-Alt-Shift-X.....Uninstall keyboard hook
**************************************************************************/

#define NOCOMM
#define _WINDLL

#include <windows.h>

#include "hotkey.h"


static HINSTANCE hInstDLL;
static HTASK      hTaskClient;

static HHOOK hHook;


/**************************************************************************
    FUNCTION: LibMain
    PURPOSE : Entry point for DLL.
**************************************************************************/

int WINAPI LibMain(HINSTANCE hInstance, WORD wDataSeg, WORD cbHeapSize,
                   LPSTR lpszCmdLine)
{
    hInstDLL = hInstance;
    return(1);
}


/**************************************************************************
    FUNCTION: WEP
    PURPOSE : Termination function for DLL.
**************************************************************************/

int WINAPI WEP(int nParameter)
{
    return(1);
}
```

```
/*****************************************************************************
    FUNCTION: HotKeyProc
    PURPOSE : Catches key msgs from queue.
*****************************************************************************/

LRESULT CALLBACK HotKeyProc(int nCode, WPARAM wParam, LPARAM lParam)
{
    LPSTR lpProg;

    MSG msg;

    int ShowState;

    if(nCode >= 0)
    {
        // Only when code is >=0 do we want to do stuff.

        switch(wParam)
        {
            case 'D' :

                // See if ctrl key is held down.

                if(GetAsyncKeyState(VK_CONTROL) & 0x8000)
                {
                    // See if shift key is held down.

                    if(GetAsyncKeyState(VK_SHIFT) & 0x8000)
                    {
                        // Launch a windowed DOS window.

                        lpProg = "doswnd.pif";
                    }
                    else
                    {
                        if(GetAsyncKeyState(VK_MENU) & 0x8000)
                        {
                            // Launch a full-screen DOS window.

                            lpProg = "dosfull.pif";
                        }
                        else
                        {
                            break;
                        }
                    }
```

```
                        // Launch a DOS box. This command doesn't really maximize
                        // the DOS box to full screen, rather it maximizes the
                        // the DOS window so it fully displays an 80x25 screen.

                        WinExec(lpProg, SW_SHOWMAXIMIZED);

                        // Eat up following keystrokes (usually a WM_SYSKEYUP).

                        while
                        (
                            PeekMessage
                            (
                                &msg,
                                NULL,
                                WM_KEYFIRST,
                                WM_KEYLAST,
                                PM_REMOVE | PM_NOYIELD
                            )
                        )
                        {
                            // Spin gears.
                        }

                        // Boog out of here without passing to def filter func.

                        return(1L);
                    }

                break;

            case 'C' :
            case 'W' :
            case 'N' :
            case 'P' :
            case 'F' :
            case 'M' :
            case 'H' :

                // See if ctrl key is held down.

                if(GetAsyncKeyState(VK_CONTROL) & 0x8000)
                {
                    if(GetAsyncKeyState(VK_MENU) & 0x8000)
                    {
                        ShowState = SW_SHOWMAXIMIZED;
                    }
```

```
else
{
    if(GetAsyncKeyState(VK_SHIFT) & 0x8000)
    {
        ShowState = SW_SHOWNORMAL;
    }
    else
    {
        break;
    }
}

switch(wParam)
{
    case 'C' :

        lpProg = "control.exe";
        break;

    case 'F' :

        lpProg = "winfile.exe";
        break;

    case 'H' :

        lpProg = "heapwalk.exe";
        break;

    case 'M' :

        lpProg = "msdos.exe";
        break;

    case 'N' :

        lpProg = "notepad.exe";
        break;

    case 'P' :

        lpProg = "printman.exe";
        break;

    case 'W' :
```

```
                    lpProg = "write.exe";
                    break;

            default :

                    lpProg = "";
                    break;
        }

        if(*lpProg)
        {
            // Launch application.

            WinExec(lpProg, ShowState);
        }

        // Eat up following keystrokes (usually a WM_SYSKEYUP).

        while
        (
            PeekMessage
            (
                &msg,
                NULL,
                WM_KEYFIRST,
                WM_KEYLAST,
                PM_REMOVE | PM_NOYIELD
            )
        )
        {
            // Spin gears.
        }

        // Boog out of here without passing to def filter func.

        return(1);
    }

    break;

case 'Z' :

    if
    (
        (GetAsyncKeyState(VK_CONTROL) & 0x8000) &&
        (GetAsyncKeyState(VK_SHIFT) & 0x8000) &&
```

```
        (GetAsyncKeyState(VK_MENU) & 0x8000)
    )
    {
        HWND hWndActive;

        BYTE FileName[60];

        // Spawns another instance of current app.

        if(!(hWndActive = GetActiveWindow()))
        {
            break;
        }

        if(
            GetModuleFileName
            (
                GetWindowWord(hWndActive, GWW_HINSTANCE),
                FileName,
                sizeof(FileName)
            )
        )
        {
            WinExec(FileName, SW_SHOWNORMAL);

            // Eat up following keystrokes (usually a WM_SYSKEYUP).

            while
            (
                PeekMessage
                (
                    &msg,
                    NULL,
                    WM_KEYFIRST,
                    WM_KEYLAST,
                    PM_REMOVE | PM_NOYIELD
                )
            )
            {
                // Spin gears.
            }

            return(1L);
        }
    }
```

```
        break;

    case 'X' :

        if
        (
            (GetAsyncKeyState(VK_CONTROL) & 0x8000) &&
            (GetAsyncKeyState(VK_SHIFT) & 0x8000) &&
            (GetAsyncKeyState(VK_MENU) & 0x8000)
        )
        {
            // With a press of Ctrl-Shift-Alt-X, pass a
            // message to the client app so it can
            // remove itself from memory. When the app
            // receives this message, HWND will be null
            // to indicate a task message as opposed to a
            // window message.

            PostAppMessage(hTaskClient, WM_QUIT, 0, 0L);

            // Eat up following keystrokes (usually a WM_SYSKEYUP).

            while
            (
                PeekMessage
                (
                    &msg,
                    NULL,
                    WM_KEYFIRST,
                    WM_KEYLAST,
                    PM_REMOVE ¦ PM_NOYIELD
                )
            )
            {
                // Spin gears.
            }

            return(1L);
        }

        break;

    default :

        break;
}
```

```
    }

    // Pass control to next filter in chain.

    return((DWORD) CallNextHookEx(hHook, nCode, wParam, lParam));
}



/****************************************************************************
    FUNCTION: InstallHook
    PURPOSE : Installs keyboard hook.
****************************************************************************/

VOID WINAPI InstallHook(VOID)
{
    // Remember task handle for future call to PostAppMessage. This is more
    // reliable than placing in LibMain, since LibMain could possibly be
    // called on via a Windows task, and not the task of HotApp.

    hTaskClient = GetCurrentTask();

    // Set up hook func for key trapping.

    hHook = SetWindowsHookEx(WH_KEYBOARD, (HOOKPROC) HotKeyProc,
                        hInstDLL, NULL);

    MessageBox(NULL, "HotKey installed", "INFORMATION",
                MB_OK | MB_ICONINFORMATION);
}



/****************************************************************************
    FUNCTION: RemoveHook
    PURPOSE : Uninstalls keyboard hook.
****************************************************************************/

VOID WINAPI RemoveHook(VOID)
{
    // Unhook the hook.

    UnhookWindowsHookEx(hHook);

    MessageBox(NULL, "HotKey uninstalled", "INFORMATION",
                MB_OK | MB_ICONINFORMATION);
}
```

Index

 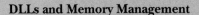

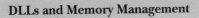
G

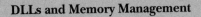
H

I-J

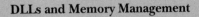

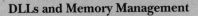

 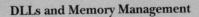
Q

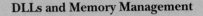

T

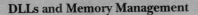

X-Z

Sams—Covering The Latest In Computer And Technical Topics!

Audio

Advanced Digital Audio	$39.95
Audio Systems Design and Installation	$59.95
Compact Disc Troubleshooting and Repair	$24.95
Handbook for Sound Engineers: The New Audio Cyclopedia, 2nd Ed.	$99.95
How to Design & Build Loudspeaker & Listening Enclosures	$39.95
Introduction to Professional Recording Techniques	$29.95
The MIDI Manual	$24.95
Modern Recording Techniques, 3rd Ed.	$29.95
OP-AMP Circuits and Principles	$19.95
Principles of Digital Audio, 2nd Ed.	$29.95
Sound Recording Handbook	$49.95
Sound System Engineering, 2nd Ed.	$49.95

Electricity/Electronics

Active-Filter Cookbook	$24.95
Basic Electricity and DC Circuits	$29.95
CMOS Cookbook, 2nd Ed.	$24.95
Electrical Wiring	$19.95
Electricity 1-7, Revised 2nd Ed.	$49.95
Electronics 1-7, Revised 2nd Ed.	$49.95
How to Read Schematics, 4th Ed.	$19.95
IC Op-Amp Cookbook, 3rd Ed.	$24.95
IC Timer Cookbook, 2nd Ed.	$24.95
RF Circuit Design	$24.95
Transformers and Motors	$29.95
TTL Cookbook	$24.95
Understanding Digital Troubleshooting, 3rd Ed.	$24.95
Understanding Solid State Electronics, 5th Ed.	$24.95

Games

Master SimCity/SimEarth	$19.95
Master Ultima	$16.95

Hardware/Technical

First Book of Modem Communications	$16.95
First Book of PS/1	$16.95
Hard Disk Power with the Jamsa Disk Utilities	$39.95
IBM PC Advanced Troubleshooting & Repair	$24.95
IBM Personal Computer Troubleshooting & Repair	$24.95
Microcomputer Troubleshooting & Repair	$24.95
Understanding Fiber Optics	$24.95

IBM: Business

10 Minute Guide to PC Tools 7	$ 9.95
10 Minute Guide to Q&A 4	$ 9.95
First Book of Microsoft Works for the PC	$16.95
First Book of Norton Utilities 6	$16.95
First Book of PC Tools 7	$16.95
First Book of Personal Computing, 2nd Ed.	$16.95

IBM: Database

10 Minute Guide to Harvard Graphics 2.3	$9.95
Best Book of AutoCAD	$34.95
dBASE III Plus Programmer's Reference Guide	$24.95
dBASE IV Version 1.1 for the First-Time User	$24.95
Everyman's Database Primer Featuring dBASE IV Version 1.1	$24.95
First Book of Paradox 3.5	$16.95
First Book of PowerPoint for Windows	$16.95
Harvard Graphics 2.3 In Business	$29.95

IBM: Graphics/Desktop Publishing

10 Minute Guide to Lotus 1-2-3	$ 9.95
Best Book of Harvard Graphics	$24.95
First Book of Harvard Graphics 2.3	$16.95
First Book of PC Paintbrush	$16.95
First Book of PFS: First Publisher	$16.95

IBM: Spreadsheets/Financial

Best Book of Lotus 1-2-3 Release 3.1	$27.95
First Book of Excel 3 for Windows	$16.95
First Book of Lotus 1-2-3 Release 2.3	$16.95
First Book of Quattro Pro 3	$16.95
First Book of Quicken In Business	$16.95
Lotus 1-2-3 Release 2.3 In Business	$29.95
Lotus 1-2-3: Step-by-Step	$24.95
Quattro Pro In Business	$29.95

IBM: Word Processing

Best Book of Microsoft Word 5	$24.95
Best Book of Microsoft Word for Windows	$24.95
Best Book of WordPerfect 5.1	$26.95
First Book of Microsoft Word 5.5	$16.95
First Book of WordPerfect 5.1	$16.95
WordPerfect 5.1: Step-by-Step	$24.95

Macintosh/Apple

First Book of Excel 3 for the Mac	$16.95
First Book of the Mac	$16.95

Operating Systems/Networking

10 Minute Guide to Windows 3	$ 9.95
Best Book of DESQview	$24.95
Best Book of Microsoft Windows 3	$24.95
Best Book of MS-DOS 5	$24.95
Business Guide to Local Area Networks	$24.95
DOS Batch File Power with the Jamsa Disk Utilities	$39.95
Exploring the UNIX System, 2nd Ed.	$29.95
First Book of DeskMate	$16.95
First Book of Microsoft Windows 3	$16.95
First Book of MS-DOS 5	$16.95
First Book of UNIX	$16.95
Interfacing to the IBM Personal Computer, 2nd Ed.	$24.95
The Waite Group's Discovering MS-DOS, 2nd Edition	$19.95
The Waite Group's MS-DOS Bible, 4th Ed.	$29.95
The Waite Group's MS-DOS Developer's Guide, 2nd Ed.	$29.95
The Waite Group's Tricks of the UNIX Masters	$29.95
The Waite Group's Understanding MS-DOS, 2nd Ed.	$19.95
The Waite Group's UNIX Primer Plus, 2nd Ed.	$29.95
The Waite Group's UNIX System V Bible	$29.95
Understanding Local Area Networks, 2nd Ed.	$24.95
UNIX Applications Programming: Mastering the Shell	$29.95
UNIX Networking	$29.95
UNIX Shell Programming, Revised Ed.	$29.95
UNIX: Step-by-Step	$29.95
UNIX System Administration	$29.95
UNIX System Security	$34.95
UNIX Text Processing	$29.95

Professional/Reference

Data Communications, Networks, and Systems	$39.95
Handbook of Electronics Tables and Formulas, 6th Ed.	$24.95
ISDN, DECnet, and SNA Communications	$49.95
Modern Dictionary of Electronics, 6th Ed.	$39.95
Reference Data for Engineers: Radio, Electronics, Computer, and Communications, 7th Ed.	$99.95

Programming

Advanced C: Tips and Techniques	$29.95
C Programmer's Guide to NetBIOS	$29.95
C Programmer's Guide to Serial Communications	$29.95
Commodore 64 Programmer's Reference Guide	$24.95

Developing Windows Applications with Microsoft SDK	$29.95
DOS Batch File Power	$39.95
Graphical User Interfaces with Turbo C++	$29.95
Learning C++	$39.95
Mastering Turbo Assembler	$29.95
Mastering Turbo Pascal, 4th Ed.	$29.95
Microsoft Macro Assembly Language Programming	$29.95
Microsoft QuickBASIC Programmer's Reference	$29.95
Programming in ANSI C	$29.95
Programming in C, Revised Ed.	$29.95
The Waite Group's BASIC Programming Primer, 2nd Ed.	$24.95
The Waite Group's C Programming Using Turbo C++	$29.95
The Waite Group's C: Step-by-Step	$29.95
The Waite Group's GW-BASIC Primer Plus	$24.95
The Waite Group's Microsoft C Bible, 2nd Ed.	$29.95
The Waite Group's Microsoft C Programming for the PC, 2nd Ed.	$29.95
The Waite Group's New C Primer Plus	$29.95
The Waite Group's Turbo Assembler Bible	$29.95
The Waite Group's Turbo C Bible	$29.95
The Waite Group's Turbo C Programming for the PC, Revised Ed.	$29.95
The Waite Group's Turbo C++Bible	$29.95
X Window System Programming	$29.95

Radio/Video

Camcorder Survival Guide	$ 14.95
Radio Handbook, 23rd Ed.	$39.95
Radio Operator's License Q&A Manual, 11th Ed.	$24.95
Understanding Fiber Optics	$24.95
Understanding Telephone Electronics, 3rd Ed.	$24.95
VCR Troubleshooting & Repair Guide	$19.95
Video Scrambling & Descrambling for Satellite & Cable TV	$24.95

For More Information,
See Your Local Retailer
Or Call Toll Free

1-800-428-5331

All prices are subject to change without notice. Non-U.S. prices may be higher. Printed in the U.S.A.

Programming Is Easy
With Books From The Waite Group!

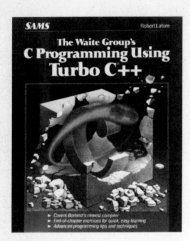

The Waite Group's C Programming Using Turbo C++
Robert Lafore

This book has been updated for the latest version of Borland's Turbo C++ compiler and provides tips, hints, tricks, and strategies to help professional and experienced programmers master Turbo C++.

794 pages, 73/8 x 91/4, $29.95 USA
0-672-22737-1

The Waite Group's Turbo C++ Bible
Naba Barkakati

A user-friendly guide to the Turbo C library, this book contains debugged real-world examples for each routine that will suit both novice programmers and software developers.

1,000 pages, 73/8 x 91/4, $29.95 USA
0-672-22742-8

Enhance Your Operating System With Books From The Waite Group!

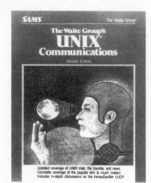

Installing the Disk

Windows Programmer's Guide to DLLs and Memory Management comes with a disk that includes all the code listings in the book plus the Colonel utility. The code listings and the Colonel utility must be installed separately.

To install the code listings from the disk, follow these steps:

1. Start Microsoft Windows.

2. Insert the disk into the appropriate drive.

3. From the File Manager, create a directory and copy the files from the disk to that directory.

4. Read the disknote.wri file for information on each of the files on the disk, including the correct procedure for using the compression/ decompression utility.

Colonel requires Windows 3.1 to run; it will not work under Windows 3.0.
To install the Colonel utility:

1. Create an empty directory on your hard disk.

2. Copy the following Colonel files from the Colonel subdirectory on the disk:

   COLONELS.EXE
   DEMYSTS.HLP
   DEMYSTS.DLL
   README.TXT

3. Add COLONELS.EXE to a program group in the Windows Program Manager.

License Agreement

By opening this package, you are agreeing to be bound by the following agreement.

This software product is copyrighted, and all rights are reserved by the publisher and author. You are licensed to use this software on a single computer. You may copy and/ or modify the software as needed to facilitate your use of it on a single computer. Making copies of the software for any other purpose is a violation of the United States copyright laws.

This software is sold *as is* without warranty of any kind, either expressed or implied, including but not limited to the implied warranties of merchantability and fitness for a particular purpose. Neither the publisher nor its dealers or distributors assumes any liability for any alleged or actual damages arising from the use of this program. (Some states do not allow for the exclusion of implied warranties, so the exclusion may not apply to you.)